WOMEN IN TH⏤ ⏤⏤⏤ ⏤⏤⏤⏤

EAST

Women in the Ancient Near East provides a collection of primary sources that further our understanding of women from Mesopotamian and Near Eastern civilizations, from the earliest historical and literary texts in the third millennium BC to the end of Mesopotamian political autonomy in the sixth century BC. This book is a valuable resource for historians of the Near East and for those studying women in the ancient world. It moves beyond simply identifying women in the Near East to attempting to place them in historical and literary context, following the latest research. A number of literary genres are represented, including myths and epics, proverbs, medical texts, law collections, letters and treaties, as well as building, dedicatory, and funerary inscriptions.

Mark W. Chavalas is Professor of History at the University of Wisconsin-La Crosse, where he has taught since 1989. Among his publications are the edited *Emar: The History, Religion, and Culture of a Syrian Town in the Late Bronze Age* (1996), *Mesopotamia and the Bible* (2002), and *The Ancient Near East: Historical Sources in Translation* (2006), and he has had research fellowships at Yale, Harvard, Cornell, Cal-Berkeley, and a number of other universities. He has nine seasons of excavation at various Bronze Age sites in Syria, including Tell Ashara/Terqa and Tell Mozan/Urkesh.

ROUTLEDGE SOURCEBOOKS FOR THE ANCIENT WORLD

WOMEN IN THE ANCIENT NEAR EAST

A Sourcebook

Edited by
Mark W. Chavalas

Routledge
Taylor & Francis Group

LONDON AND NEW YORK

First published 2014
by Routledge
2 Park Square, Milton Park, Abingdon, Oxon OX14 4RN

Simultaneously published in the USA and Canada
by Routledge
711 Third Avenue, New York, NY 10017

Routledge is an imprint of the Taylor & Francis Group, an informa business

British Library Cataloguing in Publication Data
A catalogue record for this book is available from the British Library

Library of Congress Cataloging in Publication Data
A catalog record for this book has been requested

ISBN: 978-0-415-44855-0 (hbk)
ISBN: 978-0-415-44856-7 (pbk)
ISBN: 978-0-203-73702-6 (ebk)

Typeset in Baskerville
by Taylor & Francis Books

MIX
Paper from
responsible sources
FSC
www.fsc.org   FSC® C013604

Printed and bound by CPI Group (UK) Ltd, Croydon, CR0 4YY

CONTENTS

CONTENTS

LIST OF CONTRIBUTORS

Mary R. Bachvarova is an Associate Professor in the Department of Classical Studies at Willamette University, Oregon. Her research focuses on cultural interaction between Greece and Anatolia in the Late Bronze Age and Early Iron Age.

Mark W. Chavalas (PhD UCLA) is Professor of History at the University of Wisconsin-La Crosse, where he has taught since 1989. Among his publications are the edited, *Emar: The History, Religion, and Culture of a Syrian Town in the Late Bronze Age* (1996), *Mesopotamia and the Bible* (2002), and *The Ancient Near East: Historical Sources in Translation* (2006), and he has had research fellowships at Yale, Harvard, Cornell, Cal-Berkeley, and a number of other universities. He has nine seasons of excavation at various Bronze Age sites in Syria, including Tell Ashara/Terqa and Tell Mozan/Urkesh.

Billie Jean Collins is an instructor in Middle Eastern and South Asian Studies at Emory University and Acquisitions Editor for the Society of Biblical Literature. She is author of *The Hittites and Their World* (2007), editor of *A History of the Animal World in the Ancient Near East* (2002) and co-editor of *Anatolian Interfaces: Hittites, Greeks and their Neighbors* (2008).

Harriet Crawford has worked extensively on the archaeology of the third millennium in south Mesopotamia and surrounding regions. She is the author of *Sumer and the Sumerians* and editor of *The Sumerian World*, which came out in December 2012. Now retired from her post at the Institute of Archaeology, University College London, she is a Reader Emerita at UCL and a senior Fellow at the McDonald Institute in Cambridge.

Alhena Gadotti (PhD, The Johns Hopkins University) is a Sumerologist specializing in Sumerian Literature of the Old Babylonian Period. Her doctoral dissertation, soon to be published with DeGruyter, discusses *Gilgamesh, Enkidu and the Netherworld* in the larger framework on a posited Sumerian Gilgamesh

Cycle. In addition, Professor Gadotti works on the Old Babylonian scribal curriculum, as well as on the representation of women in Sumerian documents. She is currently Assistant Professor of History at Towson University, MD.

Sarah Melville is an Associate Professor of ancient history at Clarkson University. Her research focuses on Neo-Assyrian history, particularly during the period from the ninth to the seventh centuries BC. Her publications concerning women include a monograph, *The Role of Naqi'a/Zakutu in Sargonid Politics*, and several essays.

Cécile Michel is Senior Researcher at the National Center of Scientific Research, Maison de l'Archéologie et de l'Ethnologie, Nanterre. She has published several books on the Old Assyrian documentation and is preparing a volume dedicated to Assyrian and Anatolian women.

Karen Nemet-Nejat was the first woman to receive her PhD in Ancient Near Eastern Languages, History and Cultures (with Distinction) at Columbia University. She is the author of *Daily Life in Ancient Mesopotamia*, *Cuneiform Mathematical Texts as a Reflection of Everyday Life in Mesopotamia* and *Late Babylonian Texts in the British Museum*. She has held a Kohut Fellowship at Yale University, was part of an NEH Fellowship cataloguing mathematical tablets at Yale University, and received a grant from the Max Planck Institute for the History of Science, Berlin and the Frei Universität Berlin for a seminar on the history of mathematics. She has taught at the Bosphorus University in Istanbul, Turkey, Yale University, and University of Connecticut. Her interests include ancient literature, Mesopotamian mathematic, and matching objects in texts with those in real life. She is currently writing *Yale Oriental Series no. 16*.

Martha T. Roth is Dean of Humanities and the Chauncey S. Boucher Distinguished Service Professor of Assyriology in the Department of Near Eastern Languages and Civilizations, the College, and the Oriental Institute at the University of Chicago. From 1996 to 2011 she served as the third Editor-in-Charge of the 26-volume *Chicago Assyrian Dictionary*, the first volume of which was published in 1956 and the last volume published in 2011. Roth is the author or editor of several books, articles, and edited volumes, including *The Series An-ta-gal = Saqu, Materials for the Sumerian Lexicon 17* (1985); *Babylonian Marriage Agreements, 7th–3rd Centuries B.C.* (1989); and *Law Collections from Mesopotamia and Asia Minor* (1995; 2nd edition 1997; 2nd rev. edition 2000).

JoAnn Scurlock received her BA and PhD in Assyriology from the University of Chicago. She is the author of *Magio-Medical Means of Treating Ghost Induced Illnesses in Ancient Mesopotamia* and with Medical Professor Burton Andersen *Diagnoses in Assyrian and Babylonian Medicine. Sourcebook for Mesopotamian Medicine* is forthcoming in the series *Writings from the Ancient World*. She co-edited *In the*

Wake of Tikva Frymer-Kensky and *Creation and Chaos: A Reconsideration of Hermann Gunkel's Chaos Kampf Hypothesis.* She has published over 80 articles on medicine, magic, mythology, religion, law, social organization and armies of Mesopotamia and surrounding lands. She taught history for many years at Elmhurst College.

PREFACE AND
ACKNOWLEDGEMENTS

By the mid 1990s, I had taught at the university level for over a decade, successfully avoiding incorporating the topic of women into my lectures. Whenever students would ask me about women, I had a pat answer: "We really don't know enough to make an intelligent synthesis of the material." However, I should have answered, "I really don't know enough to make an intelligent synthesis of the material." As one might guess, the students were not satisfied with my response. In 1995, I was selected to participate in a National Endowment for the Humanities Summer Institute, "The Image and Reality of Women in the Ancient Near East Societies" at Brown University. Though I was aware of most of the documents we viewed during that five-week session, I had not considered using primary source documents in such a "raw" manner. I subsequently created two undergraduate courses, "Women in the Ancient World" and "Women in World History," at the University of Wisconsin-La Crosse, where I had students read primary sources with the benefit of a small selection of secondary sources. However, the student needs both. The rationale for this work, then, is to provide a selection of primary sources on women in the ancient Near East, along with detailed historical and textual notes.

I want to thank the University of Wisconsin-La Crosse College of Liberal Studies for my sabbatical, taken in the fall of 2006. During that time, I was able to prepare the groundwork for this volume. I am also grateful to Routledge Publishing, as they had extraordinary patience with me as this project was very slow in coming together. It is no simple matter to recruit an array of veteran scholars to translate and comment on cuneiform texts in a quick and timely fashion.

Though Abelard relates that Heloise tried to console him about their failed marriage plans by telling him, *"What possible harmony could there be between pupils and nursemaids, desks and cradles, books or tablets and distaffs, pen or stylus and spindles?"* (*The Letters of Abelard and Heloise*, tr. B. Radice, London: Penguin, 1974/2004, p. 14), my wife Kimberlee and our six children (five still at home) have been fully supportive of my eccentric academic endeavors. To them I am always grateful.

Mark W. Chavalas, La Crosse, WI, June, 2012

INTRODUCTION

Mark W. Chavalas

For over two millennia, the prevailing opinion about women in the ancient Near Eastern world came from the famous Greek historian, Herodotus (ca. 484–425 BC), who expressed his irritation at Babylonian sexual and marriage practices:

> Once a year in every village all the maidens as they attained marriageable age were collected and brought together into one place, with a crowd of men standing around a crier would display and offer them for sale one by one, first the fairest of all; and then, when she had fetched a great price, he put up for sale the next most attractive, selling all the maidens as lawful wives. Rich men of Assyria who desired to marry would outbid each other for the fairest; the ordinary people, who desired to marry and had no use for beauty, could take the ugly ones and money besides; for when the crier had sold all the most attractive, he would put up the one that was least beautiful, or crippled, and offer her to whoever would take her to wife for the least amount, until she fell to one who promised to accept least; the money came from the sale of the attractive ones, who thus paid the dowry of the ugly and the crippled. But a man could not give his daughter in marriage to whomever he liked, nor could one that bought a girl take her away without giving security that he would in fact make her his wife. And if the couple could not agree, it was a law that the money be returned. Men might also come from other villages to buy if they so desired. This, then, was their best custom; but it does not continue at this time; they have invented a new one lately [so that the women not be wronged or taken to another city]; since the conquest of Babylon made them afflicted and poor, everyone of the people that lacks a livelihood prostitutes his daughters.
>
> ...The foulest Babylonian custom is that which compels every woman of the land to sit in the temple of Aphrodite and have intercourse with some stranger once in her life...Once a woman

1

has taken her place there, she does not go away to her home before some stranger has cast money into her lap, and had intercourse with her outside the temple; but while he casts the money, he must say, "I invite you in the name of Mylitta" (that is the Assyrian name for Aphrodite). It does not matter what sum the money is; the woman will never refuse, for that would be a sin, the money being by this act made sacred. So she follows the first man who casts it and rejects no one.

(excerpts of Herodotus I:196–99)

Scholars have long debated as to the meaning of these passages, especially the section concerning Mylitta. Was Herodotus describing a "rite of passage" (i.e., a rite that serves to define girls as ready for marriage), a practice of collecting offerings at the sanctuary (temple prostitution), a ritual of sexual hospitality, or something else?

Herodotus was not the only ancient source for this "shameful" custom, although other writers described it in a very different context. Strabo (c. 64 BC–AD 24) mentioned similar customs in his *Geography* (XVI:1, 20). His discussion was most certainly dependent upon the Herodotean version, as he included mention of the other Babylonian customs described by Herodotus (e.g., Babylonian medical practices). Strabo presented the story as "all women" who need to do this, without any social differences, similar to the Herodotean view. However, he changed Herodotus' amount of money to be paid from "whatever is offered" to "however much is acceptable."

The Hellenistic Period *Letter of Jeremias* in the apocryphal book of Baruch (VI:42–43), set during the Babylonian exile, stated that:

And their women, girt with cords, sit by the roads, burning chaff for incense; and whenever one of them is drawn aside by some passer-by who lies with her, she mocks her neighbor who has not been dignified as she has, and has not had her cord broken

(*New American Bible*)

Over nearly a one-thousand-year period (c. 450 BC–AD 430) numerous other classical, biblical, and Patristic sources either alluded to this custom (although not every source connected it to Babylonian women in particular) or described the base nature of Babylonian sexual customs (probably based upon the Herodotean account).

As one might expect, the modern scholarly view of Babylonian women and sexual customs has been greatly influenced by these classical sources. The modern concept of "sacred" prostitution stemming from Babylonia can be traced to W. Robertson Smith, a nineteenth-century Semiticist who argued that there were sacred prostitutes at the temples of Semitic deities, though he failed to provide any concrete evidence for such (1889, 455). His writings were a great influence upon Sir James Frazer, the great anthropologist, who postulated that ancient sacred prostitution was simply an early evolutionary stage of marriage that had survived in the Near East. Frazer also modified Herodotus' description of "amateur" prostitution by viewing the women as full-time sacred prostitutes, showing that ancients had a "mystical sexual fervor" and an "irresponsible desire to reproduce that sought expression in rite" (1906, 21–24). Thus, because of ancient and early modern authorities, it has been naively assumed that Babylonian (i.e., Mesopotamian) women were sexually free and that temple prostitution was a viable profession. Both Classical and Near Eastern scholars followed Smith and Frazer's lead on this issue. Lewis Farnell argued that the eastern idea of temple prostitution was "abhorrent to the genuine Hellenic, as it was to the Hebraic sprit." For him, it was perhaps an example of the religious acting out of a vegetation ritual to insure fertility (1911, 275–77).

With the discovery and subsequent decipherment of a vast corpus of cuneiform sources in the mid-nineteenth century, the scholarly world has been afforded an opportunity to evaluate Babylonian (or rather, Mesopotamian) women from indigenous sources. However, the mere existence of these sources did not immediately change scholarly views. For example, though Delitszch denied Herodotus' historical reliability, he uncritically accepted the idea of Mesopotamian sacred prostitution in Uruk, a southern Mesopotamian city (1915, 87–102). Langdon accepted Herodotus' description of Mesopotamian customs and postulated that the temple in Babylon was probably near the city wall to make it more convenient for women to be chosen for indiscriminate adultery, which he saw as a "dark and immoral feature of the Ishtar cult" (1914, 73). Thus, though not early all twentieth-century Mesopotamian scholars espoused Frazer's evolutionary concepts, they did for the most part uncritically accepted the idea of temple prostitution in the ancient Near East.

What Herodotus was precisely referring to in his discussion may never be fully understood (although I am working on this problem, which will be the subject of another research project; Chavalas, in prep.). However, the massive cuneiform corpus is a minefield of information from which one can draw many conclusions concerning the nature and status of women in Mesopotamia; hence the purpose of this volume.

Nature and objectives

This work should be viewed as a supplemental textbook for a course on women's or ancient Near Eastern history, similar to my general work on historical sources (Chavalas, 2006). Students of women's history typically are required to read secondary source material concerning the area and period in question, but often are not required to read the primary sources in translation, usually because they are not available. Thus, we have made available in one volume selected documents concerning women, and thus filling a void in women's and in ancient Near Eastern historical studies. In this way, the student will be able to directly evaluate the primary source material. Because of the nature of the material, I have conscripted a group of scholars to contribute up-to-date translations and historical commentary on the documents in question. However, I emphasize that these have been selected based upon availability, and are thus not a comprehensive set of documents. In many respects, this work should be considered as a "materials for the study of women in the ancient Near East." For those interested in having an overview of the ancient Near East, I suggest Marc van de Mieroop's text (2007).

Although gender studies have permeated nearly every historical field and discipline, they have only begun to make their way into Assyriology, the study of the civilizations of ancient Mesopotamia. Moreover, Assyriologists (those who study Mesopotamia) have not until recently taken a lead in theoretical considerations concerning gender, but have followed general trends. Much of previous studies has simply been to identify women in the cuneiform record, which is not such a simple task, as many personal names were not gender specific. There have been, however, conferences devoted to the study of the women in the ancient Near East (e.g., Durand, 1987). Unfortunately, the most well-known work concerning Near Eastern women has been the popular book by the non-Assyriologist Gerda Lerner (1986), which describes the evolution of patriarchy from a so-called matriarchal society as early as the prehistoric Anatolian site Catal Huyuk in the seventh millennium BC. Assyriologists have largely ignored this book except for some implicit statements by Frymer-Kensky (1992) who exposed its shortcomings. She argued that Lerner employed a faulty use of empirical data and had no command of the primary sources. At any rate, it is preferable to study gender roles in Mesopotamia within its own cultural context, incorporating gender into the mainstream of the study of Mesopotamia, shedding classical (e.g. Herodotus) and Victorian preconceptions about Middle Eastern women made from assumptions about other cultures.

Theoretical conceptions of gender in Mesopotamia were broached by Asher-Greve (1985). Moreover, Bahrani's *Women of Babylon: Gender and Representation in Mesopotamia* (2001) has been a welcome addition to the growing number of works on ancient Near Eastern women. Her work is an historical and art historical study of the prevailing concepts of femininity in Assyro-Babylonian society, setting out to analyze how Mesopotamians defined sexuality and gender roles by way of representation. She does not simply set out to, "find women in the historical record" nor do a comparative study of Mesopotamian and Classical women, both of which have been adequately done in the past. Thus, Bahrani provides an overview to feminist theory, feminist art criticism, the body and nudity, images of the elite, the position of Ishtar, and the image of Mesopotamian women in nineteenth-century European art. Thus, this is not a definitive study of gender in Mesopotamian antiquity, but an attempt to look at constructions of feminine sexuality and gender roles. Bahrani goes far to debunk the theory of the "mother goddess," pointing out flaws in the methodology of Lerner and Marija Gimbutas (e.g., 1991), rejecting their ideas as modern myths of utopian matriarchy. Thus,

4

her work has been of immense help for the scholar who has heretofore simply cataloged information about gender, but can now engage in theoretical approaches. In fact, Bahrani's work has been of great help in formulating this present work.

Based upon these considerations, I have created a primary source textbook that has excerpts of Mesopotamian and other ancient Near Eastern (specifically Hittite) texts and other primary source materials, which further an understanding of women in the context of ancient Near Eastern history. The work will survey the period in Mesopotamia from the earliest historical and literary texts (mid-third millennium BC) to the end of Mesopotamian political autonomy in the sixth century BC. However, there are many lacunae in terms of subject matter and region, as will be discussed later.

It is essential for students of history to read primary sources in translation; hence, the rationale for this book. In other words, I will work on this book with the intention that it will be considered a readable and affordable anthology of ancient Near Eastern historical texts concerning women in translation. Although one finds source books like this one for a number of areas of history (e.g., Lefkowitz and Fant, 1992; and Rowlandson, 1998) there are no books of this kind for historical texts in Mesopotamia in English. This is in part because of the difficulty of translating the material. One cannot simply edit old translations, as they are out of date quickly in this rapidly changing field. Thus, I have conscripted a veritable "army" of scholars to make new translations of excerpts of Mesopotamian (and nearby ancient Near Eastern) historical texts. The translator has also provided historical-critical commentary on the text in question, as well as a bibliographic list for further reading on the subject. However, it has been written in a manner that will make it accessible to those in the general public who are interested in women's history in general and the ancient Near East in particular.

The decipherment of the cuneiform writing script is barely 150 years past, and sometimes it is impossible for the modern student to fathom the enormous difficulties involved, not only in the decipherment of the cuneiform writing system, but the ongoing task of translating the dead languages of Akkadian (and then Sumerian) into modern languages. The cuneiform writing system has presented severe problems for the reconstruction of Mesopotamian history and civilization. Even to this day, the scholar of Mesopotamian history encounters new values for cuneiform signs, let alone fundamental issues concerning the transcription, transliteration, and translation of the document in question. In fact, Assyriologists have often concentrated in working out philological difficulties so that historical reconstruction and historiographic reflection have often been relegated to an afterthought, and the learned information has not been made available to a wider public. Furthermore, because of its philological emphasis, the discipline of Mesopotamian studies has traditionally been empirical in its approach, and has been somewhat immune until recently to new-fangled ideas of historical research. Some researchers have often indiscriminately equated all sources as potentially historical. This is why the recent upsurge in the translation and publication of primary source materials is so critical to an understanding of Mesopotamian and women's history.

Instead of searching for categories where women are described, this sourcebook will be "text based." In other words, we will locate documents that describe the nature and status of women and attempt to provide some taxonomic order to them. I prefer the structure provided in W. Hallo and K.L. Younger, *The Context of Scripture* (1997–2002) for ancient Near Eastern texts, where the documents are separated by language rather than period. Thus, I have attempted to create three distinct language categories: Sumerian, Akkadian, and Hittite, recognizing that this is only representative of the myriad of languages used in the ancient Near East. However, one will see that there is a great deal of linguistic "cross over," especially in the realm of Sumerian and Akkadian. In fact, Mesopotamia is often categorized in the early periods as a Sumero-Akkadian cultural enterprise. Thus, the chapters in this volume are not rigidly divided by language. The material in this volume on Mesopotamian law (with codes in Sumerian and Akkadian) is combined in one chapter.

It is hoped that this will be a volume that scholars and students will use to make more definite determinations concerning the nature and status of women in this region and period. Moreover, not all textual genres will be represented with each tradition. Many will perhaps think of texts (and even language groups) that were not included in this volume. However, the choices have been selective and not exhaustive.

Overview of chapters

Each contributor is a recognized specialist in ancient Near Eastern studies. They were given a great deal of latitude to determine which texts to select, based upon import, relevance, and accessibility. In many cases, the entire text was not selected, but rather only the portion that was relevant to understanding the nature and status of women will be used. Each chapter has commentary on each text, as well as a bibliography for further reading.

The contributors are experts in the field of ancient Near Eastern studies (languages, history, and archaeology), but not necessarily in the field of feminist studies. This will be made clear from the outset, as the translator will spend a good deal of time working with textual and language issues. However, I think this is fundamental to preparing the groundwork for studying women in antiquity.

Harriet Crawford prepares the groundwork in her article on women in third millennium BC Mesopotamia. After warning us of our own cultural bias, she shows rather convincingly that women were engaged in professional activities at the outset of historical writing. Moreover, they engaged in these activities in a so-called "parallel universe," "within which they were largely autonomous (from men) and from which they made major contributions to public life." Crawford goes far to show us that "a re-balancing of our picture of life in

Mesopotamia" is in order so we are able to more accurately assess their nature and status.

We will concern ourselves in the remaining chapters with the study of primary sources. Alhena Gadotti begins with a study of the divine in Sumerian literature. She forcefully argues that "the portrayal of women in Sumerian literature had everything to do with real women." In fact, she believes that the "'divine feminine' replicates on a divine level the biological, social and cultural roles women had in 'real life'."

Dr Gadotti tackles women in Sumerian proverbs in the next chapter, from which, as she states, "a multi-faceted and multilayered image of the feminine emerges." However, one must be aware that the proverbs were not fashioned with us in mind, i.e., to provide us with needed information about women. Gadotti argues that though these scribal texts seem to say much about daily life, they have "very little to say about women and their activities." One gets the idea that the study of women in the ancient Near East is a very complicated affair, and much of the textual data cannot always be taken at face value.

Taken out of context, Martha Roth's translation of Mesopotamian laws concerning women would cause one to think they were very passive. While this may be to some extent true in the legal and social sphere, it is a much too simplistic conclusion. One can quickly view Hammurabi Law 153 to understand that women were not always passive, as the legal experts decided on the consequences of a woman who had taken a "contract" out on her husband. At any rate, women's so-called legal passivity does not begin to tell the full story of the nature and status of women in the ancient Near East.

Karen Nemet-Nejat spends a great deal of time providing background to the Gilgamesh Epic, after which she provides information about the female cast of characters in the Epic. Though none of them have major roles, the story cannot move forward without them. She also discusses the purpose and audience for the work itself. Dr Nemet-Nejat shows that much background effort is involved before one even discusses the nature and status of women as derived from the Gilgamesh Epic. She works in a similar vein in the Descent of Ishtar. Moreover, she shows that Akkadian wisdom literature, although highly dependent upon Sumerian antecedents, expressed views about women that were not always consistent with Sumerian models.

The study of women in ancient letters is an altogether different enterprise than other literary genres. They, of course, were not meant for a public audience. In fact, they are perhaps more "authentic" in their depictions. The time periods discussed (Old Assyrian merchant letters and Neo-Assyrian royal correspondence) are drastically different in time, space, social class, and purpose. It appears that a number of women from Assur in the Old Assyrian period were able to compose their own letters to their husbands (and make grammatical errors, to boot). However, Cécile Michel concludes that these women, who stayed in Assyrian while their husbands were away for years at a time in central Anatolia, exhibited strong personalities and were considered as equals. Sarah Melville's treatment of

Neo-Assyrian letters, a millennium after the Old Assyrian material, shows a collection of royal women who are perhaps not unlike their Old Assyrian counterparts in strength of purpose and assertiveness.

Dr Melville also analyzes the treatment of women in Neo-Assyrian documents, as royal women were involved in treaties and building, dedicatory, and funerary inscriptions. Similarly, Dr Nemet-Nejat provides translations of oracles concerning women, who were often prophets.

Mary Bachvarova's treatment of women in Hurro-Hittite stories shows "a sense of respect for women's power to conceive and to seduce and manipulate men through their sexuality, but the misogynistic attitude of the ancient Greeks and Romans is refreshingly absent." Likewise, Billie Jean Collins shows the great diversity of female roles in Hittite ritual.

Few, if any, generalizations concerning women can be made in studying the myriad of texts in this volume. However, we hope they will provide a datum point for further research. Moreover, they are also an impressive sampling for those who are at the beginning of their studies.

Please note: Certain authors have used abbreviations, which are explained at the end of their chapters, before the bibliography.

Also, upper half brackets … mark material that is partially preserved (i.e. partially effaced) and so is somewhat insecure, as opposed to material enclosed in full brackets [.], which is completely lost in the original text and is restored based on an educated guess by the scholar.

Bibliography

Asher-Greve, J., 1985. *Frauen in altsumerischen Zeit.* Malibu: Undena.

Bahrani, Z., 2001. *Women of Babylon: Gender and Representation in Mesopotamia.* London: Routledge.

Chavalas, M.W., 2006. *The Ancient Near East: Historical Sources in Translation.* Oxford: Blackwell.

——, in prep. Herodotus and the "Shameful" Babylonian Custom.Unpublished m/s.

Delitztsch, F., 1915. Zu herodots babylonischen Nachrichten, *Fs. Eduard Sachau*, ed. G. Welf. Berlin: G. Reimer, 87–102.

Durand, J.M., 1987. *La femme dans le proche-orient antique: compte rendu de la 23e Rencontre Assyriologique Internationale (Paris, 7–10 Juillet 1986).* Paris: Editions Recherche sur les Civilisations.

Farnell, L., 1911. *Greece and Babylon: a Comparative Sketch of Mesopotamian, Anatolian and Hellenic Religions.* Edinburgh: T. & T. Clark.

Frazer, J.G., 1906. The *Golden Bough, vol. 1 part 4: Adonis Attis Osiris: Studies in the History of Oriental Religion.* London: Macmillan and Co.

Frymer-Kensky, T., 1992. *In the Wake of the Goddesses.* New York: Free Press.

Gimbutas, M., 1991. *The Civilization of the Goddess.* San Francisco: HarperSanFrancisco

Hallo, W., and K.L. Younger Jr. 1997–2002. *The Context of Scripture,* 3 vols. Leiden: Brill.

Herodotus. 1920–25. *Histories.* Cambridge: Harvard University Press. tr. A.C. Godley.

Langdon, S., 1914. *Tammuz and Ishtar: A Monograph upon Babylonian Religion and Theology.* Oxford: Clarendon Press.

Lefkowitz, M., and E. Fant. 1992. *Womens' Life in Greece and Rome*, 2nd edn. Baltimore: The Johns Hopkins University Press.

Lerner, G., 1986. *The Creation of Patriarchy*. New York: Oxford University Press.

Rowlandson, J., 1998. *Women and Society in Greek and Roman Egypt*. Cambridge: Cambridge University Press.

Smith, W. Robertson, 1889. *The Religion of the Semites: The Fundamental Institutions*. New York: Meridian Books.

Van de Mieroop, M., 2007. *A History of the Ancient Near East, Ca. 3000–323 BC* (Oxford: Blackwell, 2nd edn.).

1

AN EXPLORATION OF THE WORLD OF WOMEN IN THIRD-MILLENNIUM MESOPOTAMIA

Harriet Crawford

Attempts to reconstruct and understand the past are, by the nature of the evidence, always incomplete. Some artefacts and some groups are far more visible in the past record than others and are therefore easier to identify. Men's activities are generally easier to identify than women's and the public sphere, often thought to be predominantly male, is more accessible than the private. This inevitable incompleteness is exacerbated by the fact that scholars have frequently been rather selective in their fields of study, interested only in certain areas: in specific classes of artefacts, such as seals or metalwork; in the activities of certain classes of person; or in constructing a certain picture of the past. This approach can mean that even such evidence as exists is not fully exploited or is distorted, but with persistence and ingenuity it is possible to throw light on less visible and more neglected areas.

It is generally accepted today that there are other reasons too for this imbalance in the fields of study. In the past the relative lack of women in the archaeological profession and their generally junior status contributed to a certain myopia in scholars and to a tendency to overlook the female world of the past. For example, Trigger has written that in the 1980s "It was also demonstrated that the marginalization of women (in archaeology) had resulted in biased and androcentric interpretations of archaeological evidence" (Trigger 2006:458). Since then the situation has changed, more women are to be found in senior positions and a more holistic approach to the study of the past has begun to emerge, but problems still remain and new approaches and new models are still needed (Gilchrist 1999).

In addition, all models of the past are consciously or unconsciously coloured by the cultural and ideological background of the interpreter. This can be a particular problem when western scholars are dealing with non-Western European societies. One minor example of such a cultural bias, which is frequently quoted in the literature dealing with women in the past of Mesopotamia, is the concept of the harem, which defines the place of many women in Islamic times. This model, largely derived from the writings of early travellers in the Islamic world, coloured much of the early Western work on women in pre-Islamic times, too, even though it has yet to be shown that it is a relevant model. Recent work suggests that it is almost certainly an inappropriate concept in Mesopotamia in the later third millennium BC (al Zubaidi 2004). The issue of the veiling of women, another "oriental" custom, has also been much discussed, but there is little or no evidence for this custom either, prior to the later second millennium. Both these stereotypes need to be excluded from studies of women in early Mesopotamia (Bahrani 2001, Westenholz 1990).

Initially, scholarly work on the role of women in the early states of south Mesopotamia concentrated mainly on the professional roles of individual women. This paper will begin by reiterating and expanding the evidence for professional women, especially in the later part of the third millennium, and will then go on to suggest that these women were often based in a world that was distinct from that of men and that might best be described as a parallel universe from which they made major contributions to public life. Finally the paper will consider the relationship between the male and female worlds. It is hoped that these proposals will lead to a re-balancing of our picture of life in Mesopotamia and to a more accurate assessment of the complexity and sophistication of society in the second half of the third millennium. Finally, some new questions for future research will be briefly explored.

The evidence: potential and problems

We are fortunate that there is relevant evidence to be found in a range of different fields. Archaeologically there are representations of women in a number of media. Some of the most informative evidence is found on cylinder seals, sometimes accompanied by inscriptions. There are also female figures on inlays and votive statues in the round, which again are occasionally inscribed. Problems can arise because of the difficulty of identifying the sex of some of the figures represented on both seals and inlays. Unless the figure is naked to the waist, or bearded, it is sometimes difficult to distinguish the sex, as both male and female are known to have worn their hair long at some periods, and in a bun at others. One well-known example of such a quandary is provided by the seals of the early third millennium showing people with pig-tails weaving and pot-making. These figures are usually thought to be female, but the male "page" on the Uruk vase wears his hair in a similar fashion.

If we accept that domestic buildings are well adapted to the practical and social needs of their inhabitants, they too can provide us with generic evidence for the domestic life of non-elite women. In the third millennium, house plans show no evidence for the seclusion of women, although the situation may have been different in the royal households. There is the possibility of a women's quarter in the Mari palace. However, there is no word for such an area in the

Mari texts (Ziegler 1999:7 and 17). Graves, with one or two exceptions, are not very informative, as bone preservation in Mesopotamia tends to be bad and much of the evidence was uncovered before anthropological examination of bones became a standard procedure, so that scientific attribution of sex is often not available, or even possible. Nor is it easy to deduce the sex of a body from its associated items as it is now widely accepted that our own preconceptions of male/female activities can produce a circular argument. The position is further complicated as there is now some evidence for the deposition of objects in graves by mourners and these offerings reflect the sex of the mourner rather than that of the primary burial.

Iconography on these goods can be misleading too. There is sometimes an implicit assumption that seals found in graves that bear scenes showing women as the main actors probably belonged to females, but two male burials from Ur (PG1422 and PG1850, Woolley 1934), have produced lapis seals with females as the main figures in presentation scenes. In the first grave the seal was worn by the main male burial, so was not an offering. It could perhaps be tentatively suggested that these particular males were high-ranking servants in a female household, owning seals that validated their appointments by the female head of the household as officials in such an establishment (Winter 1987 and below). The opposite is also true and females could have seals with combat scenes on them, a scene more often associated with men. A fine example comes from Mozan where seal impressions of a daughter of Naram-Sin of Agade called Tar'am Agade, who was married to the ruler of Urkesh, carry a combat scene of a type that seems to have been used exclusively by members of the royal family of both sexes (Buccellati and Buccellati 2002). A study of sealings from the archive of Ur-Utu dating to the early second-millennium Old Babylonian period has found that women chose the same subjects as men (Colbow 2002:90).

We are fortunate in having textual records, too, covering a number of relevant fields, of which the most important from our point of view is the administrative, followed by the economic, dedicatory and literary ones. Use of such sources also presents problems, not only because of the well-known bias of such texts towards the public institutions, but also that caused by the difficulty of identifying female names with certainty in Sumerian (Van de Mieroop 1999 chap.5). Further difficulties are introduced by the fact that that some Sumerian words, such as DUMU, are not necessarily gendered and so can stand for child as well as son.[1] Gemebau/baba daughter of Enentarzi sanga of Ningirsu at Lagash, is described in her dedicatory inscription as DUMU, yet the statue and her name are undoubtedly female. The name means slave of the goddess Bau/Baba (Bahrani 2001:101). These factors taken together would seem to indicate that the number of women in all types of evidence, both visual and textual, has probably been considerably underestimated, as in the case of uncertainty there is an (unconscious) bias on the part of scholars towards identifying participants in public life as male.

Studies of modern traditional societies in the Arab world can also broaden our understanding of the possible ways in which women live and how they may contribute to public life, although such studies can do no more than this and certainly cannot be taken as paradigms for earlier societies.

The scope of this paper

It is not possible to make broad generalisations about the world of women that hold good across time and space; their situation changes in response to many factors: social, economic and political. For example, early industrialisation and the increase in demand for manufactured goods, especially textiles and garments, in third-millennium Mesopotamia had a major impact on the lives of women. The manufacturing process was moved from the home into "factories" run by the palace and the temple or by rich individuals. The majority of the workers in these institutions seem to have been women and their children, who thus became institutionalised for the first time and reliant at least in part on rations provided by the employer (Pollock 1999:220, Wright 1996). There were also opportunities for professional advancement and some women rose to be foremen in charge of twenty or so weavers with higher wages, though the foremen could also be male. The position of women can also alter in response to political or ideological change in ways that need to be further explored. For example, the advent of the Amorites to power at the end of the first-quarter of the second millennium seems to have brought considerable social change in its wake in south Mesopotamia (Sharlach 2007). In the modern world we can point to the changes that took place in the lives of women in Afghanistan with the rise to power of the Taliban.

This study will therefore focus on south Mesopotamia in the period from the third to the early second millennium when there is for the first time enough evidence from a variety of sources to allow us to examine the world of women in some detail. The conclusions reached are relevant only to this area and time. The evidence for our chosen period does not cover all women equally, but is slanted in favour of the top and bottom echelons of society, and to the urban rather than the rural. The top echelons of society created most of the records that have survived and these deal largely with their own activities and concerns. The records also deal with the working women who formed a crucial part of the large royal and upper class households, which characterised the organisation of society. The professional women in the middle ranks are not so well documented, and rural and nomadic women are barely mentioned at all. Modern parallels suggest that their lives may have been substantially different to those of their urban sisters (Abu Lughod 1993).

Royal women

The exemplar of the professional woman was the queen who exercised real power both within her sphere and outside it. Her court was staffed by professional people, both male and female, and was hierarchical in its organisation. She exercised this power in much the same spheres as her husband having religious, diplomatic, administrative and economic responsibilities. She does not seem to have had legal or military duties. In addition to running large agricultural estates, it must be remembered that a household or oikos of the third millennium produced saleable commodities, especially textiles. These were produced under factory conditions by hundreds of workers (Maekawa 1973/4) and were probably sold in order to acquire goods and materials that the household did not produce itself. The wives of state governors sometimes held high positions in the royal women's households (Glassner 1989:33).

The role of the queen in both the Early Dynastic and Ur III periods can be reconstructed in some detail. Her ceremonial role is shown, for example, on the Banquet seals popular in the later Early Dynastic period (c.2,600–602,200BC), which show women at public functions, usually together with a man, but a few examples of women-only banquets are also known. For example, two seals from the Royal Cemetery show only women as the main actors. The first is U.11871, a lapis seal from PG1163, which has a women as the main figure and which is also unusual in being a single-register seal. The second, U.10872, is also of lapis and is a two-register seal, which shows two women in the top register and one in the lower. It comes from PG800, the grave of the lady Puabi, who was probably a queen and is one of three belonging to her. The possession of three seals in itself indicates her involvement in administrative affairs as they were used to sign and validate documents, and the main figure in the banquet may represent Puabi herself performing her public functions. In addition to Puabi's seal, U.12380 from the Great Death Pit, PG1237, although worn, seems to show three women banqueting on the top register, while the lower shows an animal combat (Woolley 1934). This seal, like the others mentioned, is of lapis, a prestigious material indicating high rank in its possessor. It seems from these all-women seals that, whatever the precise nature of the ceremony, it could be carried out by women on their own.

There is no certainty that all examples of this type of seal illustrate actual royal banquets, some may be religious ceremonies, for example, while others may depict less exalted households, but they all show an apparent equality in standing between the male and female participants. The plaques representing banquet scenes also show male and female drinkers the same size.[2] It is interesting to note that in both media the women are occasionally shown drinking from straws like their male partners, but more often are shown drinking from cups. (Men may also be shown drinking from cups so this is not an exclusively female attribute.) Presumably the straws were used for drinking unfiltered beer, while cups might hold wine or some other beverage. The public aspect of banqueting would also, incidentally, argue against the seclusion of royal women.

It is also possible that some of the banquet seals may show the royal couple entertaining foreign dignitaries, as some show three or four main figures. Others could show the funerary rituals, which involved feasting with the royal women of the past (Glassner 1989:89). We know from texts at Mari that the queen would receive foreign delegations together with her husband, so that there is no doubt that she was an active part of the diplomatic process as well as the ceremonial (Ziegler 1999:7). At Lagash the queen exchanged gifts with the wife of the ruler of Adab (Prentice 2010). In addition, women of the royal family had an important though passive diplomatic role as the brides of foreign rulers with whom alliances were formed. Once married these women transmitted useful information back to their home country and could act as intermediaries. They travelled to their new homes with a large entourage and must have had a considerable cultural impact as well as a diplomatic one. Royal women were given as wives of high officials within the kingdom, perhaps to ensure their loyalty, while foreign women of high status also decorated the courts of Mesopotamian kings.

It is difficult to identify the precise type of activity taking place on the banquet seals and this is partly because the various spheres of activity that we have mentioned in fact overlap considerably. The demarcations between sacred and secular did not exist in the forms to which we are accustomed and, equally, it is difficult to distinguish between diplomacy and trade in the exchange of goods. Administrative duties included all the other areas of activity.

Another public or quasi-public function of elite women that took place within the female world is shown on some of the so-called presentation or audience scene seals, which show a single seated woman receiving homage. As with the comparable male scenes it is often difficult to tell whether the main seated figure is human or divine. In the absence of a horned crown, or of divine symbols, it seems reasonable to suggest that the seated figure is human. Such seals again occur at Ur in the Royal cemetery in both male and female graves. They apparently show the queen bestowing positions on her senior officials, an interpretation that has already been suggested by Winter for the male version of the scene (Winter 1991). For example, U.7954 is of lapis with a gold cap and both registers show a presentation to a female figure. From the same grave, apparently that of a woman, U7956, also of lapis, shows a double presentation. In the top register a woman is presented to a goddess and in the lower to a human female. The material of which these seals are made and the subject matter both suggest that they were the property of important officials, while the iconography suggests that they held these positions in a female household, although we have already seen that iconography is not a very reliable indicator. There are also a few presentation seals that seem to show more domestic scenes, such as the royal nanny in the presence of the queen and her children at Urkesh (Buccellati and Buccellati 1995/6). A particularly charming audience scene, also of lapis, shows Amar-Ashtar, a servant of Tutanapsum, another of Naram-Sin's daughters and entu priestess of the god Enlil, standing before her mistress who wears a most unusual tiara (Asher-Greve 2006:68 fig.15).

We know that royal women had specific cult duties, both ceremonial and administrative, even when they were not priestesses themselves. For example, the archives from Puzrish-Dagan, an animal collection point, show that in the Ur III period one of Shulgi's queens, Shulgi-Simtu, had responsibility for supplying animals for a variety of cult purposes. Interestingly, most of the animals originated from other women (Van de Mieroop 1999:158). Inscribed votive statues, common in the second half of the third millennium, demonstrate the overlap between the spheres that today we would call religious and secular. The representations of women, which Bahrani regards as portraits, in some sense of the word (Bahrani 2001:118) were dedicated by royal and non-royal women alike to gods and goddesses to pray for the life of their patrons, whether male or female, royal or commoner. Male statues are more numerous, but it is of interest that women's statues apparently stood side by side with them in the temples and that women had the resources to commission such items. Hymns and prayers written by women have also survived, most notably those by Enheduana, daughter of Sargon of Agade to whom we will return.

Some of the administrative duties of the queen have already been alluded to. She was responsible for the running of the women's world in the palace and often of a complex business that farmed large areas of land and a number of manufacturing enterprises whose surplus goods were used to buy in materials and goods not available locally. Some of the practicalities were certainly delegated to officials, but the overall responsibility remained that of the queen. Well-to-do elite women probably had similar responsibilities, although on a smaller scale. It is difficult to know whether the giving of presents by the wife of one ruler to another should be regarded as diplomacy or trade. Baranamtara, wife of Lugalanda of Lagash, and head of the E-Bau temple estate in that city exchanged gifts with the wife of the ruler of Adab, but we are not told why (Lambert 1953:58, Prentice 2010).

No doubt the women of the royal households also had considerable political influence even if they did not have official power in the world of men. We know, for example, that in historical periods the choice of a successor was often heavily influenced by senior women in the Abbasid court and in particular by the queen mother (Kennedy 2004 chap.7). The Velide or queen mother in Ottoman times could also exercise great political power and was frequently a very wealthy woman in her own right, using her wealth to build mosques and hospitals (Mansell 1995 chap.4).

The heavy administrative duties that were carried out by elite women meant that there was a need for professionals in a number of fields to assist them, although these professional people did not have to be exclusively female. We have seen that male officials carried seals, which apparently recorded their appointment by women, but we also have evidence for women in a number of key posts, most notably that of scribe (Ziegler 1999:8). Scribe is a flexible term, which covered a large number of roles such as surveyor and accountant, and sometimes merely meant a literate and educated person. A recent article has shown that female scribes were as highly educated as their male counterparts, although it is not clear if they attended special schools or studied with the men (Lion and Robson 2005). It should also be remembered that the scribe of the underworld was female and in the third millennium the patron deity of scribes, Nisaba, was also a woman, both indications of the importance of female members of the profession. In the second millennium the role of patron was subsumed by Nabu a male god.

Other female professions for which there is evidence include those women who worked in the service of the gods in more menial capacities, the divine barber Kindazi was female, for example (al Zubaidi 2004:131) and those carrying out similar tasks in the households of royal and elite women. At Mari, in the household of the queen, where again we have the fullest documentation, there were cooks, bakers, millers and drawers of water, many of whom were female. However, there is a mid-third-millennium seal from Mozan, which is inscribed with the name of the queen's head cook, who is male, and the seal shows him at work in his kitchen (Buccellati and Buccellati 1995/6). This surely marks the beginning of a tradition, which lasts to this day, where head chefs tend to be male! Any large household employed farm labourers, reed cutters, potters and so on, as well as weavers, spinners, tanners and other textile workers, all of which were tasks undertaken by women. Singers, dancers and musicians of both sexes also formed part of the palace households and were graded according to their expertise. Such musicians are to be seen on both plaques and seals playing a variety of instruments, which certainly included harps, lyres and cymbals, as well as drums. Perhaps rather more unexpected is the presence of female guards or gate-keepers at Mari (Ziegler 1999:8).

We have evidence from the Mari texts for a female doctor and for wet nurses, nannies and midwives, while the seals once again provide us with confirmation. There is a fine, somewhat earlier, third-millennium inscribed seal, from Mozan, which shows the royal nanny approaching a seated female, presumably the queen, with a child on her knee (see above; U.10757). A rather comparable seal from Ur was found in a so-called second-dynasty grave. It shows a seated female, again with a child on her knee, and three standing females approaching her, two of whom carry vessels with handles. It is not inscribed, but the similarity with the Mozan seal is striking. A seal originally from the Erlenmeyer collection is inscribed as belonging to Ninkalla midwife of the (goddess) Baba. The top register shows the midwife being presented to the seated goddess by her personal guardian, while the lower register shows a row of scorpions above water birds, geese or swans perhaps, swimming across the design. Another seal from Yale[3] shows a very similar scene, although the seated female on the top register is apparently human rather than divine, and the lower register has the water birds though not the scorpions. The inscription reads SAG.SHA DUMU LUGAL.BI and as the figure being presented is female it is tempting to see this as another occasion when DUMU means child rather than son and to suggest that we have the seal of another midwife.

A final representation of midwives may perhaps be seen on the shell plaque mentioned above from Mari where two priestesses are seen bending over an elaborate bed covered with sheepskins. Unfortunately the plaque is broken, so the figure on the bed is lost. The scene has also been interpreted as part of a ritual for obtaining omens through dreams (Asher-Greve 1987). Gula, the goddess of healing, was female, although the profession was certainly not a female monopoly as we know of male ashipu priests and others active in the medical world.

We have already seen that elite women were active in the commercial world overseeing the production and marketing of textiles. There is limited evidence for the participation of other women too. Foster describes the activity of a female merchant in the Sargonic period called Amar-é who apparently specialised in land lease and who invested her profits with various agents, while her husband, also a merchant, had separate business interests. There is also evidence for other female entrepreneurs so that Amar-é does not seem to have been unusual (Foster 1982:33). In addition, women are known to have bought and sold property; Asher-Greve refers to a kudurru of ED1/II date, which records the sale of land by one priestess to another (Asher-Greve 1985:169). The stela of Usumgal also shows a woman as one of the main protagonists in a deed of sale. Legal documents from approximately the same period refer to women buying and selling property and acting as guarantors for a third party (Van de Mieroop 1989:57). Finally, women could enter into contracts, act as witnesses and had certain legal rights. Owen (1980) has described a case where a widow successfully sued her brother-in-law for a share of the estate of her deceased father-in-law and won. Women were also inn-keepers, as we know from the Epic of Gilgamesh, and apparently also acted as money lenders.

Hierarchy and professionalism

There is good evidence for a social hierarchy within these early royal households. At Mari and in Sumer there were both principal and secondary royal wives, as well as princesses and concubines (Ziegler 1999:44). Ration lists, which give details of the food and raw materials issued to members of the staff, also point to hierarchical ordering, while the earlier ration lists from the temple of Bau at Lagash paint a similar picture, with rations varying from 72 silas to only 18 among the female workers. It is also clear that there are two main classes of women here of which the ones receiving 18 silas are described as purchased and may have been prisoners of war or perhaps debt slaves (Maekawa 1973/4:92 note 23, Prentice 2010). It seems that this differentiation is also sometimes visible in funerary material. Gansell has recently shown that differences in the ornaments worn by the attendants in the royal graves at Ur suggest a degree of stratification here too (Gansell 2007).

We have already mentioned the presence of high-ranking women in the priesthood, which was the most important profession open to women. In many ways the lives of the most senior of them, often of royal birth, must have mirrored those of the lives of the queens we have just described, for they were regarded as the spouse or queen of the city god whom they served. The best known of these royal priestesses is undoubtedly Enheduanna daughter of Sargon of Agade, while an Akkadian seal is inscribed with the name of Aman-Eshtar servant of Tudanapshum entu priestess at Nippur. It seems likely that Tudanapshum was a daughter of Naram-Sin, although her filiation is not entirely clear (Michalowski 1981:75). We also know of princesses as priestesses from the Mari archive (Ziegler 1999:46). Temples were in control of important estates with large numbers of dependent workers throughout the period under discussion and the final responsibility for the administration of these estates, and for the manufacture of goods for trade, no doubt rested on the high priestess as it did on the queen. The gods are known to have visited each other at major festivals and we can suggest that their priestesses, their spouses, went with them and that diplomatic contacts were maintained between the city states to facilitate such interaction.

We have evidence for less exalted priestesses as well so we can suggest that priestly households were as stratified as those of royalty. A seal from Ur, U 9315, is inscribed with the name of He-Kun-Sig priestess of Pabilsag, who was worshipped in a small neighbourhood chapel, while Asher-Greve lists three different words for priestess, nin-dingir, lukur and nu-gig (Asher-Greve 1985:184, see Westenholz forthcoming for a fuller discussion of the nomenclature of the priesthood), which she suggests may describe the different ranks within the priesthood. Alternatively they may refer to the different functions that the holder performed. For example, Gelb (Gelb et.al. 1991:17) lists a "lamenter" on his list of female professions and there is also evidence for a female interpreter of dreams (Asher-Greve 1987). Gilgamesh, for example, takes his dreams to his mother Ninsun to be interpreted when he dreams in rather cryptic terms of the coming of Enkidu (George 1999:10/11). There has been considerable debate about whether women were actually allowed to pour libations to the gods themselves, as on the Enheduanna plaque a nude male is shown performing this ritual (Winter 1987). However, there are rare seals that show women carrying out this task so that the fact that the libation is poured by a male on the Enheduanna plaque is probably a sign of her eminence, not of a prohibition on her doing so. A fine Agade seal, which shows a woman pouring a libation to a goddess from one of the Diyala sites, is illustrated by Frankfort (Frankfort 1955 no.987 pl.92).

The differences in status suggested above may also be shown in the representational evidence, where women who appear to be priestesses are depicted wearing a variety of different headdresses. The best known of these is probably the hat with ribbons hanging down over the ear, which is worn by Enheduanna on the famous plaque from Ur, while the priestesses depicted on a number of plaques and statues from the temples at Mari wear high bulbous hats apparently made of felt. A shell plaque, which probably comes from the Dagan temple at Mari, depicts a group of women weaving and carrying out other, possibly ritual, duties. Three different headdresses are shown: the bulbous hat, a swathed turban and a neat little bonnet. Judging from their activities the women in the bulbous hats, who are not shown weaving, may have held the higher status, but all three groups wear cylinder seals, so the difference in status may not have been great and they may all have had administrative duties of some sort (Dolce 1978 nos M295/7).

The question of the existence of the professional temple prostitute is still unresolved; there is the colourful account of Herodotus and later of Strabo, but the evidence for their presence in earlier times is not strong. Yamauchi (1973) claims that cultic prostitution was one of the so-called *me*, the building blocks of Sumerian civilisation, and many scholars regard the erotic plaques found in the Old Babylonian and Old Assyrian periods as further evidence for this custom. In reality the majority could as easily be regarded as charms to bring luck or fertility to the home, while some may even have been an early sex aid. Assante would go further and questions the whole concept of cultic prostitution in Mesopotamia, seeing it as being based on a nineteenth-century attitude towards the east and women in particular, and on Fraser's *Golden Bough*. She argues that some of the terms used in the cuneiform literature, which, for example, notes rations issued by the great state institutions to prostitutes, have also been misinterpreted (Assante 2003). These are powerful arguments but do not explain Herodotus's stories. It has recently been suggested that his account rests on a misinterpretation of actual Babylonian rites (Reallexikon 2006:18 and 19).

Relations between the male and female world

The evidence for the relationship between the male and female worlds is often indirect and circumstantial, but archives from two third-millennium public institutions on the southern plain, one from the Bau temple at Lagash and one from the animal-processing plant at Puzrish Dagan, as well as the slightly later archive from Mari, indicate that high-ranking women, once appointed, ran important bodies as independent entities without male supervision. In the case of the archives of the Mari palace, dating to the early second millennium, there are letters sent by the king Zimri-Lim to his queen while he was travelling round his domains entrusting her with a variety of tasks and leaving her effectively as regent in his absence, although major decisions seem to have been left till his return (Ziegler 1999:43). The perceived separateness of these two worlds in early Mesopotamia may also be illustrated by the existence of a language known as *emesal*. There is some controversy about this language; it was a variant of Sumerian, which, according to Edzard (1995:2115), was used mainly in the literary quotation of the speech of goddesses and women. Others see it as a specialised dialect used for certain types of poetic and cultic compositions (Black 1991:23). It is interesting and a little unexpected that in her hymns to Inanna Enheduadda daughter of Sargon of Agade does not once use *emesal* (Whittaker 2002:637). We have no evidence for its use by women in their everyday lives, but its existence is of some significance in this debate and may indicate that it was used to underline the separateness of the world of women whether divine or not.

The "banquet" shown on the banquet seals discussed earlier is one of the few areas where the world of men and women appear to meet on equal terms. On the banquet seals of the later third millennium, where a male and female figure are shown together drinking, and less frequently eating, the figures are the same size, probably indicating a similar status. Size is frequently used to denote relative social standing in Sumerian iconography. The so-called Ur standard, for example, which shows a formal all-male banquet on one side, depicts the main figure, the king, as a head taller than any of his companions who are thought to be his military commanders.

Bearing in mind the evidence we have reviewed, the model of a parallel universe seems an attractive one. This model also proposes that the female world was as stratified and as professional as that of men (Westenholz 1990) and that it operated in almost all the same fields, except the military and the legal. It also underlines the fact that many women wielded important power, both within their world and outside it. Women in the third millennium BC were professionally involved in administration, in religion, in diplomacy and in the economy. Van de Mieroop has already proposed a somewhat similar view in his study of the Bau temple archive and the material from Puzrish Dagan. As a result of the evidence from these two archives he says "the involvement of women in the economy was usually interacting with other women as if in a world parallel to the one where men worked" (Van de Mieroop 1999:158). These other women were most probably other elite females running similar, though smaller, institutions. He also states that "royal women were involved in public life, parallel to their husbands, perhaps primarily in contact with other women" (op. cit. p.159).

It is accepted that many of these professional women owed their positions ultimately to their male relatives, to husbands, fathers or brothers, but our evidence emphasises that, once appointed, women formed an independent and vital part of the public as well as the private spheres. Some women may also have attained high office by virtue of their own birth and talents, and both men and women benefited from the patronage exercised by their highly placed female relatives (Wright 2008). It should be stressed again that neither the male nor the female world was exclusive to one gender or another, men and women worked in both spheres, and men could be subordinate to women in the women's world. It can further be suggested that there was relatively little contact between the two worlds, except for the purposes of procreation and on certain formal occasions, although no doubt love matches occurred; this is another area that needs exploring. Evidence from recent anthropological work on women in traditional Arab societies seems to show a similar pattern (Altorki 1986).

In summary, for the periods under discussion, men and women carried out similar tasks in their separate worlds and shared some functions, apparently on an equal basis, as indicated by the Early Dynastic banqueting seals. Both made important contributions in the public sphere. It is also possible to quote examples where, in the literary world at least, it was apparently the female who dominated. It was after all Inanna who sent Dumuzi into the Underworld as her substitute, and a goddess, Ereshkigal, who initially ruled the Underworld. A similar picture of female dominance can be seen on the Uruk vase where the main male figure is presenting his offerings to a female, whether she is goddess or priestess (Black et al. 2004:75, Moortgat 1969: pl.21).

Discussion

The evidence presented here raises the profile of professional women in Mesopotamia in the period under study. It also suggests a new and more complex interpretation of the relationship between men and women, while stressing the differences visible within the world of women.

Nineteenth-century notions of the harem and the subservient place of women oversimplify and misrepresent the realities of life for elite and middle-ranking women in the later third and early second millennia in Mesopotamia. These notions seem to reflect the orientalising view of many early scholars who frequently ignored women altogether. It is more accurate to suggest that, at least in the upper echelons of society, there were, effectively, two parallel universes, which operated in similar fields and in similar ways. The evidence quoted in this paper demonstrates that women made important contributions in the public, as well as the private, spheres. They had ceremonial, administrative and economic roles in both the palace and the temple sectors of society. When men and women met for ceremonial purposes they seem, from the evidence of the banqueting scenes, to have met on a basis of equality.

Women controlled large households composed of professional men and women and it seems likely that they exercised considerable political influence as well, although direct evidence is slight. The social lives of these elite women probably revolved largely around their families and their social peers, as it does in traditional societies today (for example, Abu Lughod 1998:260) and contact with the male world was limited. The concept finds some support in anthropological studies of the world of Arab women in the immediate past and in historical work on both the Abbasid and Ottoman periods, as well as further afield. However, such power as women wielded in the male-dominated world of traditional societies is wielded by stealth or by older post-menopausal women.

It is accepted that there is no direct link between these historical and anthropological examples and the archaeological period under discussion, but the comparisons serve to remind us of other possible life-styles. It is also interesting to note that the activities of these more modern women seem to be more restricted than those of the women in early Mesopotamia. Unlike their Mesopotamian counterparts they have little contact with administration or the economy, except on a domestic scale. However, the anthropological literature frequently states that their social lives, as in the past, are oriented around same-sex groups, usually composed of kin, and that within such groups there is great freedom from the surveillance of men (Abu Lughod 1998:260). Elizabeth Fernea depicted such a parallel society in her account of a year spent in a small town south of Baghdad in the early 1960s, where her social contacts were exclusively with the women. Her evidence for this parallel society, which in practice operated within strict limits, paints a vivid picture of the lives of such women and their society, which included some professional women such as a reader of the Koran (Fernea 1968). This particular profession seems to continue today. In the cave of Abraham at Urfa, Syria, in May 2007, a woman was observed reading from the Koran to a group of other women listening intently (pers. obs.). Until very recently important events in the life of the family were also celebrated this way in Baghdad, when a female reader called a *mullayah* would recite the Koran to an all female audience.[4]

Women from the middle stratum of society were also active in a number of professional fields from the priesthood to midwifery and commerce. We may propose that their households echoed those of the elite, but on a much smaller scale. Sadly, we know virtually nothing of the lives of village and nomadic women, who no doubt also played significant roles in the economy and in family life. It cannot be assumed that their lives were similar to those of the urban women. Ultimately, however, in all spheres and at all levels, the male world was in control and many, if not most, women owed their social and professional positions to their male relatives, but within their own worlds they enjoyed power and freedom.

Changes in the social relationship between men and women

The situation of women seems to have changed and to have become considerably more restricted by the end of the second millennium, judging from the evidence of the Middle Assyrian laws (Roth 1997). Asher-Greve (2002:17) suggests that the change began earlier and that women were more visible in public life before the Akkadian period, but evidence presented recently by Rita Wright shows that they retained most of their status and power into the Ur III period (Wright 2008). It is true that women are far less visible on cylinder seals after the Agade period, though this is partly explained by the change in fashion, which meant that banquet scenes are no longer found. The reasons for the absence of women in public life after this are not clear, but it seems likely that it was due to a complex tissue of reasons. The emergence of stratified state societies, which Engels saw as linked to the declining power of women, may have played a role (Wright 2007); increasing prosperity may have been another factor. If women's work is no longer central to the economy, some at least can be removed from the workforce by prosperous families and secluded. Seclusion then becomes a mark of wealth and status and will be copied by other aspiring families.

Paradoxically, prosperity can have the opposite effect as well. Increasing wealth and foreign travel have begun to liberalise the lives of elite women in Saudi Arabia in a type of silken revolution. One result of this liberalisation in the upper echelons of Jeddah society is that young couples are increasingly deciding to live in their own home rather than moving into the paternal home, as has been traditional. This has resulted in the increasing importance of the nuclear rather than the extended family, and in increasing freedom for younger women who are reinterpreting and modifying the prevailing ideology (Altorki 1986:150/3). Altorki also observed that many of the old female support systems, which were based on the extended family, are beginning to break down in Jeddah and it seems likely that the paradigm of parallel universes ceases to be appropriate with the breakdown of the extended family as women then begin to mix more widely and freely with men and there is no longer a critical mass of women in a single household.

As the population increased there would have been a demand for increased production in every field. This in turn would tend to lead to greater profession-alization, more rigorous training and the exclusion of women from the skills that were previously learnt in the home. Another factor may relate to the shifts in the composition of the population of Mesopotamia in the second millennium. We know almost nothing of the social customs of the Amorites or the Kassites, for example, and the Assyrians in the north did not always have the same customs as the Sumerians of the south. It is possible that their women may not have enjoyed the same freedom as those in the south and that with their arrival in Sumer, their customs began to prevail. Such economic and social attitudes may each have played a part in the social change that apparently took place with the increasing seclusion of women by the Middle Assyrian period.

This paper has tried to show that if we continue to use the old models of subservient women in a male-dominated society, we distort the historical reality and neglect the important role played by women from all walks of life, but especially from the highest social class, in the public as well as the private life of south Mesopotamia in the later third and early second millennia BC. It is suggested that a more accurate picture can be gained by viewing the female world as being, in most respects, a mirror-image of the male and as forming what may be called a parallel universe in all spheres of life. This inquiry has also raised new questions and suggested new areas for research. First, it needs to be determined if the position of women at the period under review was the last phase of a long development from a postulated prehistoric, matriarchal society; and, second, the reasons for the decline in the status of women in the second millennium need to be further investigated.

Notes

1 I am most grateful to Professor Geller for this information.
2 The plaque of Ur-Nanshe showing him carrying a basket of bricks attended by members of his family shows one female who is either his wife or his daughter and who is much smaller than the main figure. This might suggest that she is his daughter, although there is something of a circular argument here!.
3 Buchanan, Briggs.1981. *Early Near Eastern Seals in the Yale Babylonian collection.* Yale, collection no.561.
4 I am grateful to Dr Lamia al Gailani for this information.

Bibliography

Abu Lughod, Lila. 1993. *Writing Women's Worlds*. Berkeley: University of California Press.

——, 1998. The marriage of feminism and Islamism in Egypt. In: *Remaking Women*. ed. Abu Lughod, Lila. Princeton University Press: 243–69.

Altorki, Soraya. 1986. *Women in Saudi Arabia*. New York: Columbia University Press.

Asher-Greve, J. 1985. *Frauen in altsumerischer zeit*. Malibu: Undena.

——, 1987. The oldest female oneiromancer. In: *La Femme dans le Proche-Orient Antique*. ed. Durand, J.M. Editions Recherche sur les Civilisations, Paris 1987: 27–31.

——, 2002. Decisive sex, essential gender. In: *Sex & Gender in the Ancient Near East. Proceedings of the XLVII th Rencontre Internationale*. ed. Parpola, S. and Whiting, R. Helsinki: The Neo Assyrian Text Project, 11–26.

——, 2006. The "Golden Age" of women: status and gender in third millennium Sumerian and Akkadian art. In: *Images and Gender*. Orbis Biblicus et Orientalis 220. ed. Schroer, S. Fribourg: Academic Press, 41–81.

Assante, Julia. 2003. From whore to hierodule: the historiographic invention of Mesopotamian sex professionals. In: *Ancient Art and its Historiography*. ed. Donahue, A.A. and Fullerton, M.D. New York: Cambridge University Press, 13–47.

Bahrani, Zainab. 2001. *Women of Babylon: Gender and Representation in Mesopotamia*. London: Routledge.

Black, Jeremy. 1991. Eme-sal cult songs and prayers. In: *Velles Paraules: Ancient Near Eastern Studies in Honour of Miguel Civil on the Occasion of his Sixty-Fifth Birthday*. ed. Michalowski, P., Steinkeller, P., Stone, E.C. and Zettler, R.L. Sabadell: Editorial AUSA, 23–37.

Black, J., Cunningham, G., Robson, E. and Zolymi, G. ed. 2004. *The Literature of Ancient Sumer*. Oxford University Press.

Buccellati, G., and Buccellati, M.K. 2002. Tar'am–Agade, daughter of Naram-Sin at Urkesh. In: *Of Pots and Pans*. Papers presented to David Oates in honour of his 75th birthday, ed. Al-Gailani-Werr, L., Curtis, J., Martin, H., McMahon, A., Oates, J. and Reade, J. et al. London: Nabu publications, 11–31.

——, 1995/6. The royal storehouse of Urkesh: the glyptic evidence from the south-west wing. *Archiv für Orientforschung* 42/3:1–32.

Buchanan, B. 1981. *Early Near Eastern Seals in the Yale Babylonian Collection*. New Haven: Yale University Press.

Colbow, G. 2002. Priestesses, either married or unmarried and spouses without title: their seal use and their seals in Sippar at the beginning of the second millennium BC. In: *Sex & Gender in the Ancient Near East. Proceedings of the XLVII th Rencontre Internationale*. ed. Parpola, S. and Whiting, R. Helsinki: Neo-Assyrian Text Corpus Project, 85–90.

Dalley, Stephanie.1984. *Mari and Karana*. London: Longman.

Dolce, R. 1978. *Gli intarsi Mesopotamici dell'epoca Protodynastca*. 2 vols. Rome: Istituto di studi del Vicino Oriente.

Edzard, D.O.1995. The Sumerian Language. In: *Civilizations of the Ancient Near East*. ed. Sasson, J.M., IV:2107–16. New York: Scribner.

Fernea, Elizabeth Warnock. 1968. *Guests of the Sheik*. London: Robert Hale.

Foster, B.R. 1977. Commercial activity in Sargonic Mesopotamia. *Iraq* 39, 31–43.

——, 1987. Notes on women in Sargonic society. In: *La Femme dans le Proche-Orient Antique*, ed. Durand, J.M. Paris: Editions Recherche sur les Civilisations, 53–61. Bethesda: CDL Press.

Franfort, Henri. 1955. *Stratified cylinder seals from the Diyala*. Oriental Institute Publications LXXII Chicago: Oriental Institute.

Gansell, A.R. 2007. Identity and adornment in the third millennium BC Mesopotamian "Royal cemetery at Ur". *Cambridge Archaeological Journal* 17, 29–46.

Gelb, I.J, Steinkeller, P. and Whiting, R.M. 1991. *Earliest Land Tenure Systems in the Near East: Ancient Kudurrus*. Oriental Institute Publications 104. Chicago: Oriental Institute.

George, A. 1999. *The Epic of Gilgamesh*. London: Penguin.

Gilchrist, Roberta. 1999. *Gender and Archaeology*. London: Routledge.

Glassner, J.J. 1989. Women, hospitality, and the honour of the family. In: *Women's Earliest Records*. ed. Lesko, B. Atlanta: Scholars Press, 71–90.

Hallo, W.W. 1976. Women of Sumer. In: *The Legacy of Sumer*. ed. Schmandt-Besserat, D. Biblioteca Mesopotamica 4. Undena: Malibu, 23–40.

Kennedy, Hugh. 2004. *The Court of the Caliphs*. London: Weidenfeld & Nicolson.

Lambert, W.G. 1953. Textes commerciaux de Lagash (époque présargonique). *Revue d'Assyriologie 47*, 57–69.

Lion, B. and Robson, E. 2005. Quelques textes Paléo-Babyloniens rédigés par des Femmes. *Journal of Cuneiform Studies 57*, 37–54.

Maekawa, K. 1973/4. The development of the E-mi in Lagash during the Early Dynastic III. *Mesopotamia 8/9*, 77–144.

Mansell, P. 1995. *Constantinople*. London: John Murray.

Michalowski, P. 1981. Tudanapšum, Naram-Sin and Nippur. *Revue d'Assyriologie 75*, 173–76.

Moortgat, Anton. 1969. *The Art of Ancient Mesopotamia*. London: Phaidon.

Owen, D.I. 1980. Widows' rights in Ur III Sumer. *Zeitschrift für Assyriologie* 70, 170–84.

Pollock,Susan. 1999. *Ancient Mesopotamia*. Cambridge: Cambridge University Press.

Prentice, R. 2010. *The Exchange of Goods and Services in Presargonic Lagash*. Münster: Ugarit Verlag.

Reallexikon der Assyriologie *Band 11.1/2* 2006.

Roth, M.T. 1997. *Law collections from Mesopotamia and Asia Minor. SBL Writings from the Ancient World*, 2nd edn. Atlanta: Society of Biblical Literature.

Sharlach, Tonia. 2007. Social change and the transition from the Third Dynasty of Ur to the Old Babylonian kingdoms. *Regime Change in the Ancient Near East and Egypt*. Proceedings of the British Academy 136. ed. Crawford, Harriet. Oxford: Oxford University Press for The British Academy, 61–72.

Trigger, B.G. 2006. *A History of Archaeological Thought*, 2nd edn. Cambridge: Cambridge University Press.

Van de Mieroop, Marc. 1989. Women in the economy of Sumer. In: *Women's Earliest Records*. ed. Lesko, B. Atlanta: Scholars Press, 53, 66.

——,1999. *Cuneiform Texts and the Writing of History*. London: Routledge.

Westenholz, J.G. 1990. Towards a new conceptualization of the female role in Mesopotamian society. *Journal of the American Oriental Society 110*, 510–21.

——, 2013. In the service of the gods: the ministering clergy. In: *The Sumerian World*, ed. Crawford, H. London: Routledge.

Winter, Irene. 1987. Women in public: the disk of Enheduanna. In: La Femme dans le Proche-Orient Antique, ed. Durand, J.M. Paris: Editions Recherche sur les Civilisations, 189–201.

——, 1991. Legitimation of authority through image and legend. *The Organisation of Power*, 2nd edn. ed. Gibson, McG. and Biggs, R.D. Studies in ancient Oriental Civilization 46.Chicago: Oriental Institute.

Whittaker, G. 2002. Linguistic anthropology and the study of emesal as (a) women's Language. In: *Sex & Gender in the Ancient Near East. Proceedings of the XLVII th Rencontre Internationale.* ed. Parpola, S. and Whiting, R. Helsinki: Neo-Assyrian Text Corpus Project, 633–44.

Woolley, C.L. 1934. *The Royal Cemetery. Ur Excavations* II. 2 vols. London: British Museum.

Wright, K.I. 2007. Women and urban society in Mesopotamia. In: *Archaeology and Gender.* ed. Hamilton, S., Whitehouse, R.D. and Wright, K.I. Walnut Creek California: Left Coast Press, 199–245.

Wright, Rita.P. 1996. Technology, gender and class: worlds of difference in Ur III Mesopotamia. In: *Gender and Archaeology.* ed. Wright, Rita. P. Philadelphia: University of Pennsylvania Press, 79–110.

——, 2008. Gendered relations and the Ur III dynasty: kinship, property and labor. In: *Gender Through Time in the Ancient Near East.* ed. Bolger, D. Lanham: Altamira Press, 247–80.

Yamauchi, E.M. 1973. Cultic prostitution. In: *Orient and Occident: Studies Presented to Cyrus H Gordon.* ed. Hoffner H.A. Jr. Alter Orient in Altes Testament Band 22. Kevelaer: Butzon und Bercker, 213–22.

Ziegler, Nele. 1999. *Le harem de Zimri-Lim.* Mémoires de NABU 5. Paris: Société pour l'étude du Proche-orient ancient.

al Zubaidi, Layla. 2004. Tracing women in early Sumer. In: *Ungendering Civilization*, ed. Pyburn, K.A. London: Routledge, 117–135.

2

THE FEMININE IN MYTHS AND EPIC

Alhena Gadotti

The study of women in Sumerian literature has received only limited attention thus far.[1] This is in contrast with many other fields of ancient studies.[2] For instance, in both biblical and classical scholarship, monographs have appeared that shed light on the relations between women's social roles and the images of women in literary documents.[3] Thus, in her discussion on the image of women in Athenian literature of the fifth century, Sarah Pomeroy pointed out that "[t] he mythology about women is created by men and, in a culture dominated by men, it may have little to do with flesh-and-blood women."[4] Indeed there is a great divide between how heroines were portrayed in Greek tragedy and comedy, and actual women living in ancient Greece.

The case of Mesopotamia, however, is quite different. As I have shown elsewhere, the portrayal of women in Sumerian literature had everything to do with real women.[5]

In the present contribution, I will focus on the portrayal of the *divine feminine*. In other words, I will primarily discuss what Sumerian compositions have to say about the goddesses of the Mesopotamian pantheon.[6] My study does not aim to be exhaustive, nor is this possible given the breadth of the topic. It does, however, attempt to highlight some facets of the divine feminine, which scholars have in the past overlooked.[7]

To an extent, this survey will show that the divine feminine replicates on a divine level the biological, social and cultural roles women had in "real life". Interestingly enough, however, when one looks at the image of actual women in Sumerian literature, the emphasis is on different aspects of the feminine.[8] Among the Old Babylonian Sumerian literary compositions where named mortal women play a central role, one finds only eight individuals:[9] the ideal mother;[10] the ideal wife;[11] two princesses who have been appointed as priestesses;[12] two sisters;[13] an old and wise woman assisting the king of Uruk;[14] and a tavern-keeper who became queen of Kiš.[15]

In the Old Babylonian Sumerian literature corpus, which provides the epigraphic evidence for this investigation, goddesses are usually found in traditional familial roles: young unmarried women, mothers and daughters, sisters, spouses, widows. The survey here presented reflects this state of affairs.[16] Thus, for instance, the goddess Ninlil/Sud exemplifies a woman's sexual as well as social growth: she is depicted as the adolescent virgin on the edge of womanhood, who develops into a mature woman and she transitions from a restricted and local function to become the spouse of Enlil, the head of the Sumerian pantheon (*Enlil and Ninlil* and *Enlil and Sud*). Ninlil's mother, Nisaba, is the mother who offers valuable and pertinent advice and enables the young girl to cross the threshold into womanhood (*Enlil and Ninlil* and *Enlil and Sud*). Ninhursaga, on the other hand, is another embodiment of the mother: in the composition here discussed she primarily represents the feminine reproductive powers (*Enki and Ninhursaga*). Finally, the Ninmah of *Enki and Ninmah* is the mother of mankind.

Geštinana is the devoted sister, who offers aid and advice to her unfortunate brother Dumuzi (*Dumuzi and Geštinana*, *Dumuzi and His Sisters*, and *Dumuzi's Dream*).[17] In *Dumuzi and Geštinana* and *Dumuzi and His Sisters*, not incorporated in the present discussion, Geštinana is always at her brother's side and attempts to protect him and rescue him from the destiny Inana has decreed for him.[18] In *Dumuzi's Dream*, she interprets the dream Dumuzi had about his impending death (see below).[19]

More complex to classify is the multifaceted Inana, who has been the subject of several studies (for instance, Bruschweiler 1987; Harris 1991; Glassner 1992; Westenholz 1998, 2009) and whose nature still eludes scholars. The complexity of her nature is evidenced by the compositions belonging to the so-called Inana and Dumuzi cycle—to be distinguished by the Inana and Dumuzi love songs. Inana is alternatively the ruthless spouse willing to sacrifice her husband in order to survive death (*Inana's Descent to the Netherworld*; *Dumuzi and Geštinana*) and the bereft woman mourning the loss of her betrothed (*Inana and Bilulu*). However, the Inana and Dumuzi songs (not included in this survey) depict her as the enthusiastic young spouse (Sefati 1998).

Of mothers and daughters

Enlil and Ninlil *and* Enlil and Sud

Enlil and Ninlil (*EN*: Behrens 1978; Cooper 1980; Leick 1994: 42–46) and *Enlil and Sud* (*ES*: Civil 1983; Wilcke 1987; Leick 1994: 46–47) are two related compositions narrating how Enlil, the patron deity of the city of Nippur and chief god of the Sumerian pantheon, found a spouse. Despite sharing a common *topos*, namely Enlil and Ninlil's "love story," the two tales are radically different, and they will be treated separately. An important corollary to this *topos* is the value of virginity (Leick 1994: 47), as we will see.

In *EN* and *ES*, goddesses appear in traditional roles. The main female character is the young unmarried girl, Ninlil/Sud, who becomes a woman by the completion of the story, and her wise mother, Nunbaršegunu/Nisaba, who advises her in women-related matters. In *ES* only, a third goddess plays a secondary role: Aruru, Enlil's sister, accompanies Sud into the wedding chamber, thus helping her to transition from her paternal house to the house of her husband (*ES* ll. 146–47).

Enlil and Ninlil

EN is "a coming-of-age scenario, which describes the transition of the two main characters [i.e. Enlil and Ninlil] from adolescence to full adulthood."[20] The setting is the city of Nippur, the centrality of which emerges from the very first lines of the composition, describing the city and its main geographical features (ll. 1–9). Even the main protagonists of the story are defined in terms of their relations to Nippur (ll. 10–12).

The story proper opens with Nunbaršegunu, Ninlil's mother, warning her daughter about Enlil, his "wondering eye" and womanizing attitude. If the young Ninlil were to meet him, she should refuse him at all costs (ll. 13–22).

As expected, things go according to Nunbaršegunu's fears. Enlil meets Ninlil while the latter is bathing along the banks of the Numbirtum canal and falls in lust (or was it love?) with her. After having approached her to no avail, Enlil enlists the help of his minister, Nuska, and eventually kidnaps and rapes Ninlil (ll. 23–53).[21] Because of his crime, Enlil is expelled by Nippur and forced into exile (ll. 54–63). His long journey appears to lead him to the Netherworld.

Despite having been raped, or maybe because of it, a now pregnant Ninlil follows Enlil in his peregrinations and has *consensual* intercourse with him three more times (Gadotti 2009b). From the rape, Suen-Ašimbabbar, the Moon God, is born (inferred from l. 53). From the ensuing couplings, Ninlil gives birth to three chthonic deities: Nergal-Meslanta-ea, Ninazu and En-bililu. The composition ends with a praise to both Enlil and Ninlil.

Key to the present survey are the figures of Nunbaršegunu and Ninlil. Nun-bar-še-gunu is another name for the goddess Nisaba.[22] In this composition, she is described as Nippur' wise woman (l. 12 um-ma) and represents the voice of maturity and experience. This is evidenced not only by the epithet used to define her, but also by line 22, which explicitly states:

In giving her (Ninlil) advice, she provided her with wisdom.[23]

She is clearly aware of the threat Enlil represents and, at least initially, is successful in protecting her daughter from his sexual overtures.

More nuanced is the figure of Ninlil. As pointed out by Leick (1994: 42), she is primarily identified in terms of her age group (l. 11, ki-sikil tur) and this label is fundamental in understanding her role. She is a young unmarried woman, a virgin, who finds herself transitioning into fully-fledged womanhood in a violent manner, through an act of rape that leaves her pregnant. By the end of the composition, her transformation is complete: the doxology hails her as Mother (l. 153, ama) Ninlil. From other sources, most notably ES, it is assumed she has taken her rightful place as Father Enlil's wife in Nippur. As nicely summarized by Leick (1994: 46), both Enlil and Ninlil "achieved the transition from the socially powerless state of being tur to full adulthood and the top position in the city's hierarchy (…)." According to Leick, this was obtained by means of what she labels "reproductive efficiency" (1994: 46). Indeed, the transformation Ninlil undergoes from daughter to young unmarried woman to pregnant woman to mother seems to bear this conclusion.

However, nowhere in *EN* is there mention of Enlil and Ninlil's wedding.[24] Modern scholars assume this is the logical result of the two deities' peregrinations, but the text is silent in this matter. It is in *ES* that one finds a detailed description of the nuptials, as we shall see.

ENLIL AND NINLIL: THE TEXT

1. There was a city, there was a city, the one in which we dwell.
2. Nippur was the city, the one in which we dwell.
3. Dur-ĝešinmbar was the city, the one in which we dwell.
4. The Sala was its bright river.
5. The Wine Quay was its quay.[25]
6. The Asar Quay was its quay, the one where the boats set their anchor.
7. The Honey Well was its well with fresh water.[26]
8. Nunbirtum was its branching canal.
9. Should someone measure it from there, its field was fifty sar.[27]
10. Enlil was its young man.
11. Ninlil was its young woman.
12. Nunbaršegunu was its old woman.
13. At that time, the mother who bore her gave advice to the young woman,
14. Nunbaršegunu gave advice to Ninlil:
15. "(In) the bright river, woman, (in) the bright river do not bathe![28]
16. "Ninlil, do not walk along the banks of the Nunbirtum canal!
17. "The one who has bright eyes, the lord, the one who has bright eyes will look at you!
18. "The Great Mountain, Father Enlil, will look at you!
19. "The shepherd who decides the fates, the one who has bright eyes, will look at you!
20. "He immediately will have intercourse with you, he will kiss you!
21. "After he has happily poured his semen in you, he will leave you!"
22. In giving her this advice, she provided her with wisdom.

As predicted by Nunbaršegunu, Enlil spots Ninlil and propositions to her (ll. 23–29). Ninlil, however, refuses, providing the following explanation:

30. "My vagina is small, it does not know how to stretch.
31. "My lips are small, they do not know how to kiss.

32. "My mother will hear of it and she will slap my hand.

33. "My father will hear of it and he will lay hold of me.

34. "Then, upon my telling about it to my girlfriend, she will not speak to me … !"[29]

Enlil is not deterred, but after having consulted his loyal minister Nuska, he seizes Ninlil and rapes her (ll. 35–51).

52. In having intercourse with her this once, in kissing her this once,

53. He ejaculated the seed of Suen-Ašimbabbar into her womb.

Because of his crime, Enlil is captured, tried and sent into exile by the assembly of the gods (ll. 54–62).[30] Curiously, however, Ninlil follows him:[31]

63. Enlil went. Ninlil followed.

64. Nunammir went.[32] The young woman pursued him.

65. Enlil spoke to the man (in charge) of the city gate:

66. "City gatekeeper, man of the bolt,

67. "Man of the bar, man of the bright bolt,

68. "Your lady, Ninlil, is coming.

69. "When she asks you about me,

70. "You must not reveal to her where I am!"

71. Ninlil spoke to city gatekeeper:

72. "City gatekeeper, man of the bolt,

73. "Man of the bar, man of the bright bolt,

74. "Where has Enlil, your lord, gone?" she said.

75. Enlil answered as the man of the city gate:[33]

76. "My master, o loveliest one, has not told me.

77. "Enlil, o loveliest one, has not told me.

78. "I will make my aim clear and [I will explain my words].

79. "You may [fill] my wombs once it has become empty."

Ninlil answers:

80. "Enlil, lord of all lands, [had intercourse with me].

81. "Just as Enlil is your lord, I am your lady."

82. "If you are my lady, let my hand touch your … !"[34]

83. "The seed of your lord, the bright seed, is in my womb.

84. "The seed of Suen, the bright seed, is in my womb."

To this, Enlil replies:

85. "My lord's seed may go up to the heavens! Let my seed go down to the netherworld!

86. "Let my seed go down to the netherworld as if it were my lord's seed!"[35]
87. Enlil, (disguised) as the city gatekeeper, made her lie down in the bedchamber.
88. He had intercourse with her there, he kissed her there.
89. In having intercourse with her this once, in kissing her this once,
90. He ejaculated the seed of Nergal-Meslamta-ea into her womb.

Enlil's journey continues and he disguises himself twice more, first as the man of the Idkura, (ll. 91–115) and then as SI.LU.IGI, the man of the ferryboat (ll. 117–40).[36] He has intercourse with Ninlil and impregnates her with Ninazu (ll. 116) and En-bilulu (l. 141), respectively. The composition ends in an abrupt manner. After the last sexual encounter, the praise to Enlil (ll. 143–52) is followed by the doxology, commemorating both Enlil and Ninlil:

153. For the praise spoken for Mother Ninlil,
154. Praise be to Father Enlil.

Enlil and Sud

The setting of *ES* is quite different from *EN*. The overall tone is more bucolic, and the composition shares many images and literary *topoi* with the Inana-Dumuzi songs, especially in so far as the marriage rituals are concerned.

The beginning of the composition is not very well preserved, but it is clear that it narrates the birth of Sud, daughter of Nisaba and Haia, who becomes Ninlil after marrying Enlil.[37] As she grows up into an attractive woman Sud catches the eye of Enlil who, as specifically stated by the composition, has yet to be given a wife in the Ekur, Enlil's temple in Nippur (l. 9). Enlil approaches Sud, but, differently from *EN*, where the intent is sexual intercourse, in *ES*, the god of Nippur is looking for a bride and is clear about his intentions (ll. 11–16). However, he mistakes Sud for a prostitute, an error for which he will have to atone (ll. 15–16 and l. 66, where Nisaba clearly states that "amends have been made" for the case of mistaken identity). On account of her inexperience, Sud appears to misunderstand Enlil's intentions (ll. 17–21), but he reiterates his wishes (ll. 22–25). Sud, however, retreats in her abode.

Enlil requests the help of his minister, Nuska, like he had done in *EN*. The task entrusted to the minister is, however, quite different: Nuska is sent to Eresh to formally request Sud's mother her hand in marriage (ll. 27–43). Nuska carries out his order and Nisaba consents to Enlil's request (ll. 44–73) and Nuska returns to Nippur after having spent some time as a guest at the divine court of Ereš (ll. 74–102).

At this point, the preparations for the wedding can begin and the composition presents a long list of bridal gifts, which are delivered to Eresh (ll. 103–36). After a short speech in which Nisaba advises and blesses her daughter, Sud is taken into the Ekur, where she marries Enlil (ll. 137–47). The marriage is then consummated (ll. 148–49) and Enlil decrees his new wife's fate, as well as the fate of the daughter they will have (ll. 150–69). Finally, Sud officially becomes Ninlil (ll. 170–74) and the composition ends with a doxology celebrating both Enlil and Ninlil (l. 175).

As evidenced by this summary, the basic difference between *EN* and *ES* lies in the dynamics of Enlil and Ninlil's interaction. Whereas in *EN* Ninlil is first a victim and only ultimately Enlil's legitimate spouse, in *ES*, Ninlil (as Sud) is the designated wife all along.

Sexuality is not central to *ES*. Rather, the focus is on the proper social behavior to be upheld in the matter of matrimony. Approaching the potential bride is clearly not an option, even if she may be a prostitute. Proper etiquette must be followed.

The female protagonists central to the plot are mother and daughter—Nisaba and Sud, two different incarnations of Nunbaršegunu and Ninlil of *EN*. However, whereas Nunbaršegunu played a very marginal role in *EN*, as Nisaba she is one of *ES*'s pivotal characters. Like her counterpart Nunbaršegunu, Nisaba is the wise older woman, offering advices to her young unmarried daughter (ll. 139–45). However, she also represents the patriarchal authority in arranging her daughter's marriage. It is Nisaba, and not Haia, who is Enlil's referent in the marriage agreement.

Similarly to *EN*, Sud (Ninlil) is described in terms of age-category (ki-sikil, l. 6). However, in this composition there is a stronger emphasis on Sud's physical attributes, which had found only a passing mention in *EN*. In l. 6, Sud is said to be "full of charms and delight" (hi-li ma-az ba-an-du$_8$-du$_8$). Key in the interpretation of this passage is the Sumerian term hi-li, which (Leick 1994: 74 with references) summarized as follows:

> [it] has several connotations, but basically expresses the notion of something that is conductive to the inducement of sexual desire, similar to the Greek term *kharis*, and hence often translated as 'charm' or 'sex-appeal', although neither of these lexemes are able to convey the semantic range of the Sumerian word. People possess hi-li, Inanna is its divine personification, the object of desire is also invested with hi-li.

In general, the terminology used in *ES* line 6 is revealing of Sud's maturity: she is a grown-up girl, and not a young one (ki sikil tur). She is desirable and appears to have reached the age of consent, which in turn makes her a suitable sexual partner. This is a major change from Enlil and Ninlil, where Ninlil herself emphasizes her youth and inexperience.

Sud's maturity and poise is also evident from the way she easily dismisses Enlil as a potential suitor because he has misunderstood her for a prostitute (ll. 14–26). At the same time, however, she conforms to the norm by accepting her mother's consent to her wedding.

A secondary but important role is played by Aruru, Enlil's sister and one of the major mother-goddesses in second millennium Mesopotamia.[38] In *ES*, she leads Sud to the bridal chamber, thus accompanying her in the transition from her paternal household to the house of the husband.

ENLIL AND SUD: THE TEXT

The first five lines of the composition are not very well preserved. Nevertheless, it is clear that they describe the conception of Sud, born to Haia (l. 2) and Nun-bar-še-gunu (l. 3).

6. [The ...] of the young girl grew up, she became full of charms and delight.
7. In the [...] of the house of Nisaba, at the gate of the Ezagin,
8. [...] stood as an object of admiration, like a large, beautifully shaped cow.
9. At that time, Enlil had not yet been given a spouse in the Ekur.
10. The name had not yet appeared in the Kiur.
11. After having travelled through Sumer and until the limits of heaven and earth, he lifted his head to ...
12. Enlil, the Great Mountain, searching throughout the land, stopped at Ereš.
13. He looked around and found the woman of his heart.
14. He approached and, filled with joy, spoke to her:
15. "I want to adorn you with the mantle of ladyship! After standing in the street ...
16. "Now, I trust in your beauty, even if you have no honor".[39]
17. With the strength of her youth, Sud answered Enlil:
18. "I want to stand proudly at our gate, who is smearing my reputation?
19. "What are you looking at? Why are you coming here?[40]
20. "Young man, [...] from my sight!
21. "[...] deceived my mother[41] and enraged her(?)."
22. Enlil addressed Sud for a second time:
23. He spoke to her again while standing near her:
24. "Come, I wish to speak to you, I want to say a word to you: be my wife!
25. "Kiss me, my sister of the beautiful eyes. This is in your hands."
26. The words had not yet left his mouth that she had already entered the house before him.

Possibly realizing his mistake, Enlil hastens to summon Nuska and sends him to Eresh, entrusting him with the following speech, which the minister has to repeat to Nisaba (ll. 27–30):

31. "I am an unmarried man, I send you a message concerning my wishes.
32. "I want to take your daughter in marriage, give me your consent.
33. "I want to send you presents in my name, accept my bridal gifts.
34. "I am Enlil, the offspring born of Anšar, the most illustrious one, the lord of heaven and earth.
35. "Let your daughter's name be Ninlil, let it be spread through all lands.
36. "I will bestow upon her the Gagišua as her storehouse,
37. "I will give her as a gift the Kiur as her beloved chamber,
38. "Allow her to live with me in the lofty Ekur, allow her to determine the fates.
39. "Allow her to distribute the mes among the Anunna, the great gods.[42]
40. "As for you, I will place in your hand the life of the Black-headed people.
41. "When you arrive there, the attractive woman whom I chose will be standing by her mother.
42. "Do not go to her empty-handed, but bring to her a treasure with your left hand!"

Nuska swiftly carries out Enlil's order (ll. 44–59) and the speech clearly appeases Nisaba, who accepts the proposal on behalf of her daughter and entertains Nuska at her court before sending him back with her own demands (ll. 60–102). After a long list of bridal gifts (ll. 103–38), which marks the beginning of the preparation for the wedding, we find Nisaba advising her daughter in the matter of marriage:

139. "May you be Enlil's favorite wife, may he speak sweetly to you.
140. "May he embrace you, (who are) the most beautiful one, and may he say to you: 'Beloved, open wide!'
141. "The two of you should not forget attractiveness and pleasure, but should make them last a long time.
142. "You two make love on the hill and afterwards have children.
143. "Having entered the house and dwelling there, may abundance be before you and may joy be after you.
144. "May the people be equal to you upon your path, may they …

145. "May the fate I decreed for you come to pass. Go proudly
into the lofty house".

The composition concludes with the consummation of the marriage (l. 149:
"Enlil made love to his wife and took great pleasure in it") and the blessing of
Sud, who is granted powers and functions, as well as the blessing of Nisaba –
Ašnan, Enlil and Ninlil's daughter. Sud finally becomes Ninlil, who is praised
with her husband Enlil in Nippur.

Of different mothers

Enki and Ninhursaĝa *and* Enki and Ninmah

As I pointed out in the introduction, various goddesses embody different aspects
of motherhood within the Old Babylonian Sumerian literary corpus. We already
discussed the case of Nisaba/Nunbaršegunu and her advisory role. We also
briefly touched upon the development of Ninlil into a mother, described in both
EN and *ES*, albeit in different forms. I would here like to turn to two goddesses
who are more traditionally associated with motherhood, to the point that they
qualify as mother-goddesses: Ninhursaĝa and Ninmah.[43]
   Ninhursaĝa is the protagonist of the problematic *Enki and Ninhursaĝa*. Ninmah
aids and then challenges Enki in matter of creations in the entertaining *Enki and
Ninmah*. In both compositions, Enki is the protagonist and the two goddesses are
to an extent secondary to his pivotal role. At the same time, however, these two
characters inform us about various aspects of Mesopotamian motherhood.

Enki and Ninhursaĝa

Enki and Ninhursaĝa (*EnNinh* Alster 1974; Attinger 1984; Leick 1994: 30–41; Gadotti
2009b) is an Old Babylonian composition known only from three manuscripts.[44]
The plot focuses on "Enki's relationship with female deities and aspects of sexuality and fertility."[45] In particular, it addresses Enki's abnormal sexual behavior,
which translates in several cases of rape and incest, as well as the consequences
of such behavior.
   Two goddesses stand out in the *EnNinh*: Ninhursaĝa and Uttu. The former,
who is addressed also as Nintur and Damgalnuna, plays several roles: she is
Enki's spouse and the mother of one of his daughters, Ninnisig; she provides
Uttu with sound advise in dealing with Enki; she curses Enki because of
his crimes and she ultimately saves his life.
   Ninhursaĝa's interaction with Uttu, a minor deity associated with weaving,
reminds us of Nisaba and Sud in *ES*, despite the fact that the dynamics and the
rationale behind Ninhursaĝa's advices are different. Technically speaking, Ninhursaĝa is Uttu's great-grandmother (Ninhursaĝa → Ninnisig → Ninkura →

(Nin-imma) → Uttu), but she takes upon herself the same role Nisaba had *vis-à-vis* Sud in order to break the vicious cycle Enki has initiated by impregnating his daughters with a child destined to endure her mother's fate.

Uttu is depicted both as the obedient daughter—she duly follows the instructions Ninhursaĝa gives her—and as the young bride. The latter is harder to explain, but it may be seen as part of Ninhursaĝa's plan to trick Enki and thus put a stop to his sexual excesses.

ENKI AND NINHURSAĜA: THE TEXT

The setting of *EnNinh* is the land of Dilmun, depicted in bucolic terms as "virginal" and "pristine," a place devoid of illnesses, old age, but also of the markers of civilizations (ll. 1–28). The ensuing thirty lines (29–62) describe the origins and developments of the land of Dilmun, after which Enki has sex with Nintur/Damgalnuna/Ninhursaĝa.[46]

63. By himself, the wise one, toward Nintur, the mother of the land,
64. Enki, the wise one, toward Nintur, the mother of the land,
65. He was digging his phallus into the dykes,
66. He was plunging his phallus into the reed beds.[47]
67. The august one pulled his phallus aside,
68. He cried out: "No man take me in the marsh."
69. Enki cried out:
70. "By the life's breath of heaven I adjure you.
71. Lie down for me in the marsh, lie down for me in the marsh. What a joy!"
72. Enki ejaculated Damgalnuna's seed.
73. He poured semen into Ninhursaĝa's womb.
74. She received the semen in (her) womb, Enki's semen.

Ninhursaĝa becomes pregnant and after nine months she gives birth to Ninnisig (ll. 75–87). Once Ninnisig reaches adulthood, Enki sees her in the marshes, becomes infatuated with her and rapes her, impregnating her with Ninkura (ll. 88–107). The latter suffers the same fate as her mother, as she catches Enki's eyes and is forced to have sexual intercourse with him (ll. 108–19). Ninkura in turns gives birth to Uttu (ll. 120–26).[48]

Uttu is however to have a different fate, thanks to Ninhursaĝa's intervention:

127. Nintur said to Uttu:
128. "Let me advise you, you should take heed of my advice.
129. "Let me speak words to you, you should heed my words.
130. "From the marsh, one man is able to see up here, [he is able to see up here, he is].

131. "From in the marsh Enki is able to see up here, [he is able to see up here, he is].
132. "He [will set] eyes [on you]."

Although the composition is not well preserved, it is clear that Ninhursaĝa gives Uttu specific instructions about how to handle Enki, and Uttu follows them (133–46). Furthermore, Uttu's preparations for Enki's arrival closely resemble those of a bride eagerly waiting for her groom (ll. 147–51). In order to safely approach Uttu's abode, Enki disguises himself as a gardener and is welcomed by Uttu (ll. 152–77). The ensuing encounter between Enki and Uttu is not rape, but rather a failed attempt at seduction. This is clear from the following lines, in particular ll. 186–87:

178. Uttu, the exalted woman, placed herself to the left for him, waved the hands for him.
179. Enki aroused Uttu.
180. He embraced her, lying on her limbs.
181. He touched her thighs, he touched her with the hand.
182. He embraced her, lying on her limbs.
183. He made love to the young one and kissed her.
184. Enki poured (his) semen into Uttu's womb.
185. She received the semen in (her) womb, Enki's semen.
186. Uttu, the beautiful woman, said: "Woe, my thighs." She said: "Woe, my body, woe, my heart."
187. Ninhursaĝa removed (Enki's) semen from (her) thighs.

After having gathered Enki's seed, Ninhursaĝa proceeds to create a set of different plants (ll. 188–97). Possibly in order to determine their destiny,[49] Enki devours the plants that have just been born from his failed intercourse with Uttu (ll. 198–219). The ingestion of the plants, which may be interpreted as an alimentary incest, causes Ninhursaĝa to curse Enki:

220. Ninhursaĝa cursed the name "Enki" (as follows):
221. "Until the day he dies, I shall never look upon him with eye of life."

At this point, the composition becomes very cryptic. However, it is clear that Enki has fallen ill and the Anuna-gods are in a panic. The only way Enki can recover is through Ninhursaĝa's intervention.

222. The Anuna sat down in the dust.
223. But a fox was able to speak to Enlil:
224. "If I bring Ninhursaĝa to you, what will be my reward?"
225. Enlil answered the fox:

226. "If you bring Ninhursaĝa to me,
227. "I shall erect two birch trees for you in my city and you will be renowned."

The ensuing twenty lines are very fragmentary. The fox seems to be able to convince Ninhursaĝa to head to the place where the Anuna are gathered, since when the narrative resumes, we find the goddess there (ll. 247–53). She addresses Enki directly, inquiring about his health according to the following pattern:

257. "My brother, what part of you hurts you?"
258. "The locks of my hair (Sumerian **siki**) hurt me."
259. "She gave birth to Nin**siki**la out of it."[50]

It appears that Enki's ingestions of the plants he had generated with his sperm had caused his ills. Ninhursaĝa intervenes by carrying the failed pregnancies to term (ll. 254–71). A new set of goddesses is born, whose destiny Ninhursaĝa establishes (ll. 272–80). The composition ends with a praise to Enki (l. 281).

Enki and Ninmah

Commentators have often noted that *Enki and Ninmah* (*EnNinM*: Benito 1969: 1–76; Klein 1997; Leick 1994: 26–29) is an extremely obscure myth.[51] The fragmentary state of the composition hinders scholars' attempts to decipher its most complex parts. To an extent, the story looks like a *tençon* or debate poem, where the main characters are not personifications of natural phenomena, seasons or agricultural tools, but rather gods. Klein (1997: 516) also pointed out the composite nature of this composition. Most notably, it contains two very different story-lines: the creation of mankind (ll. 1–43), a theme known from other Mesopotamian compositions; and the contest between Enki and Ninmah, which takes place during a banquet celebrating the creation of mankind (ll. 44-end).

The female protagonists of this composition are the mother-goddesses, and in particular Ninmah. She is a multifaceted character, as she is depicted at the same time as extremely capable and absurdly incompetent.

In the first part of the story, Ninmah is a very valuable asset in the creation of mankind. She not only directly participates in the creative process; she also assigns to man his traditional task of carrying baskets.

In the second part of the composition, however, she is depicted as an incompetent deity, unable to provide even one solution. Although it is tempting to blame Ninmah's failure on the alcohol she consumed and on the fact that her opponent is the trickster of the Sumerian pantheon, Enki, I believe there is more at stake here. The comic character of the composition has long been recognized. And what is more comic than a supposedly experienced mother-goddess, who just aided in creating mankind, unable to fix a bunch of pitiful individuals?

A secondary, albeit important, function is played by Namma, Enki's mother and one of the most ancient deities of Eridu.[52] She urges her son Enki to intervene and free the gods of their burden. In addition, she plays an active role in the creation of mankind by selecting a lump of clay from the Apsu—Enki's domain. Although the passage is in part fragmentary, it seems that Namma herself gives birth to the first man with the aid of Ninmah and the other mother-goddesses.

ENKI AND NINMAH: THE TEXT

EnNinm begins in the far-away past (ll.1–3), when the gods were created and the goddesses were taken in marriage (ll. 4–7). This is a time of labor for the gods, who begin to complain about their fate (ll. 8–11). The stage is set for Enki's intervention.

12. At that time, the one who has great wisdom, the creator of all the great gods,
13. Enki, within the deep Engur, in the subterranean water, the place the inside of which no other god may admire,
14. (Enki) lay on his bed, he did not wake up from his sleep.
15. Weeping, the gods were saying: "He is the cause of the lamenting!"
16. To the one who lay down, to the one who lay and did not wake up from his bed,
17. Namma, the primeval mother who gave birth to the all gods,
18. Brought the gods' tears to her son:
19. "You are really lying there, you are really asleep there!
20. " ... you are not waking up.
21. "The gods, your creatures, ... they are breaking their backs.[53]
22. "Son of mine, wake up from your bed! After you have sought out your skill from your own wisdom,
23. "And you have created a substitute for the gods, they shall be freed from their toil!"[54]

Enki's answer to his mother Namma is as follows:

30. "Mother of mine, the creature that you planned will indeed come into existence. Impose upon him the work of carrying baskets.
31. "After you have kneaded clay (gathered) from the top of the abzu;
32. "The birth-goddesses[55] will nip off the clay. After you have brought the body into existence,
33. "Ninmah shall act as your assistant;

34. "Ninimma,[56] Šuziana, Ninmada,[57] Ninbarag,[58]
35. "Ninmug,[59] ŠAR.ŠAR.GABA[60] and Ninguna,[61]
36. "They shall stand by as you give birth.
37. "My mother, after you have decreed his fate,
38. "Ninmah shall impose upon him the work of carrying baskets".

The gods, delighted of having been relieved of their arduous tasks, gather in celebration and, during the banquet, Ninmah challenges Enki (ll. 45–51):

52. Enki and Ninmah drank beer and their hearts became filled with elation.
53. Ninmah said to Enki:
54. "The body of a human being may be either good or bad.
55. "It is on account of my will that I make a fate good or bad."
56. Enki replied to Ninmah:
57. "I will counterbalance the fate you decide, be it good or bad."

Ninmah fashions six maimed or defective individuals. For each of them, Enki is able to decree a satisfactory fate, which enables them to "have bread", i.e. to be able to support themselves and thus lead a fulfilling life despite their impairments (ll. 58–79).[62] Of interest for our investigation is the fifth creature:

72. Fifth, she (Ninmah) fashioned a woman who could not give birth.
73. Enki looked at the woman who could not give birth,
74. He decreed her fate: he made her stand in the woman's estate.[63]

It is now Enki's turn to test Ninmah's abilities as mother-goddess, and he does so by creating Udmul (ud-mu-ul, l. 95), a weakling afflicted by many diseases (ll. 80–101).[64]

The god of wisdom subsequently challenges Ninmah to establish for Udmul a destiny, which will allow him to support himself (ll. 102–11). Ninmah's answer, or at least its first part, is lost in a ten-line gap (ll. 110–21?).[65] When the text resumes, however, it is not clear what is happening, since Ninmah's speech makes no sense in the present context (ll. 122–28). What is clear, however, is that she fails, since Enki removes Udmul from her lap (l. 131) and decrees his fate himself:

132. "Ninmah, your work shall be supervised (?). You seized for me what is imperfect; who can oppose this?[66]
133. "The one, my creation, who has your back, shall pay you homage![67]

134. "On this day, my penis shall be praised, your assembled wisdom is abundant indeed!"[68]

After a few other unclear lines, the doxology proclaims Enki's superiority over Ninmah:

140. Ninmah could not rival the great lord Enki.
141. Father Enki, your praise is sweet!

Of sisters

Dumuzi's Dream *and* Dumuzi and Ĝeštinana

In origins, Ĝeštinana was an agrarian deity associated with grapes (her name means the "Grape/Wine of Heaven").[69] In the extant Sumerian literary documents, Ĝeštinana embodies the devoted sister. The important role of sisters in the Sumerian pantheon has already been pointed out by Westenholz (1998: 69), although not explored in depth.

Dumuzi's dream

Dumuzi's Dream (*DD*: Alster 1972; Katz 2003: 301–8) is an Old Babylonian literary composition known from copies primarily from Nippur and Ur. It belongs to the Inana-Dumuzi cycle and, from the narrative viewpoint, it comes after *Inana's Descent to the Netherworld*.[70] *DD*'s premise is a dream Dumuzi has, which foretells his impending death. In order to better understand the message of the dream, Dumuzi enlists the help of his sister Ĝeštinana, who reveals to him the deep meaning of his vision. *DD*, however, also focuses on Dumuzi's repeated attempts to escape the galla-demons sent to seize him and take him to the land of the dead as Inana's substitute.[71]

DD is extremely informative about the role of women in an advisory capacity. Besides offering a detailed portrait of Ĝeštinana, Dumuzi's sister, it also introduces the figure of Belili, the old woman (um-ma) in whose home Utu hides Dumuzi when the latter pleads him for help (ll. 192–226).[72] It is worth mentioning that the name of Belili is consistently written with the divine determinative, thus indicating her divine status in the Mesopotamian universe.

Ĝeštinana, on the other hand, has a dual role: a familial one, that of devoted sister; and a more practical one—in fact, in *DD* her sisterly role is further developed as she is the divine personification of the woman as a scribe, a dream interpreter and a woman in an advisory capacity.[73]

Her scribal skills are only mentioned briefly in *DD* (l. 21). Conversely, the storyline is based upon her expertise in interpreting dreams. Indeed, she is invoked as the wise woman "who knows the meaning of dreams" (l. 22) and it is precisely because of this competence that Dumuzi consults with her.

DUMUZI'S DREAM: THE TEXT

The composition opens *in medias res* (l. 1 reads "His heart was filled with tears. He went out to the steppe"). Dumuzi, terrified by his looming sense of foreboding, seeks the help of his sister (ll. 1–18). He describes her as follows:

19. "Bring, bring, bring my sister!
20. "Bring my Ĝeštinana, bring my sister!
21. "Bring my scribe proficient in tablets,[74] bring my sister!
22. "Bring my singer expert in songs, bring my singer!
23. "Bring my knowledgeable girl,[75] bring my sister!
24. "Bring my wise woman who knows the meanings of dreams,[76] bring my sister!
25. "I will relate the dream to her."[77]

Dumuzi proceeds to tell Ĝeštinana about his dream (ll. 26–40), which she interprets as foreseeing Dumuzi's imminent death (ll. 41–69). Dumuzi immediately decides his course of action: he orders Ĝeštinana to go to the mound and act as a desperate woman, most likely in order to sidetrack the demons hunting him (ll. 70–83). Ĝeštinana consults with her girlfriend, who confirms the demons are approaching. As such, she acts exactly like Dumuzi has described them:

84. Ĝeštinana bent her neck.
85. Her girl friend Ĝeštindudu [gave her] coun[sel]:
86. "The big one, who bind the neck, are coming for him, […] are coming for him!"
87. "My adviser and girlfriend! Are they coming?"
88. "I will show you the ones who bind the neck!"

Upon Ĝeštinana's advice (ll. 89–91), Dumuzi decides to hide in the grass and warn Ĝeštinana not to reveal his hiding place if she does not wish him dead (ll. 91–109). In the ensuing lines 110–29, we find a detailed description of the demons, rich in proverbial references. The demons try to bribe Ĝeštinana into revealing Dumuzi's whereabouts, but she does not accept their gifts (ll. 130–38). Forced to acknowledge that Ĝeštinana will never betray her brother, the demons decide to ask an unnamed friend of Dumuzi's, who promptly betrays him (ll. 139–50).

Having finally managed to capture Dumuzi, the demons are on their way back to the netherworld when the lad invokes Utu's help on account of the fact he is his brother-in-law (ll. 151–73). Utu accepts to help and turns Dumuzi into a gazelle. He finds refuge at Ku-bireš, but the demons catch up with him (ll. 173–91).

In his second attempt to find a safe haven from the galla-demons, Dumuzi begs Utu to hide him in the house of the old woman Belili (é um-ma ᵈbe-li-li, ll. 192–99). Utu acquiesces and Dumuzi escapes his hunters yet again (ll. 200–204):

205. He approached the house of old woman Belili.
206. "Old woman! I am not just a man. I am the husband of a goddess!
207. "Once you have poured some water, I shall drink it!
208. "Once you have sprinkled some flour, I shall eat it!"
209. After she had poured water and sprinkled flour, he sat down inside (the house).
210. (Then) the old woman left the house.
211. When the old woman left the house,
212. The demons saw her.
213. "If the old woman did not know of Dumuzi's whereabouts,
214. "She would indeed look frightened!
215. "She would indeed scream in a frightened way![78]
216. "Come, let us go to the house of Old Woman Belili!"
217. They caught Dumuzi at the house of Old Woman Belili.

Once again, Dumuzi is carried away in fetters (ll. 218–26). In his last attempt to gain freedom (ll. 227 fl), Dumuzi asks to be sent to the "holy sheepfold, my sister's sheepfold" (l. 234) and as customary, Utu grants him his wish (ll. 235–39). When Dumuzi reaches his sister's abode, this is what he finds:

240. Ĝeštinana cried towards the heavens, she cried towards the earth.
241. Her cries covered the horizon completely like a cloth, they were spread out like linen.
242. She scratched her eyes, she scratched her face.
243. She scratched her ears in public.
244. She scratched her buttocks in private.
245. "My brother, I will wander around in the streets, I will … !"
246. "If Ĝeštinana {…} [Dumuzi's] whereabouts, would not look frightened!
247. "(But) she is indeed looking frightened!
248. "She is indeed screaming in a frightened way!
249. "Come, let us go to the sheepfold and cow-pen!"[79]

The remainder of the composition sees the demons hunting for Dumuzi in the sheepfold (ll. 250–60) but Dumuzi has died. The doxology states that this is a "širkalkal for the dead Dumuzi" (l. 261).

Dumuzi and Ĝeštinana

This very short composition (*DĜ*: Katz 2003: 289–300) is known only from two manuscripts from Ur.[80] Although these two sources do not belong to *Inana's Descent* (Sladek 1974: 28), the similarities between the two compositions are numerous. I have incorporated the text in my discussion because it allows us to gain a better understanding of Ĝeštinana's character. In this composition, it is her role of devoted sister which is mostly emphasized.

Like *DD*, *DĜ* begins *in medias res*.[81] The netherworld demons are in Uruk, where they manage to capture Inana. However, she hands over Dumuzi, apparently in exchange for her own freedom (ll. 1–21).

Dumuzi asks for Utu's intervention and requests to be turned into a gazelle and to be allowed to find refuge in Ĝeštinana's abode (ll. 22–32). As usual, Utu agrees to help and Dumuzi safely reaches his sister's house (ll. 33–37). Upon his arrival, this is Ĝeštinana's reaction:

38. Ĝeštinana looked at her brother.
39. She scratched her cheeks: she scratched her nose.
40. She looked at her sides: she put on her garment.
41. (She said): "I will intone a lament of misfortune for the unfortunate lad![82]
42. "O my brother! O my brother, lad who has not fulfilled those days!
43. "O my brother, shepherd Ama-ušumgal-ana,[83] lad who has not fulfilled those days and years!
44. "O my brother, lad who has no wife, who has no children!
45. "O my brother, lad who has no friend, who has no companion!
46. "O my brother, lad whose goodness does not extend (anymore) to his mother!"[84]

The following ten lines depict the demons searching for Dumuzi (ll. 47–56). They finally reach Ĝeštinana's house and begin interrogating her (ll. 57–58). However, she refuses to disclose her brother's whereabouts and the demons decide to torture her:

59. "Show us where your brother is," they said to her.
60. But she spoke not a word to them.
61. They afflicted her loins with a skin disease, but she spoke not a word to them. They scratched her face with … , but she spoke not a word to them.
62. They … the skin of her buttocks, but she spoke not a word to them.
63. They poured tar in her lap, but she spoke not a word to them.
64. So they could not find Dumuzi at the house of Ĝeštinana.

Despite Ĝeštinana's unwillingness to cooperate, the demons discover Dumuzi's hiding place and capture him (ll. 65–71). The last two preserved lines of the composition are of great interest Ĝeštinana seems to offer herself as a substitute for her brother:[85]

> 72. His sister was wandering about the city like a bird on account of her brother's fate:
> 73. "Brother of mine, I shall carry away the great misfortune, come, I shall … "[86]

Inana Bereft

As I pointed out in the introduction, Inana has been the subject of many studies. Here, I limit myself to discuss an overlooked composition called *Inana and Bilulu* (*IB*: Jacobsen and Kramer 1953; Bottéro and Kramer 1989: 330–37). In it, Inana is depicted as a grieving betrothed, a role for her quite unusual.[87] The composition is known only from one Nippur manuscript and focuses on Inana's grief in the aftermath of Dumuzi's death.[88] In this tradition, Inana had not caused her husband's death. Rather, Bilulu, an old woman (um-ma), is responsible for this, apparently together with her son Ĝirĝire. Central to the composition is Inana's curse of Dumuzi's killers (ll. 98–121 and the parallel ll. 111–21). This curse brings about the physical metamorphosis of the people involved, as we shall see.

Interesting for the present investigation is the figure of Bilulu, otherwise unknown in the Sumerian literary corpus. A possible parallel may exist with the figure of the old woman Belili, who, according to *DG*, provides Dumuzi with a safe place.[89] In *DG*, **Belili's** house has a positive connotation, since it is a temporary haven in which Dumuzi finds respite from the galla-demons. In *IB*, on the other hand, **Bilulu's** house is the place of Dumuzi's death.

That there may be a contamination between the good Belili and the evil Bilulu is evidenced by *IB* l. 67, which reads: [é um]-ma ᵈbe-li-li-šè, "To the house of the old woman Belili" (instead of the expected Bilulu). In the past, ingenious interpretations have been put forward in order to account for the presence of Belili in this section. In particular, Kramer (Jacobsen and Kramer 1953: 187–88) states that this line refers to the fact that:

> Dumuzi is no longer in his sheepfold, since he has "carried off his soul" to the house of Mother Belili, presumably in the netherworld. (…) Dumuzi did not meet his death by having his head smashed in, (…) Bilulu had nothing to do with Dumuzi's death, and (…) Inana did not decide to kill Bilulu in order to avenge Dumuzi.

Kramer's interpretation of this portion of the composition differs drastically from Jacobsen's. The latter opts (at least implicitly) for emending ᵈbe-li-li in l. 62

to ᵈbe-lu-lu. In his opinion, Dumuzi was indeed killed in Bilulu's house, by Bilulu and her son Ĝirĝire (1953: 163).

I find Jacobsen's interpretation more convincing, especially in light of ll. 67–73. As such, I have followed it here. However, both Jacobsen and Kramer fail to address the larger inter-textual implications the figure of Belili/Bilulu raises. In particular, it seems there existed in the Dumuzi–Inana cycle an ambivalent character, the old woman, who could play both a positive or negative role in Dumuzi's vicissitudes.[90]

In *IB*, Bilulu's name is consistently written with the divine determinative, thus suggesting she was a (local?) deity, possibly associated with weather phenomena.[91] In addition, she is referred to in age-related terms: her most common epithet is old woman (um-ma, for instance in ll. 67, 81, and 92, among others).[92] In addition, however, she is also a matriarch (bur-šu-ma, l. 82),[93] as well as her own lady (nin ní-te-na-ka, l. 82). The insistence of the text on Bilulu's age is not coincidental: in Mesopotamian tradition, as in other societies, old age is often synonym of wisdom. However, in Bilulu's case, she seems to lack such gift. On the one hand, the composition is at times very fragmentary, so that one cannot appreciate the full extent of Bilulu's involvement in Dumuzi's death. On the other hand, Inana's curse is first and foremost cast against Bilulu. This suggests she was directly involved in Dumazi's death, which in turn indicates a lack of wisdom on the old matriarch's part: she attacked and killed Inana's betrothed and a god in his own right.

Inana's curse is very specific as to Bilulu's ultra-mundane fate: not only is her name to be forgotten (l. 100), but she becomes a water-skin. On a final note, she is to become the protective spirit (ᵈlamma) of the steppe.

Inana and Bilulu: *the text*

1. She can make the lament for you, [Dumuzi, the lament for you, the lament, the lamentation,] reach [the desert].
2. She can make it reach [the house] Arali.
3. She can make it reach Badtibira.
4. She can make it reach Dušuba.
5. She can make it reach the shepherding country, the sheepfold of Dumuzi.

The next twenty lines are missing, but when the text resumes, Inana is still weeping about Dumuzi's death.

27. "O Dumuzi of the fair-spoken mouth, of the beautiful eyes," she sobs tearfully.
28. "O you of the fair-spoken mouth, of the beautiful eyes," she sobs tearfully.
29. "[…], spouse, lord, sweet as the date,

30. "O Dumuzi!" she sobs and sobs tearfully."
31. Bright Inana [...],
32. [...]
33. The mistress [...]
34. The maiden Inana ... [...]
35. She was pacing in the chamber of the mother who bore her,
36. In prayer and supplication, she stood by her respectfully:[94]
37. "Mother of mine [...] I shall go to the sheepfold!
38. "Ningal, mother of mine [...] I shall go to the sheepfold!
39. "My father has shone forth for me; humbly I shall [...].
40. "Suen has shone forth for me; humbly I shall [...]"
41. Like a messenger of the mother who bore her, she went out from the chamber;
42. Like a messenger of Mother Ningal, she went out from the chamber.
43. My lady has vast knowledge. She is very much capable.
44. Bright Inana has vast knowledge. She is very much capable.
45. The beer stored in remote days, in far-away days ...

The composition breaks off for about twenty lines and when it resumes it seems that Inana is informed by a servant that Dumuzi has been murdered in Bilulu's house:[95]

67. "In the old woman, Bilulu's, [abode ...],
68. "There, the shepherd, (his) head having been hit [...];
69. "Dumuzi, (his) head having been hit [...];
70. "Ama-ušum-gal-ana, (his) head having been hit [...].
71. "The sheep of my master, of Dumuzi, [...] in the steppe.
72. "Inana, a shepherd, who is not Dumuzi,
73. "Was returning the sheep at my master's sheep's side!"[96]

Inana's reaction to the news is as follows:

74. The lady created a song for her young husband, she fashioned a song for him.
75. Bright Inana created a song for Dumuzi, she fashioned a song for him:
76. "O you who lies at rest, shepherd, who lies at rest, you stood guard!
77. "Dumuzi, you who lies at rest, you stood guard!
78. "Ama-ušumgal-ana, you who lies at rest, you stood guard!
79. "Standing by day, you stood guard over my sheep(?)![97]
80. "Lying by night, you stood guard over my sheep(?)!"
81. At that time, the son of old woman Bilulu,

82. Matriarch and her own mistress,[98]
83. Ĝirĝire, his own man,[99]
84. Ĝirĝire the apt one,[100] a knowledgeable man,
85. Was filling pen and fold with his captured cattle;
86. He was stacking his piles of grain.
87. In haste, he disbanded (the victims) he had stricken with his weapon.[101]
88. Child of none, friend of none, Širru of the haunted steppe,
89. Sat before him and was talking with him.
90. On that day what did the lady carry in her heart?
91. What did bright Inana carry in her heart?
92. To kill the old woman, Bilulu! This is what she carried in her heart!
93. For her beloved spouse,[102] for Dumuzid-ama-ušumgal-ana
94. To make (his) resting place pleasant: this is what she carried in her heart!
95. My lady [went] to Bilulu in the haunted steppe.
96. Her son Ĝirĝire […] its wind.
97. Child of none, friend of none, Širru of the haunted steppe, […].
98. Bright Inana entered the alehouse.
99. She sat into a seat (and) began to determine (their) fates:[103]
100. "Begone! I have killed you. It is indeed so. With you, I shall also destroy your name.[104]
101. "You shall become the water-skin for cold water, which is used the desert!
102. Her son Ĝirĝire, together with her,[105]
103. "(The two of them) shall become the protective god of the steppe and the protective goddess of the steppe!
104. Child of none, friend of none, Širru of the haunted steppe,
105. "Shall wander in the steppe and count the flour.
106. "When water is libated and flour sprinkled for the lad who wanders in the steppe,
107. "The protective god of the steppe and the protective goddess of the steppe shall call out:
108. "'Libate!' They shall call out: 'Sprinkle!'
109. "So that he shall be in the place from which he disappeared, in the [steppe]!
110. "Old woman Bilulu shall gladden his heart!"

Inana's curse is fulfilled (ll. 111–24) and after yet another gap (ll. 125–36), the composition resumes by describing a francolin pondering on the best way to sooth Dumuzi's heart (ll. 137–48). The passage is not very clear and somewhat damaged. However, both Dumuzi's mother and sister are mentioned, and when the text becomes clear again, it is Ĝeštinana who intones a lament for her brother (ll. 155–61). This is followed by a praise to Inana (ll. 162–65) after which she herself intones another lament for Dumuzi (ll. 166–73). This in part parallels the opening lines of the composition, which concludes as follows:

174. How truly she proved the equal to Dumuzi, [avenging him].
175. By killing Bilulu,
176. Inana proved equal to him!
177. An ulila song of Inana.[106]

Notes

1 See Asher-Grave and Wogec 2002 for bibliographical references.
2 Harris 1997.
3 Brenner 1985; Brenner and Fontaine 1997; Pomeroy 1975.
4 Pomeroy, 1975: 96.
5 Gadotti 2011.
6 For a survey on goddesses in the Ancient Near East see Westenholz 1998.
7 For example, Inana is treated only briefly in this survey, whereas more space has been given to her sister-in-law, Ĝeštinana.
8 Gadotti 2011.
9 For the distinction between named and unnamed female characters see Gadotti 2009a. For a general discussion about importance of named characters see Veldhuis 2004: 70–71.
10 Šat-Eštar in the *Message of Lu-dingira to His Mother* for which see Civil 1964 and Çiğ and Kramer 1976.
11 Nawirtum, protagonist of the *Elegy for the Death of Nawirtum* (Kramer 1960).
12 Ninšatapada, in one literary letter included in the *Correspondence of the King of Larsa* (Brisch 2007) and Enheduana, in *Ninmešara* (Zgoll 1997).
13 Peštur and Enmebaragesi, Gilgameš' sisters in *Gilgameš and Huwawa* A (Edzard 1991; Michalowski 2003).
14 Sagburu, who aids Enmerkar king of Uruk to defeat his arch-nemesis, the king of Aratta, in *Enmerkar and Enšukešdana* (Berlin 1979).
15 Kubaba, mentioned only briefly in the *Sumerian King List* (Jacobsen 1939).
16 Goddesses also performed other functions. Westenholz (1998: 68) points out "moral and spiritual enforcement, royal legitimation and local tasks" in addition to the familial and the creative roles addressed here.
17 For *Dumuzi and Ĝeštinana* see Sladek 1974: 225–39; for *Dumuzi and his Sisters* see Black 2004; for *Dumuzi's Dream* see Alster 1972.
18 In *Dumuzi and Ĝeštinana*, Ĝeštinana does not reveal her brother's hiding place even when the galla-demons torture her (ll. 57–64).
19 A similar role is played by Ninsun, Gilgameš' mother, in the *Epic of Gilgameš*.
20 Leick 1994: 42.
21 See Scurlock 2003 for a different interpretation.
22 For Nun-bar-še-gunu see Cavigneaux and Krebernik 2001d: 615.
23 Sumerian na šag$_4$ X mu-ni-in-de$_5$ mu-uš-túg ĝeštug mu-na-zé-èĝ (one manuscript preserves the variant ĝeštug mu-na-an-šúm).
24 Leick (1994: 47) reminds us that "[t]he legal texts show clearly that defloration, especially of a free girl, was a serious offence 'against the property of another person',

specifically the girl's father or her betrothed husband (...). In Sumerian times it was sanctioned by forcing the man to marry the girl." This is exactly what happens in *EN*.

25 Following Cooper 1980: 184 rather than ETCSL (Electronic Text Corpus of Sumerian Literature) (http://etcsl.orinst.ox.ac.uk/), which preserves the Sumerian kar-ĝeština.

26 Following Cooper 1980: 184.

27 A sar is a unit of length.

28 For the correct interpretation of this form as a prohibitive and not an affirmative see Cooper 1980: 180–81.

29 For this problematic line, see Gadotti 2009.

30 The text never mentions where specifically the gods exile Enlil. Leick (1994: 44) seems to imply that Enlil and Ninlil remain in the neighborhoods of Nippur. Cooper's (1980: 179) suggestion that "the banished Enlil is on his way to the Nether-world (he is crossing the i₇-kur-ra river)" is, however, more convincing, especially in light of the chthonic nature of the deities born from the second, third and fourth intercourses.

31 Ninlil's behavior is puzzling. Cooper (1980: 180) claimed that "[t]he psychological portrait of Ninlil, who followed the man who raped her, yet had to be tricked into repeated acts of intercourse with him, is an early attestation of the well-known ambivalence of the victim toward the oppressor, especially in sexual contexts." More likely, in accordance to Mesopotamian customs, Enlil had by the time of the exile been forced to marry Ninlil, and therefore she was bound to him. If a man rapes an unmarried young woman, who is not betrothed, he must marry her (see especially Lafont 1999: 133–71).

32 Nunnamir (Sumerian ᵈnu-nam-mir) is common epithet for Enlil.

33 From this line and its parallels it is clear that Enlil assumes the identity of the gate-keeper, the man of the Idkura and the ferryman. The reasons behind this action are unclear but see Gadotti 2009.

34 Sumerian NE.ÉŠ-zu šu-ĝu₁₀ hé-tag-ga. The meaning of the term NE.ÉŠ is obscure, although it must be a body part.

35 These lines are keys in understanding the overall meaning of the second part of the composition. Possibly because he was sent into exile to the Netherworld, and he was bringing along his spouse Ninlil and their child, Suen-Ašimbabbar, Enlil needed to provide substitutes who would take their place there. Therefore, he impregnates Ninlil three more times, thus generating three deities who will take the place of Enlil, Ninlil and Suen in the Netherworld (see Cooper 1980: 180 and Scurlock 2003: 66). This interpretation is strengthened by the fact that the three deities born, Nergal, Ninazu and En-bililu, are all traditionally associated with the Netherworld.

36 The reading of the ferryman's name is unclear.

37 For the reading and meaning of Sud see Civil 1983: 44.

38 Westenholz 1998: 77.

39 Lines 15–16 are keys to understand the nature of Enlil's transgression: the Sumerian reads: e-sír-ra un-gub-bu ba-[...] / nam-zil-zil á-šè nir im-te-ĝál lú téš nu-tuk-tuku-un. Civil (1983: 46) points out that '[t]he straightforward marriage plot is complicated by a case of mistaken identity. Enlil finding Sud 'standing in the street' (...) mistakes her for a prostitute. Nowhere are we explicitly told that Sud is taken for a kar-kid, but the expression sila-a gub-ba, the way she is treated by Enlil, and the repeated use of the verb šu – kár 'to smear the reputation,' as well as the need for the insult to be corrected by marriage, leave no doubt that Enlil took her for a lady of the street". Although I agree with Civil's overall interpretation, I do not see any mistreatment on Enlil's part, nor do I believe that the marriage proposal is the solution to address the mistake made. Rather, Enlil wishes to marry Sud, *even if* she is a prostitute and upon realizing she is not, he follows the proper channels to make it happen.

40 For this line see Civil 1983: 61.

41 *um-mi-ia* is preserved in ms. V, a Neo-Assyrian bilingual (Sumerian and Akkadian) exemplar of the composition (see Civil 1983: 48 fn. 52).

42 For the meaning and significance of the *mes* in Mesopotamia see Farber 1990.

43 Heimpel 2000; Cavigneaux and Krebernik 2001b.

44 One manuscript was found at Nippur, one at Ur and one is unprovenanced.

45 Leick 1994: 30.

46 The fact that Ninhursaĝa is addressed with three different names complicates the understanding of the narrative. However, it is clear that one deity is intended here.

47 For these lines see Cooper 1989: 89 and Leick 1994: 31–32.

48 One manuscript (AO 6724 = TCL 16 62) adds a third episode: Ninkura gives birth to Ninimma, who is also raped by Enki. The child of this sexual act is Uttu.

49 This seems implied by line 219: "Enki determined the destiny of the plants, he knew them deeply."

50 A word play is clearly in place between the part of Enki's body and the deity it creates: beside the play between siki and Nin-sikil-la, one finds Nin-kiri-u-tud (written nin-kìri-ù-tud, literally the "Lady born from the nose"), who indeed emerged from the nose (kìri); Ninkasi (written nin-ka-si) from Enki's mouth (ka); Nazi (na-zi), born from Enki's throat (zi); Azimua (á-zi-mú-a) from the arm (á); Ninti (nin-ti) from Enki's ribs (ti) and Ensag from Enki's side (zag).

51 A nice summary of the various interpretations of this composition can be found in Leick 1994: 28–29.

52 See Wiggerman 1998 for information about Namma's mythology, cult and traditions.

53 Sumerian has gú-bi im-tu$_{10}$-tu$_{10}$-ne, literally "they are hitting their neck."

54 What Enki is urged to create is, in Sumerian, a kíĝ-sig$_{10}$, technically an alternate spelling for kíĝ-sig$_7$, a "late afternoon meal." This meaning hardly fits the context, as already recognized by Benito 1969: 52, who opted for a more suitable translation, "substitute," based on the Akkadian parallels found in Atrahasis. Klein, on the other hand, attempted a more literal translation and offered "a worker comparable(?) to the gods" (1997: 517), breaking down the nominal chain into its two component, kíĝ "to work," and sig$_{10}$ "to equal" (lit. one who works who is equal to the gods). Either interpretation works.

55 Sumerian SIG$_7$.EN SIG$_7$.HI is only attested in *EnNinm* (ll. 26, 32, and 46) and generally understood as birth goddesses.

56 Focke 1998 and 2000.

57 Cavigneaux and Krebernik 2001a.

58 Cavigneaux and Krebernik 2000a.

59 Cavigneaux and Krebernik 2001c.

60 With the exception of the unknown ŠAR.ŠAR.GABA, all goddesses listed here are known from other sources as deities associated with childbearing and midwifery. See above and Krebernik 1996: 502–16.

61 Cavigneaux and Krebernik 2000b.

62 As Leick (1994: 27) puts it "[t]he aetiological message is clear: such beings were fashioned by a drunk goddess but their employment is sanctioned by Enki's wisdom."

63 There are two versions of the destiny of the woman who could not give birth (Sumerian munus ù-tu-ud): é-mí-a-ke$_4$ àm-ma-ni-in-dù, "He made her stand in the woman's estate," or uš-bar mu-ni-in-du$_8$ é-mí-a-kam àm-ma-ši-in-dím, "He made her *stand* (as a) weaver, he fashioned her for the woman's estate". In the latter, I take the verb du$_8$ as a phonetic variant of dù (aural error on the part of the scribe).

64 Klein 1997: 516 fn. 1 reads the name ud-mu-ul and interprets it either as "the-day-was-far-off" or as "my-day-is-far-off". In his opinion, this refers either to an unborn child or to a very old man. For a detailed discussion of the term see Kilmer 1976.
65 See Leick 1994: 228 for a summary of the suggested reconstructions of this break.
66 Sumerian ^dnin-mah kíĝ-ĝá-zu hé-bí-lá-lá šu nu-du₇ ma-dab₅ a-ba-àm saĝ mu-un-ĝá-ĝá. For saĝ – ĝá-ĝá, "to oppose, confront, advance," see Karahashi 2000: 135–36.
67 Reading lú me²-dím²-ĝu₁₀ eĝer-zu-šè tuku-a kiri(not ka)-bi šu hé-bí-ĝál. The first hemistich is problematic due not only to the poor state of preservation of some of the signs, but also to the unparalleled sequence eĝer-zu-šè tuku-a, literally "the one who has to your back."
68 The comic effect of this line is derived by the fact that Enki praises *Ninmah's* wisdom, and not his own, despite the goddess' failure at finding for Udmul a suitable fate. Enki's praise of his penis refers to his own creative powers (Leick 1994: 29).
69 The figure of Ĝeštinana has thus far not been the subject of many studies. See Edzard 1957–71 and Katz 2003: 397–401.
70 Alster (2004: 581) claims however that *DD* "depicts Dumuzi as a guiltless victim of an unavoidable fate, not as the sufferer of a fate he had himself provoked by his thoughtless behavior" as it is the case in *Inana's Descent*.
71 For the nature and powers of the galla-demons, as well as their attestation in literary and archival documents, see Katz 2003: 127–54.
72 For the possible contamination between the house of the old woman Belili, where Dumuzi finds refuge, and the house of the old woman Bilulu, where Dumuzi is killed, see below under *Inana and Bilulu*.
73 For an overview of female sages in Mesopotamia see Harris 1990.
74 Sumerian dub-sar im zu-ĝu₁₀.
75 Sumerian lú-bàn-da šag₄ inim-ma zu-ĝu₁₀.
76 Sumerian um-ma šag₄ ma-mú-da zu-ĝu₁₀.
77 For *DG* ll. 19–25 see now Selz 2008: 19.
78 These lines are extremely problematic. The Sumerian reads as follows:

213. tukum-bi ud-da um-ma ki ^ddumu-zi tìl-la nu-ub-zu
214. igi ní te-a na-bar-bar-re.
215. gù ní te-a na-dé-dé-e.
216. ĝá-nam-ma-an-zé-en é um-ma ^dbe-li-li-šè ga-an-ši-re₇-dè-en.

The translation offered here is the only one that makes sense. Belili is neither worried nor frightened because she knows Dumuzi is safe in her house. This is what gives away Dumuzi's location and it also explains why Ĝeštinana makes such a public display of emotions while hiding her brother.
79 Ll. 246–49 are uttered by the demons.
80 Sladek 1974: 29–34 and 225–39.
81 The composition is known only from two *imgida*. Therefore, it is not too far-fetched to suggest we may not have its beginning.
82 The Sumerian reads as follows: ĝuruš áĝ-gig-ra i-lu áĝ-gig-ga hu-mu-ni-íb-bé. The usage of *emesal* áĝ-gig for níĝ-gig and the presence of a precative verbal forms indicate Ĝeštinana is the speaker.
83 Another name for Dumuzi.
84 Sumerian ĝuruš ama-ni sag₉-ga-ni nu-du₈. A literal translation "the lad whose goodness does not spread (= extend) to his mother" makes no sense in the context, since the text lists what Dumuzi will lose by dying so young, and not his alleged faults. As such, I opted for supplying "anymore," thus implying that Dumuzi's death will prevent his mother from enjoying his goodness.

85 Sladek 1974: 32–33.
86 The Sumerian reads as follows:

72. ning-e na-áĝ šeš-na-šè iri-a mušen-gin7 im-ma-an-níĝin-níĝin
73. šeš-ĝu10 áĝ-gig-ga gal šu ga-de6 ĝá-na me ga-an-te

Sladek (1974: 236) translates the second hemistich of l. 73 as follows: "let me be *the fitting one* (?)" (emphasis his), but offers no rationale for such translation. His suggestion is however compelling in light of *Inana's Descent* ll. 407–9 (for which see Sladek 1974: 32). In these lines, Inana promises Dumuzi the following:

407. "You for half the year and your sister for half the year.
408. "When you are demanded, on that day you shall stay;
409. "When your sister is demanded, on that day you shall be released".

L. 407 must refer to a six-month long sojourn in the netherworld the two siblings will have to endure in Inana's stead.

87 As already noted by Jacobsen and Kramer 1953: 169 fn. 9, it is not clear whether, in *IB*, Dumuzi and Inana are married or simply betrothed. The usage of the term "nitalam" to describe Dumuzi (l. 93) may point to marriage.
88 The manuscript, published by Jacobsen and Kramer 1953, is a four-column tablet, which must have preserved the entire composition.
89 This parallel was already noted by Jacobsen and Kramer 1953: 182.
90 A more detailed discussion of Belili/Bilulu in the Dumuzi-Inana cycle must for the present be set aside, but I plan to return to it in a future study.
91 Jacobsen and Kramer 1953: 167–69.
92 Jacobsen and Kramer 1953: 183 point out that "the term um-ma (…) denotes primarily the wise and skilled woman and can be used without the implication of advanced age". This observation does not take into account the presence of bur-šu-ma, which strengthens the notion that old age was indeed Bilulu's defining feature. For the role of older women in Mesopotamian society see Harris 2000.
93 For bur-šu-ma see PSD B *s. v.* 188–89, in particular 189.
94 I translated the verb with a singular form although it is clearly a plural form: mu-un-na-sug8-ug.
95 That Dumuzi was assassinated is suggested by the usage of the verb saĝ–re, "to hit/ strike (in) the head" (cf. saĝ ĝeš-ra, "to kill").
96 This passage suggests Dumuzi was killed in order to steal his sheep.
97 Sumerian DI-ĝu10. I here follow Jacobsen and Kramer 1953: 183, who render DI as sig8 and suggest it may be a phonetic writing for si6 = *immeru*.
98 Bilulu is described as um-ma (l. 81), bur-šu-ma (l. 82) and nin ní-te-a-ka (l. 82). The first two terms are not problematic, but the third is difficult to understand. I opted for a literal translation "her own mistress," which reflects both the Sumerian and Bilulu's reality: there is no husband in the picture.
99 Sumerian lú AŠ-àm. This can be solved either as lú dili-àm "a single man" or as lú rim5-àm, "a perfect man." Considering that Ĝirĝire is anything but perfect, the former seems more likely.
100 Sumerian ĜÍR-gunu.ĜÍR-gunu-e àm-túm. Jacobsen and Kramer 1953: 183 solve the first three signs as ul4-ul4-e and translate this line as "he is worthy of (-e) directing" and point out that "the coincidence of the writing of this word and of ul4-ul4-la in l. 92 with that of the name of Ĝirĝire is rather striking". I think, on the other

hand, that GÍR-gunu.GÍR-gunu-e is a variant writing of Bilulu's son's name, ĝír-ĝír-e. As such, I translated as "Girĝire was suitable and knowledgeable man."

101 Sumerian ul₄-ul₄-la šíta tag-ga-na ság mu-un-ne-dug₄. The graphic play between ul₄-ul₄-la and ĝír-ĝír-e has already been noted by Jacobsen and Kramer 1953: 183. For ság – dug₄, "to push back, to hunt, to kill" but also "to disperse" see Attinger 1993: 655 fl. Attinger 1993: 662 translates this line as: "En hâte, il (Girgire) dispersait loin d'eux (des propiétaires des victimes?) (ses frappés de la masse =) les victimes qu'il avait abbatues avec la masse." This translation has been used here.

102 Sumerian nitalam.

103 I disagree with Jacobsen and Kramer's interpretation of these lines (1953: 164). They think that Inana crossed the haunted steppe and reached an alehouse where people gathered after a long day of labor. In my opinion, the alehouse refers to Inana's abode. Her association with alehouses is well documented in Mesopotamian literature (see Allred 2009).

104 Sumerian ĝen-na ba-ug₅-ge-en na-nam-ma-am₃ mu-zu ga-ba-da-ha-lam-e. In *Inana and Shukaletuda*, Inana cursed Shukaletuda, the gardener who had raped her, with similar words. The only concession she made for him was that his name would be remembered (l. 296): ĝen-na ba-ug₅-ge-en nam-ĝu₁₀ mu-zu nam-ba-da-ha-lam-e: "Begone! I have killed you. What is it to me? Your name, however, shall not be forgotten!"

105 Whereas Inana addresses Bilulu directly in ll. 100–101, she speaks of her and her son in the third person in ll. 102–3. This may be a mistake on the scribe's part.

106 The colophon identifies *IB* as a ù-líl-lá, a "lament", of Inana (that is performed by her). To my knowledge, this is the only composition labeled as ù-líl-lá.

Bibliography

Allred, L. (2009) "*The Ancient Mesopotamian Tavern*," paper presented at the 219th Meeting of the American Oriental Society, Albuquerque, March 16th 2009.

Alster, B. (1972) *Dumuzi's Dream. Aspects of Oral Poetry in a Sumerian Myth.* Copenhagen: Akademik Forlag.

——. (1974) "Enki and Ninhursag," *Ugarit Forschungen* 10: 15–27.

——. (2004) "Myth and sacred narratives: Mesopotamia," in S. Iles Johnston (ed.) *Religions of the Ancient World: A Guide.* Cambridge: The Belknap Press of Harvard University Press, 580–82.

Asher-Greve, J. and M. F. Wogec (2002) "Women and gender in the ancient Near Eastern cultures: bibliography 1885–2001 AD," *NIN* 3: 33–114.

Attinger, P. (1984) "Enki et Ninhursaĝa," *Zeitschrift für Assyriologie* 74: 1–52.

Attinger, P. (1993) *Eléments de linguistique sumérienne. La construction de du₁₁/e/di «dire».* Göttingen: Vandenhoeck and Ruprecht.

Behrens, H. (1978) *Enlil und Ninlil. Ein sumerischer Mythos aus Nippur.* Rome: Biblical Institute Press.

Benito, C. (1969) *"Enki and Ninmah" and "Enki and the World Order,"* unpublished dissertation, University of Pennsylvania.

Berlin, A. (1979) *Enmerkar and Ensuhkešdanna. A Sumerian Narrative Poem.* Philadelphia: The University Museum.

Black, J. (2004) "Dumuzi and his sisters," *Orientalia* NS 73: 228–34.

Bottéro J. and S. N. Kramer (1989) *Lorques le Dieux Faisaient l'Homme.* Paris: Éditions Gallimard.

Brenner, A. (1985) *The Israelite Woman. Social Role and Literary Type in Biblical Narrative.* Sheffield: JSOT Press.

Brenner A. and C. Fontaine (eds) (1997) *A Feminist Companion to Reading the Bible. Approaches, Methods and Strategies.* Sheffield: Sheffield Academic Press.

Brisch, N. M. (2007) *Tradition and the Poetics of Innovation: Sumerian Court Literature of the Larsa Dynasty (c. 2003–1763 BCE).* Münster: Ugarit-Verlag.

Bruschweiler, F. (1987) *Inanna: la Déesse Triomphante et Vaincue Dans la Cosmologie Sumérienne. Recherche Lexicographique.* Leuven: Éditions Peeters.

Cavigneaux, A. and M. Krebernik (2000a) "Nin-BARAG," *Reallexicon der Assyriologie* 9: 335–336.

——(2000b) "Nin-gun(a/u)," *Reallexikon der Assyriologie* 9: 375–77.

——(2001a) "Nin-mada," *Reallexikon der Assyriologie* 9: 462.

——(2001b) "Nin-mah," *Reallexikon der Assyriologie* 9: 462–63.

——(2001c) "Nin-muga, Nin-zed, Nin-zadim," *Reallexikon der Assyriologie* 9: 471–73.

——(2001d) "Nun-bar-še-gunu," *Reallexikon der Assyriologie* 9: 615.

Civil, M. (1964) "The 'Message of Lú-dingir-ra to His Mother' and a group of Akkado-Hittite 'Proverbs'," *Journal of Near Eastern Studies* 23: 1–11.

——. (1983) "Enlil and Ninlil: the Marriage of Sud," *Journal of the American Oriental Society* 103: 43–66.

Cooper, J. S. (1980) "Critical review of Hermann Behrens, Enlil und Ninlil," *Journal of Cuneiform Studies* 32: 175–88.

——(1989) "Enki's member: eros and irrigation in Sumerian literature," in H. Behrens, D. Loding and M. T. Roth (eds) *dumu-e₂-dub-ba-a: Studies in Honor of Å. W. Sjöberg.* Philadelphia: The University Museum Press, 87–89.

Çiğ, M. and S. N. Kramer (1976) "The ideal mother: a Sumerian portrait," *Belleten* 40: 413–21.

Edzard, D. O. (1957–71) "Geštinanna," *Reallexikon der Assyriologie* 3: 299–301.

——. (1990) "Gilgameš und Huwawa A. I. Teil," *Zeitschrift für Assyriologie* 80: 165–203.

——. (1991) "Gilgameš und Huwawa A. II. Teil," *Zeitschrift für Assyriologie* 81: 165–233.

Farber, G. (1990) "me," *Reallexikon der Assyriologie* 7: 610–13.

Focke, K. (1998) "Die Göttin Nin-imma," *Zeitschrift für Assyriologie* 88: 196–224.

Focke, E. (2000) "Nin-imma," *Reallexikon derAssyriologie* 9: 384–86.

——. (2009) "Why it was rape: the conceptualization of rape in Sumerian literature," *Journal of the American Oriental Society* 129: 73–82.

Gadotti, A. (2011) *"Presence in Absentia: Portraits of the Feminine in Sumerian Literature,"* *Journal of the American Oriental Society* 131: 195–206.

Glassner, J.-J. (1992) "Inanna et les me," in M. de Jong Ellis (ed.) *Nippur at the Centennial.* Philadelphia: University of Pennsylvania Press, 55–86.

Harris, R. (1990) "The female sage in Mesopotamian literature (with an appendix on Egypt)," in J. G. Gammie and L. G. Perdue (eds) *The Sage in Israel and the Ancient Near East.* Winona Lake, IN: Eisenbrauns, 3–17.

——. (1991) "Inanna-Ishtar as Paradox and a Coincidence of Opposites," *History of Religions* 3: 261–78.

——. (1997) "Images of women in the Gilgamesh Epic," in J. Maier (ed.) *Gilgamesh: A Reader.* Wauconda, IL: Bolchazy-Carducci Publishers, Inc., 79–94.

——. (2000) "Old(er) women," in *Gender and Aging in Ancient Mesopotamia.* Norman, OK: University of Oklahoma Press, 88–118.

Heimpel, W. (2000) "Ninhursaga," *Reallexikon der Assyriologie* 9: 378–81.

Jacobsen, Th. (1939) *The Sumerian King List*. Chicago, London: The University of Chicago Press.

Jacobsen Th. and S.N. Kramer (1953) "The myth of Inana and Bilulu," *Journal of Near Eastern Studies* 12: 160–88.

Karahashi, F. (2000) *Sumerian Compound Verbs with Body-Part Terms*, unpublished dissertation, University of Chicago.

Katz, D. (2003) *The Image of the Netherworld in the Sumerian Sources*. Bethesda, MD: CDL Press.

Kilmer, A. (1976) "Speculations on Umul, the first baby," in B. L. Eichler, J. W. Heimerdinger and Å. W. Sjöberg (eds) *Kramer Anniversary Volume. Cuneiform Studies in Honor of Samuel Noah Kramer*. Neukirchen-Vluyn: Butzon & Bercker, 265–70.

Klein, J. (1997) "Enki and Ninmah," in W. W. Hallo (ed.) *The Context of Scripture I: Canonical Compositions from the Biblical World*. New York & Leiden: Brill, 516–18.

Kramer, S. N. (1960) *Two Elegies on a Pushkin Museum Tablet: A New Sumerian Literary Genre*. Moscow: Oriental Literature Publishing House.

——. (1987) "The woman in ancient Sumer: gleanings from Sumerian literature," in J.-M. Durand (ed.) *La Femme dans les Proche-Orient Antique*. Paris: Éditions Recherche sur les Civilisations, 107–12.

Krebernik, M. (1996) "Muttergöttin A I," *Reallexikon der Assyrologie* 8: 502–16.

Lafont, S. (1999) *Femmes, Droit et Justice dans l'antiquite Orientale. Contributions a l'Etude du Droit Penal au Proche-Orient Ancient*. Freiburg: Vandenhoeck & Ruprecht.

Leick, G. (1994) *Sex and Eroticism in Mesopotamian Literature*. London and New York: Routledge.

Michalowski, P. (2003) "A man called Enmebaragesi," in W. Sallaberger *et al.* (eds) *Literatur, Politik und Recht in Mesopotamien. Festschrift für Claus Wilcke*. Wiesbaden: Harrassowitz, 195–208.

Pomeroy, S. (1975) *Goddesses, Whores, Wives and Slaves*. New York: Schocken Books.

Scurlock, J. (2003) "But was she raped? A verdict through comparison," *NIN* 4: 61–103.

Sefati, Y. (1998) *Love Songs in Sumerian Literature. The Critical Edition of the Dumuzi-Inanna Songs*. Ramat-Gan: Bar Ilan University Press.

Selz, G. J. (2008) "The divine prototypes," in N. M. Brisch (ed.) *Religion and Power: Divine Kingship in the Ancient World and Beyond*. Chicago: University of Chicago Press, 13–31.

Sladek, W. (1974) *Inanna's Descent to the Netherworld*, unpublished dissertation, the Johns Hopkins University.

Veldhuis, N. (2004) *Religion, Literature and Scholarship: the Sumerian Composition «Nanše and the Birds»*. Leiden and Boston: Brill & Stix.

Westenholz, J. G. (1998) "Goddesses of the ancient Near East 3000–1000 BCE," in L. Goodison and C. Morris (eds) *Ancient Goddesses. the Myth and the Evidence*. Madison: The University of Wisconsin Press, 63–82.

——. (2009) "Inanna and Ishtar – the dimorphic Venus goddesses," in G. Leick (ed.) *The Babylonian World*. New York: Routledge, 332–47.

Wiggermann, F.A.M. (1998) "Nammu," *Reallexikon der Assyrologie* 9: 135–40.

Wilcke, C. (1987) "Die Schwester des Ehemannes (/erib/)," in J.-M. Durand (ed.) *La Femme dans les Proche-Orient Antique*. Paris: : Éditions Recherche sur les Civilisations, 179–87.

Zgoll, A. (1997) *Der Rechtsfall der En-hedu-Ana*. Münster: Ugarit-Verlag.

3

SUMERIAN WISDOM LITERATURE

Alhena Gadotti

Defining wisdom literature is not an easy task, especially when dealing with ancient societies.[1] In his most recent work on the topic, *Wisdom from Ancient Sumer* (2006), Bendt Alster provides a wide-range definition of wisdom as "not only an attitude, but a number of very different attitudes that may come to light in literary works belonging to various text types, or genres".[2] In addition, he rightly stresses that this term "does not do justice to the subtleties of the ancient cultures".[3] Therefore, wisdom-oriented texts written in Sumerian may not necessarily be considered as such in other civilizations.[4]

Alster classifies as wisdom texts the following Sumerian compositions: didactic compositions, including the so-called father-to-son instructions; practical instructions; dialogues and disputations; schools compositions; the proverbs collections; the riddle collections; morality tales; fables; folktales; and satires.[5]

Alster's categorization raises the issue of an etic vs. emic definition of literary genres, which have plagued the field of ancient Near Eastern Studies for quite a while.[6] Most notably, scholars debate the validity of applying modern (i.e. Aristotelian) labels to ancient compositions (both in Sumerian and Akkadian, as well as in Hebrew, Hittite, Aramaic and Egyptian), written before such labels were actually developed. This problem is complicated by the fact that all of the above-mentioned languages have native terms, which may be understood as literary categorizations.[7]

Unfortunately, developing an emic classification of Mesopotamian literature is a task that cannot be satisfactorily addressed here. Since, however, Alster's is a valid heuristic framework within which to set the present investigation, I will use his classification as a starting point to investigate the image and portrayal of women in wisdom literature. In what follows, I will discuss the Sumerian Proverb Collections: two didactic compositions, namely *The Instructions of Shuruppak* and the *Counsel of Wisdom*; and two Sumerian folktales, *The Old Man and the Young Girl* and *The Three Ox-Drivers from Adab*.[8] These are the only wisdom texts mentioning women and/or addressing some specific aspects of the feminine.

From these documents, a multi-faceted and multilayered image of the feminine emerges. It is, however, important to stress that the purpose of wisdom literature is *not* to talk about women, or to even provide information *about* women (see below). The only exceptions may be two Sumerian dialogues, known as *Two Women A* and *Two Women B*. However, these two compositions still await publication, and they have not been incorporated in this survey.

Women in Sumerian proverbs[9]

Sumerian proverbs have a long history, spanning from the Early Dynastic (2600–2500 BCE) to the Neo-Assyrian periods (seventh century BCE). Tablets containing proverbs are ubiquitous in the Ancient Near East. The earliest examples come from Abu Salabikh, and the latest were uncovered in the library of Assurbanipal at Nineveh. The largest corpus is, however, the Old Babylonian one (1900–1800 BCE), which is the topic of this section. Although some of tablets are of unknown provenance, the majority have been found at Nippur and Ur. Manuscripts were also unearthed at Kish and Sippar, as well as in the Elamite capital, Susa.

Interpreting proverbs is notoriously difficult, even more so for a society as far removed from ours as Mesopotamia is. Attempting to derive from them a general picture of the status of women within Mesopotamian society is even more challenging, mainly for two reasons: first, most of the surviving proverbs cannot be understood unless they are seen within the larger framework of scribal education, as Veldhuis demonstrated in his works on scribal education at Nippur (1997, 2000); second, women are very much underrepresented in this corpus.

Despite Alster's optimistic comment that the Sumerian proverb collection contains information about "a women's daily routine, family relationships, good and bad manner, the good man, the liar, legal proceedings, Fate, the palace, the temples and their gods, as well as historical and ethnic allusions" (Alster 1997: xxviii), the present discussion shows that these proverbs have very little to say about women and their activities.

Sumerian proverbs tend to depict women in traditional roles: young unmarried and married women (SP 1.148 and 1.149 and 1.12, respectively), mothers and daughters (SP 1.185), sisters (SP 1.148 and 1.149, albeit indirectly) and caregivers (SP 3.2). Social status *may* be a defining feature (SP 1.50 and SP 3.41, paralleled by SP 28.25). Indeed, several proverbs deal with the role and responsibilities of female servants (SP 3.41, SP 21 Sec. A 6–11 and SP 21 Sec. A 16 = *The Lazy Slave Girl*).

Some of the proverbs address women's roles and opportunities *vis-à-vis* their male counterparts. For instance, women's sexuality is depicted in negative terms, especially when compared to men's sexuality (SP 1.156, albeit of difficult interpretation). Women's rearing is also viewed in opposition to men's, as illustrated by SP 1.185. Women's incompetence is stressed *vis-à-vis* a man's resourcefulness (SP 28: 21–22).

A discussion on women in proverbs needs to address the issue of the proverbs written in the *emesal* dialect of Sumerian (among others SP 1.108, 1.125–26,

1.150, 2.99–101).[10] Although its precise nature is still under debate, *emesal* is employed in Sumerian literary compositions when goddesses, women or the gala-priests speak. In addition, *emesal* is found in cultic laments.[11]

Proverbs containing *emesal* forms are problematic, even when it is certain a woman is speaking,[12] because of the proverbs' curricular settings: some of these adages may have very little to do with what *women had to say* within the Old Babylonian society. Rather, they may have been a means to an end: to teach students how to properly use *emesal*.

Here, I discuss only proverbs with *emesal* forms, in which it is unequivocal a woman is speaking (SP 1.125–26//14.41–42, 1.169, 1.176, 1.187//SP 7.74, 3.41//7.73). One exception is SP 21 Sec. A 6–11. The collection uses *emesal* forms often, but the nature of the speaker is unclear. However, the text is about women, more precisely female servants.

The texts

1.12
Something that has not happened since time immemorial:
A young girl did not fart on her spouse's lap![13]
1.50
Pea-flour is suitable for all women within the palace.[14]
1.125
My husband heaps up for me,
My son measures out to me,
My lover shall pick the bones from the fish for me.[15]
1.126
A plant as sweet as a husband does not grow in the steppe.[16]
1.148–49
Young girl: your brother does not appreciate you.
Whom do you appreciate?
Young girl: your brother is like me.
The brother should live like I do.[17]
1.156
(If) a male is aroused, he eats salt.
(If) a female is aroused, she is dragged in the mud.[18]
1.169
Sons-in-law, what have they brought!
Fathers-in-law, what have they spread out![19]
1.176
I am the lady who wears large garments.
I shall cut my loincloth.[20]
1.185
A mother silences her chattering daughter.
A mother does not silence her chattering son.

1.187
The ferryboat is [filled] with men:
My husband shall not board!
3.2
A nursemaid looks at the parapet as if she were a king's daughter.[21]
3.41
When she (the lady) went out of the house and she (the slave-girl) came in from the street,
The latter (the slave-girl) set up the meal for her lady.[22]
3.104
A dog moves,
A scorpion moves,
(But) my man does not move.[23]
21 Sec. A 6–11
6. At dusk, the female servant roams around as if it were midnight.[24]
7. While the dirt had not become apparent to the female servant, to her mistress it looked more and more abundant.[25]
8. Dusk is the joy of the daughter-in-law.[26]
9. It is not precious for her: she is the ... female servant.
10. The female servant took out the balag-instrument. The Mistress of Heaven (Inana) was seated in the bottom dike / village.[27]
11. The female servant of the palace speaks constantly.[28]
28: 21–22
When a man walks about, he finds something,
When a woman walks about, she loses something.

Women in the *Instructions of Shuruppak*

The *Instructions of Shuruppak* has a very long manuscript tradition. The earliest exemplars date to the Early Dynastic period (ca. 2700–2600 BCE) and were uncovered at Abu Salabikh and Adab.[29] The composition was very popular during the Old Babylonian period. As to be expected, the bulk of manuscripts has been unearthed at Nippur and Ur, but the *Instructions* is well known in other cities, such as Kish and Susa. There also are several tablets of unknown provenance, which contain different sections of the *Instructions*.[30] Monolingual Akkadian as well as bilingual Akkado-Hurrian translations also exist and are a testimony to the popularity of this composition.[31] In this discussion, I will focus on the Old Babylonian Sumerian version.

The *Instructions* consists of a collection of father-to-son advices expressed in gnomic form.[32] The composition is more informative about the status of women than the proverbs discussed above. On the one hand, a misogynist attitude is expressed throughout this composition: there is an emphasis on the dangers of dealing with both female servants and women (for instance ll. 49, 118 and 193). In addition, the father cautions the son about women's unreliable nature (l. 209). At the same time, however, the *Instructions* highlights the importance of women as caregivers (ll. 265–67 and 264), as well as the need to have a competent woman in charge of your household (l. 215, with a possible word-play between house-hold/field/legitimate progeny). Therefore, a certain level of ambiguity emerges from this text. This is evident from the views expressed, for instance, by the above mentioned l. 215 and l. 220, which states a woman with possessions will ruin a household.

The text

49. Do not have sexual intercourse with your slave girl. She will neglect you.[33]

...

118. A weak wife is always caught by fate.[34]

...

193. When you bring a slave-girl from the mountains, she carries with her both goods and evils.

...

208. You should not take a wife during your festival.
209. (Her) heart is for hire; (her) appearance is borrowed.
210. The silver is borrowed; the lapis lazuli is borrowed.
211. The dress is borrowed; the linen garment is borrowed.[35]
212. (...) it is not equal (?).

...

215. One should place a trustworthy woman in a reliable field.[36]

...

220. A woman with possessions brings the house to its rump.[37]
221. A drunkard drowns the harvest.
222. A female catcher, at(?) the ladder, (the place where) not even two men speak,[38]
223. Flies into the houses like a fly.[39]
224. (Like) a she-donkey, she recites words on the street.[40]
225. (Like) a female pig, she suckles her child on the street.
226. A woman who pricked herself begins to cry,
227. And holds the spindle which pricked (?) her in her hand.
228. She enters every house;
229. She peers into all streets.
230. And upon the roofs, she keeps saying: "Leave!"
231. She looks up to all the parapets.[41]
232. She ... where there is a quarrel.[42]

...

256. Do not ... an ewe:[43] you will have a girl.

257. Do not throw a lump (of earth) into the money-chest: you will have a boy.[44]

258. Do not abduct a wife; do not raise an outcry.[45]

259. At the place where the wife has been abducted, the force is crushing.

260. "Oh the foot, oh the neck!" (they say) "Let us go around in circle!"

261. "Let us make the great man bow down with one single arm!"

...

264. The nursemaids of the women's chamber[46] decide the destinies for their lords.

265. Do not speak an arrogant word to your mother; there will be hatred caused against you.

266. Do not seize in your mouth your mother and god's words![47]

267. A mother is like Utu, who gives birth to mankind.

Women in the *Counsels of Wisdom*[48]

Women are mentioned sporadically in the *Counsels of Wisdom*, an Old Babylonian composition thus far known from seven manuscripts, four of which were unearthed at Nippur.[49] The *Counsels of Wisdom* is not very well preserved. However, from the available material, it is evident that the text focuses on a set of rules and regulation about how to properly behave in society.

Among others, we find an exhortation to pay attention to the words uttered by one's parents (ll. 76–77); general advice to maintain amicable relations with one's sister (l. 82), in a larger section encouraging the perpetuation of good family relations (ll. 80–83). Furthermore, there is an invitation to treat both female and male neighbors as if they were one's sibling (ll. 183–84). Therefore, the emphasis appears to be on the clan and the community.

At the same time, however, the *Counsels of Wisdom* advocates caution when dealing with noisy female neighbors, as they might be interested in one's possessions (ll. 194–95).

The text

76. "You should pay attention to [the words of your father as if they were the words of your god].

77. "You should pay attention to the words of your mother as if they were the words of your god(dess).[50]

...

80. "You should know to fear your brother.
81. "You should listen to the words of your older brother as if they were the words of your father.
82. "You should not let the heart of your older sister become angry. Let the curse return to the mouth (which uttered it).
83. "You should know to [...] your brothers, since it is edifying.

...

183. "A son of the city quarter was treated as if he were your brother; a female neighbor of the city quarter was treated as if she were your sister.
184. "For as long as you live, you should not ... to your drinking parties.[51]

...

194. "Secondly, as for the noisy female neighbors of the city quarter,[52]
195. "(if) they (wish to) pull out your possessions, you should hide them."

Women in *The Old Man and the Young Girl* and *The Three Ox-Drivers from Adab*

The Old Man and the Young Girl, recently re-edited by Alster (2006: 384–90), is known from four Old Babylonian manuscripts, three of which have been found at Nippur.[53] The text is not very well preserved and difficult to understand,[54] as both the beginning and the end are lost. The tale narrates an old man's health problems and the solution offered by a sekrum (see below) to solve his ills: to marry a young girl (ll. 19–21).

The story has four protagonists: the old man, whose declining physical abilities prompts him to seek the advise of an unnamed king (ll. 9'–11'); the king, who listens to the old man's predicament and then seeks the advice of a sekrum (ll. 12'–17'); the sekrum, who offers a practical solution for the old man's ailments, namely to marry a young woman (ll. 18'–23'(?)); and finally, the young woman, whose youth is supposed to restore the old man's lost prowess (ll. 37'–41').[55]

Of interest for our purposes are the young girl and the sekrum. The young girl embodies the solution to the matter at hand, namely the old man's decline. The terminology employed to describe her (ki-sikil tur in line 19', ki-sikil in ll. 37' and 40') indicates that she is a virgin.[56] Although we only see glimpses of her in the very short composition, it is evident that she exemplifies the young unmarried woman on the edge of womanhood. Her youthful enthusiasm for her wedding emerges in the final lines of the tale, where she invites her girlfriends to dance in celebration of the upcoming nuptials (l. 21).

It is, however, the sekrum who plays a pivotal role in *The Old Man and the Young Girl*, as she finds the solution to the problem. Understanding who she is, however, not an easy task. The word sekrum[57] is an Akkadian loanword into Sumerian from the term *sekretum*. Von Soden translates the latter "Abgesperrte" or, more broadly "eine Frauenklasse".[58] The editors of CAD S, on the other hand, translate *sekretum* as "(a woman of his rank, possibly cloistered); (a woman of the palace household, court lady)."[59] Whereas the first meaning is attested in Old Babylonian legal and literary documents, the latter is often used to describe courtly women in foreign courts, especially Elam.[60] In addition, the term *sekretum* is often applied to royal women within the Neo-Assyrian court.

Alster (2006: 385–86) translates sekrum as "cloistered woman".[61] However, I find the translation "court lady" more suitable to the present context, since the tale has a court setting and it is the king himself who asks for her advice.

The court lady plays an important role also in the story of *The Three Ox-Drivers from Adab*,[62] known only from two Old Babylonian manuscripts.[63] Here, the king turns to her for help in the matter of the three men who had sought the king's advice on the account of a quarrel that arose among them.[64] *The Old Man and the Young Girl* and *The Three Ox-Drivers from Adab* share a common literary *topos*: a king, unable (or unwilling) to address a matter himself, consults with a court woman, who offers a feasible solution.

Although the evidence is limited to two literary documents, which almost certainly used the same repertoires of motifs, it emerges that there existed a literary tradition in which a woman acted as a counselor to the ruler. This tradition does reflect a state of affair that is well documented from the Mari archives.[65]

The Old Man and the Young Girl: *the text*

The beginning of the composition is lost, but it appears that an old man laments his loss of vigor before the king (ll. 1'(?)–11') and possibly seeks advice:

12'. The king did not answer,
13'. (But) entered (the abode of a) court lady,
14'. And repeated the speech (of the old man) to the court lady.
15'. "(I was) an exceptional man, whose chest was very strong.
16'. "My blood was fine, my … , … , (and) …
17'. "were multicolored. My … barley had no god." Thus he said.
18'. The court lady replied to the king:
19'. "My [lord], suppose the old man took a young girl as a wife.
20'. […] and the old man will regain his youthfulness,
21'. [… and the young girl] will become a mature woman."

The ensuing fourteen lines contain a dialogue between the king and the old man. The latter asks the old man a question difficult to understand (l. 25'): "Why has your ... ?".[66] The old man's answer is convoluted (ll. 26'-35'), and rich in metaphors and obscure references, which seem to stress yet again the man's loss of vigor.[67]

26'. The old man replied to the king:
27'. "I (was once) a youth, (but now) my god, my strength, my protective god,
28'. "My youthfulness abandoned my loins as a runaway donkey.
29'. "My black mountain produced white gypsum;
30'. "My mother sent to me a man from the woods, and he gave me ... ;[68]
31'. "My mongoose,[69] which ate redolent food, does not even stretch towards a jar of ghee;
32'. "My teeth, which ground hard food, do not chew hard food (anymore);
33'. "My urine flew (?) in a strong wall (i. e. abundantly); ... ;[70]
34'. "My son, who fed me oil and cream, does not give me food (anymore);
35'. "And my young female servant, whom I bought, is like an evil galla-demon!"
36'. The king paid attention to the words of the old man,
37'. The king spoke to the young girl:
38'. "When I have given him (the old man) to you, he shall lie on your lap like a young man.
39'. "Come, your servant shall make a speech (?),[71] your house shall be adorned."
40'. Upon leaving the palace, the young girl (said):
41'. "[Dance], dance all young girls, move around!"[72]

The rest of the composition is lost, although we can safely assume the nuptials brought about the desired effects.

The Three Ox-Drivers from Adab: *the text*

Three men from Adab are involved in a dispute about the rightful ownership of a calf. In order to solve the matter, they go to consult an unnamed king (ll. 1–15).

16. The king did not answer them, but entered (the abode of) a court lady.
17. The king asked the court lady for advice.

The ruler explains the problem to the court lady by reporting the story he heard from the three men from Adab (ll. 18–30). The advice of the court lady is lost in a long lacuna (ll. 31–68), although her solution to the problem may be preserved in ll. 65–88, which may "contain her speech repeated by the king to the three men. The missing lines 33-ca. 53 would thus have been identical with 65–85 (? Or 88?), but approximately 15 lines of the composition would still be missing".[73]

Be that as it may, the solution the woman offers is not clear. Like in *The Old Man and the Young Girl*, the language is convoluted and rich in double entendre and word play. The text itself recognizes that the dispute among the three men from Adab was settled "with skillful words" (ll. 93–94).

89. When the king came out from (the abode of) the court lady,
90. Each man, whose heart [...], his heart was satisfied.
91. The man who was angry with his wife left his wife;
92. The man who [...] ... dropped. ... [74]
93. With skillful words,[75] the citizens of Adab,
94. With skillful words, their matter was settled.
95. Panigingarra, their sage, the um-mi-a, the god of Adab, was the clerk.

Notes

Abbreviations follow standard Assyriological practices.
1 See Alster 2006: 18–21 for an exhaustive summary of the proposed definitions of wisdom literature as well as the problems these definitions pose.
2 Alster 2006: 21.
3 *Ibidem.*
4 Or indeed by different scholars studying the same civilization, as nicely illustrated by Alster's summary of the problem, 2006: 20–21.
5 Alster 2006: 22–23.
6 See most recently Holm 2007.
7 See Holm 2007: 271 for a list of examples.
8 *The Lazy Slave Girl* and *The Fowler and His Wife* (Alster 2006: 370–72 with previous bibliography) have not been included in the discussion.
9 Abbreviations and numbering follow Alster 1997. For definition and classification of the proverbs, see Alster 1997: xiii–xvi. For the concept of "proverb collection" see Alster 1997: xvi.
10 For *emesal* see Schretter 1990. See also Black 1991; Whittaker 2002 and Cooper 2005.
11 Black 1991; Cohen 1974, 1981 and 1988; Cooper 2005.
12 Alster 1997: 355 does so in the case of SP 1.150, which reads: mà-a-gin$_7$-nam šim-bi líl-lá-àm u$_5$ lí bar-šèg-gá hé-gu$_7$-e, "It is like me: antimony paste is air. Processed fat(?) that shall be eaten in the cold". The meaning of the proverb is unclear and it cannot be excluded that the speaker is a gala priest.
13 The meaning of this proverb is obscure. Alster does not comment at all. Pedagogical reasoning may lay behind this proverb. Sumerian Proverb Collection one, 1–59(?) focuses on the readings of the GAR sign, which with a few exceptions (SP 1.4–5, 1.19, 1.47–50 and 1.54–57) is found at the beginning of each of these proverbs. GAR is to be read níĝ ("thing", but also "possession, something") in SP 1.1–3,

1.6–7, 1.9–18, 1.20, 1.23–25, 1.27–30, 1.3237, 1.44–45. It is to be read ninda ("food, bread") in SP 1.8–9, 1.21–22, 1.26, 1.31, 1.38–43, 1.46, 1.51–53 and 1.58–59 (?). After the latter, the IRI sign becomes prevalent in he opening position. Note that 1.47–50 deal with food, thus retaining a content association with the proverbs dealing with ninda. More specifically, 1.47 opens with zíd-gu, pea flour; 1.48 begins with dabin, barley flour; 1.49 begins with a-šà-ga ninda (to be translated "what food is in the field") and 1.50 also begins with zíd-gu. SP 1.12 is encapsulated in a set of four proverbs (1.10–11.13) exploring the grammatical possibilities of níǵ at the head of a sentence.

14 Alster 1997: 346, suggests that "[t]he implication seems to be that a special type of fine flour was appropriate for women of high social rank". This interpretation, however, clashes with SP 1.46, which reads: "Pea-flour of the home-born slaves is mixed with honey and ghee, (still) there is no end to their laments". The latter suggests that honey and ghee improve the quality of pea-flour.

15 As already noted by Alster 1997: 353, this proverb provides a snapshot of marriage bliss as seen from the woman's point of view. The man's is found in SP 3.112.

16 See Alster 1997: 353 with reference for the meaning of this proverb.

17 Problematic couplet. The difficulties stem from the translation of the verb saǵ ... kal. I here follow see Karahashi 2000: 140, and opt for a meaning "to appreciate", rather that "to choose", for which see Alster 1997: 354. Alster suggests that the proverbs may have originated "in the formalities preceding the marriage. This can be taken as evidence that the girl actually was asked to express her opinion as to the man she wanted to marry, and not merely to rely on her brothers choice". Familial law of the Old Babylonian period makes this explanation unlikely (see Westbrook 2003: 385 and, for in depth discussion, Westbrook 1982 and 1988). Rather, 1. 148–49 consists of an exercise in grammar and the use of rhetorical devices, in particular parallelism (1.148: saǵ nu-mu-re-eb-kal-le vs. saǵ mu-e-kal-le-en; 1.149 (quoted in full): ki-sikil šeš-zu ǵe₂₆-e-gin₇-nam// šeš ǵe₂₆-gin₇ hé-til-le).

18 Alster 1997: 355–56 claims that in this line zi-ga-àm "most likely means 'aroused' in the sense of having lost one's temper". However, an allusion to the šag₄ zi-ga rituals cannot be excluded. The proverb may have a sexual connotation, and I interpret it as such. A woman's arousal seems to be seen as a negative event, as witnessed by im-ma gíd, "to drag into the mud". A man's arousal appears more problematic to interpret. The expression mul gu₇, "to eat salt", is ambiguous, as already noted by Alster 1997: 355, with reference.

19 As explained by Alster 1997: 356, these lines refer to the specific roles of sons-in-law (who had to pay a pre-agreed sum to the bride's parents) and fathers-in-law within marriage practices. The reference to the fathers-in-law is, however, more ambiguous than Alster's comment indicates. He suggests the father-in-law mentioned in the proverb to be the groom's father, who ultimately provided the bride price. However, this is not necessarily the case, since the groom acted often alone in the transaction (Westbrook 2003: 386). The lack of a possessive pronoun seems to support this idea.

20 According to Alster 1997: 357 "this [proverb] presumably ridicules a woman who is so proud of her fine clothing that she scorns her own underwear, a characteristic of an *homme nouveau*". I find this explanation unsatisfactory. Rather, Lambert 1967: 98, cited by Alster, *ibidem*, may be correct in suggesting that the adage stresses the incredible riches of the woman, who has so much clothing she can forego underwear.

21 As already noted by Alster 1997: 376, this proverb stresses the fundamental role played by a nursemaid in the rearing of rulers. This notion is also found in the *Instructions of Shuruppak* (l. 264).

22 Problematic proverb, paralleled by SP 28: 25. The problem is not only grammatical but of interpretation (see Alster 2006: 381). In particular, it is not clear whether the

female servant is actually fulfilling her duties or rather taking advantage of her mistress' absence to enjoy her possessions. A polemic against unreliable servants may indeed be meant here. This theme is attested elsewhere in the corpus. For example SP 21 Sec. A 16, known as *The Lazy Slave Girl* (Alster 1997: 256–57 and 442–44 and 2006: 370–71), also addresses the roles and functions of servants—both male and female—within one's household. The text, curiously written in *emesal*, clearly states that servants will have to face a life of tribulations should the lord and/or lady of the household die.

23 Although in this case the husband is the victim of his wife's ridicule (see along these lines Alster 1997: 387), this proverb may also allude to his inadequate sexual performances, by means of a word play between ĝír, "scorpion" and ĝír "knife, dagger", a phallic symbol.

24 *Emesal* gi₄-in is used instead géme. Alster 1997: 442 suggests that "the slave girl is eager to do things after dusk which she might not do in daylight". A possible explanation may be found in SP 21 Sec. A 8 (see below).

25 Similarly to SP 3.41 and *The Lazy Slave Girl*, this proverb shows a polemic against the ineptitude of servants. Specifically, the mistress sees dirt where the female servant does not.

26 The sense of this proverb is clear: it refers to the joys of the wedding bed (as indicated by the use of the term daughter-in-law). This proverb may also clarify the meaning of SP 21 Sec **A 6**. The latter may refer to the female servant after dark sexual activities.

27 See Alster 1997: 442 for problems.

28 For za-ra–du₁₁, "to speak constantly, to chatter" see Attinger 1993: 754.

29 See Alster 2006: 46–47 for the composition's publication history and ample bibliography.

30 Alster 2006: 52–53.

31 For the Akkadian version see Lambert 1960; for the bilingual Akkado-Hurrian see Krebernick 1996 and Wilhelm in Alster 2006: 204–8.

32 Line numbering follows Alster 2006.

33 For discussion of the variants see Alster 2006: 121. The translation is based on the Akkadian version.

34 Dies (?).

35 See the parallel in SP 4.18, already noted by Alster 2006: 210. The sense of these lines is clear: choosing a wife during a festive occasion is not advisable, since women tend to dress up to the nines precisely with the intention of catching a husband.

36 I here follow Alster and others, 2006: 164, and read gán instead of é, preferable in this context.

37 Reading munus bar-šu-ĝál-e é dúr-bi-šè mu-un-**túm** rather than mu-un-**ĝen**.

38 Sumerian munus šu-HA ᵍᵉˢkur₅ lú min-e da nu-sá. This line is extremely problematic. According to Alster 2006: 166, "[t]he intent seems to be that a fisher-woman is so busy meddling into everyone's affairs, that she is compared to a ladder that not even a couple of men can make stand upright". He translates the unknown compound verb da – sá as "to lean the side (in order to align)" (*ibidem*). Note however the parallel ki lú-da nu-di in *Inana's Descent* 180 and *Dumuzi's Dream* 244: *in private* (lit. in the place where no man speaks).

39 The symbolism of this imagery is well established, as illustrated by Alster 2006: 166. The woman is busy or, in modern terms, she is a busy body.

40 Although not reflected by the Sumerian grammar, this sentence and the following one must be understood as comparisons between the busy woman and a female ass and a pig, respectively. This is evidence by the usage in line 225 of dumu-ni (her child) instead of the expected dumu-bi (its child), and already noted by Alster 2006: 166.

Furthermore, this is also proved by the fact that the text chooses not to use the Sumerian term for piglet, zé-eh.

41 Sumerian bàd-si bàd-si-a igi mu-ši-x-íl-íl(?)-e. For igi – íl, "to look upwards/downwards", see Karahashi 2000: 125–26. I take bàd-si bàd-si-a as the semantic object of the verb (often marked by the locative, as illustrated by Karahashi's survey) rather than as the location from which the woman is looking.

42 Sumerian ki du$_{14}$-dè ĝál-la-šè zi im-[…]-RI. The verb is preserved only in one manuscript, K1 (from Kish). Alster 2006: 94 and 167 suggests a verb "to breath" (zi – pa-an), although he recognizes the problem posed by K1. Without additional data, I prefer to leave the verb untranslated.

43 For áš – du$_{11}$, see Attinger 1993: 445–50. He renders this sentence as follows (1993: 450): "n'injurie pas une agnelle", preferring the meaning of áš – du^{11} = ezērum. Alster 2006: 168 opts for "to abuse", an extrapolation on the primary meaning of the verb "to curse" (Akkadian arārum) and suggests the possibility the verb was here used as an euphemism. A third, and not well attested meaning for this verb, namely "to desire" (Akkadian hašāhum), may not be excluded in this context (see Attinger 1993: 446–47). It remains that the action brought upon the kid is a malicious one, which results into the fathering of daughters. In light of the ensuing line 257, this may not be interpreted as evidence for the idea that having daughters is worse than having sons. It is clear from the couplet that both sons and daughters are perceived as potential sources of future problems.

44 Alster 2006: 169 interprets the "throwing [of] a lump of clay into a money chest as symbolic of a son dispersing a fortune". However, this explanation makes no sense since the birth of a son is the consequence of this action and not its cause. For mi-si-sahar as "money chest" see Alster 2006: 113 with reference.

45 Ll. 258–61 form a unit of difficult interpretation. Commentators have raised the question of the speaker both in l. 258 and ll. 260–61 (see Alster 2006: 169 with reference). As for l. 258, I do not see the need to imply a change of speaker here. It stands to reason that Šuruppak is still advising his son about the appropriate course of action. The situation is admittedly more complex for ll. 260–61, where a change of speaker seems more likely. Alster's suggestion that the speaker in ll. 260–61 may be the people in the woman's household, cannot be completely set aside, although it is not completely convincing.

46 Rather than "the wet-nurses of the milk of mercy" preferred by Alster 2006: 170. Cf. SP 3.2 for the important role of nursemaids in the rearing of rulers.

47 Contra Alster 2006: 171, with discussion and previous bibliography.

48 Alster 2006: 221–26 for sources and publication history and 241–64 for edition, translation and commentary. Line numbering follows Alster 2006.

49 Alster 2006: 225–26. The provenience of the three remaining manuscripts is uncertain.

50 This advice echoes the one offered by The Instructions of Shuruppak ll. 265–67.

51 Sumerian [e]n-na ud-til-la-ta ki-kaš-dé-a-ta šu nam-na-e-díb-bé. Alster 2006: 253 and 263 opts for translating šu – díb as "to oblige someone to, to take advantage of his/her presence" and translate the line as "as long as you live, you should not oblige (?) him (/her) at your drinking parties".

52 Sumerian mìn-kam-ma-šè usar ká-gi$_4$-a igi-du$_8$-du$_8$-meš.

53 Alster 2006: 384. The fourth, BM 54699 = CT 42, 36, is of unknown provenance.

54 Line numbers follow Alster 2006.

55 Ll. 24'–36' list the afflictions the old man has to endure in his golden years. As already noted by Alster 2006: 385, the language is highly metaphorical and may have been an exercise in scribal erudition.

56 Cooper 2002.

57 The term is written either sé-ek-ru-um (ll. 13'–14') or sé-ek-rum (l. 18'), depending on the manuscript.

58 AHw 1036, *s.v. sekretum.*
59 CAD S, 215.
60 See the examples listed in CAD S 215 and 216, respectively.
61 See Alster 2006: 389 for a discussion of the term.
62 See also Alster 2006: 389. For the edition of this text see Alster 1991–93 and Alster 2006: 373–83. The similarities between the two tales are such that Alster treated them together in a chapter on "Sumerian Folktales" (2006: 373).
63 Alster 2006: 373. TCL 16, 80 and 83, of unknown provenience, may date to the Kassite period (Cavigneaux 1987), but CBS 1601 from Nippur is certainly Old Babylonian. In the *Three Ox-Drivers from Adab*, sekrum is always written sé-ek-rum (ll. 16–17 and 89).
64 See Alster 1991–93: 29–31 for a summary of the composition.
65 See Batto 1974 for the role of women at Mari. As pointed out by Harris 1990: 14, the best example of a woman counselor is the tavern-keeper Siduri "who advises Gilgamesh on how to cope with the reality of death" in Tablet X of the Standard Version of the *Epic of Gilgamesh* (ll. 1–91).
66 The question is problematic not only because the line is badly preserved, but also because it appears out of context. The Sumerian reads a-na-aš-àm /dam(?)\-zu a-ra-pag-pag-g[e] (see Alster 2006: 386 for variants and 389 for interpretation). Since the reading of the fifth sign is problematic (Alster 2006: 389), I left it untranslated. Equally problematic is the verbal chain a-ra-pag-pag-ge (so far unparalleled). The verb pag has two basic meanings: "to shut in", which Alster adopted in his edition (2006: 386 and 389) and "to leave behind" (see, for example, Ea II 284: (pag) pa-[a]g: HU = [*e-ṣe*]-*e-ru* and Secondary Proto-Ea/Aa no. 22 ii 19': pa-ag = pag(HU) = *e-ṣ-ru*). Line 25' could therefore be translated as "Why has your ... become shut in/ been left behind?". Alternatively, the old man could be made the subject of the verb: "Why have you left your ... behind?". Neither solution is completely satisfactory and the old man's answer does not help clarifying what question has been asked.
67 For the interpretation of these lines see Alster 2006: 389.
68 Sumerian ama-ĝu$_{10}$ tir-ta lú mu-e-ši-in-gi$_4$ šu-dab$_5$-ba ba-an-šúm-m[u]. Although Alster's suggestion that "the man turning toward the old man from the woods and apparently causing him paralysis (šu-dab$_5$?) is perhaps metaphorical for the old man having to walk on crutches" is plausible, it does not explain the significance and the meaning of the old man mother's presence. Also problematic is the translation of šu-dab$_5$(-ba). As a compound verb, šu – dab$_5$ means "to seize", from which Alster most likely derived the translation "paralysis". The term is at present not attested in the *Lists of Diseases*, and I cannot offer an alternative translation.
69 Alster 2006: 389 interprets ^{d}nin-ka$_6$, "mongoose" as a metaphor for the old man's nose. However, in the bilingual version of Ugumu Sec. D line 16 (MSL 9, 69), ^{d}nin-ka$_6$-ĝu$_{10}$ is equated to Akkadian *ši-ku-ku-tu*, lit. "little mongoose" and appears in a section devoted to parts of the arm (cf. also CAD Š/II *s. v. šikkukūtu*). This meaning is in my opinion more fitting, as the mongoose represents a portion of the arm (a muscle? a tendon?), which is now unable to stretch to reach the jar of ghee mentioned in the second half of the line.
70 Sumerian kàš-ĝu$_{10}$ iz-zi kala-ga i-bùr(?)-e IM-ĝu$_{10}$-ta ì-DU-zé-en. The second-half of the line is obscure to me. See Alster 2006: 389 for possible readings.
71 eme–ak, literally "to make tongue" is amply discussed by Alster 2006: 390, with reference. See also, however, Attinger 2005: 222. A sexual connotation seems unlikely in the present context. As such, I kept a more literal translation.
72 Sumerian [gu$_4$-ud-da-an-z]é-en gu$_4$-ud-da-an-zé-en ki-sikil tur-tur-re PI-PI-en-zé-en. Alster 2006: 388 translates the last verbal chain with "rejoice". This form is otherwise

unattested. The possible parallel with the onomatopoeic verb wu-wa(PI.PI)–za, most recently discussed by Black 2003: 46, should be dismissed (see also Alster 2006: 390). Rather, this may be a form of the verb bu / wu, "to chase around, to move about" (Akkadian *našarbuṭu*, CAD N/II 60 *s. v.*), which fits nicely the context of dance and celebration described by the line.

73 Alster 1991–93: 29–30.
74 Sumerian lú me-ni me-ni ba-an-da-/šub\ (?). This line is problematic, since the meaning of me is not clear. See Alster 2006: 381 and 383 for previous translations. Also note that the reading of the verb šub is not certain.
75 Sumerian inim galam-galam-ma.

Bibliography

Alster, B. (1991–93) "The three ox-drivers from Adab", *Journal of Cuneiform Studies* 43–45: 27–38.

——. (1997) *Proverbs of Ancient Sumer*, Bethesda, MD: CDL Press.

——. (2006) *Wisdom from Ancient Sumer*, Bethesda, MD: CDL Press.

Attinger, P. (1993) *Eléments de Linguistique Sumérienne. La Construction de du₁₁/e/di «dire»*, Fribourg Suisse & Ruprecht Göttingen: Editions Universitaires Vandenhoeck.

——. (2005) "A propos de AK «faire» II", *Zeitschift für Assyriologie* 95: 208–74.

Batto, B. F. (1974) *Studies on Women at Mari*, Baltimore: The Johns Hopkins University Press.

Black, J. (1991) "Eme-sal cult songs and prayers", *Aula Orientalis* 9: 23–36.

——. (2003) "Sumerian noises: ideophones in context", in W. Sallaberger, K. Volk and A. Zgoll (eds) *Literatur, Politik und Recht in Mesopotamien: Festschrift für Claus Wilcke*, Wiesbaden: Harrassowitz Verlag, 35–52.

Cavigneaux, A. (1987) "Notes Sumérologiques", *Acta Sumerologica* 9: 45–66.

Cohen, M. (1974) *Balag-Compositions: Sumerian Lamentation Liturgies of the second and the first millennium BC*, Malibu, CA: Undena Publications.

——. (1981) *Sumerian Hymnology: The Ershemma*, Cincinnati: Hebrew Union College.

——. (1988) *The Canonical Lamentations of Ancient Mesopotamia*, Potomac, MD: Capital Decisions Ltd. Press.

Cooper, J. (2005) "Virginity in Ancient Mesopotamia", in S. Parpola and R. Whiting (eds) *Sex and Gender in the Ancient Near East*, Helsinki: The Neo-Assyrian Text Corpus Project, 91–112.

——. (2006) "Genre, gender and the Sumerian lamentations", *Journal of Cuneiform Studies* 57: 39–47.

Harris, R. (1990) "The female 'sage' in Mesopotamian literature (with an Appendix on Egypt)", in J. G. Gammie and L. G. Perdue (eds) *The Sage in Israel and the Ancient Near East*, Winona Lake, IN: Eisenbrauns, 3–17.

Holm, T. (2007) "Ancient Near Eastern literature: genres and forms", in D. C. Snell (ed.) *A Companion to the Ancient Near East*, Oxford: Wiley-Blackwell, 269–88.

Karahashi, F. (2000) *Sumerian Compounds Verb with Body-Part Terms*, unpublished dissertation, University of Chicago.

Krebernik, M. (1996) "Fragment einer Bilingue", *Zeitschift für Assyriologie* 86: 170–76.

Lambert, M. (1967) "Recherches sure les proverbes sumériens, 1", *Rivista degli Studi Orientali* 42: 75–99.

Lambert, W. W. (1960) *Babylonian Wisdom Literature*, Oxford: Clarendon Press.

Schretter, M. (1991) *Emesal-studien: sprach-und literaturgeschichtliche Untersuchunger zur sogenannten Frauensprache des Sumerischen*, Innsbruck: Verlag des Instituts für Sprachwissenschaft der Universität Innsbruck.

Veldhuis, N. (1997) *Elementary Education at Nippur. The List of Trees and Wooden Objects*, Groningen.

——. (2000) "Sumerian proverbs in their curricular context", *Journal of the American Oriental Society*, 120: 383–99.

Westbrook, R. (1982) *Old Babylonian Marriage Law*, unpublished dissertation, Yale University.

——. (1988) "Old Babylonian marriage law", *Archiv für Orientforschungen* Beiheft No. 23, Berger: Horn.

——. (2003) "Old Babylonian period", in R. Westbrook (ed.) *A History of Ancient Near Eastern Law*, Leiden and Boston: Brill, 361–430.

Whittaker, G. (2002) "Linguistic anthropology and the study of Emesal as a women's language", in S. Parpola and R. Whiting (eds) *Sex and Gender in the Ancient Near East*, Helsinki: The Neo-Assyrian Text Corpus Project, 633–44.

4

AKKADIAN WISDOM LITERATURE

Karen Nemet-Nejat

Introduction

Near Eastern didactic literature has been referred to as "wisdom literature," a term borrowed from the Bible, because Biblical literature was known to the public before Akkadian works came to light. Mesopotamian wisdom literature was compared to the Biblical Books of Job, Proverbs and Ecclesiastes;[1] however, the word "wisdom" (nēmequ) was not as prominently mentioned in Akkadian literature as it is in Biblical Literature (ח כ מ ה).[2]

In the Bible wisdom stressed moral and ethical behavior as a philosophy.[3] According to Akkadian literature, wisdom came from the gods, and specialists were trained in specific disciplines to intercede between mankind and the gods.[4] Colophons were added to copies, describing texts as "secret," communicating the information only to "experts" or "initiates" and forbidding its revelation to "non-initiates"; the tablet was described as "sacred property" belonging to the gods.[5]

Wisdom literature was reinforced by proverbs, popular sayings, instructions, fables (also known as contest literature) and riddles.[6] Here the focus was on practical teaching and advice so that all people might achieve a successful life.[7]

Kitchen noted, "The authors of wisdom literature, were as often collectors and revisers of treasured lore rather than its actual inventors."[8] Authors were seldom known unless they were mentioned in texts, their names appeared in acrostics, in certain versions of the texts and as the work by or for the king.

In the first millennium the gods or "sages of the past" were connected with various compositions, thereby authenticating these works, although sometimes earlier catalogs of literature list these works without authors.[9] Regardless, of purported authorship, all compositions were believed to be revealed, explained, proclaimed or approved by a god; in other words, the source of authorship was considered to come from an outside source.[10] Literary libraries consisted of standard texts copied by successive generations with some new texts added.

Among the longer narrative Near Eastern wisdom pieces are *The Poem of the Righteous Sufferer*, *The Theodicy* and *The Dialogue of Pessimism*. Women are seldom mentioned in the major works; nonetheless, a few general quotes are necessary in order to understand the tenor of Mesopotamian wisdom literature.

Most extant Babylonian wisdom literature was attested in Assyria, with the exception of an occasional proverb. Like many pieces of literature from Mesopotamia, the question remained as to who was the audience.

Major narrative works of Akkadian wisdom literature

The Righteous Sufferer

The Righteous Sufferer began with the words "I will praise the Lord of Wisdom," a hymn to Marduk, which occurred at the beginning of this poem Ludlul I: 1–40.[11]

The speaker, perhaps, Shubshi-meshre-Shakkan, a governor, during the early thirteenth century BC, was mentioned throughout the poem.[12] In his monologue, Shubshi-meshre-Shakkan, described how he was abandoned by the gods, removed from his office and estates, and was stricken with numerous sicknesses. The "Babylonian Job" stated that he never neglected his duties to the gods; therefore, he did not understand why he was being punished. He assumed the gods compensated people for their good deeds (with prosperity) and punished them for neglecting the duties to their gods. Though "goddess" appeared, it was only in a phrase parallel to "god"; she had no special position within the poem.

> One year to the next, the appointed time passed,
> I turned around and there was truly evil.
> Wickedness was increasing; I do not find righteousness.
> I called to my god, but he did not pay attention,
> I implored my goddess, but she did not listen
> The diviner could not determine the future through his divination.
> The dream interpreter could not elucidate my case with libanomancy.
> I called to the dream spirit, but he did not libanomancy (observation of smoke).
> The exorcist could not appease divine anger with his rituals.
> (Lambert BWL, 38, *Ludlul* II: 1–9)

> The day of worshiping the gods was joyful for me;
> The day of following the goddess was my profit and gain.
> (Lambert BWL, 38, *Ludlul* II: 25–26)

> My god did not help me; he did not take my hand.
> My goddess did not pity me; she did not go by my side.
> (Lambert BWL, 46, *Ludlul* II: 112–13)

Beaulieu stated that this composition was "the first wisdom text that connected physical disease and divine abandonment" of the righteous sufferer; therefore, the skills of the physician, who practiced the earliest form of medicine as an herbalist and surgeon, and, the exorcist, who performed a variety of procedures in order to restore relations between a sufferer and his god.[13] This dialog between two friends concerning divine justice illustrated theological erudition:[14]

> What is good to oneself is an offense to a god.
> What is despicable to oneself is good to one's god.
> Who knows the reasoning of the gods in heaven?
> Who understands the counsel of the underworld gods?
> Where could human beings learn the way of a god?
> (Lambert BWL, 40, *Ludlul* II: 34–38)

The poem ended with all of the speaker's afflictions being removed, and his being restored to his former life. Because of similar themes of the "righteous sufferer," both the Akkadian text and the prose of Job exhibit many parallels.[15]

The Theodicy

The concept of theodicy was based on innocent suffering and was a dialog between a sufferer and a friend about divine justice.[16] The sufferer complained of the injustices in his life, and the friend answered with conventional ideas of Babylonian piety. The sufferer gave examples of those who have served the gods but, nonetheless, were afflicted with suffering and hardship; the friend asserted that, at the proper time, piety would be rewarded with prosperity. His friend also explained that not only the sufferer must have sinned in some way, but also no one knew the will of the gods.

The beginning of each stanza, when read vertically, formed an acrostic, "I, Saggilkinamubbib, the incantation priest, a supplicant of the god and king."

XXIII *Sufferer*

> I have looked at the world, and the evidence is the opposite.
> The god does not bar the way of the evildoer.
> A father drags his boat along the canals.
> While his first born lies sprawled on the bed.
> How do I profit from having bowed down before my gods?
> I even bow down before my inferior.
> The rich and prosperous treat me as inferior.
> (Lambert BWL, 85 *The Theodicy*, XXIII: 243–53)[17]

Friend XIV

> Able one, learned one, he who masters knowledge,
> When your heart is angry, you treat the god with disrespect.
> The mind of the god, like the innermost heaven, is remote.

Knowledge of it is difficult, so that people can not understand it.[18]
(Lambert BWL, 86, *The Theodicy*: XXIV 254–57)

Originally, this poem was thought to be a complaint from a righteous sufferer about unjust punishment. But, the friend concluded that the punishment was the result of an individual's sin.[19] In the final verse of the poem (XXVII), the sufferer asked his friend for sympathy, the help of his personal god and goddess, and the guidance of Shamash.

The Dialogue of Pessimism *or* (The Obliging Slave)

The Dialogue of Pessimism, also called, *The Obliging Slave*, was a satiric dialog between a master and his slave, in which the master suggested a course of action, and the slave obsequiously agreed with him. The master immediately changed his mind pointing out the foolishness of what he has proposed, and the slave quickly offered arguments in support of his master's latest point of view. The dialog was both amusing and cynical.[20] In the final stanza, the master asked the slave what was the best course in life, to which the slave replied suicide, "to break my neck and your neck, to be thrown in the river." The master stated that he will kill the slave first. The slave answered that the master could not manage to live three days by himself, i.e., the slave was indispensable.[21]

Two sections in this dialog referred specifically to women in an unflattering way:

"Slave, obey me." "Yes, master, yes."
"I will build a home and have children."
"Have, master, have. Build a [home and have] children.
[The man who builds] a home [and has children ...]"
["No, slave,] no"
"[...] door called 'The Trap.'
[...] small, two-thirds an idiot."
"[...] I will burn and depart and return.]
I will wait for my adversary."
"How about that—I will not build a home." "Do not build a home."
"A man who builds a home, breaks up his father's home."
(Lambert BWL, 144, 146, *The Dialogue of
Pessimism*: 29–38)[22]

"Slave, oblige me." "Yes, master, yes."
"I will love a woman." "So, love, master, love.
A man who loves a woman forgets depression and melancholy."
"No, slave, I will definitely not love a woman."
"Definitely, do not love, master; definitely, do not love.

A woman is a well—a well, a trap, a ditch.
A woman is a sharp iron dagger that cuts a man's throat."
(Lambert BWL, 146, *Dialogue of Pessimism*: 46–52)[23]

"Slave, oblige me." "Yes, master, yes."
"I will make loans." " So make loans, master, make (loans).
"A man who makes loans, [his grains remain] his grain and his interest increases."
"No slave, I will certainly not make loans."
"Don't make loans, master, don't make (loans).
Making loans is like loving a woman but returning (them) is like childbirth.
They will eat your grain; while continually cursing you.
And deprive you of the interest on your grain."
(Lambert BWL, 148, *Dialogue of Pessimism*: 62–69)

The Dialogue of Pessimism has been viewed several ways.[24] Foster indicated that the original intent of some passages in Akkadian literature and letters may have been considered humorous today; however, we cannot be certain how people in ancient times regarded them.[25]

Greenstein's analysis provided two possible interpretations for understanding the last exchange between the master and servant: (1) the master could not have survived without his servant, on whom he depended for approval; or (2) since life was short, the master could only survive three days without his servant.[26]

I believe there is another possibility: *The Obliging Servant* may be a form of contest literature; much like the Sumerian school literature. The master first took a positive position and then offered negative reasons for not proceeding with his initial plan. Throughout this "debate," whatever course of action the master suggested, the slave obliged his master with supporting statements. However, in the final exchange between the master and servant, the ending was unexpected— the servant disagreed with his master's stance. Therefore, the meaning of the final stanza would appear to be that the master would be unable to survive without his servant on whom he depended for approval.

Other types of wisdom literature

Proverbs, instructions and riddles comprised the earliest known sub-categories of wisdom literature.[27] Proverbs were probably transmitted orally. Those that made sense only at a particular period of time were quickly forgotten; however, others, which expressed a universal quality, were often passed down.

Proverbs, popular sayings and short compositions were meant both to entertain and to educate.[28] Crenshaw noted that proverbs were descriptions of daily life; they neither judged nor recommended action.[29] Most proverbs were written in Sumerian, of which some were translated into Akkadian.

Proverbs

A proverb (from the Latin *proverbium*), is an anonymous, concrete saying based on daily life; the language was usually general, and metaphors were frequently used.[30] The choice of subjects in proverbs has led to the conclusion that proverbs were not scribal rhetoric, but, rather, belonged to an oral tradition, drawing on subjects from daily life, which rarely represented the viewpoint of the scribes.[31] Some proverbs were truncated, further suggesting an oral tradition.[32] Of course, not every abbreviated saying represented a proverb.[33]

Akkadian proverbs occurred when Akkadian became important within the culture of Mesopotamia. Both Sumerian and Old Akkadian were spoken in Mesopotamia in the third millennium BC, so that both languages contributed to literacy in Mesopotamia.[34] The precise date at which each language continued to be spoken has been debated by scholars. However, after Sumerian was no longer spoken, it continued to be used in literary, scholarly and religious texts, and was preserved in writing until the first or second millennium AD.

Sumerian proverbs constituted the oldest major collections of proverbs in the world. The earliest proverb collections date to Early Dynastic period (2600–2550 BC); these included a collection of misogynistic proverbs in a Sumerian dialect called eme-sal, literally "the tongue/language of a woman" or "the fine tongue," which may have originated from a regional dialect or the dialect of a particular group, such as women and performers.[35] For the most part, eme-sal forms were related to the genre of the text and; however, no text was written completely in eme-sal.[36]

The Early Dynastic (2600–2500 BC) version of Shuruppak's Instructions has been viewed as a series of proverbs; they were written in eme-gir$_{15}$, perhaps, to be translated as "native tongue," i.e., Standard Sumerian according to native Sumerian sources; in fact, ems-gir$_{15}$ was called "Sumerian" in Akkadian.[37]

Most proverbs were written in Sumerian, of which some were translated into Akkadian. Surprisingly, there is no single word in Sumerian that means "proverb," so that we cannot be certain that an actual proverb or saying was quoted. However, in Akkadian, *têltum* was often used to suggest an oral saying.

Sumerian proverbs have been found both singly, on lenticular (round) tablets, as well as in larger collections. Proverbs were part of elementary education, that is, to practice writing and learning Sumerian.

Sumerian proverbs were diverse and included humor, social consciousness, scribal education, legal proceedings, historical allusions, bilingual proverbs, extracts from literary texts, parallels to lexical texts and short stories.[38] Sumerian school dialogs, which were essays about school life, were often cited in proverbs; these may have been contemporaneous with scribal education.[39] Short stories have been found among Sumerian proverbs, e.g., (1) *The Fox and the Dog* in which the fox thought if he stayed in his den forever, the dog could not harm him (Alster, *Proverbs*, SP 8 sec. B 2), parallel to (2) *The Boy and the Gardener*, a brief anecdote about a gardener who tried to catch a boy, who was presumed to be stealing fruit from the garden, so the boy hid in a place where the gardener could not reach him but where they could converse. The gardener threatened the boy who was too scared to come out and, therefore, may have never been able to go home again (which Alster, *Proverbs*, SP 13.48); (3) *Nanne*, a fictitious ruler of the Ur III period, who was unable to finish anything he started (Alster, *Proverbs*, SP 3 B 1); and (4)*The Fowler and His Wife*, which poked fun at the Fowler's sexuality (Alster, *Proverbs*, 21 A5; artu 2, 120, no. 36).

There are 26 collections of Sumerian proverbs, a few minor collections and the unprovenanced proverbs of the Schøyen Collection. Some proverbs were bilingual, being written in both Sumerian and Akkadian. Lambert noted that different forms of the same proverb have been found in Hebrew and Egyptian literature in which proverbs were organized by the initial word or sign.[40]

To date, collections of Akkadian proverbs have not been found. Akkadian proverbs were not as well known because they were not part of Assyrian and Babylonian academic education. Perhaps native Akkadian proverbs were rejected because they were spoken by the general public and not considered literature in their own right.

Akkadian proverbs usually appeared as translations of some Sumerian proverbs in bilingual editions. The Babylonians and Assyrians adopted only a portion of the Sumerian collections, translating them first in the Old Babylonian Period (1900–1600 BC) as part of scribal education. Why certain Sumerian proverbs were chosen for translation into Akkadian remains a mystery.

Akkadian proverbs also have been found in letters. The Mesopotamians were "indefatigable letter writers," and much of their correspondence has survived. Most extant letters dealt both with business and a variety of topics, and some included proverbs.

The Kassite scribes (c. 1595–1158 BC), who later collected and organized the traditional literature of the Babylonians and Assyrians, had at their disposal bilingual proverbs and may have rejected the genre of Akkadian proverbs because they were spoken by the general populace. Perhaps the best way of viewing both Sumerian, Akkadian and bilingual collections is as a group of entries or sayings, in which the context remains unknown.[41]

The following are Akkadian proverbs from bilingual collections of Sumero-Akkadian proverbs; these proverbs describe how women were perceived during the time when the Akkadian language came into use.

The importance of marriage

The importance of marriage in ancient Near East is reflected in the proverbs:

A husband who does not support a wife,
DITTO, a child,
The husband is a liar,
who cannot support himself.
(SP 1.153 = SP 3.9b = Lambert BWL, 255: 11–14)[42]

The ability to support a wife and children was considered an indicator of wealth and status.

A house without an owner
(Is like) a woman without a husband.
(Lambert BWL, 229 iii 20–21)

Rib-Addi, ruler of Byblos in the Amarna period, and a loyal vassal to the king, changed this proverb slightly and quoted it four times to the Egyptian king as:

My field is like a woman without a husband because
it lacks a cultivator.
(See Lambert BWL, 232–33)

Who is rich? Who is wealthy?
For whom do I reserve my vulva?
(Lambert BWL, 227, K4347+ ii 19–20)

This proverb referred to choice of a future mate, and clearly virginity was important in Mesopotamia, as in most patriarchal societies.

The next proverb in this same collection stated:

Whom you love, you bear his yoke.
(Lambert BWL, 227, K4347+ ii 21–22)

It may have referred to a woman's position as subject to her mate, as well as his economic situation.

The young girl said to her friend:
(Alster, CUSAS 2, 108–9, MS 3279:11)

This line may refer to the myth of *Martu and the Nomad*.

Her girlfriend answers her.
(Alster, CUSAS 2, 111, MS 3279:14)

Alster suggested that MS 3279: 11 and 14 might have referred to *Martu's Marriage*, a short myth in which a nomad and princess fell in love. Her friend warned her against marrying a nomad because of his uncivilized ways. Perhaps, this was a truncated proverb. "My girlfriend, why would you marry Martu?" Adgar-kidug replied to her girlfriend: "I will marry Martu!" Martu was read in Sumerian as MAR.TU, the Amurru, who lived on the steppe and raided the agricultural produce of the Sumerians and Babylonian.

Propriety

Propriety was important because virginity was valued in a young woman's marriage. A faithful wife provided insurance that the children were those of the marital union and that her husband was the father:[43]

> Don't laugh with a married girl, the slander (arising from it) is [great].
> > (Alster, 2005, 63, *Instr. of Shuruppak,* #33)[44]

> Don't sit in a chamber with a man's wife.
> > (Alster, 2005, 63, *Instr. of Shuruppak,* #34)

Sexual relations

Sexual relations were also described:

> Intercourse brings on lactation.
> > (Lambert BWL, 241, K4347+ obv. ii 43–44)

There is no scientific evidence for this proverb. It probably reflected the folk wisdom of the time.

> Since time immemorial (something) which has not happened,
> A young girl has not farted during sex with her husband.
> > (Alster, 1997, SP 1.12 = Lambert BWL, 260, BM 98743: 5–10)

The phrase "since time immemorial" may have pointed to the ironic tone of common decency as flatulence was embarrassing to the ancient Mesopotamians in less intimate circumstances.[45] In Akkadian the proverb is a declarative statement, but in Sumerian, it is a question.[46]

Cooper described this as a folklore theme of a young married girl on her wedding night, perhaps, either humorous or tragic.[47] "A young girl" refers to the age of marriage, since girls usually married as teenagers with their husbands being ten years older.

> An Amorite said to his wife,
> "You will be the man

I will be the woman."
[...] I became a man
[...] female
[...] male
(Lambert BWL, 226, K 2024 obv. i 1–7)

Lambert suggested that this Middle Assyrian proverb concerned transvestitism, a practice condemned in Deuteronomy 22:5. The Amorites were known for perversion, as well as the men of Sodom, Corinth and Bulgaria, and the women of Lesbos. The proverb may also refer to anal intercourse or the woman being on top of the man, since the missionary position was the most common position in intercourse.

Has she become pregnant without sexual intercourse?
Has she become fat without eating?
(Lambert BWL, 241, K 4347 obv. ii 40–42)

This is a humorous proverb relating to pregnancy. The proverb appears as a quote in Akkadian, similar to "They say" at the beginning.

I go into my house,
You plow the field in order to be satisfied,
When you plow the meadows, having (sexual) desire
   (OR: being sexually potent),
It means abundance for all.
(Alster, CUSAS 2, 52–54, MS 3323:2,3,5,6)

This proverb is replete with metaphors—rather unusual among proverbs, particularly Akkadian proverbs.

Adultery

Adultery was viewed negatively.

The oral proverb states: "In court, the word of a sinful woman exceeds her husband"
(Harper, ABL no. 403 obv. 13–15 = Lambert BWL, 281).[48]

In court, what an adulterous woman said carried more weight than her husband's words. Adultery could only be proven in court if the husband caught his wife having sexual intercourse with another man.[49]

Just as the old proverb says, "A bitch in her haste, gave birth to blind puppies."
(Lambert BWL, 280, ARM 1:5 obv. 10–13)[50]

This proverb was from a letter of Shamshi-Adad, the king of Assyria in 1700 BC, which was written to his son Yashmakh-Adad, the regent of Mari, to emphasize that Yashmakh-Adad was wasting time by putting his troops in danger by engaging with the enemies. Samshi-Adad told his son to be patient because he will soon be at his son's side with reinforcements to engage the enemy in a decisive battle without unnecessary risk.[51]

Alster has traced this proverb through time and place from the unilingual Sumerian proverb: "As long as the bitch? is helpless [from ...], the puppies will not open their eyes." This proverb also appears in slightly perverted form in Aristophanes *Pace*, and in an almost identical form by Archilochus ("an old saying: A bitch in a hurry gave birth to blind puppies in a perverted) in Turkey, (Byzantine) Greece, Italy and other European countries. That is, the meaning of the proverb in the west suggests that the hasty bitch does not wait the full time for gestation and, therefore, gives birth to defective puppies.[52]

The proverb has even been found in a present day collection of Baghdadi Arabic proverbs, in which the cat replaced the dog, as in Italian, Iranian and Turkish sources. A Judeo-Arabic form preserves the original with the dog whelping, which may have passed from Akkadian through Aramaic to spoken Arabic, thereby making it the oldest surviving proverb.

This was the only proverb that Shamshi-Adad did not explain in his correspondence; however, its use through time has suggested some meaning. I believe that the reference was to Shamshi-Adad's upbraiding his son, Yashmakh-Adad here. Elsewhere, Shamshi-Adad compared Yashmakh-Ahad to his brother who was a true leader in raising an army and fighting, while Yasmakh-Adad ran around with women. As for puppies being born blind, they are not blind in the true meaning of the word. When born, their vision is not developed for several months, but they do see shadows.[53]

(My wife said), "Liar,
One who pursues the vulva,
Unreliable, (one who)
Has two sickles."

(Alster, *Proverbs*, SP 1.158 = Lambert BWL,
p. 255, K 8338: 7–10)

The Early Dynastic Version #42 is a precursor to this proverb:

"The treacherous man is in constant pursuit of vulvas."

(Alster, *Proverbs*, p.xxvii)

In the anatomical lexical lists, the male genitalia had only five entries; whereas, the female genitalia had twenty-one entries listed with the exterior genitalia followed by the vagina and uterus.[54] Sickles is most likely a metaphor for testicles.

Mesopotamia was a patriarchal society, which became increasingly so from the Old Babylonian Period until the first millennium BC. Terms for a legal marriage varied by time, tribe, ethnic group, class, religion and place.[55] However, in daily life, this proverb suggested that a woman found her husband's cheating ways unacceptable.

Female slaves and workers

Female slaves and workers were viewed in the following ways:

> He who speaks humbly,
> His wife is a female slave.
>> (Alster, *Proverbs,* SP 7.44 = Lambert BWL, 236 obv. iii 3–4)[56]

The position of the wife, who was a slave, affected the husband's status.

> Don't have sexual intercourse with your slave girl,
>> she will neglect you.
>>> (Alster, *Wisdom*, Instr. of Shuruppak, p. 67, #49)

> I, a slave girl, have no authority
> over my lady. My husband, I shall pluck.
>> (Alster, *Proverbs,* SP 19 Sec. D 11 = UET 6/2 386)

Plucking sheep was probably one of the duties of a slave girl.

> I do not know the nether stone for grinding for flour:
> if (the millstone) disappears, I will not be upset.
>> (Alster, CUSAS 2, 29–30, MS 2065:3)

The Akkadian version described the feeling of female workers, whose work was monotonous. The sound of the work was like a song, as noted in Sumerian eme-sal words, "as they say" and "song." The noise was long and lasted all day. This proverb had no parallel. This sound of the grinding was noisy; it was associated with hearth and home, so to speak. The lack of this song is associated with desolation.[57]

> My vulva is fine;
> according to my people, it is used up (or: finished) for me.
>> (Lambert BWL, 242, K4347 obv. iii 14–16)

This is the complaint of an old prostitute defending her ability to continue her work. According to Assante, no word existed for a (secular) prostitute in cuneiform documents; rather, bartering for sexual favors "in the pre-coinage societies of Mesopotamia and Egypt" was common, so that no vocabulary was needed.

Note in this proverb no word is actually used with the meaning "prostitute," which is implied. However, even without a secular word for prostitutes, we know they existed.[58]

The status of women

The status of women seemed to be of little importance in ancient Mesopotamian society:

> Now my father and lord should pay attention to my words even
>   if I am a woman.
> (ARM 10: 31 r 7'–10')[59]

> A woman who carried out the rites of the gods,
> (Who) increased the rules the kingship forever.
> How did Enlil, the great lord act?
> He despised her foundations like the foundations of chaff.
> (Alster, *Proverbs*. SP 3.45 = Lambert BWL, 266,
BM 38596. obv. i 2–9)

The proverb referred to a woman who carried out the rituals of a king, but Enlil despised her actions, as women's roles decreased in the professions and religious life through time. In daily life, the gradual loss of women's professions and clerical positions may be dated from the Old Babylonian period to the first half of the first millennium.[60]

Only part of this Sumerian proverb was translated into Akkadian. A possible truncated version of the proverb may have been written in Sumerian; however, this raised several questions. To what did the lance refer? Did it allude to the consequences due to war or drought caused by Enlil's lance?[61]

> What did Enlil make? Chaff!
> The lance struck. It went into the flesh.
> (Alster, 1997, SP 3.25)

> (They say) Daughter-in-law, what you did to her mother-in-law;
> They (your own daughters-in-law) will do to you.
> (Lambert BWL, 261, VAT 10810 obv. 10–12)

All of these examples of Akkadian proverbs showed the importance of the reputation of a young woman, her marriage and virginity. Sexuality was usually openly described, and adultery was frowned upon. A woman's position within society was of little importance, and slaves and female workers received little respect. Akkadian proverbs, though few in number, seemed to express the popular culture.

Popular sayings

Popular sayings were common in both Babylonia and Assyria. The Assyrian tablet, VAT 8807, contains a series of anecdotes, grouped by subject, such as animals, insects and people. Lambert noted the similarity of this category to unilingual Sumerian proverbs; however he retained "Sayings," as its own category.[62]

> The circumspect (temple) prostitute slanders an evil woman/
> female demon.
> (But only) at Ishtar's command the noble's wife is slandered.
> (Lambert BWL, "Popular Sayings," 218, rev. iv: 6–7)[63]

The section to which the saying above belongs described a number of malcontents: the male prostitute who complained about his pimp, the briber who stood at the court, the maligner who spoke cunningly but pejoratively before the ruler, and animals.

> A rutting horse, as he mounts a mare,
> Whispers in her ear as he rides her,
> "Let the foal you bear be a swift runner; like me,
> Do not make it like a donkey which carries a load."
> (Lambert BWL, "Popular Sayings," 218, rev. iv: 15–18)[64]

Only extant phrases in "Popular Sayings" referred to women as " female slave(s)," "house of a second-rank wife," "sister," and "mother"; however, because the context was broken, these "Popular Sayings" did not elucidate the perception of women (Lambert BWL, "Popular Sayings," 216, rev. iii: 35–41).

Instructions (precepts and admonitions)

Instructional "wisdom" occurred within the *Book of Proverbs* in the *Old Testament*. Detailed studies have often compared the *Book of Proverbs* in the *Old Testament* to cultures within the ancient Near East.[65]

The advice was practical and included a variety of topics. The instructions were directed to "my son," a phrase common to instructional literature throughout the ancient Near East.[66] "My son" may refer either to a fictitious paternal relationship, a close relationship between a teacher and student, or the composition read by a writer to a reader.[67]

1. *The Instructions of Shuruppak* were attributed to the divine Ninurta[68] and to the king of the last antediluvian city, Shuruppak, the home of the Sumerian Noah. Ninurta was known as both a farmer and a warrior god. In The *Farmer's Instructions*, Ninurta gave detailed instructions to the farmer on cultivating the crops and preparing the fields throughout the year.[69] His symbol was the plow. In

Ninurta's role as a warrior god, Assyrian kings were devoted to him to help them fight their enemies. However, the unilingual Akkadian version was badly broken, and the only reference to women was the phrase "a man's daughter [...]."

2. In the *Counsels of Wisdom*, a variety of topics were directed to "my son" (Lambert BWL, 201: 81) and possibly a fragment, which might belong to the beginning of this tablet (Lambert BWL, 106, K 13770).

Among these various pieces of advice two passages regarding women are the following:

> Do not honor a female slave in your house.
> She must not rule your bedroom like a wife.
> [...]
> Let your people tell you thus:
> The house that a female slave rules, she will disrupt.
> (Lambert BWL, 102, *Counsels of Wisdom*, ll. 66–67, 70–71)

followed by:

> Do not marry a follower of Ishtar, whose husbands
>   are numerous,
> (Or) A follower of Ishtar dedicated to a god,
> (Or) A prostitute,[70] whose intimates are many.
> When you are in trouble, she will not support you,
> When you are in a dispute, she will mock you.
> There is no respect or obedience in her nature.
> If she controls your house, get her out.
> Her attention is directed to the footsteps of another.
> Variant: She disrupts the house she enters, (and) her partner
>   will not be stable.
> (Lambert BWL, *Counsels of Wisdom* ll. 72–80)

3. *Counsels of a Pessimist*, a small oblong tablet, may have been an extract from a larger text. The text may be advice either to a particular person or to the reader.[71] The listener was advised to pray for children. Two lines followed with the words "first-born son" and "daughter."

4. *The Advice to a Prince* warned a Mesopotamian king and his officers against abusing power through taxation, forced labor and unlawful seizure of land. The form was similar to omens, that is, "If *x*, then *y*," except the all important "if" of omens is omitted from the text. Also, the text contained many ideograms. The style of the piece suggested that it was written in the first millennium BC. The text has only been found in the Ashurbanipal's library.

The purpose of the text was to protect the rights of the citizens. Should those in power ignore the admonitions, then punishment would follow, for example, rebellion, chaos, devastation of the land, and abandonment by the gods.[72] A foreigner was mentioned in Lambert BWL, 112:9 and 114:40. The king, presumably a native, was warned to protect the rights of the citizens of Sippar, Nippur and Babylon. Women did not appear in this text.

5. A bi-lingual Akkadian and Hurrian fragment was found at Ras Shamra (Ugarit). The River Ordeal was mentioned in terms of bringing cases before the gods of the river when the facts were in dispute. Immersion in the Divine River brought a verdict of guilt (downing) or innocence (survival). There was a play on the Akkadian words "answer" and "son" in the line about the River Ordeal in the following:

> Deposit silver for a oath; you can take it from the gods.
> Respect the oath and assure your well-being.
> Swear (falsely), and answer completely to the River Ordeal
> for his life.
> His wife will never have a son.
>
> (Lambert BWL, 116: 1–4)

6. *Instructions on Various Professions*, an Old Babylonian tablet from Sippar, was very difficult to interpret. All of the admonitions advised "give up evil" and "seize righteousness"; the tablet referred to a barber, a prostitute, and a scribe.

> (They said) to the prostitute of evil, "Come to an agreement
> with us,"
> "If I consent [...]"
> They slapped her cheek, [sober or drunk]![73]
> "Go! Go off! The one who receives will provide for you.[74]
> The one who does not receive will not provide for you."
> [...]
> "Give up evil. Seize
> righteousness."
>
> (Lambert BWL, 118, CBS 1399: 10–17)

7. *The Instructions of Shupe-Awilum* is in poor shape. A father, Shupe-awilum,[75] advised his son on a variety of topics. The tablet was found at Emar and Ugarit (in Syria), as well as Hattusha, the Hittite capital (in Anatolia in Turkey). Foster used the Hittite version.[76] Lambert suggested that the speaker may have been the flood hero, i.e., the Babylonian Noah, of other myths.[77] *Shupe-Awilum* may have been a garbled combination of names.[78]

> "Do not open your heart to the woman you love.
> Even if she has your seal [of your strong room] that you know.
> Know the wealth that is in your strong room. Be aware!
> Do not let your wife know what is in your purse.

Since our ancestors established this from earlier times,
Our fathers divided the sacrifices for the gods.
They sealed the loop with a lump of clay.[79]
Keep your cylinder seals ring safe on its ring
Surround the door bolt with a loop, thereby guard your house.
Let your seal be the only opening to your capital.
Whatever you see, leave it within.
When you need it, you can give it to her."

(The Instructions of Shupe-Awilim ii 16–27)[80]

Akkadian "instructions" offered practical advice on a variety of topics, but advice concerning women was clearly misognystic as shown throughout the literature. Prostitutes, religious devotees who were prostitutes, slave women and even beloved wives were not to be trusted.

Fables or contest literature

Fables in the sense of Aesop's fables, which were short stories about animals used to teach a moral lesson, were not part of Akkadian literature. Akkadian fables were similar to Sumerian fables, which became popular throughout the Near East.[81] Some of these fables have been listed in catalogs.[82]

Lambert suggested that fables, like proverbs, did not become part of the Akkadian academic curriculum because they were considered an oral genre of the common people. The extant Akkadian dialogs began with a mythological beginning, which was followed by a debate between two contestants, either animals or plants, as to their qualities.[83] A god or king decided which one prevailed.

These dialogs may have been performance pieces that were meant to be recited or sung, perhaps, accompanied either by instruments or by a choir.[846] The fables were written at different periods, found at different sites and showed varying degrees of scribal knowledge.[85] Five Babylonian fables have been found, some in poor condition.

1. *The Tamarisk and the Date Palm* has been found in one Old Babylonian version and two Middle Assyrian versions. The basic "story line" of the fable can be reconstructed by using the three versions. The fable opened with a mythological beginning in the assembly of the gods in which both Shamash and Ishtar were seated in the center. Shamash was the sun god and the god of judgment; Ishtar was his sister, the planet Venus and the goddess of love and war. The gods decided to give kingship to humankind. The king planted both trees and held a banquet under the Tamarisk. In this setting both the tamarisk and the palm tree debated their merits. Though the judgment of the king is missing, the palm tree won the debate, noting that its leaves, wood, sap and fruit were all staple elements in the economy.

Traces of this myth are found in a Pahlavi fable, *The Assyrian Tree*, and Strabo spoke of hearing a Persian song enumerating 360 uses of the palm tree; also, a fragment of this text is preserved in Callimachus.[86]

All references to women appeared as parallel phrases, which did not shed light on understanding on how women were viewed, for example:

> The Tamarisk:
> Think about your furnishings in the king's palace. What is
>   mine is found
> in the king's palace? The king eats from my dish. The queen
> drinks from my cup.
>   (Lambert BWL, *The Tamarisk and the Date Palm*. b/c: 153)

Otherwise, women or goddesses appeared in broken context, e.g., "Like a slave girl who […] to her mistress";[87] "The temple priestess sprinkled water […] she takes and they praise and make a festival";[88] "I am the substitute for Nisaba";[89] and "The impoverished, the widow, the poor man […]."[90]

2. *The Fable of the Euphrates Popular*,[91] also in poor condition, appeared to be a debate between the poplar and the laurel. Other trees were mentioned such as the pomegranate-tree, the cedar, the cypress, the tamarisk, the date palm (referred to as "the king of trees"). Women were not mentioned in what survived of this fable.

3. In Akkadian literature, *The Fable of Nisaba and Wheat*, Nisaba has the general meaning of grain, but, as the first speaker, Nisaba was referred to as the goddess of the underworld. The only connection between Nisaba and the underworld inferred is that plants received nourishment from the world below.

The beginning of the fable, a fragment, was probably spoken by Nisaba and concluded with a possible prayer for an abundance of food in the land. Various gods were mentioned, including Aruru, the birth goddess, "May Aruru, mother of the gods, let offspring prosper."[92]

The mythological beginning was followed by a diatribe by wheat:

> Wheat opened his mouth and spoke,
> Saying to Nisaba, the lady of the underworld,
> "Why, Nisaba, do you fight in the land?
> You have quarreled with every plant.
> You have created strife; you incited evil.
> You say malicious things; you utter […]
> You brought hatred between the Igigi and Anunnaki.[93]
> […] you flood[94] (the land) as well.
> […] your you continued to place in every corner of the world.
> You gather up settlements; you destroy creatures."
> Nisaba heard the terrible words,

[...] she cried in pain.
[...] she herself created a plan
[...] she asked her friend.
   (Lambert BWL, 169, *The Fable of Nisaba and Wheat*, ll. 25–38)

Nisaba was castigated rather than portrayed as a goddess who brought life to the world by her nourishing the plants from below.

The light itself illuminates the darkness.
[...] by not looking he examined [...]
Nisaba shines among all the gods [...]
Let Nisaba's voice become loud, let her shout not [...]
Let her food be sweeter than [...]
Let all the lands submit and bring their tribute
Let what she has planted constantly grow luxuriously [...] let it
   last long.
Let her offspring, living creatures, and the black-headed people
   (Akkadians) [...]
Let those whom Aruru created bow at her feet.
Let her make their statues high; let her make their countenance
   radiant,
Let all mankind worship Nisaba!
Let the animals of the steppe (and) the wild animals praise her
   greatness!
Nisaba is unique; giver of life [...]
Man beyond count, constantly praise [...]
Let invoking her not cease; let her name not [...]
   (*The Fable of Nisaba and Wheat*, BWL, 172, iv: 5–19)

The last section was a hymn to Nisaba, suggesting, that she had been judged the winner of the contest.[95]

4. *The Fable of The Ox and the Horse*, was once a fable of significant size from Ashurbanipal's library, but only a small portion is extant. A half-line indicating the usual mythological introduction remains, "When exalted Ishtar." No reference to women remained as the two animals debated their importance. Presumably, the horse referred to his importance in war, and the ox to the use of his hide in making implements of war.
This fable became widespread due to the breeding and training of horses by the Mitanni (ca. 1500 BC). A Mitanni scribe may have been the author of a manual for training horses, though it was written in Hittite.[96]

5. *The Fable of the Fox* involved three animals: the fox, the wolf and the dog. The fable, found in thirteen fragments, was described as a "huge tablet." The story line can be more or less reconstructed.

The wolf, the dog and the fox, each in turn, complained and threatened the others. The animals boasted about their abilities. The dog was the leader of the pack of dogs and bitches; he guarded the city, both people and property and was entrusted with the flocks. The animals hurled insults at each other; they went to Shamash to judge their case. At the end of this fragmentary tablet the fox worshiped Enlil. The fox was most probably the winner.

Humans were not mentioned. As for female animals, two short phrases, which referred to female dogs in the dog's boasts as a leader of a pack, such as "Shining, the bitches (like the stars) of the sky […]" and "Let the bitches tear apart […] like a teasel."[97] These phrases do not elucidate the characteristics of a woman.

Riddles

There are no extant collections of Akkadian riddles. Riddles may have been a transition between popular sayings and didactic poetry, with the surprise element directed toward teaching.[98] Few Akkadian riddles have been identified but, to date, most have nothing to do with women, and others are often badly broken.[99]

Abbreviations

ABL   *Assyrian and Babylonian Letters.*
ARM   *Archives Royales de Mari.*
Alster, CUSAS 2   Alster, B., 2007. *Sumerian Proverbs in the Schøyen Collection,* Cornell University Studies in Assyriology and Sumerology, 2 vols, Bethesda: CDL Press.
CAD   *Chicago Assyrian Dictionary.*
CANE   Sasson, J.M., (ed.), 1995. *Civilizations of the Ancient Near East,* 4 vols, New York: Charles Scribner and Sons; Hendrickson Publishers edition, Peabody: MA, 2000, 2 vols.
CBS   Museum siglum of the University Museum in Philadelphia (Catalogue of the Babylonian Section).
COS   Hallo, W.W. (ed.), *The Context of Scripture: Canonical Compositions from the Biblical World,* vol. 1, Leiden & New York: Brill, 1996.
K   Museum siglum of the British Museum in London (Kuyunjik).
Lambert BWL   Lambert, W.G. 1960. *Babylonian Wisdom Literature,* Oxford, Clarendon Press; Revised, 1996, Winona Lake: Eisenbrauns.
OIS   Oriental Institute Seminars, Chicago: The University of Chicago Press.
SAACT   State Archives of Assyria Cuneiform Texts.
SBLSym   Society of Biblical Literature Symposium Series.
SP   Gordon, E., *Sumerian Proverbs*
UET   Ur Excavations, Texts.

VAT   Museum siglum of theVorderasiatisches Museum, Berlin
(Vorderasiatische Abteilung. Tontafeln)

Notes

1 Crenshaw, 1993, 801–3. To these, Ecclesiasticus (Sirach), the Wisdom of Solomon from the Deutero-canon may be added from the Apocrypha.
2 Hallo, 1992, 234–37.
3 Lambert, 1997, 30–42.
4 Beaulieu, SBLSym, 18.
5 Van der Toorn, SBLSym 26.
6 Lambert BWL, 1–2; Foster, 1996, 44: 1; T.L. Holm, 2005, 282.
7 Foster, 1996, 44.
8 Kitchen, 1977, 71.
9 Foster, 1991, 15.
10 Foster, 1991, 14–15; idem., 1996, 20–21.
11 Wiseman, 1980, 101–7; Annus and Lenzi, 2010.
12 Foster, 1996, 306; Annus and Lenzi, 2010, xvii.
13 Beaulieu, 2007, 10–11. See also Abusch, 1998.
14 von Soden, 1994, 223.
15 Bricker, 2000, 208.
16 Lambert and Gurney, 1954, 65–99.
17 These are the last lines of this part of the Sufferer's complaint about the injustice of man's situation; the first four lines of the Friend's speech followed. Each section of the dialog is approximately eleven lines long, sometimes broken and difficult for the reader to understand out of context.
18 Grayson, 1980, 95–97; Denning-Bolle, 1987, 218. "But wisdom, where can it be found? And where is the place of understanding? Man does not know its value. It is not found in the land of the living" (Job 28:12–13, my translation).
19 Bricker, 2000, 207–8 added that people are evil because the gods created man to sin. He concluded that this poem is not a theodicy.
20 Foster, 1996, 23, described this text as humor that subtly became satire so that this text was difficult to classify; see Lambert BWL, 139–41.
21 Grayson, 1980, 97, viewed *The Dialogue of Pessimism* quite differently; he saw this dialog as illustrating how any action could lead either to success or failure and that death was inevitable part of life.
22 See Alster, 1997, Proverb SP 1.153 = SP 3.9b = Lambert BWL, 255, K 8338 11–14. The text is broken and ll. 35–36 probably belong to another section.
23 Hallo, COS, 496.
24 This discussion refers to the last exchange between the master and the servant.
25 Foster, CANE, 2459. Crenshaw, CANE, 2455 suggested that *The Dialogue of Pessimism* may have been a form of entertainment, that is, an intellectual exchange at banquets based on the servant's remark, thereby playing an important role in early education. However, the slave's remark about banquets occurred in Lambert BWL, 144, *The Dialogue of Pessimism*, ll. 12–13 and is a part of the slave's sycophantic behavior with his master. Therefore, the educational aspect remains uncertain.
26 Greenstein, 2007, SBLSym 57, n. 3.
27 Hallo, 1992, 863.
28 Foster, 1996, 44.
29 Crenshaw, CANE, 2447.
30 Alster, CUSAS 2, 3–4.

31 Charpin, 2004, 481–508; Alster, 1997, xvii; Alster, CUSAS 2, 2.

32 Alster, 1997, xvii.

33 Alster, CUSAS 2, 12–13.

34 Rubio, 2007, 1327; Alster, 1997, xvi.; Cooper, 2010, 331.

35 Michalowski, 2006, 169–70, indicated that eme-sal was neither spoken nor a true dialect, pointing to its only characteristic being verbal prefixes, since it is known only through writing.

36 Rubio, 2007, 269.

37 Rubio, 2005, 84–85.

38 Alster, CUSAS 2, 7–9, 13 n. 55.

39 Alster, CUSAS 2, 2–5.

40 Alster, CUSAS 2, 19.

41 Alster, CUSAS 2, 5.

42 Lambert, 1963, 63–64, traced the proverb from the Early Dynastic Period III from Fara to Sumerian and Akkadian. Numerous references are listed under Alster, 1997, vol. 1, SP 3.9; CAD, s.v. *sarru*, 180–81; Gordon, 1959, 495–96; Alster, 1997, 356; Lambert BWL, 255. Cf. Jacobsen, 1959, 469.

43 Cooper, 2002, 105 and n. 92.

44 See Alster, 2005, *The Instructions of Shuruppak*, 56–100.

45 Cooper, 2002, 99 n. 52.

46 Jacobsen, 1959, 547; Alster, 1997, 29. Cf. Gordon, 1959, 111–13 for various possible interpretations on the last line of the proverb.

47 Cooper, 2002, 98.

48 Harper, ABL vol. 4.

49 Roth, 1988, 195.

50 Dossin and Finet, 1978.

51 Moran, 2002, 87–99.

52 Moran, 2002, 92–93.

53 See Durand, 2006, 29. I would like to thank Professor J.M. Sasson for noting the articles by W.L. Moran and J–M. Durand and our discussions of this proverb, at the 222nd American Oriental Society in Boston, MA, 2012, where I gave an abbreviated version of Akkadian proverbs, entitled, "The Image of Women in Akkadian Proverbs." Of course, all errors are my own.

54 Cooper, 2002, 101, 106.

55 Assante, 2006, 125, discussed this issue in terms of the nuances of various forms of marriage and quasi-marriage.

56 Alster, 1997, 412; cf. Lambert BWL, 236, K4327+ iii 3–4, translated this section as "The wife of him who cannot talk well is a slave-girl."

57 Civil, 2006, 121–38; Tigay, 1995, 374–76.

58 Assante, 2006, 117–32. For prostitution see M. Stol, CANE 492–4; Nemet-Nejat, 1999, 101, 107–8.

59 Dossin and Finet, ARM 10.

60 Assante, 2006, 125, dated women's gradual loss of power beginning after the Old Babylonian period, that is to say, after the date of these proverbs.

61 Alster, 1997, 380.

62 Lambert BWL, 214.

63 CAD, Š$_2$, 67b, s.v. šarrabu.

64 Compare the broken saying about a dog mounting his wife (Lambert BWL, "Popular Sayings," 216 iii 29–31); the text is broken.

65 Kitchen, 1977, 69.

66 Lambert BWL, 92.

67 Kitchen, 1977, 96.; Lambert BWL, 96.

68 See Black and Green, 1992, 172–73.
69 Civil, 1994.
70 Assante, 2006, 117–32.
71 See Lambert BWL, 107 for discussion.
72 See Lambert BWL, 110–11 for discussion of this text.
73 Stol, 1987, 383–87, with transliteration, translation and commentary by Wasserman and Streck, 2009, n. 12 who suggested restoring "drunk and sober strike your cheek!" This curse is found in other myths.
74 In both lines 13 and 14, the expressions are turned around, i.e., here sober and drunk as opposed to the usual drunk and sober, and provide and receive instead of receive and provide.
75 Foster, 1996, 320–25, ii ll. 17–27 under the heading of "Wisdom of Ugarit." Horowitz, 2007, 45–49, presented a preliminary translation with references to the Biblical *Book of Proverbs* and *Ecclesiastes*.
76 The Akkadian version can also be found in Nougayrol. no. 163, pp. 277–83 ii 16 with notes on pp. 283–90, ll. 16–27.
77 Lambert BWL, 93–94.
78 See Foster, 1996, 330, n. 1 and Beaulieu, SBLSym 5.
79 Foster, 1996, 332 n. 1, indicated that the reference was to a strong room that had a peg with a ring covered with clay, and was sealed so no one could enter without breaking the seal.
80 Line numbers are according to, Nougayrol, 1968, 278–79; CAD, s.v. qullu, 298, Foster, 1996, 332.
81 Lambert BWL, 151.
82 Lambert BWL, 151.
83 Lambert BWL, 150.
84 A. L.Oppenheim, 1974, 250–54. For a cross-cultural study, see Paglai, 2009, 63.
85 Lambert BWL, 151–52.
86 Lambert BWL, 154.
87 Lambert BWL, 160, rev. 6.
88 Lambert BWL, 160, rev. 7–8.
89 Lambert BWL, 160, rev. 20; Nisaba was the goddess of grain and eventually became the goddess of writing, as cane was broken to create a stylus for writing on clay.
90 Lambert BWL, 160 rev. 20.
91 Neuman and Parpola, 1983, 1141, n. 2;CAD, s.v. ṣarbu, 109.
92 *The Fable of Nisaba and Wheat*, Lambert BWL, 170 obv. i 23.
93 They are the gods of heaven and the gods of the underworld, respectively; see Black and Green, 1992, 27.
94 Mesopotamians believed that *apsû* was the underground freshwater from which springs, wells, rivers and lakes were replenished. See Black and Green, 1992, 27.
95 Lambert BWL, 168.
96 Lambert BWL, 175.
97 Lambert BWL, 196, c = VAT 10349: 11 and 13. See Oracle #74 in Nissinen, 2003, 108 for these rodents.
98 Crenshaw, CANE, 2447.
99 See N. Veldhuis, 2000, 67–94.

Bibliography

Abusch, T., 1998. "The Internalization of Suffering and Illness in Mesopotamia: A Development of Mesopotamian Witchcraft Literature," *Studi Epigrafici e Linguistici sul Vicino Oriente Antico* 15, 49–58.

Alster, B., 1974. *The Instructions of Shuruppak. A Sumerian Proverb Collection*, Copenhagen: Akademisk Forlag.

——, 1997. *Proverbs of Ancient Sumer*, 2 vols, Bethesda: CDL Press.

——, 2005. *Wisdom of Ancient Sumer*, Bethesda: CDL Press.

——, 2007. *Sumerian Proverbs in the Schøyen Collection*, CUSAS, 2 vols, Bethesda: CDL Press.

Annus, A. and Lenzi, A., 2010. *Ludlul bēl nēmeqi: The Standard Babylonian Poem of the Righteous Sufferer*, SAACT, vol. 7, Helsinki: The Neo-Assyrian Text Corpus Project.

Assante, J., 2006. "What Makes a Prostitute? A Prostitute: Modern Definitions and Ancient Meanings", in *Prostitutes and Courtesans of the Ancient World*, Faraone, C.A. and McClure, L.K. (eds), Madison: University of Wisconsin Press, 117–32.

Beaulieu, P.A., 2007. "The Setting of Babylonian Wisdom Literature," in *Wisdom Literature in Mesopotamia and Israel*," Clifford, R.J. (ed.), SBLSym 36, Atlanta: Society of Biblical Literature, 3–19.

Black, J. and Green, A., 1992. *Gods, Demons and Symbols of Ancient Mesopotamia: An Illustrated Dictionary* (illustrations by Tessa Richards), Austin: University of Texas Press.

Black, J.A., Cunningham, G., Fluckiger-Hawker, E, Robson, E., and Zólyomi, G., 1998. *The Electronic Text Corpus of Sumerian Literature* (http://www-etcsl.orient.ox.ac.uk/), Oxford: University of Oxford.

Bottéro, J., 1992. *Mesopotamia, Writing, Reasoning, and the Gods*, Chicago: The University of Chicago Press.

Bricker, D.P., 2000. "Innocent Suffering in Mesopotamia," *Tyndale Bulletin* 51, 193–214.

Charpin, D., 2004. 'Lire et écrire en Mésopotamie: une affaire de spécialistes?' *Comptes-rendus des séances de l'année … – Académie des inscriptions et belles-lettres*, 148, 481–508.

Civil, M., 1994. *The Farmer's Instructions: A Sumerian Agricultural Manual*, Aula Orientalia Supplementa 5, Barcelona: Sabadell.

——, 2006. "The Song of the Millstone," in *Shapal tibnim mû illakû: Studies Presented to Joaquín Sanmartín on the Occasion of His 65th Birthday*, Del Olmo Lete, G., Feliu, L. and Millet, A. (eds), *Aula Orientalis Supplement* 22, Barcelona: Sabadell, 121–38.

Cooper, J., 2002. "Virginity in Ancient Mesopotamia," in *Sex and Gender in the Ancient Near East, Proceedings of the 47th Rencontre Assyriolgique Internationale, 2001*, Parpola, S. and Whiting, R.M. (eds), Helsinki: The Neo-Assyrian Text Corpus Project, 91–112.

——, 2010. "'I Have Forgotten My Burden of Former Days!' Forgetting the Sumerians in Ancient Iraq," *Journal of the American Oriental Society* 310, 327–34.

Crenshaw, J.L., 1993. "Wisdom Literature", in *The Oxford Companion to the Bible*, Metzger, B.M. and Coogan, M.D. (eds), New York: Oxford University Press, 801–3.

——, 1995. "The Contemplative Life in the Ancient Near East," in CANE IV, 2445–57.

Denning-Bolle, S., 1987. "Women and Dialogue in the Ancient near East", *Numen* 34/2, 214–34.

Dossin, G., 1950. *Correspondance de Shamshi Addu et ses fils*, Archives Royales de Mari, vol. 1, Paris: Impr. nationale.

Dossin G., and Finet, A., 1978. *Correspondance Féminine*, ARM 10, Paris: Librairie Orientaliste Paul Geuthner, S.A.

Durand, J.M., 2006. "Dictons et proverbes à l'époque amorrite," *Journal Asiatique* 36, 3–38.

Foster, B.R., 1991. "On Authorship in Akkadian Literature," *Annali dell'Istituto Orientale di Napoli* 51, 17–32.

——, 1995. "Humor and Wit in the Ancient Near East," in CANE IV, 2459–69.

——, 1996 *Before the Muses: An Anthology of Akkadian Literature*, 2 vols, 2nd edn, Bethesda: CDL Press.

Gordon, E.I., 1959. *Sumerian Proverbs:* Glimpses *of Everyday Life in Ancient Mesopotamia*, Philadelphia: The University Museum of the University of Pennsylvania.

Grayson, A.K., 1980. "Babylonia" in *The Penguin Encyclopedia of Ancient Civilizations*, Cotterell, A. (ed.), London: Penguin Books, 89–101.

Greenstein, E., 2007. "Sages with a Sense of Humor," in *Wisdom Literature in Mesopotamia and Israel*, Clifford, R.J. (ed.), SBLSym 36, Atlanta: Society of Biblical Literature, 55–

Hallo, W.W. (ed.), 1992. "Sumerian Literature," in *Anchor Bible Dictionary*, vol. 6, Freedman, D.N. (ed.), New York: Doubleday, 234–37.

———, 1996. *The Context of Scripture: Canonical Compositions from the Biblical World*, vol. 1, Leiden: Brill.

Harper, R.F., 1896. *Assyrian and Babylonian Letters Belonging to the Koyunjik Collection of the British Museum*, vol 4, Chicago: The University of Chicago Press.

Holm, T.L., 2005. "Ancient Near Eastern Literature: Genres and Forms," in *A Companion to the Ancient Near East*, Snell, D.C. (ed.), Oxford: Blackwell, 282–88.

Horowitz,V., 2007. "The Wisdom of Shupe-awilum—A Deathbed Debate between Father and Son," in *Wisdom Literature in Mesopotamia and Israel*, Clifford, R.J. (ed.), SBLSym 36, Atlanta: Society of Biblical Literature, 37–51.

Jacobsen, Th., 1959. "Additional Notes," in *Sumerian Proverbs: Glimpses of Everyday Life in Ancient Mesopotamia*, Gordon, E.I. (ed.), Philadelphia: The University Museum of the University of Pennsylvania, 547–50.

———, 1980. "Sumer," in *The Penguin Encyclopedia of Ancient Civilization*, Cotterell, A. (ed.), London: Penguin Books, 223–27.

Katz, D., 2003/4. "RBC 2000—Out of Prison, into the Netherworld, or, Perhaps a Love Charm," *Jaarbericht van het Vooraziatisch-Egyptisch Genootshap, Ex Oriente Lux*, 38, 71–76.

Kitchen, A.K., 1977. "Proverbs and Wisdom Books of the Ancient Near East: the Factual History of a Literary Form," *Tyndale Bulletin* 28, 69–114.

Lambert, W.G., 1960. *Babylonian Wisdom Literature*, Oxford: The Clarendon Press; revised 1995, Winona Lake: Eisenbrauns. [Lambert BWL].

———, 1963. "Celibacy in the World's Oldest Proverbs," *Bulletin of the American Schools of Oriental Research* 169, 63–64.

———, 1997. "Some New Babylonian Literature," in *Wisdom in Ancient Israel: Essays in Honour of J.A. Emerton*, Day, J. (ed.), Cambridge: Cambridge University Press, 30–42.

Lambert, W.G. and Gurney, O. R., 1954. "The Sultantepe Tablets (Continued) III: The Poem of the Righteous Sufferer," *Anatolian Studies* 4, 65–99.

Landsberger, B. and Jacobsen, Th., 1955. "An Old Babylonian Charm against *merhu*," *Journal of Near Eastern Studies*, 13, 14–21; and additions and corrigenda in *Journal of Near Eastern Studies* 16, 1958, 56–58.

Michalowski, P., 2006. "The Lives of the Sumerian Language," in *Margins of Writing: Origins of Cultures*, OIS 2, Sanders, S. (ed.), Chicago: University of Chicago Press, 159–84.

Moran, W.L., 2002. "Puppies in Proverbs—From Shamshi-Adad to Archilocus?" *The Most Magic Ward: Essays on Babylonian and Biblical Literature*, Catholic Biblical Quarterly Monograph Series 35, Washington: The Catholic Biblical Association of America, 87–99.

Nemet-Nejat, K., 1999. "Women in Ancient Mesopotamia", in *Women's Roles in Ancient Civilizations: A Reference Guide*, Vivante, B. (ed.), Westport: Greenwood Press, 85–114.

Neuman,J. and Parpola, S., 1983. "Wind Vanes in Ancient Mesopotamia about 2000–1500 B.C.," *Bulletin of Meterological Society*, 1141–43.

Nougayrol, J. et al. 1968. *Ugaritica* V, Mission de Ras Shamra 16, Paris: Librairie Oreintaliste Paul Geuthner.

Oppenheim, A.L., 1974. *Ancient Mesopotamia: Portrait of a Dead Civilization*, Chicago: The University of Chicago Press; Revised by Erica Reiner.

Paglai, V., 2009. "The Art of Dueling with Words: Toward a New Understanding of Verbal Duels across the World," *Oral Tradition* 24/1, 61–88.

Roth, M.T., 1988. "She Will Die by the Iron Dagger: Adultery and Neo-Babylonian Marriage," *Journal of Economic and Social History of the Orient* 31, 186–206.

Rubio G., 2005. "The Languages of the Ancient Near East," in *A Companion to the Ancient Near East*, Snell, D. (ed.), Malden: Blackwell Publishing, 79–94. Paperback Edition, 2007.

——, 2007. "Sumerian Morphology," in *Morphologies of Asia and Africa I-II*, Kaye, A.S. (ed.), Winona Lake: Eisenbrauns, 1327–79.

Saggs, H.W.F., 1984. *The Might That Was Assyria*, London: Sidgwick & Jackson.

Sasson, J.M. (ed.), 1995. *Civilizations of the Ancient Near East*, 4 vols, New York: Charles Scribner and Sons 1995; Hendrickson Publishers edition, Peabody: MA, 2000, 2 vols.

Stol, M., 1987. "Two Old Babylonian Literary Texts," in *Language Literature and History: Philological and Historical Studies Presented to Erica Reiner*, Rochberg-Halton, F. (ed.), New Haven: American Oriental Society, 383–87.

——, 1995. "Private Life in Ancient Mesopotamia", in CANE I, 469–501.

Tigay, J., 1995. "Some Archaeological Notes on Deuteronomy," in *Pomegranates and Golden Bells: Studies in Biblical, Jewish, and Near Eastern Ritual, Law and Literature in Honor of Jacob Milgrom*, Wright, D.P., Freedman, D.N. and Hurvitz, A. (eds), Winona Lake: Eisenbrauns, 373–80.

Uther, Hans-Jorg, 2006. "The Fox in World Literature: Reflections on a Fictional Animal," *Asian Folklore Studies* 65, 133–60.

Van der Toorn, Karel, 2007. "Why Wisdom Became a Secret: On Wisdom as a Written Genre," in *Wisdom Literature in Mesopotamia and Israel*," Clifford, R.J. (ed.), SBLSym 36, Atlanta: Society of Biblical Literature, 21–36.

Veldhuis, N., 2000. "Kassite Exercises: Literary and Lexical Extracts," *Journal of Cuneiform Studies* 52, 67–94.

von Soden, W., 1965. "Das Fragen nach der Gerechtigkeit Gottes im Alten Orient," *Mitteilungen der deutschen Orient-Gesellschaft* 96, 41–59.

——, 1994. *The Ancient Orient: An Introduction to the Study of the Ancient Near East*. Translation by Donald G. Schley. Grand Rapids: William B. Eerdmans Publishing Company.

Wasserman, N., and Streck, M., 2009. "Translation and commentary,"<http://cdli.ucla.edu/search/result.pt?-sort=id_text&-op_id_text>

Wiseman, D.J., 1980, "Ludlul: A New Text of the Babylonian Poem of the Righteous Sufferer," *Anatolian Studies* 30, 101–7.

5

MEDICINE AND HEALING MAGIC

JoAnn Scurlock

Ardat-lilî and lilû

Adolescent demonic pests

Human adolescence is a difficult period of transition between childhood and adulthood. The death of a young man or woman in the flower of youth is also a tragic event, deeply felt, and attended by feelings of guilt, which translate to the idea that ghosts of such persons might have legitimate reasons for haunting the living. When, then, ancient Mesopotamian scholars needed an explanation for the stresses experienced by adolescents, and diseases or conditions that seemed disproportionately to afflict them, they attributed these stresses, diseases or conditions to a class of demons, *lilû*, *lilîtu* and *ardat lilî*, who were recruited from among young persons who died just before or just after marriage and who usually victimized persons of the opposite sex but of the same age as themselves.

For example, the adolescent female *ardat lilî* was responsible for Gilles de la Tourette syndrome, a disorder primarily affecting boys in the first two decades of life, which combines the explosive and uncontrollable verbalization of obscene words with jerking and gyrating movements of the head, pelvis or arms.

Gilles de la Tourette syndrome 1[1]

If he continually cries out: "My insides, my insides!," he continually raises his pelvic region, his confusional state(s) come over him (and) when they come over him, he continually talks in a frightful manner, "hand" of [*ardat lilî*].

Gilles de la Tourette syndrome 2[2]

If his illness enters and leaves (and when his confusional state comes over him), he continually talks in a frightful manner, "hand" of *ardat lilî*.

Even normal teenagers have a tendency to nervous behavior, fainting spells and false seizures. Western medicine follows Hippocrates in associating such behavior with "hysterical" women. According to the "father of medicine" the cause of this condition was that women's uteruses periodically went AWOL, careening about the body in search of insatiable sexual satisfaction. Ancient Mesopotamians, by contrast, attributed this type of illness to a non-sexist class of demons, which allowed them to notice that both boys and girls were afflicted, if in slightly different ways.

Hysteria 1[3]

If a woman is ill and her affliction always afflicts her in the evening and she continually takes her clothes off, it is an affliction of *lilû*.

Hysteria 2[4]

If the top of his head[5] ⌐continually feels as if split in two all⌐ [day/night long], he continually has sexual desires, and the bedding is continually turned around him, (and) like one who lays himself down on top of a woman, he has an erection, "hand" of ⌐*ardat lilî*⌐.

Both sexes are prone to "hysterical" pseudo-seizures. Modern physicians recognize these seizures by non-physiologic events, such as a twitching of all four extremities without loss of consciousness or by careful attention to avoid injury by moving away from a wall or bed edge while having convulsions. Hysterical seizures may also have frankly sexual overtones, with pelvic thrusting or genital manipulation. Genuine seizures are followed by a postictal state, for the absence of which the ancient physician checked by asking the patient to get up afterwards.

Hysteria 3[6]

If he shudders and he can get up (afterwards), he talks a lot and he continually ⌐jerks⌐, for a woman, *lilû*, for a man, *lilîtu*; he can get up (afterwards).

In addition, there are some mental disorders, as for example, schizophrenia, in which patients develop characteristic symptoms in adolescence or early adulthood. These may be recognized by slurred speech, dissociative states and visual hallucinations. These, too, were attributed to the *lilû* class of demons.

Mental illness 1[7]

If [his] mentation [is altered] (and) his ⌐words⌐ hinder each other in his mouth ... *ardat lilî* or *lilû*.

Mental illness 2[8]

If his limbs are as still as those of a healthy person, (and) he continually opens his eyes and, when he sees the one who afflicts him, he talks with him and continually changes his self, "hand" of *lilû*, messenger of his god.

Unhappy ghosts[9]

The *lilû*-demons and their female counterparts the *lilîtu* or *ardat lilî*-demonesses were hungry for victims because they were the spirits of young men and women who had themselves died young. Enkidu answers Gilgamesh's questions on the fate of such persons as follows: "Did you see the woman who never gave birth?" "I saw (her)." "How does she fare?" "Like a ruined (?) pot, she is cast down violently, she gives no man joy." "Did you see the young man who did not strip the garment from his wife's lap?" "I saw (him)." "How does he fare?" "You offer (him) a helping rope, and he weeps over the helping rope." "Did you see the young woman who did not strip the garment from her husband's lap?" "I saw (her)." "How does she fare?" "You offer (her) a helping reed, and she weeps over the helping reed."[10]

If a girl had the misfortune of dying prematurely before the fulfillment of life's expectations, her ghost was forever doomed to prowl the earth in the form of a *lilîtu* or *ardat lilî*-demon. Fulfillment, in *ardat-lilî* texts, is defined not only in terms of children, but also the experiencing of sexual pleasure and the increase in social status (and freedom of movement) represented by growing up and becoming a wife and mother.

Poor ardat-lilî[11]

Ardat-lilî slips in a man's window; young girl not fated (to be married); young woman who was never impregnated like a woman; young woman who was never deflowered like a woman; young girl who never experienced sexual pleasure in her husband's lap; young girl who never removed a garment in her husband's lap; young woman whose garment-pin a good man never loosened; young women in whose breasts there never was milk, who cries in pain; young girl who was never filled with sexual pleasure in the lap of a young man, who never had her fill of desire; young girl who never had (her own) women's quarters, whom they did not call by the name: "mother"; young girl who in desolation mistreated (her) cheeks; young girl who never rejoiced with (other) young girls; young girl who was never seen during her(!) city's festival, does not raise her eyes; young girl who was snatched away from a husband in her women's quarters; young girl who never had a husband, never gave birth to a child; young girl who never had a husband, never brought forth a child; young girl who never had a husband, never had a child; young girl who was snatched away from a husband, snatched away from a child; young girl who was driven from her father-in-law's house; *ardat-lilî* who was driven out the window like the wind; *ardat-lilî* whose ghost (when she died) was not in her mouth; *ardat-lilî* whose heartache carried her (down) to the nether world; *ardat-lilî* whom the "hand" of Ištar mistreated in the (family) nest; *ardat-lilî* who roams outside in the broad steppe.[12]

The obvious solution to this problem was to find the *ardat-lilî* the husband she needed and to dispatch the two of them, bound together in perpetual and indissoluble marriage to the Netherworld. Ghosts who received regular *kispu*-offerings were expected not to bother the living, a promise enforced inter alia by the Anunnaki gods who attended Ereškigal, queen of the Netherworld.

Ardat-lilî *gets a husband*[13]

You pull out a white and a black hair from a virgin she-goat and you twine a double thread and you bind it to the heads of those figurines (of *ardat-lilî* and *lilû*) and you make them face the setting sun and you draw (a circle) of flour (around them, saying): "May they sit in place for their *kispu*-offerings and may they be satisfied at the gate of the Anunnaki. Anunnaki, great gods, make them swear; make them swear by heaven and earth so that the patient's[14] burden may be loosened."[15]

What is interesting about these texts is that not only were adolescent girls' concerns taken seriously by ancient Mesopotamians, but they were given universal value. If a boy had the misfortune of dying prematurely before the fulfillment of life's expectations, his ghost was forever doomed to prowl the earth in the form of a *lilû*-demon. Fulfillment, in *lilû*-texts, is defined not only in terms of experiencing of sexual pleasure but also the increase in social status (and personal honor) represented by growing up and becoming a husband and father.[16] It is clear from these passages that, as in the modern Middle East, the young man's living room was the street.

Poor lilû[17]

[Young man] who always sits, silent and ⌈alone⌉, [in] the street; [young] man who cries bitterly in the grip of his death-demon; young man to whose fate silence was attached; young man to whom his mother, crying, gave birth in the street; young man whose body grief has burnt; young man whose god has ⌈evilly bound⌐ him; young man whose goddess has cut him off; young man who never married a wife, never raised a child; young man who never experienced sexual pleasure in his wife's lap; young man who never removed a garment in his wife's lap; young man who was driven out of the house of his father-in-law.

The slurred speech, dissociative states and visual hallucinations of adolescent mental disorders found ready explanation in the persistent and irresistible temptations offered by the *lilû* class of demons.

Mad about you[18]

They continually confront the one who does not possess a personal god. They put their hands on his hands; they put their feet on his feet; they put their neck on his neck. They make him change his self. "I am the son of a prince," he tells her. "I will fill your lap with silver and gold." "You be the wife, and I will be your husband," he tells her. "I will make your riches (as abundant) as the fruit of the garden."

As with the *ardat lilî*-demon, the solution was to find the *lilû* a wife, complete with money bound into the hem, as if this were a human marriage. Indeed, the same ritual was used, regardless of the sex of the perpetrator or victim.

Lilû *gets a wife*[19]

Bind a [girdle] (on them) [and] put shoes on their feet and give them a tied water skin and tie a money bag (filled) with silver and gold into their hem and (saying): "Let it assign you *kispu*-offerings in the steppe,"[20] make them stand at the base of an acacia and you make them face the setting sun and you draw a (circle of) flour (around them, saying): "I have made you swear by the great gods—you should go away. You shall not cross the magic circle of Ea (and) the erected reed hut of Marduk, son of Eridu.

Until you have distanced yourself from the house, (and) until you have withdrawn from the city, you shall not eat bread; You shall not drink water. You shall not taste seawater, sweet water, bitter water, Tigris water, Euphrates water, well water, canal water (standard offerings to ghosts). If you try to fly up to heaven, may you have no wings; if you try to be detained on earth, may you have no dwelling place. [Let] the young man, son of his god [be cleansed]; let him be purified.

Love magic

Seduction charms

The course of true love never ran any smoother for ancient Mesopotamians than it does for us. The medical corpus has left us this description of "love sickness".

Love sickness[21]

If he continually flutters about, he is continually insolent, he continually talks with himself (and) he continually laughs for no reason, he is sick with love sickness; it is the same for a man and a woman. If depression continually falls upon him, his breath is continually short, he eats bread (and) drinks water/beer but it does not agree with him, he says "Ua my heart!" and he is dejected, he is sick with love sickness; it is the same for a man and a woman.

First marriages were arranged; however, it was possible for a young couple to force their parents to agree to let them marry by making it public knowledge that they had slept together.[22] In Assyria, at least, widows were also free to move in with a man or let a man move in with them, becoming legally married after two years of cohabitation. Problems arose when one of the parties was not agreeable, giving rise to spells, quasi-legitimate and downright sorcerous, to persuade a reluctant young lady or wealthy widow to cooperate.

Inanna/Ishtar was goddess of liminality who turned men into women and oversaw the transition between childhood and adulthood. She was patroness of prostitutes and gave success (and failure) in love, in or out of wedlock. *Entu*-priestesses were virginal spouses of divinities. However, the cynical equivalent of our expression "where there's a will, there's a way" was: "The *entu*-priestess, in order not to get pregnant, has you have intercourse with her in her buttocks."[23]

Irresistible me[24]

Beloved, beloved, you(m.) whom Ea and Enlil established (as the beloved), I will surround you(m.) (with a magic circle) as surely as Ištar sits on a dais (and) Nanaya sits in a sanctuary. Entu-priestesses love burning (and) married women hate their husbands; cut off for me her high-held nose and put her nose under my foot! Just as her love has become higher than me, so may my love become higher than her love!

Who really ate that apple[25]

The beautiful woman has come forth (as) love—Inanna, fond of apples and pomegranates, has come forth as potency. Rise! Fall! Love stone, go straight for me! Rise! Inanna, you truly are the one who does (it) via the anus![26] She has presided over love.

Recitation for cases where a woman looks at a man's penis.

Its ritual: You recite the recitation three times either over an apple or a pomegranate. You give it to her (and) have her suck their juices. (Wherever) that woman goes, you will be able to make love to her.

Getting a woman to respond favorably to lame or offensive pick-up lines is a perennial male problem. The Mesopotamian Don Juan in the know armed himself for battle. The hardwoods and the obsidian invoked durable emotions: "Your love is true obsidian, your (coital) laughter true gold."[27] *Saḫlû* was used to make a spicy condiment, and the shelduck tongue suggested continual twittering chatter. The shelduck was presumably chosen not merely for its noisiness, but for the fact that such birds nested in holes (*ḫurru*). According to a commentary,[28] this category of love charm was particularly valuable in loosening the tongues of women with rich legacies.[29]

The perfect pick-up line[30]

(To) get a woman to talk, you wrap *mēšu*-wood, *taškarinnu*-boxwood, obsidian(!), saḫlû-plant (and) the tongue of a shelduck in sheep's wool. If you put (it) at the head of your bed, wherever that woman goes, she will not be able to stop talking (and) you will be able to make love to her.

Charms for wives with impotent husbands

What is striking about Mesopotamian treatments for impotence is the extent to which the female partner was expected to participate by reciting playful sex talk. Donkeys are proverbial for their disproportionately large genitals, and goats for the ease with which they get excited. Comparing the male partner to an animal does not surprise, but that the woman should wish to be thought of as a dog is amusing in modern context. Also interesting is the sexual aggressiveness of the image of the female spider luring male victims into her web, hardly the slavishly passive female of imagined "patriarchal" societies.

Love is a bitch[31]

Let the wind blow; let the mountains ⌜quake⌝. Let the clouds gather; let the raindrops fall. Let the donkey stiffen up so that he can mount the jenny; Let the gazelle buck repeatedly mount the she-goat of the plain.[32] May a goat buck be tied at the head of my bed; may a ram be tied at the foot of my bed. The one at the head of my bed get it up! Love me! The one at the foot of my bed get it up! Adore me! My genitals are the genitals of a bitch; his penis is the penis of a dog. (May my genitals hold his penis fast) as the genitals of a bitch hold fast the penis of a dog. May your penis go as long as a *mašgašu*. I sit in a spider's web of (coital) laughter; may I not miss the prey: Spell (and) Recitation.

Recitation for potency.

Its ritual: You pour powdered magnetic hematite (and) powdered iron [into] *pūru*-oil. You recite the recitation seven times over it. If the ⌜man⌝ repeatedly rubs his ⌜penis⌝ (and) the woman her genitals (with it), he ⌜should be able to mount (her) repeatedly⌝.

Performance anxiety[33]

Let the wind blow; let the orchard sway. Let the clouds gather; let the raindrops fall. May my erection be (like) the flowing waters of a river. May my penis be (taut as) a harp string. May it not come down (prematurely) from inside her: Spell (and) Recitation.

Its ritual: You take a harp string (and) tie three knots (in it). You recite the recitation seven times. If you tie it on his right or left hand, he should have potency.

As may be gathered, anal intercourse was a favored method of birth control, and seems to have been enjoyed by both parties.

Sex for pleasure, not procreation[34]

I am a daughter of Ningirsu, the releaser. My mother is a releaser; my father is a releaser. I who have come, I really can release. May the penis of so-and-so (the male partner) be a stick of *martû*-wood. May it "kill" the anus of so-and-so (the female partner); may he never be sated with her charms: Spell (and) Recitation.

Charms for ending marital quarrels

As everywhere, ancient Mesopotamian husbands and wives did not always get along. Among the curses in Esarhaddon's Oath of Allegiance, on a par of horror with having to eat the flesh of one's own children, is this curious imprecation: "Just as a snake and a mongoose do not enter the same den to lie down together but think only of cutting each other's throats, may you and your wives not enter the same house and not sleep on one bed; (and only) think about cutting each other's throats!"[35] To solve these problems, ancient Near Easterners devised a sort of anger-management strategy using magic. In Hittite, this took the form of Maštigga's Ritual for Domestic Quarrel.[36] In Akkadian, a series of charms under the aegis of Ištar (who was also the planet Venus) brought the recalcitrant husband back into line.

20. Speechless with anger[37]

Goddess of goddesses, Ištar is ⌜male⌝ (in sexual appetite); she makes (even) experienced women blush.[38] She makes (even) the ⌜impotent⌝ able to make love. She makes every angry person return to the womens' quarters. I cry out to you, ⌜Ištar⌝; I have extracted your cusp, Ištar (Venus), in the midst of the heavens.[39] Because he will not tell me what is on his mind; because he is so angry that he will not speak with me. Put truth in him, put truth in me, in what I say, in what he says, in our trouble(?).[40] The recitation is not mine; it is the recitation of Ištar (and) Nanaya. Ištar told (it) to me and I am (just) repeating it.

⌜Recitation⌝ for a woman whose husband is angry with her.

Before [Ištar], you set up [an offering arrangement]. You put 12 emmer flat breads on ⌜top [of the offering arrangement]. You set out a [censer (burning)] juniper on *ašāgu*-thorn coals. You put […] oil on the offering table. You pour […]-wood into it. You recite the recitation [7 times] over it before Ištar. [When the] ⌜offering arrangement has subsided and the censer has used up its ration, you let [the woman] say whatever afflicts her heart and then you rub her ears with the oil.[41]

Magnetic attraction[42]

[…] Let us bathe in the pure river and come up so that my friend may return. Enuru recitation; ⌜recitation to return an irate person.

Its ritual: (The woman) raises magnetic hematite in her right (hand and) an iron *magurru*-boat in her left. She recites this recitation three times. While reciting, he has her touch the death wound of a sheep.

Recitation: I have cried out to you, Ištar, friend(f.) of the great gods. Truly, [you] live in the heavens, the seat of [your] godship. Ištar, now, return the recalcitrant. Though he be angry, let him return to me; though he be hateful, make him speak with me., etc.

109

Women's health

Excessive bleeding

The fact that there were collections of therapeutic texts devoted exclusively to women's problems suggests that obstetrics and gynecology may have been a separate subspecialty of ancient Mesopotamian medicine. The ancient physician devised treatments for amenorrhea, menorrhagia and infertility, uterine prolapse and vaginal infections. He also provided birth control and attempted to predict the sex of unborn children. Most importantly, he attempted to treat uterine bleeding and gastro-intestinal problems during pregnancy, prevent miscarriages and deal with post-partum complications, including child-bed (puerperal) fever. As was generally the case in ancient Mesopotamian medicine, herbal medicines (which included plant estrogens), were supplemented by psyching up the patient with what we would probably term "magic". In this charming spell, the gods, including Marduk, head of the Babylonian pantheon, are detailed to help put a stop to excessive bleeding.

Dam it up![43]

⌐Spell⌐ (and) Recitation: Carnelian (color) (is) her blood. (In) the ⌐carnelian⌐ branch canal, will they dry up the waters [with] a carnelian *mirtu*-tool?[44] ⌐Who⌐ can tell (it) to merciful Marduk? Let them dam (it) up ⌐with⌐ a carnelian *mirtu*-tool.[45] < *Adāru*-wood, (and) lapis lazuli, [will dam up (the canal)]; *ašlu*-rush will dry up (the waters) >.

⌐Recitation⌐ for stopping a woman's bleeding.

Its ⌐ritual⌐: You twine together white wool (and) red wool. You tie seven ⌐knots⌐. You dribble *ḫurātu* (on the knots). < Whenever (you tie one of the) knots >, you recite the recitation seven times. If you tie it on her hip region, she should recover.

Post-partum complications

Illnesses suffered by women shortly following delivery include bloating, diarrhea, urinary tract infection, bleeding, uterine atony and child-bed (puerperal) fever. Urinary tract infections are common in pregnancy, and when they cause inflammation of the urethra, the pain during urination can be severe.

Bloating[46]

If a woman gives birth and subsequently is inflated with "wind", you grind *kukru* (and) *burāšu*-juniper. You mix (it) with winnowed beerwort. If you completely bandage her vulva (with it), she should recover.

If a woman gives birth and subsequently becomes distended and is inflated with "wind", if you have her smell dust from a copper kettledrum, she should recover.

Alternatively, you grind *burāšu*-juniper. If you have her drink (it mixed) with first quality beer, she should recover.

If a woman is colicky and inflated with "wind", if you have her smell dust from a copper kettledrum, she should recover.

Diarrhea[47]

If a woman (gives birth) and subsequently her bowels are loose, you grind *kukru* (and) have her eat it with *mersu*-confection made with *isqūqu*-flour (and) ghee. Her bowels should [...]

If a woman (gives birth) and subsequently she has a flowing of the bowels, you grind *isqūqu*-flour, emmer flour, sheep kidney fat, ox fat, *kibrītu*-sulphur (and) *kisibirrītu*-coriander. You mix (it) together with sheep fat, pour (it) into wax (and) boil (it). If you have her eat (it), [she should recover].

If loose bowels afflict a woman in confinement, you soak emmer groats, dates (and) [... in ...] in a *namzītu*-vessel. In the evening, you [...]. If you have her drink it [...].

Urinary tract infection[48]

If a woman gives birth and subsequently her pubic region stings (and) her lower abdomen (hypogastric region) continually hurts her intensely, "striking" has seized that woman. You bandage her with hot dregs of beerwort. You grind *lišān kalbi* (and) "fox grape". You boil (it) in beer, filter (it) and pour(?) (it) into her vulva. You have her drink *imḫur-lim* (mixed) with wine.

Viral infection[49]

If "wind" blasts a woman and she is about to give birth and (the appearance of) her skin/body continually changes (for the worse), to cure her, you boil these eleven plants: *kukru*, *kasû*, *nīnû*, *burāšu*-juniper, *ḫašû*, *nuḫurtu*, *saḫlû*, flax seed, *šammi ašî*, *ṭūru*-aromatic (and) "white plant" in first quality beer and oil. If she takes (it), she should recover.

Alternatively, you boil these five plants: *ḫašû*, *nuḫurtu*, *šūnû*-tree, dates (and) *aṣuṣimtu* in first quality beer. You pour (it) into her vagina.

Child-bed (puerperal) fever[50]

If a woman (gives birth) and subsequently her umbilical area (feels) supple (but) she cannot stop the sweat from coming, you grind *biṣṣūr atāne*-shell (and) pour (it) on it.

Alternatively, you dry (and) grind *dadānu*-thorn, *šakirû*, *lišān kalbi*, *šammi bu'šānu* and *sikillu* in equal proportions. You mix (it) with *biṣṣūru*-shell (and) *erēnu*-cedar resin. You scatter (it) on her umbilical area (and) bandage (it) over.

If a woman gives birth and subsequently she [continually] has internal fever, she vomits and [...], the blood of her confinement has been ⌜locked⌝ up inside her; that woman, while giving birth [...]. You grind wheat flour, powdered ⌜roasted⌝ *kasû*, powdered *šūnû*-tree, *kukru*, *burāšu*-juniper, [...], sesame residue (and) "dove dung" with a stone pestle. [You mix (it)] with beer-wort (and) [...].

Alternatively, [you ...] winnowed beerwort, *kukru*-aromatic, *burāšu*-juniper, baluḫḫu-aromatic, roasted *kasû*, *nuḫurtu* (and) [...]. You pour roasted *saḫlû* (and) *buṭuttu*-pistachio into it. You mix (them) with oil (and) wind them into burls with a cloth. [You insert (it)] into [her] ⌜vagina⌝. She takes (it) up and keeps (it) there. As soon as it has changed (color) and her body has become swollen, she takes it out. Then you have her mix together honey (and) [...]. If she blows it into her body with a lead tube, she should recover.

Alternatively, you mill grind together *kukru*, *burāšu*-juniper, *kasû*, *šupuḫru*-cedar, *ballukku*-aromatic, *nuḫurtu*, *su'ādu*, *tiyātu*, *ṭūru*-aromatic, *baluḫḫu*-aromatic resin, *antaḫšum*-vegetable, *šunḫu*, *šammi ašî* (and) winnowed beerwort. You boil (it) in *asu*-myrtle oil and beer (and) wind (it) into a burl. You sprinkle (it) with oil (and) insert (it) into her vagina.

Alternatively, you grind (and) mix wheat flour, powdered roasted *kasû*, powdered *šūnû*-tree, *burāšu*-juniper, *baluḫḫu*-aromatic, *šigūšu* flour, *ḫalluru*-chick pea flour, *kakku*-lentil flour, sesame residue, "dove dung", flax seed, *ḫarubu*-carob flour (and) winnowed beerwort in equal proportions. You bandage (her with it).

Alternatively, you roast together (and) grind *ḫašû*, *nuḫurtu*, *šammi ašî*, *kukru*-aromatic, *burāšu*-juniper, *kasû*, "white plant" (and) flax seed. You boil (it) with beerwort (and) *abukkatu* resin (mixed) with oil (and) pour (it) into her vagina. You wrap (it) in a tuft of wool (and) insert (it) into her vagina.

Alternatively, you grind *azukirānu* (and) insert (it) into her vagina (mixed) with oil and beer. You mix *su'ādu*, *baluḫḫu*-aromatic resin (and) *burāšu*-juniper with beerwort (and insert it into her vagina).

Alternatively, you mix *kukru*, *šammi aši*, *saḫlû*, salt, *ṭūru*-aromatic (and) assorted incense. If you have her drink (it), she should recover.

Alternatively, you mix together *kukru*-aromatic, *burāšu*-juniper, *kasû*, *šammi aši*, *ṭūru*-aromatic, *su'ādu*, *sikkatu*-yeast (and) winnowed beerwort. The woman takes (it). She should massage her lap with boiled beer. If she takes (it), she should recover.

Alternatively, you pour *šūšu*, *šūnû*-tree, *aktam*, *kasû*, "sweet reed", *barirātu* and *argannu* into water. You boil (it and) repeatedly bathe her with it.

If a woman (gives birth) and subsequently she (has) fever (and) *li'bu* and dark spots accumulate(?) on her flesh and her veins (and) inside she contains pus, to soothe it, you repeatedly bathe her with *kasû* juice and *buṭnānu* infusion.

Alternatively, you bake (gazelle) dung from the early part of the year in an oven (and) bathe her (with it). You pour oil and beer into her vagina. You make 1 *qû* of powdered *šūšu*, 1 *qû* of powdered sesame residue, 1 *qû* of malt flour, 1 *qû* of *kukru*-aromatic flour and 1 *qû* of burāšu-juniper flour into a dough with *kasû* juice. You let (it) cool in a magic circle (and) bandage (he)r over the canal (with it).

Alternatively, you cool *karāšu*-leek with milk and rub her gently with it. You insert it into her vagina.

If a woman (gives birth) and subsequently her insides give her a sharp pain and inside she contains pus, you grind *kasû*, roasted *kukru* and *saḫlû*. You form an acorn-shaped suppository (and) insert (it) into her vagina.

(Alternatively), you dry and grind *ḫašû*, [...] (and) *irrû* "fat". You have her drink (it mixed) with oil and beer.

The primary cause of uterine atony is that part or all of the placenta is retained in the uterus. The obvious solution is to encourage the expulsion of this material.

Uterine atony[51]

(If) a woman gives birth and subsequently she is distended, [her] excrement [...], her insides are constipated, and her waters and [her] blood have gone back [inside her].

To make her release it, you gather together these eleven plants: *kukru*-aromatic, *burāšu*-juniper, *atā'išu*, *ṣumlalû*, "sweet reed", *ballukku*-aromatic, myrrh, *ṭūru*-aromatic, *abukkatu* resin, *baluḫḫû*-aromatic resin and *atā'išu* root. You gather *ašāgu*-thorn coals into (an overturned) pottery drum and you pour those plants onto them. You have that woman sit over it. You wrap her in a cloth.

You mix *sīḫu*, *argānu*, *barirātu*, *saḫlû* and beerwort in fat from a pure cow. You wrap it in a tuft of wool and insert it repeatedly into her vagina and, if you continually do this day and night, she should experience improvement.

On the second day, you boil [...] (and bathe her with it). After she comes out (of the bath), you have the woman sit over (the fumigants). You wrap her in a cloth. You sprinkle beer onto hot bitumen. The smoke should enter her mouth and nostrils. You repeatedly rub her gently with sweet oil. If she does not experience delirium, she should recover.

If she does not experience improvement, you fill a *tamgussu*-vessel with water and beer. You pour these eleven plants together into it: *erēnu*-cedar, *šurmēnu*-cypress, *daprānu*-juniper, *kukru*-aromatic, *burāšu*-juniper, *ṣumlalû*, *atā'išu*, *sīḫu*, *argānu*, *barirātu*, *kasû* and *šūšu* seed. You boil it and filter it and bathe her with it. When she comes up (out of the bath), you rub her gently with oil. You have her enter a slaughterhouse. If she does not experience delirium, she should recover.

You mix the aforementioned plants, all of them (*erēnu*-cedar, *šurmēnu*-cypress, *daprānu*-juniper, *kukru*-aromatic, *burāšu*-juniper, *ṣumlalû*, *atā'išu*, *sīḫu*, *argānu*, *barirātu*, *kasû* and *šūšu* seed) with roasted beerwort. You collect it into a [...]-vessel. You bake it in an oven. You take it out and massage it into cloth. If you bandage her hypogastric region, her buttocks and her coccyx with it, she should recover.

Lamaštu

Ancient Mesopotamian women had particularly to fear the baneful attentions of Lamaštu, a thoroughly disagreeable hag with pendulous breasts, lion's head, donkey's ears, leopard-like body, and eagle's claws.[52] She also was less than tidy in her personal appearance and had a brown thumb, not to mention unsavory appetites.

Decamp![53]

She [...] in the street; she [...] in the corners. She is mighty; she is intractable. [...] She shines like the day. [...] She ⌈darkens⌉ the daylight; she [causes] burning with *ṣētu*-fever; she ⌈springs like a trap on⌉ the infant. She took from the lion her divine radiance; he assigned (it to) her. She took from the wolf the (evil) eye for infecting (people with fever).[54]

She crosses a river, she ⌜causes⌝ confusion in the water. She goes on a road, she ⌜blocks off⌝ its traffic. She leans on a wall, she ⌜smears (it)⌝ with mud. She leans on a *bīnu*-tamarisk, it loses its foliage. She leans on a datepalm, she strips off its dates. She leans on an *allānu*-oak or a wild *buṭnu*-terebinth, she makes it shrivel up.[55]

She continually drinks the dried(?)[56] blood of men, flesh that is not to be eaten, bones that are not to be cracked. You, daughter of Anu, have continually taken the bread of tears and wailing as (your) provision; you continually drink the dried(?) blood of men, flesh that is not to be eaten, bones that are not to be cracked.[57]

Let Anu, your father, provision you. Let Antu, your mother, provision you. Pull up your (tent) poles; roll up your (tent) ropes. Ride off to your mountain like the wild bull![58]

Let the *mašmašu*, *āšipu* of Asalluḫi, give you comb, *tudittu*-pin,[59] distaff and *kirissu*-clasp.[60] Head for the wild beasts of the steppe!

May you be smeared with the oil of *miḫru*-offerings; may you have put on shoes (that last) for ever and ever; may you carry the waterskin for your thirst. May the Brewer God give you groats, malt and beer bread; may he fill a leather pouch for you; may he give you beerwort for making beer.[61]

I have made you swear by Anu, your father (and) Antum, your mother. (I have made you swear) by Enlil and Ninlil, Ea and Damgalnunna. (I have made you swear) by Marduk and Ṣarpanitum. ... And ⌜you are made to swear⌝ by the god(s) of ⌜rivers⌝ and quays. [...][62]

Recitation for Lamaštu.[63]

Its ritual: You make a Lamaštu of clay from the river bank. You make a donkey of clay from the river bank. You provide it with provisions. You thread fourteen breads made from *šigūšu* flour on palm fibre. You put it on her neck. You pour out hot (broth) for her. You pour out water and beer for her. You cut the throat of a piglet. You put the heart in the daughter of Anu's mouth. You recite the recitation three times every day for three days before her. On the third day in the late afternoon you take her out into the steppe and you make her face the setting sun. You bind [her hands] ⌜behind⌝ her. You tie her to a *baltu*-thorn (or) an *ašāgu*-thorn. You surround her with a ⌜magic circle⌝. You make her swear an oath by heaven, earth and the Anunnaki.[64]

Fortunately for the sufferer, her unnatural appetites were equally disagreeable to the gods, despite the fact that Lamaštu was a minor divinity, a daughter of the sky-god Anu.

115

I am the daughter of Anu of heaven[65]

Recitation: "'⌐I⌐ am the daughter of Anu of heaven. I am a Sutean; I am teeth gnashing; I am brilliant! I enter the house; I leave the house. Bring me your sons so that I may ⌐suckle⌐ (them); let me ⌐put⌐ the breast into the mouth of your daughters.' Anu heard (this), wailing; (the birth goddess) Aruru-Bēlet-ilī (heard this), [her] tears flowing (and they said): 'Why should we ⌐destroy⌐ what we have created and (why) should the ⌐wind⌐ carry off what we have caused to exist? Take her and ⌐lay her to rest⌐/throw (her) in the sea. Tie her to a wild tamarisk standing to one side or to a solitary reed stalk.' Just as a corpse no longer has [life] and the stillborn child never suckled the milk of [his] mother, so may the daughter of Anu, like smoke, not be able to return to the house." [Spell and Recitation].

It is interesting to compare Lamaštu's address to her father with the speech that is supposed to cause the toothache worm to be crushed by the god Ea to the sufferer's benefit: "The worm went, weeping, before Šamaš, his tears flowing before Ea, (saying): 'What have you given me to eat? What have you given me to suck?' 'I have given you the ripe fig, the apricot (and) the apple.' 'What are they to me—the ripe fig or the apricot (and) apple? Lift me up and make me dwell between the teeth and the jaw. Let me suck the blood of the tooth and gnaw on the particles (caught) in the jaw!' ... Because you said this, worm, may Ea strike you with his mighty hand!"[66] The close similarities between these passages would seem to imply that, as in the case of the toothache worm, Lamaštu's less than edifying speech was repeated by the healer in the hope that it would make the gods irritated enough for them to force Lamaštu to cooperate in the cure.

Up from the swamp[67]

⌐She is furious⌐, she is raging, she is a goddess, she is brilliant, the ⌐daughter⌐ of [Anu]. She comes up ⌐from⌐ the [swamp] and, as a result, she is furiously furious. [The swamp is her shit]; stone/bedrock is her ⌐dung⌐.[68] The [appearance(?)] of her face is raging; deathly stillness, her charms. She continually enters the house(s) of women in confinement. She continually stands at the head of women about to give birth, (saying): "Bring me your sons so that I may suckle them; let me put the breast into the mouth of your daughters." The daughter of Anu comes before Enlil, her father, crying: "Bring me what I ask of you, my father Enlil: the flesh of mankind which is not good (to eat), the coagulated(?)[69] blood of men." (And Enlil answered): "Because you

116

asked this of me, may they make your house from clods of earth; let a young slave girl bring you a broken comb, a broken spindle (and) hot broth cooked in the embers." I have made [you] swear an oath by Anu and Antu, Enlil and Ninlil, an oath by the gates and entrances, an oath by the shaft of *ḫarbu* (and) seeder plow, (by) the abandoned child and his son. If you come back into this house and if you approach this infant; (if) you sit on the seat on which I want to sit; (and if) you take into the fold of your arms the infant which I want to take into the fold of my arms, (may you be punished). Ištar, ⌜seize⌝ the mouth of your dogs; Nanaya, put a muzzle on the mouth of ⌜your⌝ whelps. May the sleeper in his bed not awake until the sun, his advocate, rises! Spell (and) Recitation.

Its ritual. You take seven strands of red-dyed wool, bristle from a donkey from the right side, bristle from a jinny from the left side, bristle from a donkey foal, bristle from a white pig, a *ḫallulaya*-insect from the road, a tuft of hair from the right thigh of a donkey (and) wood shavings from the shaft of a *ḫarbu* (and) seeder plow. You twist (it) into three ropes (and) put them on his neck.[70]

In origin, Lamaštu was a demon of disease, probably typhoid fever, which is to this day a prominent cause of infant deaths in Iraq, and notorious for inducing abortions or premature labor in pregnant women (see below).[71] Ancient Mesopotamians imagined her as coming up from her swamp to prowl about after pregnant women, waiting eagerly for the opportunity to suckle (and kill) the newborn baby.

Baby-snatching fever[72]

Recitation: Lamaštu, daughter of Anu, by whom the gods swear, Inanna, trustworthy lady, lady of the black-headed people—may you be made to swear by heaven; may you be made to swear by earth. She is an [Elamite]; she has a large topknot.[73] She comes up from the swamp and then again goes out. [...] She is overpoweringly strong; she is teeth-gnashingly angry. [...]

She is [un]just and of low standing, the daughter of Anu. Anu her father (and) [Antu her mother], at her deeds which were not pleasing [and her ...] made her come down ⌜from⌝ [heaven]. She is endowed with ⌜wings⌝ and [flies] like a ⌜*lilītu*⌝.

Night turns to night and morning to morning for the woman whose entrance is ⌜fearsome(ly narrow)⌝.[74] The daughter of Anu daily counts the pregnant women; she goes around after those (about to) give birth. She counts up their [months]; she marks the days (of their confinement) onto the wall. For the lying-in women giving birth (this) is (her) incantation: "Bring me your sons so that

I can give them suck; let me put the breast into the mouth of your daughters."

She holds in her hands fever, cold, chills (and) frost. They (the hands) are full of ambiguous[75] (and) hidden things. Her body is covered with burning flames. Now and then, she spits venom; suddenly, she spits venom. Her venom is snake venom; her venom is scorpion venom. She murders the young men, ruins the young women (and) smites the children.

(32–35) [She ... the woman about to give birth. She makes (her) drink] the water of distress. [...] She enters the locked [house. She comes in by the window]; she slips in past the door-pivot. She ⌈suckles⌉ the infant on [her poisonous] milk.

(37–40) [She has smeared] his abdomen and then she has smeared his face. [... ; he] wails for food. ⌈Lamaštu⌉ and Labaṣu has smeared his face with poisonous venom. She has seized the ⌈chair⌉ from a place of mourning; she has gathered the ⌈dust⌉ from a place of mourning.

(41–46) Her teeth are the [teeth] of a dog; her talons are the talons of an eagle. [...]; her *tudittu*-pin[76] is broken, her breast exposed. Her [hand]s [are an *aluḫappu*-net]; her hold is limp. Her breasts are bathed [in] ⌈blood⌉.

Unpleasant as she might be, Lamaštu's continued presence was necessary in order to keep human population (literally) down to a dull roar: "Let there be an 'obliterator' (i.e., Lamaštu) among the people; let her seize the infant from the lap of the woman who bore it (lest the noise of mankind again become unbearable, tempting the gods to send another flood to destroy them)."[77]

Unloved and unlovable as she was, Lamaštu had ample reason to be disagreeable—the poor thing was hardly the vision of loveliness. Moreover, her personality profile strikingly resembles the role played in other societies by the ghosts of women who died in childbirth. It is interesting to note that, when she is being bribed to take witch figurines with her to the Netherworld, she is dressed in blue and receives *kispu*-offerings alongside the more usual gifts,[78] both attributes of ghosts. Like more ordinary hungry ghosts whose descendants no longer provided them with funerary offerings, Lamaštu inspired pity as well as fear. For this reason, although Lamaštu was treated with firmness and occasional violence, as often as not, the exorcist attempted to buy her off by making her an offering designed to send her on her way properly provisioned and/or to fulfill something of her need to mother, like the dog and pig in this ritual.

Lamaštu gets a husband[79]

Lamaštu, daughter of Anu, by whom the gods swear, ⌈Inanna⌉, trustworthy lady, lady of the black-headed people—may you be made to swear by heaven; may you be made to swear by earth. I have married you to a black dog, your slave; I have poured out for you well water (as a libation). Let up! Go away! Withdraw and distance yourself from the body of the infant, son of his god! I have made you swear by Anu and Antu. I have made you swear by Enlil and Ninlil. I have made you swear by Marduk and Ṣar-panitum. I have made you swear by the great gods of heaven and earth. If you ever return [to] this house (may you be punished)! Spell (and) Recitation.

Recitation to remove a persistent fever and Lamaštu.

Its ritual. You make a Lamaštu represented as imprisoned. You arrange offerings; you put twelve breads made from unsifted flour before her. You pour out well water for her (as a libation). You marry her to a black dog. For three days you have her sit at the head of the patient. You put the heart of a piglet in [her] mouth. You pour out hot broth for her. You put out dried bread for her. You give [her] a wooden *šikkatu*-vessel full of oil. You provide her with [provisions]. You recite the spell (every day) in the morning, noon, and evening. On the third day in the late afternoon you take her out and bury [her] in the corner of a wall.[80]

Childbirth

Prognosticating childbirth

The ancient Egyptian (and Hippocratic) method of inserting a garlic clove into the vagina and seeing whether the woman's breath smelled of garlic has no counterpart in ancient Mesopotamia. Instead the ancient physician used a test that is remarkably similar in principle to many modern medical tests that check for changes in vaginal acidity and salt, or levels of estrogen and progesterone, to determine whether or not a woman is pregnant.

Pregnancy tests[81]

You [wrap] one half shekel "white plant", a quarter shekel alum and [one shekel *tarmuš* in a tuft of wool]. You insert it [into] her ⌜vagina⌝. [She keeps it in place all night. [The next morning, (you take it out and)] you wash it. If the tuft of wool is red or streaked with blood red, [that woman is pregnant]. If that tuft of wool is green, that woman is not pregnant.[82]

If the inside of her vagina is [...] and her [...] protrudes when she is walking, do her workup over again. Her pregnancy is [...]. You have her drink the potion. If [...] her, a tampon should be worn. You have her drink *kukru*, *burāšu*-juniper, *ḫašû*-thyme, *nuḫurtu* and ⌜*abukkatu*⌝ resin < once >, twice, or three times. If she vomits, she is pregnant.[83]

Alternatively, you wrap *šambaliltu*-fenugreek in a tuft of wool and insert it into her ⌜vagina⌝. She wears it for three days and then, if the *šambaliltu*-fenugreek is speckled like myrrh/*šeguššu*-cereal,[84] that woman is pregnant.

Alternatively, you wrap "white plant" and *uḫḫūlu qarnānu* in a tuft of wool and insert it into her vagina. She wears it for three days and then, on the third day, you wash the tuft of wool with water. If the tuft of wool is [... , she is ...]. If the tuft of wool is green, red? and shiny, that woman [is ...].

Alternatively, [you wrap] Egyptian alum and [... If ...] or exudation is repeatedly seen, that woman [...]. When *burāšu*-juniper, *uḫḫūlu* and [...].

[If ...] her [...] is red and her body is [... the (usual) test] is not to be given to her. [You give her] one (tampon) of fresh *kukru* as ⌜thick⌝ as necessary to fill her up (?!).

You make (one of) the two batches of ashes into a dough with water (and) you wipe (her) off. You sprinkle (the other batch) with honey (and) pressed-out oil and when you have sprinkled it, you insert (it) once, twice, three times into her vagina. Her man should not approach her. For two days afterwards, nothing whatsoever should be given to her; they should remove what is inside her and the midwife should keep watch over her.

(This is) her test to see whether she is (still) pregnant or no (longer) pregnant. (Oops, I forgot to tell you about those two batches of ashes). You roast *usābu*-plant over a fire. You reduce (it) to ashes. In two batches, you grind (and) soften the ashes in hot pressed-out oil or you make (it) into a dough with water. You make a tampon; you may use as much as you wish.

If her womb looks abnormal,[85] so that it is stretched out (i.e., if the cervix is dilated), then you give her a tampon of fresh *kukru* as thick as necessary to fill her up and (after)wards you give her the tampon (mentioned) above, and she wears it.

If her womb sucks the tampon and it is softened by the waters, [that woman] is (still) pregnant. If the tampon stays in its original condition and her womb does not suck it, she is no (longer) pregnant; [the fruit of] her ⌜womb⌝ has been plucked out.

If (her womb) looks normal,[86] you give her the aforementioned tampon of fresh *kukru* as thick [as necessary to fill her up] and you may perform the (usual) ⌜test⌝.

Universal in sex-prediction schemes are a particular interest in variations that can be differentiated along a left–right axis. Mesopotamians shared the opinion of Chinese midwives that pregnancies with male babies are more difficult and male fetuses more demanding than female fetuses. Persian traditions (following Hippocrates) allow sexist attitudes to reverse the prediction. Men are happy and smiling and hard working; women are bad tempered and do nothing but eat and sleep; it follows that a woman who is bad tempered and wants to do nothing but eat and sleep is pregnant with a girl. It is also girls and not boys who are supposed to give their mothers bad complexions.[87]

Boy or girl?[88]

If a woman of childbearing age is pregnant and the top of her forehead is greenish, her fetus is male (var. it will be fully formed).

If the top of the forehead of a woman of childbearing age is white (and) shines, her fetus is female (var. it will become rich [i.e., fat]).

If it is dark, her fetus is female (var. it will be healthy).

If it is reddish, her fetus is male (var. it will die).

If (the top of the forehead of a woman of childbearing age) is full of 'grains', her fetus is male (var. richness [plenty of fat]).

If she is past (normal child-bearing age), her fetus is male.

If a muscle of a woman of childbearing age's forehead is reddish, her fetus is male.

If it is white, her fetus is female.

If (the blood vessels of a woman of childbearing age's temple), the lower ones to the left pulsate, her fetus is female.

If the lower ones to the right pulsate, her fetus is male.

Miscarriage

Herbal medicines[89]

You crush (and) sift these eight plants in equal proportions: ½ shekel of *tarmuš*, ½ shekel of *imḫur-lim*, ½ shekel of *imḫur-ešra*, ½ shekel of *nīnû*, ½ shekel of *uḫḫūlu qarnānu*, ½ shekel of alum, ½ shekel of *pillû* and ½ shekel of *ḫašû*. There should be no lumps left in it. You break it into tiny pieces (and) when you have broken the plants and their lumps into tiny pieces, you mix them thoroughly together. You weigh out ½ shekel of the resulting flour. Then, you mix 1 NINDA of honey into 4 NINDA of old barley beer. You mix the plants into it and you have her drink the plants while pregnant to prevent the waters from coming to the mouth (of the vagina). You recite the recitation: "Gula, great mistress, merciful mother who lives in the pure heavens" over it.

121

A perennial problem for young mothers is getting pregnant, only to suffer frequent miscarriages. Naturally, these mothers suspected that they had been the victims of sorcery. The ancient physician did not dismiss these suspicions, but allayed them by providing a means by which the woman's problem could be given to various recipients, including the very sorcerer or sorceress who had (in the patient's mind) caused the problem in the first place. Note that, although male children were obviously preferred, ancient Mesopotamian women (and/or their husbands) also desired daughters. The first ritual below promises the birth of a son as is indicated, inter alia, by the "masculine" lone-stone. The second ritual seems to have been designed for a child of either sex, whereas the choice of a female animal swaddled like a baby would seem to indicate that the third ritual was meant to deal with the specific problem of girls not coming to term.

May what is within me live![90]

THE FIRST RITUAL

(Ritual for) ⌈making bring to term(?)⌉ a woman who does not bring (her children) to term. At the setting of the sun, you isolate (her). You do her shaving onto a piece of leather and you put (it) around her neck in a new leather bag. You thread copper beads, lapis, masculine lone-stone, magnetic hematite, and *iṣbitu*-stone on red (wool). You wind three burls of red-dyed wool. You put (it) on her right hand.

And you give her bread, the short (bone) of a male sheep with its meat (still on it), (and) 2 *qû*-measures of seed grain besides. It spends the night at her head. In the morning, before the sun comes up, you suspend it from a wall. She goes and you place the bread, meat, and seed grain in a secluded place, at a crossroads, and she says five times: "The ones with names have given (them) to me; the ones without names have received (them) from me." When she has said (this), she takes off her garments and you bathe her with water. She gets up (out of the water) and dresses in another garment. And she does not look down behind her.[91]

She goes to the river and she goes down to the river. She draws water three times in a downstream direction and you recite (this) recitation over it. "You flow in a straight line (and) your waters make (things) flow in a straight line. Receive (evil) from me and take the sin, crime, offense, wrongdoing, evil (and) weakness from my body downstream with your water. May the rivers fill up (with it). May the marshes add good things. May they make the bond of my evil depart. River, you flow in a straight line (and) your waters make (things) flow in a straight line ('*šr*); cause me to give birth easily (*'šr*) so that I may sing your praises. The spell is not mine; it is the recitation of Ea and Asalluḫi. It is the recitation of Damu and Gula, the recitation of Ningirim, the mistress of recitations." Spell (and) recitation.

You say (this) three times. You give her ⌜soap-plant⌝ and you recite (this) recitation over it. "Soap-plant, soap-plant, Sîn conceived you; Šamaš made you grow; Addâ gave you water to drink from the clouds. […]. What the sorcerer did, I have washed off. What the sorceress did, I have washed off. What the caster (of spells) did, I have washed off. What the castress (of spells) did, I have washed off. What the sponsor of sorcery did, I have washed off. The sorcerer and sorceress, caster and castress ⌜did not give(?)⌝ (it to me). May it (stay) with (you); may it be imposed on you." Spell (and) recitation.

She comes up from the river. She goes to a potter's oven and takes shelter in the oven and she says as follows. "Pure oven, eldest daughter of Anu, from whose womb fire is withdrawn; hypogastric region inside which the heroic fire god makes his home. You are in good condition and your implements are in good condition. […]. You become full and then you become empty. But I am pregnant and then I do not bring to term what is in my womb. Please give me your things which are well formed. Take away the things which are not well formed. […] implements do not come out of your womb. May what is in my womb be in good health. May I see its […]. Where I live may it be pleasing." Spell (and) recitation.[92]

She goes down to a garden ⌜and⌝ takes shelter (under) a date palm and (says): "Date palm, who receives every wind, receive from me sin, crime, offense (and) wrongdoing and, where I live, (receive from me having to say) wah!, not sleeping, *di'u*, restlessness, (and) loss of infants, slaves and slave girls as many as there may be so that I may not die in my steppe. They inalterably keep coming back; it (the misfortune) is close by, downstream (and) in front. Where there is an ⌜early harvest⌝, you cause there to be a late harvest. Where there is a late harvest, you cause there to be an early harvest. You cause the ⌜broken⌝ tree to have flies (to pollinate it). You cause the tree which does not bear (fruit) to have fruit. Unhappiness (and) ill health and whatever insignificant little thing of my god and goddess I saw and stepped upon without realizing it; I don't know (what)—receive, receive it from me so that I may sing your praises." Spell (and) recitation.

Recitation. Šamaš, you are the one who entirely lights the four quarters. You are the lord of (those) above and below. You decide the case of caster and castress (of spells); you pronounce the decision of sorcerer and sorceress; you bring to an end the punishment of the wronged man and woman. She seeks you out, the woman who does not bring (her children) to term, on whom punishment was imposed, whom caster and castress (of spells) detain, whom the greeting of sorcerer [and sorceress] make bear a load, who gives birth to infants and then [...], who does not raise her infant and does not widen her relations [...], who does not look upon her relations, who is taken away and [...]. Šamaš, you are the one who entirely ⌈lights⌉ the four quarter[s]; make the woman's judgment (and) of the sorcerer [and sorceress pronounce their decision ...]".[93]

Recitation. [Ea], you are the one who created everything. You are the [...]. She seeks you out, the woman [who does not bring (her children) to term] on whom punishment was imposed. Before you [...] to the *apsû* (Ea's home and the repository of sweet water), make the woman's judgement and cancel her sin, ⌈her offense⌉ and her load. May the rivers carry (them) off. May the marshes add good things. May they make the bond of her evil depart. Make the woman escape the punishments which the caster and castress, the sorcerer and sorceress imposed; cancel (them). May she raise the infants among her male children. May she widen her relations. May she sing your praises. Spell (and) recitation.[94]

THE SECOND RITUAL

Ritual for making bring to term a woman who does not bring (her children) to term. You set out a censer (burning) juniper before Gula (goddess of healing). You pour out a libation of *miḫḫu*-beer and she (the patient) says as follows.

"Ninkarrak, ⌈exhalted⌉ mistress, your merciful mother, may the pregnant ewe of ⌈Šakkan⌉ and Dumuzi (gods of domestic animals) receive my pregnancy from me and give me her pregnancy. May she receive from me (my) inability to give birth right away and give me her ability to give birth right away."

She says (this) three times and then in the ⌈morning⌉ before Šamaš you ignite a brush pile on top of bricks. You scatter juniper. One should secure(?) a pregnant ewe which brings (its young) to term to an uprooted (pole) and two [...] carry it and the pregnant woman says as follows into the ears of the pregnant ewe.[95]

"Pregnant ewe of Šakkan and Dumuzi, take my pregnancy away and bring me your equivalent. Take away (my) inability to give birth right away and give me your ability to give birth right away."

She recites (this) three times each into both ears and, when she recites (it) she comes out from below the ewe. And when she comes out the seventh time, facing the [steppe], she spits into the ewe's mouth and she goes out to the steppe and leaves it (there).

THE THIRD RITUAL

[Ritual for] ⌜making bring to term a woman who does not bring (her children) to term⌝. [...] She places two breads (of) each (kind) at a crossroads and she takes off her garment in the midst of the crossroads and puts it back on again and then she says this spoken prayer.

"They brought (the evil) and I received (it); I brought it (back) so let them receive (it back) from me." She says this recitation three times and three times she puts out bread. She does not look down behind her.

You kill a female mouse and you have it grasp jewelry(?) (made) from cedar in its hands. You fasten *ballukku*-aromatic to its head and then you swaddle (it) with carded wool. You put (it) at a crossroads. She says this spoken prayer.

"They brought (the evil) and I received (it); I brought it (back) so let them receive (it back) from me." She says (this) and does not take (to get home) the road she took (to get there).

You repeatedly do this and this at dawn. You put (the bread and mouse) at a crossroads and she says this spoken prayer. "They brought (the evil) and I received (it); I brought it (back) so let them receive (it back) from me." She says (this) and does not take (to get home) the road she took (to get there).

You station a pregnant she-ass and the woman holds barley in the cup of her hand and crawls under the pregnant she-ass and she feeds the she-ass three times and ⌜says⌝ this spoken prayer to the she-ass. "May what is within you die (and) what is within me live." She crawls three times under the she-ass and three times she raises up barley to the she-ass.

At noon(?), you put *šigūšu*-grain at the crossroads and then you hang (it) from a window and then the pregnant woman rubs womb(?) and breast (with it). On the day of her labor pains, a girl grinds (it) and they make it into a dough with the water of her labor pains and you make a figurine of a man ⌜or⌝ you make a figurine of a woman. You go in until midnight. At midnight, you throw (it) into the street or they throw it into a road. She [...] and enters her house.

Besides sorcery, Lamaštu (see above) was a major producer of miscarriages. In her eagerness to suckle babies, this demonic midwife seems sometimes to have caused them to be born before their time. She also disturbed their sleep, before and after the birth.

She is a wolf, the daughter of Anu[96]

If (you want) sorcery not to approach a pregnant woman, (and) for her not to have a miscarriage, you grind magnetite, *guḥlu*-antimony, dust, *šubû*-stone, and dried "fox grape". You mix (it) with the blood of a male shelduck and cypress oil and if you rub (it) on her heart, her hypogastric region and her (vulva's) "head", sorcery will not ⌜approach⌝ [her].[97]

Alternatively, you take a potsherd (found) standing on edge at a crossroads and, if you bury (it) in the inner threshold, sorcery will be kept at bay.[98]

Alternatively, you bind masculine and feminine *šû*-stone on her right hand. If you recite the recitation: "He who lives in the darkness" three times over it, the sorcery will not approach her.[99]

"He who lives in the darkness, never seeing the light of the Sun, you have come out and seen the sunlight. May you be as calm as swamp water; may you sleep like the kid of a gazelle, until the rising of the Sun who releases you (from sleep)." [Spell (and)] ⌜recitation⌝.[100]

Recitation: She is furious, she is raging, she is a goddess, she is brilliant and she is a wolf, the daughter of Anu. Her foot is that of Anzu; her hands are dirty; her face has the appearance of the face of a ferocious lion. She comes up from the swamp and, as a result, her hair is loose, her *dīdu*-cloths are cut off. She walks in the tracks of oxen; she follows the tracks of sheep. Her hands are placed in flesh and blood. She comes in through the window; she slips in through the door pivot. She enters the house; she leaves the house, (saying): "Bring me your sons so that I may suckle them and your children so that I may rear them; let me put the breast into the mouth of your daughters." Ea, her "father", heard her and (said): "Instead, Daughter of Anu, directress of mankind, of your taking (the bread of tears and wailing)[101] as (your) provision and instead of having your hands laid in flesh and blood, instead of entering houses (and) leaving houses, receive from the merchant his *qannu* and his travel provisions; receive from the iron smith the bracelets appropriate to your hands and feet; receive from the silver smith the earrings appropriate to your ears; receive from the seal-cutter the carnelian appropriate to your neck; receive from the carpenter the comb, spindle, *tudittu*-pin,[102] distaff, and the *kirissu*-clasp appropriate to your thread."[103] I have made you swear by Anu, your father, Antu, your mother (and) Ea who created you. Spell (and) Recitation.[104]

You recite this recitation over the salve.[105]

Since Lamaštu caused miscarriages, it was logical to transfer the problem directly to her. Note that creation, meaning the creation of life, was something that women, as well as men, were capable of.

Lamaštu hoisted on her own petard[106]

[If a woman's children cannot] be saved, to save (them) (and) [for her to bear] only well formed male and female (children), you make [a figurine of the daughter of Anu out of] clay from the river meadows. You put […] in her hand. You fill a *burzigallu*-vessel and set it out. [You] ⌜set out⌝ [. …] and you strangle a female lamb but do not cut off its head. […] You swaddle it all over in cloth like a baby. [You provide it with] whatever it needs and place it on the river bank. [You set out] a censer (burning) juniper [and] you have her say as follows.

"You are the one ⌜who soothes⌝ the evil of my heart, the one who dispels my sin. Why do you create the evil of my heart, why do you not dispel my sin?" You have her say (this) three times and then that woman pours out a libation of beer. She puts the lamb down between her breasts. You have her say as follows.

"I did not bring my pregnancy to term. I gave birth (but) I did not create (life) (*banû*). May one who brings to term receive it from me and leave me (*wuššuru?!*) my reward (*banītu*). May I prosper (*ešēru*) and give birth safely (*šūšuru*) in the house where I dwell."

You have her say (this) three times and then you pour out first quality beer (mixed) with roasted barley flour before Šamaš. You put the shearling which is to receive (the evil) from her in her lap and you make it go to her breast. You put the figurine of the daughter of Anu (i.e., Lamaštu) and whatever (else) you (normally) put (with her) into a boat and make it cross to the other side of the river. You surround it with a magic circle and you recite this recitation.

"Mountains and rivers, seas and precious stones, heaven and earth (and) DN$_1$ whom DN$_2$ his father bore are her arraigners.

From now on, if you go to so-and-so daughter of so-and-so and return to the house where I dwell (may you be punished)! You are made to swear these things."

Difficult labor

To assist in labor, ancient Mesopotamian physicians employed a combination of massage and recitations. They also had labor-inducing potions. Particularly prominent in childbirth recitations are the moongod Sîn and the head of the Babylonian pantheon, Marduk. For more on these recitations, see below.

Inducing labor[107]

One cow of Sîn, "Maid of Sîn" (was) her name, she was richly adorned; she was luxuriant in shape. Sîn saw her and loved her. He put the shining *šubaḫu* of Sîn on her. He had her take the lead of the herd, going as herdsman after her. They pastured her on grass among the juiciest grasses; they gave her water to drink in the most satisfying of watering places. Concealed from the herd boy, without the herdsman seeing, a vigorous fat (bull) mounted the cow; he reared up (over) her tail(?).[108]

At the coming to an end of her days (and) the completion of her months, the cow became frightened; it frightened her herdsman. His face was downcast; all the herd boys mourned with him. At her bellowing; at her cries in labor, he threw himself to the ground.[109]

In heaven, the moon-crescent Sîn, heard her cry. He raised his hand towards heaven. Two protective divinities came down from heaven and one of them was carrying oil in a *pūru*-vessel. The other one brought down the water of giving birth.[110]

They smeared oil from a *pūru*-vessel onto her forehead. They sprinkled the water of giving birth over her whole body. A second time, they smeared oil from a *pūru*-vessel onto her forehead (and) sprinkled the water of giving birth over her whole body. While (they were) smearing it on a third time, the calf fell on the ground like a young gazelle. He made the calf's name "Suckling Calf". Just as "Maid of Sîn" gave birth straightaway, so may the adolescent who is having difficulty give birth. May the midwife not be kept waiting; may the pregnant woman be all right.[111]

Narundi, Naḫundi, and Nanam-gišir. (There was once) a cow of Sîn, "Maid of Sîn" (was) her name. At her bellowing, at her cries in labor, the moon crescent, Sîn, heard her cry. "Who is it, Narundi; who is it, Naḫundi?" "(It is) a cow, oh lord, who is having difficulty giving birth. Lord, pour down water from your bucket over her so that the sight of the cow 'Bride of Sîn' may be opened." May he come out like a snake; may he slither out like a little snake. Like a collapsing wall, may he not be able to lean backwards.[112] Spell (and) Recitation.

Its ritual: you pour dust from a crossroads, dust from a former threshold, dust from the upper and lower drainpipe (and) dust from a door drain into oil. You trim a thick reed at the top and base. You recite this recitation seven times over it. You fill the thick reed (with the oil) and you massage it in a downwards direction over the middle of the cash box.[113]

I am the great cow of Sîn, belonging to Sîn; I am pregnant and ready to gore. With my horn, I thrash the earth; with my tail, I make the whirlwind pass along. The boat is detained at the quay of death; the *magurru*-boat is held back at the quay of hardship. [At the command of] Ea, lord of spells, may the boat be loosed [from the quay] of ⌈death⌉; [may] the *magurru*-boat be freed [from the quay of hardship. Just like "Maid of Sîn" who] ⌈gave birth⌉ [straight away], ⌈so may⌉ [the adolescent who is having difficulty give birth]. May [the pregnant woman] ⌈be all right⌉. [May the midwife not be kept waiting;] may (the baby) come out promptly and see the light of the sun. Spell (and) Recitation.

Recitation: Run to me like a gazelle; flee to me like a little snake. I, Asalluḫi, am the midwife; I will receive you. Spell (and) Recitation.[114]

Its ritual: you buy a stick of *e'ru*-wood[115] from a shepherd. You recite the recitation seven times over it. If you lay it across her abdomen, she should give birth quickly.[116]

Recitation: (As for) the sealed woman who is made (too) narrow of womb,[117] you (Marduk = DINGIR.ŠÀ.ZU) are a god (DINGIR) and(!) also her midwife (ŠÀ.ZU); make her give birth. Spell (and) Recitation.

Its ritual: you recite the recitation seven times over a stick of *e'ru*-wood (purchased from) a shepherd and you roll it over her epigastrium in a downwards direction.

Recitation: *zalaḫ*, *izzalaḫ*, *zalaḫ* (probably meant to evoke SAL.LA.RA.AḪ, the woman having difficulty giving birth), may she live.

Recitation for a woman having difficulty giving birth.

If you have her drink *maštakal* (and) roasted barley flour (mixed) with oil and beer, she should give birth straight away.

If a woman has difficulty in giving birth, you grind together "fox grape", *lišān kalbi* (and) *maštakal*. You fill a *laḫannu*-vessel with *kurunnu*-beer and whisk these plants into it. If you have her drink (it) on an empty stomach, she should give birth promptly, etc. (more treatments follow).

The story of the moon god and his cow has quite a history. On the one hand, it stretches back to at least the Old Babylonian period and is supposed, by some, to be an Ur III composition.[118] On the other hand, Ibn Qutayba, a Muslim scholar of the ninth century AD reports: "Jesus passed by a cow which was calving in great distress. 'Oh Word of God,' the cow said, 'Pray that God may deliver me.' Jesus prayed, 'O Creator of the soul from the soul, begetter of the soul from the soul, deliver her.' The cow dropped its young."[119]

The cow of Sîn[120]

A cow is pregnant, a cow gives birth in the sheepfold of Šamaš, the pen of Šakkan. Šamaš saw her, crying; the (moon) whose rites are pure saw her, the tears coming (to his eyes). Why does Šamaš cry (and) the pure-in-rite's tears come? "For my cow which has not been opened, for my she-goat which has not given birth! ⌐Whom⌐ should I ⌐send⌐? [Whom should I] ⌐dispatch⌐ [to] the ⌐seven⌐ [and seven daughter]s of Anu? May they [...] their pot of [...] May they (the daughters of Anu) make the infant come straight out to me."[121]

Whether it be a male like a wild ram or a girl like a wild cow(?),[122] may (the infant) fall to the ground. Spell (and) Enuru. Recitation for a woman who is about to give birth.

It was the woman's job to load the boat of heaven (i.e., the fetus) with carnelian or lapis, which not only gave it life, but also determined its sex. Once the child had been born, it was essential to make sure that the child's gender corresponded with the sex that had been assigned to it. It was thus the custom for a boy to be handed, or made to look at, symbols of masculinity and for a girl to be made to take, or look at, symbols of femininity when the umbilical cord was cut.[123]

The boat of heaven[124]

(The handsome bull) having mounted the female in the pure pen, having mounted her in the fold, in the pure pen, he has deposited in her womb the true seed of mankind. The sperm deposited in her womb having coagulated, having given the male an offspring, the female put her teeth to the honey plant and fattened herself with it; she put her teeth to the honey plant, her favorite food, and fattened herself with it.

That female, it was her day, her month. It was the moment, her time of childbirth, she bent to the earth; her cries approached the sky; her cries approached the underworld; her echoing cries covered the fundament of heaven like a garment.

Like the boat of heaven, she furled her sails. She loaded the royal boat with merchandise. She loaded the boat (for carrying) carnelian and lapis lazuli with carnelian and lapis lazuli.

The wise one passed by, Asalluḥi saw her (and told his father Ea all about it and asked him what should be done, to which Ea replied): "Whatever I know, you know it too. When you have taken the [fat] of a pure cow, cream from a mother cow (and) when you have taken in hand (the things) which were placed in the abode of the divine bed-chamber[125] (and) when (while reciting) the ⌈spell⌉ of Eridu, you have taken hold of that woman's shoulders, back (and) chest, may (the waters) take free course like rain from heaven; may (she) be loosened like a ⌈knot⌉; may (the waters) flow down as if from the [teats of] the fundament of heaven.

If it is a boy, he grasps the mace (and) axe of his heroship. If it is a woman, a spindle and *kirissu*-clasp are to hand. May Gula, the meticulous administratress, (simultaneously) loosen the umbilical cord (and) reveal the destiny of the house of his father.

Recitation for a woman about to give birth. Its ritual: You mix oil and ghee and if you rub (it) on the flesh of the shoulders, (and) both sides of her chest, it should come out.

Giving birth to live children was a difficult and dangerous task. The boat (i.e., the fetus) had to be sailed across dark primordial waters (the amniotic fluid) to moor at the "quay of death" (the Netherworld) where it received a soul which had then to return and moor at the "quay of life" (the upper world).

The quay of death[126]

[Recitation: The cow of Sîn] took in [the semen] and so made clouds; the waterskin was full (i.e., her udders filled with milk). The earth was plowed up with her horn. [With her tail, she made the whirlwind pass along.] Sîn [took] the road; [before] Enlil, [he cries (and) his tears come. Why] does ⌈Sîn⌉ cry, the pure-in-rite's tears [come]? [...] Because of my cow which has not yet given birth, [because of my she-goat which has not yet] ⌈been opened⌉.[127]

The boat is [de]tained [at the quay] of difficulty ("narrows"); the *magurru*-boat is held back [at the quay] of hardship. [Whom should I] ⌈send to merciful⌉ Marduk? May the boat be loosed [from the quay] of difficulty; may the *magurru*-boat be freed [from the quay] of hardship. [Come out to me l]ike a snake; slither out to me like a little snake. May the [...] relax so that the infant may fall to the earth and see the sunlight.

[Recitation] for a woman who is having difficulty giving birth.

[Its ritual. ...] You pour oil on "sweet reed". [... You rub (it) gently] over her abdomen and hypogastric region. The infant should ⌜come out straight away⌝.

Recitation: [...] having difficulty [. ...] having difficulty. ⌜Come⌝(?) [...] Fly! Come(?) [...] Let it come out. [...] "(Who is it), Naḫundi; (who is it), Narundi?" Run like a gazelle; slither like a snake. I am [Asalluḫi]. May [...] see him. Recitation.

Recitation: The boat is ⌜detained⌝ at the quay of death; the *magurru*-boat is ⌜held back⌝ at the quay of hardship. [Come down] to me from heaven. Command Belet-ili to have mercy so that it may go straight down the road. May it come out from ⌜hardship⌝; [let it see] the sun.

Recitation for a woman who is having difficulty giving birth.

Its ritual: You whisk *pūru*-oil into [...]. [If you massage (her) in a] down[wards direction], she should give birth straight away.

[...] Her loincloths are loosened [...] Stand beside her, Marduk. Entrust life, the spell of life. (With) this storm am I surrounded; reach me.

May the boat be safe in [...]. May the *magurru*-boat go aright in [...]. May her massive mooring rope be loosened, and may her locked gate be opened. (May) the mooring rope of the boat (be moored) to the quay of health, the mooring rope of the *magurru*-boat to the quay of life. May the limbs be relaxed; may the sinews be slackened. May the sealed places be loosened; may the offspring come out, a separate body, a human creature. May he come out promptly and see the light of the sun.

Like a hailstone (which can never go back to the heavens), may the (fetus) not be able to return to what is behind him. Like one who has fallen from a wall, may he not be able to turn his breast. Like a leaky drainpipe (which cannot hold water), may none of the (mother's) waters remain.[128]

When Asalluḫi heard this, he became exceedingly concerned for her life. At the command of Ea, he exalted his name. He cast the incantation of life (and) the spell of health. He loosed (her) mooring rope; he undid [her] ⌜knotting⌝. The locked gates [were] ⌜opened⌝. The ⌜limbs⌝ were relaxed; [the sinews slackened]. The sealed places were loosened; [the offspring came out], a ⌜separate⌝ body, a [human] creature. He came out promptly and saw [the light of the sun].

Like a hailstone, he did not return [backwards]. Like one who had fallen from a wall, he did not turn [his breast]. Like a leaky drainpipe, none [of her waters] remained. The incantation of Asalluḫi, the secret of ⌜Eridu⌝, the true yes of Ea, the renowned spell which Mami requested for health('s sake and which) ⌜king⌝ [Ea] gave to help make the foetus come out straight away.

Recitation for a woman having difficulty giving birth.

Its ritual: you mix hailstone, dust from the parapet of an abandoned wall (and) dust from an overflowing drain with *pūru*-oil. If you massage (her) in a downward direction, that woman should give birth straight away.

The goddess Inanna/Ištar assisted pregnant women in their quest for live children. If she was amenable, the goddess would herself pole the (foetus) boat, ensuring successful childbirth. If not …

Steering the boat loaded with cedar[129]

[Enuru recitation. The woman who is about to give birth steers as she goes along like a ship. Pure Inanna] steers [as she goes along] like a ship. [Ninḫursag] steers [as] she ⌜goes along⌝ like a ship.[130] [She] steers as she goes along […] like a ship. She steers as she goes along the ⌜base⌝ of heaven and earth like a ship.

Like a boat (for carrying) perfume, it (her boat) is loaded (with) perfume. Like a boat (for carrying) cedar, it (her boat) is loaded (with) cedar. Like a boat (for carrying) cedar fragrance, it (her boat) is [loaded] (with) cedar fragrance. Like a boat (for carrying) carnelian and lapis lazuli, it (her boat) is [loaded] (with) carnelian and lapis lazuli; (yet) she knows not whether it is carnelian; she knows not whether it is lapis lazuli. Sum.: The boat, when it has spent time at the quay, leaves the quay. Akk: She steers to the quay of rejoicing.

Asalluḫi (Marduk) ⌜saw⌝ her, [entered the house of his father Enki (Ea) and said: "My father, the woman who is about to give birth steers as she goes along like a ship. She steers as she goes along … like a ship. She steers as she goes along the base of heaven and earth like a ship."]

[When he had repeated this, Enki answered his son Asalluḫi: "Asalluḫi, what can I tell you? What further can I add for you? What I know, you also know, and what you] know I also [know]."

"Go, my son! When [you have taken] in hand a reed of the "small marsh" of Eridu, pour into it the fat of a pure cow (and) the cream of a mother cow. Mix (it) together with dust from a crossroads[131] (and) […]."

"Break (the reed) over his (the child's) umbilical cord and then[132] [if] it is a boy, make him look at a mace; [if] it is a ⌜girl⌝, make her look at [spindle] and *kirissu*-clasp. [Let the infant] come out [into the light] of the sun (i.e. be born alive). [Recitation for a woman] who is about to give birth. [The month] of Ayyaru."

Since the month name in Sumerian (GUD.SI.SÁ) literally means "the ox comes out straight away", it was an obviously appropriate time to be delivering a child. The involvement of Marduk, the head of the Babylonian pantheon, in childbirth, is related to his role in creation. In order to create dry land, he bolted up the sky to hold back the waters. Here, conversely, his job was to unbolt them, allowing the baby to be born.

Through the unlocked door[133]

From the fluids of intercourse was created a skeleton; from the tissue of the muscles was created an offspring. In the turbulent and fearful sea waters, in the distant waters of the ocean where the little one's arms are bound, whose midst the eye of the sun does not illumine, Asalluḫi, the son of Enki, saw him. He loosened his many-knotted bonds. He made a path for him; he opened a way for him, (saying): "Paths are ⌜opened⌝ for you; ways are ⌜allotted⌝ to you." [The divine] ⌜midwife⌝ sits (waiting) for you, she who created [...], she who created all of us. She has told the lock bar: "You are released. [Your] door bolts are ⌜loosened⌝; [your] doors are ⌜left unlocked⌝." [Should he] knock at [the door], (say): "Let yourself out like a favorite child." Recitation for a woman who is about to give birth.

It is striking, especially in view of the Assyrians' fearsome reputation among modern scholars for misogyny, that the two recitations that express the greatest empathy with, and concern for, the mother (as opposed to the complex of mother and child), namely "Enveloped in the dust of death" and "Cast adrift", are provably Assyrian compositions, which have no Babylonian parallels. In Medieval Europe, women who died in childbirth were denied Christian burial; by contrast, Islam regards such women as martyrs.

Enveloped in the dust of battle[134]

The woman in travail is having difficulty giving birth; she is having difficulty giving birth. The infant is stuck fast; the infant is stuck so fast as to end (her) life. The door bolt is secure; the door is made fast against the suckling kid—that one (f) and the lamb to be plucked. The creatress is enveloped in the dust of death. Like a chariot she is enveloped in the dust of battle; like a plow she is enveloped in the dust of the forest. Like a warrior in the fray, she is cast down in her blood. Her eyes are dimmed; she cannot see.

Her lips are covered; she cannot open (them). Her eyes are clouded (with) a deathly fate or fates (Either she or the baby or both may die). Her [...] continually tremble; her ears do not hear. Her breast is not tight(ly corsetted); her headcloths are scattered. She is not covered with a cloak, (yet) she is not ashamed. Merciful Marduk, stand by and say something to her. (With) this confusion am I surrounded, so come to me. Bring forth that sealed up one, a creation of the gods, a creation of man. Let it come out and see the light. Enuru spell; a spell for a woman in travail.[135]

Cast adrift[136]

"Why are you cast adrift like a boat in the midst of the stream, your rungs broken, your ropes cut? Why, your face veiled, do you cross the river of Assur?" "How could I not be cast adrift, my ropes not be cut? On the day I bore fruit, how happy I was! I was happy; happy my husband. On the day of my labor pains, my face was overcast; on the day I gave birth, my eyes were clouded. With my hands opened (in supplication), I prayed to Bēlet-ilī (saying): 'You are the mother of those who give birth, save my life!' (But) when Bēlet-ilī heard me, she veiled her face (saying): '[...] Why do you keep praying to me?' [My husband who] ⌜wedded⌝ me gave a cry, (saying): '[Do not abandon] me, my beloved wife!' [...] over the years [...] (this) land of wrongs. [My female companion] used to go about ⌜Assur⌝; (now) she cries out in woe. [Since] those days (when) I was with my husband, (when) I lived with him[137] who was my lover, death slunk stealthily into my bedroom. He made me leave my house; he separated me from my husband (and) set my feet to a land from which I will never return."

Abbreviations

4R[2]   Henry C. Rawlinson and Theophilus Pinches. 1891. *The Cuneiform Inscriptions of Western Asia: A Selection from the Miscellaneous Inscriptions of Assyria*. Volume 4, 2nd edition. London: R. E. Bowler.

AOAT 43   Nils Heessel. 2000. *Babylonisch-assyrische Diagnostik*. Alter Orient und Altes Testament 43. Münster: Ugarit Verlag.

AUAM   Museum number of a cuneiform tablet in the Andrews University Archeological Museum.

BAM	Franz Köcher, 1963–80. *Die babylonisch-assyrische Medizin in Texten und Untersuchungen*. Berlin: Walter de Gruyter.
BM	Unpublished cuneiform tablet in the British Museum.
BRM	Albert T. Clay, 1912–23. *Babylonian Records in the Library of J. Pierpont Morgan*. New Haven: privately printed.
CAD	*The Assyrian Dictionary of the Oriental Institute of the University of Chicago*. Chicago: The Oriental Institute, 1956–2011.
CT	*Cuneiform Texts from Babylonian Tablets in the British Museum*. London: The Trustees of the British Museum.
DABM	JoAnn Scurlock and Burton Andersen, 2005. *Diagnoses in Assyrian and Babylonian Medicine*. Champaign: University of Illinois.
DPS	Esagil-kin-apli, ca. 1050 BC. *Diagnostic and Prognostic Series* SA.GIG. Borsippa.
K	Unpublished cuneiform tablet in the Kuyunjik collection of the British Museum.
KAR	Erich Ebeling, 1919–20. *Keilschrifttexte aus Assur religiösen Inhalts*. Wissenschaftliche Veröffentlichung der Deutschen Orient Gesellschaft 28, 34. Leipzig: J. C. Hinrichs.
KUB	*Keilschrift Urkunden aus Boghazköi*. Berlin: Vorderasiatische Abteilung der Staatlichen Museen.
LKA	Erich Ebeling, 1953. *Literarische Keilschrifttexte aus Assur*. Berlin: Akademie Verlag.
LKU	Adam Falkenstein, 1931. *Literarische Keilschrifttexte aus Uruk*. Berlin, Vorderasiatische Abteilung der Staatlichen Museen.
MLC	Museum number of a cuneiform tablet in the J. Pierpont Morgan library collection.
PBS 1/2	Henry F. Lutz, 1919. *Selected Sumerian and Babylonian Texts*. Publications of the Babylonian Section of the University of Pennsylvania Museum. Philadelphia.
PSD	*The Sumerian Dictionary of the University Museum of the University of Pennsylvania*. Philadelphia: The Babylonian Section of the University Museum, 1992ff.
RA	*Revue d'Assyriologie*.
STT	O.R. Gurney, J.J. Finkelstein and P. Hulin, 1957, 1964. *The Sultantepe Tablets*. London: Occasional Publications of the British Institute of Archaeology at Ankara 3, 7. British Institute of Archaeology at Ankara.
TDP	René Labat, 1951. *Traité akkadien de diagnostics et pronostics médicaux*. Paris: Académie internationale d'histoire de sciences.
UET	*Ur Excavations Texts*. London: The British Museum.
UM	Museum number of a cuneiform tablet in the University Museum of the University of Pennsylvania.

VS   Vorderasiatische Schriftdenkmäler der Königlichen/Staat-
lichen Museen zu Berlin.

YBC   Museum number of a cuneiform tablet in the Yale
Babylonian Collection.

YOS   *Yale Oriental Series: Babylonian Texts.* New Haven: Yale
University Press.

Notes

1 DPS XIII G$_2$ 18 = TDP 124 iii 25 (DABM 13.264). DABM is an abbreviation for Scurlock and Andersen, 2005.
2 DPS XVII:40 (AOAT 43.199; DABM 13.265).
3 DPS XXXVII A obv. 13 = TDP 214:13 (DABM 19.18).
4 DPS III A obv. 13–14//C obv. 4–5 = TDP 18:4–5 (DABM 12.74).
5 Restored from the preceding line.
6 DPS XXVI:82'–83' (AOAT 43.285; DABM 19.20).
7 DPS XXII:53–54 (AOAT 43.256; DABM 19.22).
8 DPS XXVI:73'–74' (AOAT 43.284; DABM 19.23).
9 The classic study is still Lackenbacker, 1971, 119–54. For an Old Babylonian exemplar, as well as corrections and commentary to Lackenbacker, see Farber, 1989a, 14–35. A previous translation of these passages appears in Foster, 1996, vol. 2, 855–57. For similar complaints, see Lackenbacker, 1971, 135–36 r. i 2'–9''; Farber, 1989a, 13–24.
10 See Shaffer, 1963, 91–92: 273–78.
11 Lackenbacker, 1971, 131–32 i 1–ii 4.
12 Restored from von Weiher, 1983, no. 7: 1'–18' and no. 6: 36–45. For how these two texts relate to one another, see Geller, 1988, 1–23. To note is that Geller's translation is not only awkward, but inaccurate as, for example, p. 19 l. 75, which translates "setting sun" as "East".
13 Lackenbacker, 1971, 134–35 iii 4'–27'.
14 See Borger, 1981, 628 ad 291ff.
15 Restored from von Weiher, 1983, no. 7 r. 5–13.
16 For further discussion, see Scurlock, 1991, 153–55.
17 Lackenbacker, 1971, 124 i 1–22.
18 Lackenbacker, 1971, 126 ii 1–18.
19 Lackenbacker, 1971, 126–28, rev. i 1'–24', ii 3'–19'.
20 For the expression, see Tsukimoto, 1985, 140–45.
21 DPS XXII:6–9 (AOAT 43.251–52; DABM 16.23–24).
22 For more on this subject, see Scurlock, 2006, 61–103.
23 This is cited as an omen in CT 31.44 iv 11, apud CAD Q 255b.
24 C. Wilcke, 1985, 42–51; the text is edited; 188–209. See also Scurlock, 1989/90, 107–12. A previous translation of this passage appears, alongside other love charms, in Foster, 1996, vol. 1, 141–47.
25 KAR 61: 1–10. This is edited in Biggs, 1967, 70–71. There was an earlier edition in Ebeling, 1925, pp. 8–15.
26 The Sumerian is barbarous and the sentiment crude, but there is really no other way to take this line.
27 KAR 158 vii 43, apud CAD R 137a.
28 BRM 4 20:61, apud CAD E 38b.
29 MUNUS *šá e-dul-la.* For the interpretation of this term, see Waetzoldt, 1990, no. 5.

30 KAR 61: 22–25. This is edited in Biggs, 1967, 71. See also Reiner, 1990, 421–23 (with a different interpretation).
31 KAR 236: 1–17//KAR 70 r. 10–24//KAR 243 obv.(!) 1–14. This is edited in Biggs 1967, pp. 32–35. A translation of the recitation appears in Foster, 1996, vol. 2, p. 871 and of the recitation and ritual in Farber, 1987a, 274.
32 For the reading, see CAD D 120b s.v. *daššu* A.
33 LKA 101 r.(!) 12–19//LKA 95 r. 6–11//STT 280 iv 37–41. This is edited in Biggs 1967, pp. 35–36. A translation of the recitation also appears in Foster, 1996, vol. 2, 869.
34 KAR 70 r. 25–30. This is edited in Biggs, 1967, 40–41.
35 S. Parpola and Watanabe, 1988, no. 6 § 71.
36 Edited in Miller, 2004, 11–132.
37 STT 257 r. 2–16. This text is unedited.
38 See CAD S 132a s.v. *sâmu* mng. 2.
39 Compare the alleged practice of bringing down the moon for purposes of witchcraft.
40 Reading *an-<ni>-ziq-ti-ni*.
41 Restored from Scheil, 1921, 21–27, no. 17 obv. i 1'–10'.
42 Scheil, 1921, no. 17 rev. ii 1'–18'; edited, 21–27. See also J.A. Scurlock, 2002, 372.
43 BAM 235: 10–16//BAM 236 r. 1'–9'. Texts relating to excessive bleeding (and the Akkadian word for the condition) are discussed in Finkel, 1980, 37–52.
44 The word is extremely rare; the choice of this particular tool (as opposed to a spade etc.) may have been dictated by the fact that *mirtu* also means "cow".
45 Compare: "A cloud, a cloud, a red cloud has risen and covered (another) red cloud. Red rain has risen and fecundated the red earth. A red flood has risen and filled a red canal. Let the red farmer bring a red plow and a red hod and let him dam up the red water" (CT 23.37 iii 65–67 [CAD S 131b s.v. *sâmu* mng e]).
46 BAM 240 (KAR 195):25'–28'. See DABM 12.116.
47 BAM 240 (KAR 195):33'–38'. See DABM 12.117–18.
48 BAM 240 (KAR 195):17'–19'. See DABM 12.120.
49 BAM 240:20'–24'. See DABM 4.15.
50 BAM 240:30'–32', 39'–66'. See DABM 12.123–25.
51 Lambert, 1969, 29–30: 1–31; edited, pp. 28–39. See DABM 12.122.
52 For details, see Farber, 1983, 444–46 and especially Wiggermann, 2000, 217–49.
53 4R² 56 (w/ K 4929) iii 5–iv 12//KAR 239 ii 1–22. See Myhrman, 1902, 160–67.
54 Restored from Nougayrol, 1969, 396 ii 3'–6'.
55 See Nougayrol, 1969, 396 ii 7'–13'.
56 For the translation, see Civil, 1982, 2 n. 4.
57 See Nougayrol, 1969, 396 ii 14'–17'.
58 See Nougayrol, 1969, 396 ii 18'–21'.
59 See Klein, 1983, 255–84 ("toggle pin").
60 For a discussion of the gifts given to Lamaštu, see Farber, 1987b, 85–105. It is there argued that *šiddu* is some sort of rolled carpet. However, it seems odd that a carpenter (see below) should provide a textile rather than something made of wood.
61 See Nougayrol, 1969, 396 ii 22'–23'.
62 Restored from Nougayrol, 1969, 396 ii 24'–28'.
63 Restored from K 4929 (See Myhrman, 1902, 196).
64 Restored from 4R² 55 rev. 31–33. Myhrman, 1902, 194–95.
65 4R² 58 iii 13–27//PBS 1/2.113 iii 2–14. See Myhrman, 1902, 178–79 and Ungnad, 1921, 69–71. A previous translation appears in Foster, 1996, vol. 2, 851.
66 CT 17.50: 7–19, 21–23.
67 4R² 58 ii 25–58//PBS 1/2.113 ii 63–85//STT 143: 2ff//*RA* 65.173: 9–19. See Myhrman, 1902, 174–77 and Ungnad, 1921, 69–71.

68 This is restored from the similar 4R² 58 ii 58. PBS 1/2.113 gives the much more polite commentary version of this line: The canebrake(!) is her(!) creation; her(!) ⌐rulerships⌐ (a pun on "dung") extend to the *apsû*.

69 For the translation, see Civil, "Lexicography," p. 2, n. 4.

70 Restored from the similar 4R² 55 no. 1: 5–9.

71 Farber, 2007, 137–45 wishes to see Lamaštu as Sudden Infant Death Syndrome (SIDS), by which he means any unspecific and untreatable condition affecting infants. This is not what is meant by Sudden Infant Death Syndrome. In any case, the condition produced by Lamaštu was both specific (otherwise it could not have been identified as Lamaštu as opposed to, say, Gula) and treatable (otherwise we would have neither medical nor magical treatments for the condition, whereas we have both). She certainly caused a fever of some sort and her inclusion in anti-miscarriage rituals indicates that, when the victim was a pregnant woman, spontaneous abortions were known to result. Whether Lamaštu's fever was specifically typhoid is another matter, but it seems likely. For more on this subject see Scurlock and Andersen, 2005, 483–85 and Scurlock, 1991, 155–59.

72 LKU 33: 1–46//4R² 56 ii 28ff//KAR 239 i 1–34. See Myhrman, 1902, 160–61.

73 She is an Elamite because she comes up (*e-lam-ma*) from the swamp. The topknot was a feature of Elamite women's headdress shown on Neo-Assyrian reliefs.

74 The expression is usually used of mountain passes. The point is that she is too narrow to give birth and, consequently, day after day passes with no baby emerging.

75 Reading *ta-pil-tim* (from *apālu*: to answer; cf. *tapalu*: pair).

76 See Klein, 1983, 255–84 ("toggle pin").

77 Atrahasīs III vii 3–4. See Kilmer, 1972, 160–77.

78 D. Schwemer, 2006, 4–5, 7, 9 rev. 20–27a.

79 4R² 56 (w/ K 4929) i 11–29//PBS 1/2 113 i 3–11. See Myhrman, 1902, 154–57. A previous translation appears in Farber, 1987a, 259–60.

80 Restored from 4R² 55 no. 1 rev. 20–25. See Myhrman, 1902, 192–93.

81 UET 7.123 obv. 1-rev. 14'. This is edited in Reiner, 1982, 124–38.

82 The translation is restored from BM 42313+43174 r. 29–32.

83 "If she vomits" is literally "and her vomiting"—the construction is an Aramaism.

84 The text consistently omits determinatives which make it unclear whether this is ŠEM.ŠEŠ or ŠE.MUŠ₅.

85 This is literally "has turned over/fallen flat on its face".

86 This is literally "has not turned over/fallen flat on its face".

87 For bibliography and further discussion, see Scurlock and Andersen, 2005, 274–79.

88 DPS XXXVI A 1–12.

89 BM 78963: 60–65.

90 von Weiher, 1998, no. 248. For fuller discussion, see Scurlock, 2002b, 209–23.

91 The family ghosts (who have names) are to give their names (i.e., live boys) to the patient and the forgotten ghosts (who have no names) are to take the patient's no-names (the stillborn male children symbolized by the offerings) in return.

92 The choice of a potter's oven is dictated by the patient's problem; it is in some sense also a womb from which fetuses (pots) regularly emerge, sometimes "whole" (also "well" in Akkadian) and sometimes cracked or broken. We may presume that the potter was paid for his oven to compensate him for the hoped-for loss of crockery.

93 This recitation was apparently meant to be recited to the setting sun to accompany the amulets.

94 This recitation was apparently meant to be recited to the river to accompany the river section.

95 As the third ritual makes clearer, she is supposed to crawl under the suspended ewe.

96 von Weiher, 1988, no. 84: 56–78. For a discussion, see Farber, 1989b, 229–30.

97 Restored from LKA 9: 7–13 and BM 42327+//BM 51246: 1–4. See Farber, 1989c, 110 § 39 and 112 § 39A.
98 Restored from BM 42327+//BM 51246: 5–6. See Farber, 1989c, 112 § 39A.
99 Restored from BM 42327+//BM 51246: 7–9. See Farber, 1989c, 112–14 § 40.
100 Restored from BM 42327+//BM 51246: 10–13. See Farber, 1989c, 112–14 § 40.
101 See Myhrman, 1902, 162: 21.
102 See Klein, 1983, 255–84 ("toggle pin").
103 For a discussion of the gifts given to Lamaštu, see Farber, 1987b, 85–105. It is there argued that šiddu is some sort of rolled carpet. However, it seems odd that a carpenter should provide a textile rather than something made of wood.
104 Restored from Thureau-Dangin, 1921, 163 rev. 13–29//Farber, 1989c, pls. 14–15: 14–38. A previous translation appears in Foster, 1996, vol. 2, 849.
105 Restored from Farber, 1989c, pls. 14–15: 39.
106 von Weiher, 1998, no. 84: 1–16. For many of the restorations and a discussion, see Farber, 1987b, 225–26.
107 BAM 248 i 37–iii 9. See Veldhuis, 1989, 239–60.
108 Compare Lambert, 1965, 286: 20–25; 1969, 31: 53–56.
109 Compare Lambert, 1965, 286: 25–29; 1969, p. 31: 56–57.
110 Compare Lambert, 1965, 286: 29–31; Lambert, 1965, 31: 57–60 (with two daughters of Anu instead of the protective divinities).
111 Compare Lambert, 1965, 286: 32–36; 1969, 31: 60–62; KUB. 4 13: 6–12. For more on this recitation, see Ebeling, 1922, 65–78 and Veldhuis, 1991. For a comparison between this and other versions of the same text, see Röllig, 1985, 260–73. Previous translations appear in Farber, 1987a, 274–76 and Foster, 1996, vol. 2, 876–77.
112 The point is that a wall that is collapsing cannot straighten up again but must keep falling, and so must the baby. For the translation, see Farber, 1987a, 276.
113 Farber, 1987a, 276 suggests taking this as "buckled belly." It refers in any case to the pregnant woman's abdominal region.
114 A previous translation appears in Foster, 1996, vol. 2, 877.
115 It is probably not irrelevant that erû means: "to be pregnant".
116 For a translation of iii 36–iv 5, see Farber, 1987a, 276–77.
117 CAD R 263b suggests that "womb" might be an irregularly constructed: "Have mercy!", referring to Marduk. In CAD Š/I 16b, the passage is therefore translated: "O Marduk, have pity on the woman having difficulty in birth, Šazu(?), you are her midwife, make her give birth."
118 Stol, 2000, 61–62.
119 This is translated in Khalidi, 2001, 108, no. 103.
120 VS 17.34: 1–18. The text is edited in van Dijk, 1972, 339–48. A previous translation appears in Foster, 1996, vol. 1, 137.
121 For restorations and interpretation, see Farber, 1990, 308.
122 See Stol, 2000, 64. He follows the suggestion of Michel and Wasserman, 1997, no. 64.
123 For a discussion, see Scurlock, 1991, 149–50.
124 VS 17.33: 1–30. The text and its parallel, UM 29-15-367, are edited in van Dijk, 1975, 52–79. See also van Dijk, 1972, 346–48.
125 See Volk, 1995, 150–51; cf. PSD A 66a.
126 BAM 248 iii 10–iv 5. See Veldhuis, 1989, 239–60.
127 The text is restored from the similar VS 17.34: 1–10 (q.v.).
128 A previous translation appears in Foster, 1996, vol. 2, 878.
129 AUAM 73.3094: 1–61. The text is edited in Cohen, 1976, 133–40. It is roughly parallel to MLC 1207, which is edited in van Dijk, 1975, 52–79.
130 The first three lines are restored from a parallel text which is edited in Farber, 1984, 311–16.

131 This has been collated by Finkel, 1980, 48 n. 25.
132 Restored from 11N-T3: 12, which is a commentary edited in Civil, 1974, 331–36.
133 YBC 4603 (YOS XI.86): 1–28. The text is edited in van Dijk, 1973, 502–7. For a discussion, see Veldhuis, 1999, 39–41. A previous translation appears in Foster, 1996, vol. 1, 138.
134 Lambert, 1969, 31: 33–50; edited, 28–39.
135 A previous translation appears in Foster, 1996, vol. 2, 875.
136 A. Livingstone, 1989. See also E. Reiner, 1985, especially pp. 86–89. A previous translation appears in Foster, 1996, vol. 2, 890. See also K. Hecker, 1989, 780–81.
137 For further discussion of childbirth in ancient Mesopotamia, see Scurlock, 1991 and Stol, 2000.

Bibliography

Biggs, R.D., 1967. *Šà.zi.ga: Ancient Mesopotamian Potency Incantations*, Texts from Cuneiform Sources 2, Locust Valley: J.J. Augustin.
Borger, R., 1981. "Review of The Assyrian Dictionary of the University of Chicago, vol. M/I-II," *Bibliotheca Orientalis* 38, 628 ad 291ff.
Civil, M., 1974. "Medical Commentaries from Nippur," *Journal of Near Eastern Studies* 33, 331–336.
——, 1982. "Studies on Early Dynastic Lexicography I," *Oriens Antiquus* 21, 1–26.
Cohen, M.E., 1976. "Texts from the Andrews University Archeological Museum," *Revue d'Assyriologie* 70, 133–40.
van Dijk, J., 1972. "Une variante du theme de 'l'Esclave de la Lune'," *Orientalia* N.S. 41, 339–48.
——, 1973. "Une incantation accompagnant la naissance de l'homme," *Orientalia* N.S. 42, 502–7.
——, 1975. "Incantations accompagnant la naissance de l'homme," *Orientalia* N.S. 44, 52–79.
Ebeling, E., 1922. "Keilschrifttafeln medizinischen Inhalts III," *Archiv für die Geschichte der Medizin* 14, 65–78.
——, 1925. *Liebeszauber im Alten Orient*, Mitteilung der Altorientalischen Gesellschaft 1/1, Leipzig: J.C. Hinrichs.
Farber, G., 1984. "Another Old Babylonian Childbirth Incantation," *Journal of Near Eastern Studies* 43, 311–16.
Farber, W., 1983. "Lamaštu" in *Reallexikon der Assyriologie*, vol. 6/5–6, Berlin: Walter de Gruyter, 444–46.
——, 1987a. "Rituale und Beschwörungen in akkadischer Sprache" in Farber, W., H. M. Kümmel, and W. H. Ph. Römer, eds, *Texte aus der Umwelt des Alten Testaments* II/2: *Religiöse Texte*. Gütersloh: Gütersloher—Gerd Mohn, 259–77.
——, 1987b. "Tamarisken-Fibeln-Skolopender" in Rochberg-Halton, F., ed., *Language, Literature and History (Fs. Reiner)*, American Oriental Series 67, New Haven: American Oriental Society, 85–105.
——, 1989a. "(W)ardat-lilî(m)," *Zeitschrift für Assyriologie* 79, 14–35.
——, 1989b. "Lamaštu, Enlil, Anu-ikṣur: Streiflichter aus Uruks Gelehrtenstuben," *Zeitschrift für Assyriologie* 79, 229–30.
——, 1989c. *Schlaf, kindchen, Schlaf! Mesopotamische Baby-Beschwörungen und Rituale*, Mesopotamian Civilizations 2, Winona Lake: Eisenbrauns.
——, 1990. "Mannam Lušpur ana Enkidu: Some New Thoughts about an Old Motif," *Journal of Near Eastern Studies* 49, 299–321.

——, 2007. "Lamaštu—Agent of a Specific Disease or a Generic Destroyer of Health" in Finkel, I.L. and M.J. Geller, eds, *Disease in Babylonia*, Cuneiform Monographs 36, Leiden: Brill, 2007, 137–45.

Finkel, I.L., 1980. "The Crescent Fertile," *Archiv für Orientforschung* 27, 37–52.

Foster, B., 1996. *Before the Muses: An Anthology of Akkadian Literature*, 2nd edn, Bethesda: CDL, 2 vols.

Geller, M.J., 1988. "New Duplicates to SBTU II," *Archiv für Orientforschung* 35, 1–23.

Hecker, K., 1989. "Hymnen und Gebete aus jüngerer Zeit" in Römer, W.H.P. and Karl Hecker, eds, *Texte aus der Umwelt des Alten Testaments II/5: Religiöse Texte*, Gütersloh: Gütersloher—Gerd Mohn, 780–81.

Heessel, N., 2000. *Babylonisch-assyrische Diagnostik*. Alter Orient und Altes Testament 43. Münster: Ugarit Verlag.

Khalidi, T., 2001. *The Muslim Jesus: Sayings and Stories in Islamic Literature*, Cambridge, MA: Harvard University.

Kilmer, A.D., 1972. "The Mesopotamian Concept of Overpopulation and its Solution as Reflected in the Mythology," *Orientalia* N.S. 41, 160–77.

Klein, K., 1983. "Tudittum," *Zeitschrift für Assyriologie* 73, 255–84.

Labat, R.,1951. *Traité akkadien de diagnostics et pronostics médicaux*. Paris: Académie internationale d'histoire de sciences.

Lackenbacker, S., 1971. "Note sur l'Ardat-lilî," *Revue d'Assyriologie* 65, 119–54.

Lambert, W.G., 1965. "A Middle Assyrian Tablet of Incantations" in *Studies in Honor of Benno Landsberger on his Seventy-fifth Birthday*, Assyriological Studies 16, Chicago: Oriental Institute, 286: 20–25.

——, 1969. "A Middle Assyrian Medical Text," *Iraq* 31, 28–39.

Livingstone, A., 1989. *Court Poetry and Literary Miscellanea*, State Archives of Assyria 3, Helsinki: Helsinki University.

Michel, C. and N. Wasserman, 1997. "Du nouveau sur šumma zikar a-li-da-ni šumma sinnišat na-ap-TA-ar-ta-ni," *NABU*, 1997/64.

Miller, J.L., 2004. *Studies in the Origins, Development and Interpretation of the Kizzuwatna Rituals*, Studien zu den Boğazköy-Texten 46, Wiesbaden: Harrassowitz.

Myhrman, D.W., 1902. "Die Labartu-Texte," *Zeitschrift für Assyriologie* 16, 141–200.

Nougayrol, J., 1969. "La Lamaštu à Ugarit," *Ugaritica 6*, Mission de Ras Shamra 17, Paris: Collège de France, 393–408.

Parpola, S. and K. Watanabe, 1988. *Neo-Assyrian Treaties and Loyalty Oaths*, State Archives of Assyria 2, Helsinki: Helsinki University.

Reiner, E., 1982. "Babylonian Birth Prognoses," *Zeitschrift für Assyriologie* 72, 124–38.

——, 1985. *Your Thwarts in Pieces, Your Mooring Rope Cut, Poetry from Babylonia and Assyria*, Ann Arbor: University of Michigan.

——, 1990. "Nocturnal Talk" in Abusch. T., J. Huehnergard, and P. Steinkeller, eds, *Lingering over Words: Studies in Ancient Near Eastern Literature in Honor of William L. Moran*, Atlanta: Scholars, 421–23.

Röllig, W., 1985. "Der Mondgott und die Kuh. Ein Lehrstück zur Problematik der Textüberlieferung im Alten Orient," *Orientalia* N.S. 54, 260–73.

Scheil, V., 1921. "Catalogue de la Collection Eugène Tisserant," *Revue d'Assyriologie* 18, 21–27.

Schwemer, D., 2006. "Auf Reisen mit Lamaštu: Zum 'Ritualmemorandum' K 888 und seinen Parallelen aus Assur," *Baghdader Mitteilungen* 37, 1–15.

Scurlock, J.A., 1989/90. "Was there a 'Love-hungry' Entu-priestess Named Eṭirtum?", *Archiv für Orientforschung* 36/37, 107–12.

——, 1991. "Baby-Snatching Demons, Restless Souls and the Dangers of Childbirth: Medico-Magical Means of Dealing with Some of the Perils of Motherhood in Ancient Mesopotamia," *Incognita* 2, 137–85.

——, 2002a. "Animals in Ancient Mesopotamian Religion" in Collins, B.J. ed., *A History of the Animal World in the Ancient Near East*, Leiden: Brill, 361–87.

——, 2002b. "Translating Transfers in Ancient Mesopotamia" in Mirecki, P. and M. Meyer, eds, *Magic and Ritual in the Ancient World*, Leiden: Brill, 209–23.

——, 2006. "But Was She Raped? A Verdict Through Comparison," *NIN* 4, 61–103.

Scurlock, J.A. and B.R. Andersen, 2005. *Diagnoses in Assyrian and Babylonian Medicine*, Urbana: University of Illinois.

Shaffer, A., *Sumerian Sources for Tablet XII of the Gilgamesh Epic*, Ph.D. Diss., University of Pennsylvania, 1963.

Stol, M., 2000. *Birth in Babylonia and the Bible: Its Mediterranean Setting*, Cuneiform Monographs 14, Groningen: Styx.

Thureau-Dangin, F., 1921. "Rituel et amulettes contre Labartu," *Revue d'Assyriologie* 18, 161–98.

Tsukimoto, A., 1985. *Untersuchungen zur Totenpflege (kispum) im alten Mesopotamien*, Alter Orient und Altes Testament 216, Neukirchen-Vluyn: Neukirchener Verlag, 140–45.

Ungnad, A., 1921. "Zu den Labartu-Texten," *Zeitschrift für Assyriologie* 33, 69–71.

Veldhuis, N., 1989. "The new Assyrian Compendium for a Woman in Childbirth," *Acta Sumerologica* (Japan) 11, 239–60.

——, 1991. *A Cow of Sîn*, Groningen: Styx.

——, 1999. "The Poetry of Magic" in Abusch, T. and K. van der Toorn, eds, *Mesopotamian Magic: Textual, Historical, and Interpretative Perspectives*, Ancient Magic and Divination 1, Styx: Groningen, 35–48.

Volk, K., 1995, *Inanna and Šukaletuda*, Wiesbaden: Harrassowitz.

von Weiher, E., 1983. *Spätbabyonische Texte aus Uruk 2*, Ausgrabungen der deutschen Forschungsgemeinschaft in Uruk/Warka 10, Berlin: Gebr. Mann.

——, 1988. *Spätbabylonische Texte aus Uruk 3*, Ausgrabungen der Deutschen Forschungsgemeinschaft in Uruk-Warka 12, Berlin: Walter de Gruyter.

——, 1998. *Uruk: Spätbabylonische Texte aus dem Planquadrant U 18, Teil 5 (= SpTU 5)*, Ausgrabungen in Uruk-Warka Endberichte 13, Mainz: Philipp von Zabern.

Waetzoldt, H., 1990. "É.DU$_8$.LA = edu(l)lû 'Nachlass'," NABU 1990/5.

Wiggermann, F.A.M., 2000. "Lamaštu, Daughter of Anu: A Profile" in Stol, M., *Birth in Babylonia and the Bible: Its Mediterranean Setting*, Cuneiform Mongraphs 14, Groningen: Styx, 217–49.

Wilcke, C., 1985. "Liebesbeschwörungen aus Isin," *Zeitschrift für Assyriologie* 75, 188–209.

6

WOMEN AND LAW

Martha T. Roth

Introduction

The texts designated "law collections" from ancient Mesopotamia are compositions written in the cuneiform script on clay tablets and stone monuments, in the Semitic language Akkadian (in various Babylonian and Assyrian dialects) and in Sumerian.[1] The distinguishing feature of the law collections is that they include provisions understood by modern scholars to be either aspirational or reflections of social and legal practice and reality. The compositions entered into the scribal schools and, as such, for generations were a means of training the classes of bureaucrats and scholars who served in the royal palace and temples; while advancing through the scribal curriculum, copying and memorizing school texts, students absorbed the vocabulary, the formulations and the fundamental concepts of legal rules.[2] While they thus may reflect the legal practices or norms that were in operation at a particular time, they were also the models—in both form and content—for the creation of new compositions.

The law collections should not be understood by the modern student as prescriptive or legislative in any legal sense. The handful of law collections are in fact complemented by many thousands of cuneiform tablets that document the daily operation of social and legal life: records of trials, witness testimony and court cases; transactional records, such as sales, leases, contracts, wills and testaments, etc.; administrative memoranda; letters; and treaties. The scholastic views on legal matters may be evidenced too from the literary corpus (myths, epics, fables, etc.), as well as from the handful of compilations of model court cases and model contracts.

Structure and conventions

Some of the exemplars representing the law collections include historical-literary prologues and epilogues that provide historical and divine justification for their publication and identify a royal sponsor or imprimatur, situating the law-giving in the context of a ruler's political ambitions and the gods' favor. This is the case for the Sumerian collections attributed to kings Ur-Namma (c. 2100) and

Lipit-Ishtar (c. 1900) and for the Akkadian collection of Hammurabi (c. 1750). Other compositions, such as the Laws of Eshnunna (c. 1800), the Middle Assyrian Laws A (c. 1050), and the Neo-Babylonian Laws (c. 700) are known only from exemplars with brief notations referencing a date or ruler; we should not exclude the possibility that they, too, were part of larger compositions with prologue-epilogue framing structures.

The present numbering of the provisions is the product of the conventions of modern scholarship, generally following the numbering assigned in the first edition of the collection. The cuneiform tablets themselves do not in any way mark the beginnings or ends of provisions: there are no punctuations, indentations, paragraphing, notations, etc. New provisions may be indicated by the conditional conjunction (Sumerian tukum-bi, Akkadian *šumma*, "if") marking a new protasis, but the conditional conjunction may also mark a secondary condition of the primary protasis—that is, a variation of the circumstance outlined in the primary protasis—rather than a completely new circumstance. In the edition presented here, such secondary provisions are indented (whether or not the secondary provision is conventionally assigned a unique number) signaling to the reader that they depend upon the circumstances outlined in the preceding provisions.

Terminology: persons, status, institutions

The law collections presented here, while all inscribed in the cuneiform script on clay tablets or stone monuments, come from an immensely long period of time (more than one thousand five hundred years), span a vast geographical area (from the Mediterranean Sea to the Zagros Mountains, from the Black Sea to the Persian Gulf) and were written in different languages and dialects (Sumerian, Old Babylonian Akkadian, Middle Assyrian Akkadian, Neo-Babylonian Akkadian). Thus the reader must not assume that a particular term or institution necessarily reflects an identical reality in any two law collections: terms such as "marriage" or "judge" may signify different culturally assumed conditions. This edition does, however, strive to present particular Sumerian and Akkadian terms consistently and with identical English translations, although the reader must remain aware that a translation of a vocabulary item is not a description of an underlying institution, and an identical translation of a vocabulary item in two law collections (separated by time and space) need not indicate identical social meaning or institutional context.[3] Noteworthy are the following English terms (with their Sumerian and Akkadian[4] equivalents, specification of law collection if unique, and provided with brief annotations and further bibliography, where appropriate).

citizen (LU, LL dumu-gi₇; MAL (fem.) *alāītu*) The implications (rights and duties) are unknown; the Sumerian term may mean "native(-born) son"; the Akkadian is derived from *ālu* "city" plus a derivative suffix, thus "one of the city" or "urban resident."

commoner (*muškēnu*, LH) A category of persons placed in contrast with "man" (*amīlu*) and "slave" (*ardu*), sometimes understood to refer to a class under royal patronage, with unique rights and privileges; for discussion and recent bibliography see von Dassow, forthcoming.

daughter (dumu-munus, *mārtu*), daughter-of-a-commoner (*mārat muškēni*), daughter-of-a-man (*mārat amīli*) See the note at "son."

husband (*mūtu*), wife (*aššatu*), first-husband (*ḫā'iru*), first-wife (*ḫīrtu*), spouse (dam) The Sumerian dam does not distinguish male and female, and it is not always clear whether the "husband" or "wife" is meant; like the Akkadian terms *mūtu* and *aššatu*, the terms reference a legally significant status for which there are socially understood duties and responsibilities (such as exclusive sexual and reproductive rights), as well as privileges (such as bearing and producing heirs), not all of which are articulated in our extant sources. The terms translated here as "first-husband" (*ḫā'iru*) and "first-wife" (*ḫīrtu*) are derived from the Akkadian verb *ḫâru*, used in LH § 155 where it is translated "to select." The precise nuance of the term, used primarily in contexts of sexual unions (humans, demons, etc.), and whether or not it signals a unique form of marriage, remain open. In polygamous marriages in which a man may have more than one "wife" (including slaves or priestesses), one woman may be designated first-ranking or primary and her offspring will take precedence in inheritance. Note that in the LL, first-spouse (*dam-nitadam*) and second-spouse (*dam-egir-ra*) may refer to chronological precedence rather than to preferential status.

maiden (*batultu*) An age category denoting marriageability; see Roth, 1987, 715–47.

male (nita, *zikaru*) The term used in the law collections to identify the "other man" or the "not-husband" in sexual behaviors.

man (lu$_2$, *amīlu*) The unmarked and default subject of the laws ("If a man … "); earlier editions translated *amīlu* in the laws as "free man" or "citizen," assuming a particular and elite class. Another term, young-man (*guruš*), is found in the LU (§§ 6 and 7) and LL (§ 30); see Jacobsen, 1993, 69–80. See also above at "commoner."

marriage gifts The customary or obligatory exchanges of gifts at marriage vary through time and dialects. Gifts that move from the groom's family to the bride's family include the ceremonial-marriage-prestation (nig$_2$-de$_2$-a [LU], *biblu* [LE, LH, MAL]), given on behalf of the groom to the bride's family; bridewealth (nig$_2$-mi$_2$-us$_2$-sa$_2$ [LL], *terhatu* [LE, LH, MAL]), given by the groom to the bride's father; and the marriage-settlement (*nudunnû* [LE, LH, MAL]) given by the husband to the wife. Gifts that move from the bride's family to the groom or his family include the dowry (sag-rig$_7$ [LU, LL], *šeriktu* [LE, LH], *širku* [MAL], *nudunnû* [LNB]) and the bridal gift (*zubullû* [MAL]).

priestess In the LH, four different terms are used to identify women dedicated to religious service: *nadītu*-priestess, *qadištu*-priestess, *šugītu*-priestess, *ugbabtu*-

priestess. Some of these women lived in cloisters or compounds, some were married but were not permitted to bear (or raise their own) children. Inheritance practices took into account their peculiar circumstances. The most comprehensive treatments of the categories of priestesses in the Old Babylonian period remain Harris, 1975; and Renger, 1967, 110–88.

prostitute (*harimtu*) See Assante, 1998, 5–96.; Roth, 2006, 21–39; Assante, 2007, 117–32.

River (ordeal) (id_2) A supra-judicial process undertaken in instances in which an individual accused of committing a wrong in secret or private, without witnesses or clear evidence, is given a particularly public decision. The most comprehensive treatment is found in Frymer-Kensky, 1977; see also Durand, 1988, 509–24.

slave (arad, *ardu*) slave-woman (geme$_2$, *amtu, amīlūtu*) The nature of chattel slavery varied greatly according to circumstances and situations, and in different periods. Persons acquired through debt or as pledges might serve for limited terms and their bodies not subject to corporal punishment; children acquired in times of famine or severe economic stress with the intention of saving their lives might be treated more as family members; offspring born to slaves might themselves acquire the status of the slave parent. For general treatments, see Mendelsohn, 1949; Westbrook, 1995, 1631–76; Dandamaev, 1984; and the several essays in Culbertson, 2011. In the law collections, slaves are contrasted with other categories of persons for purposes of assessing penalties for injuries and offenses.

son (dumu, *māru*), daughter (dumu-munus, *mārtu*), and compounds rendered here son-of-a-man (*mār amīli*), daughter-of-a-commoner (*mārat muškēni*), daughter-of-a-man (*mārat amīli*), and male-son (dumu-nita) Sumerian dumu does not specify sex (thus "child") and some editions of the laws may understand the term to include both male and female offspring; so, too, Akkadian *māru*, which is formally masculine, might be gender neutral in certain contexts. In this edition, however, dumu/*māru* and dumu-munus/*mārtu* are unambiguously rendered as "son" and "daughter," and understood to refer to a male and female of any age who is legally and socially dependent upon a head-of-household. So too the compounds identify a male or female dependent of a "man" or "commoner"; see Westbrook, 1988, 57–58; Roth, in press a; in press b; and in press c.

"take (in marriage)" The verb used in both Sumerian (tuk/du$_{12}$) and Akkadian (*ahāzu*), with the primary meaning of "to take, to seize," may be further defined by the object "wife" (Sumerian dam "spouse," Akkadian *aššatu* "wife") or "wifehood" (*aššūtu*) "to take a wife" or "to take in wifehood," thus "to marry." The object is often omitted, however, and the context may be implied. The precise and full implications of the action, either as a concrete, physical (or sexual) taking or as acquisition of legal authority, remain open. In this work, I translate "take (in marriage)" or "take (as a wife)," when the object is not expressed, and "take as a wife" when it is expressed, rather than the possibly misleading "to marry." Note that in one provision cited here, LL § 30, the verb is used first in a compound with dam and then twice without qualification in contexts suggests explicitly sexual "taking" or copulation in the first occurrence and possibly a legal relationship in the second: "If a young-man who is married (lit.: spouse-taken) *takes* a prostitute from the street, the judges order him not to go back with that prostitute, afterwards he divorced his spouse (who is) the first-spouse and gave her divorce-settlement-silver to her: he shall not *take* that prostitute."

Laws of Ur-Namma (c. 2100 BC)

King Ur-Namma, the founder of the Third Dynasty of Ur (Ur III), reigned from 2112 to 2095 BC. The composition known as the Laws of Ur-Namma (or Ur-Nammu) is known from exemplars written on clay tablets and dating to the Old Babylonian period (c. 1900–1600 BC) and one clay cylinder from the Ur III period. The tablets are all housed in museums and come from excavated contexts in southern Mesopotamia: from Nippur (Ni 3191, source A [Istanbul Archaeological Museum], and possibly 2N-T 440 [UM 55-21-71], formerly Laws of Lipit-Ishtar, source P [University of Pennsylvania Museum]); from Ur (U.7739+, source B [… Museum]); from Sippar (Si. 277, source C [Istanbul Archaeological Museum]; BM 54722+, formerly Laws of X [British Museum]). A clay cylinder originally with ten columns, unexcavated and acquired from dealers, and now in a private collection, perhaps from Umma: MS 2064.

The composition is framed by a prologue (c. 3000 words) and an incompletely preserved epilogue (c. 400+ words) with only curses preserved; between are preserved approximately 90 law provisions, formulated as casuistic clauses ("If such is the situation, then: this is the remedy or consequence"). MS 2064 (source X in Civil's editio princeps), a ten-column cylinder with "long" or "double" lines that likely held the complete composition, originally could have held between 100 and 150 law provisions in column iii through the beginning of column x.

The law provisions primarily concern economic matters and—in so far as they impact upon the economic rights and responsibilities of the elites—deal with the social, familial, economic and legal positions of women both free-born and in servitude. A few examples are presented below.

§ 4 If a slave takes (in marriage) a slave-woman of his choosing, and that slave is given his freedom: s/he[5] will not leave the household.

§ 5 If a slave takes (in marriage) a citizen: s/he shall place one male-son in the service of his master. …

§ 6 If a man deflowers the not-deflowered[6] spouse of a young-man, with guile: they shall kill that male.

§ 7 If the spouse of a young-man on her own initiative pursues a man and has sexual intercourse with him: they shall kill that woman; that male shall be given his freedom.

§ 8 If a man deflowers the not-deflowered[7] slave-woman of a man, with guile: that man shall weigh and deliver 5 shekels of silver.

§ 9 If a man divorces[8] his first-spouse: he shall weigh and deliver 60 shekels of silver.

§ 10 If he divorces a widow: he shall weigh and deliver 30 shekels of silver.

§ 11 If a man has sexual relations with the widow without a written document: he shall not weigh and deliver silver.[9]

§ 14 If a man makes an accusation of sexual intercourse with the spouse of a young-man, and the River clears her/him: the man who makes the accusation shall weigh and deliver 20 shekels of silver.[10]

§ 33 If [a ...] strikes the daughter-of-a-man and causes her fetus to drop (i.e. miscarry): he shall weigh and deliver 30 shekels of silver.

§ 34 If she dies: they shall kill that man.

§ 35 If [a ...] strikes a slave-woman of a man and causes her fetus to drop: he shall pay 10 (var. 5) shekels.

§ 36 If the slave-woman dies: he shall put in place servant for servant.

§ B2 If a man dies and has no male-son: an unmarried daughter [will be] his heir.

§ B7 If a man takes a spouse and his/her spouse divorces her/him (var.: If a woman divorces her spouse): after waiting six months the woman shall be permitted to take (in marriage) a spouse of her choice.

§ B8 If a man takes (in marriage) a spouse and his spouse dies: until the male will take (in marriage) (another woman), the dowry of his spouse shall remain with him; at the time when he will take (in marriage) (another woman), the dowry shall return to the household of her man.[11]

Laws of Lipit-Ishtar (c. 1925 BC)

King Lipit-Ishtar, fifth king of the First Dynasty of Isin, reigned from 1934 to 1924 BC. The composition known as the Laws of Lipit-Ishtar is known from more than a dozen exemplars written in Sumerian on clay tablets and dating to the Old Babylonian period (c. 1900–1600 BC), mostly from the scribal centers of Nippur as well as from Kish and Sippar.

The composition is framed by a prologue (c. 4,000 words) and epilogue (incomplete, c. 4,200 words preserved); between are preserved approximately 40 law provisions, formulated as casuistic clauses ("If such is the situation, then: this is the remedy or consequence").

The law provisions primarily concern economic matters and—in so far as they impact upon the economic rights and responsibilities of the elites—deal with the social, familial, economic and legal positions of women both free-born and in servitude. A few examples are presented below.

§ 23 If a daughter is not given (in marriage) from the house of her living father:[12] her brothers shall give her (in marriage) to a spouse.

§ 24 If a second-spouse whom he takes (in marriage) bears to him a son: the dowry which she brought from her father's house are for her son; the son of a first-spouse and the son of a second-spouse shall divide the property of their father equally.

§ 25 If a man takes a spouse, she bears to him a son, and that son lives; and a slave-woman (also) bears to him a son: the father shall free the slave-woman and her sons; the son of the slave-woman shall not divide the house with the son of her master.

§ 26 If his first-spouse dies, after his spouse he takes in wifehood his slave-woman: the son of his first-spouse shall be his heir. The son whom the slave-woman bears to her master is considered like a son of a citizen, they shall make good his house.

§ 27 If a man's spouse does not bear to him a son and a prostitute from the street does bear to him a son: he shall give grain rations, oil rations, and wool rations to the prostitute. The son whom the prostitute bears to him is his heir. As long as his spouse is living, the prostitute shall not reside in the house with the first-spouse.

§ 28 If a man's first-spouse loses her sight[13] or becomes paralyzed: she shall not be evicted from the house. Her spouse may take (in marriage) a healthy spouse;[14] the second-spouse shall support the first-spouse.[15]

§ 29 If a son-in-law enters the house of a father-in-law, performs the bridewealth (delivery/ceremony), later they evict him, and they give his spouse to his comrade: they shall restore to him two-fold the bridewealth which he brought; his comrade shall not take (in marriage) his spouse.

§ 30 If a young-man who is married (lit.: spouse-taken) takes a prostitute from the street, the judges order him not to go back with that prostitute, afterwards he divorced his spouse (who is) the first-spouse and gave her divorce-settlement-silver to her: he shall not take[16] that prostitute.

§ 33 If a man states that a not-deflowered[17] daughter-of-a-man has sexual experience (lit.: knows the penis), then it is proven that she has not had sexual experience: he shall weigh and deliver 10 shekels of silver.

Laws of Eshnunna (c. 1800 BC)

Two large tablets excavated at Tell Harmal and a third small fragment preserve a collection of approximately 60 legal provisions formulated, in Akkadian, as relative clauses ("A man who … "), apodictic statements ("The hire of a wagon is … ") and casuistic constructions ("If such is the situation, then: this is the remedy or consequence"). A brief and damaged superscription on one source has been reconstructed to refer to King Dadusha of the kingdom of Eshnunna in upper (northeast) Mesopotamia, dating the composition to the end of the nineteenth century BC.

§ 17 Should a son-of-a-man bring the bridewealth to the house of a father-in-law, and if one of the two should go to (her/his) fate: the silver shall revert to its owner.

§ 18 If he takes her (in marriage) and she enters his house, (if) either the groom or the bride goes to (his/her) fate: he shall not take out any that he brought, only its excess shall he take.

§ 25 If a man comes to claim (his bride) at the house of a father-in-law, but his father-in-law wrongs(?) him and gives his daughter to [another]: the father of the daughter shall return two-fold the bridewealth which he received.

§ 26 If a man brings the bridewealth for the daughter-of-a-man, but another without the consent of her father and mother abducts her and deflowers her: it is indeed a capital offense, he shall die.

§ 27 If a man takes (in marriage) the daughter-of-a-man without the consent of her father and her mother, and does not conclude the nuptial feast and the contract for(?) her father and her mother: (even) should she reside in his house for one full year, she is not a wife.

§ 28 If he concludes the contract and the nuptial feast for(?) her father and her mother and marries her, she is indeed a wife: the day she is seized in the lap of a man, she shall die, she will not live.

§ 29 If a man should be captured during a raiding expedition or patrol(?), or a razzia has carried (him) off, (even if) he reside in a foreign land for [a long time], should another take (in marriage) his wife and she bear a son: when he returns he shall take back his wife.[18]

§ 30 If a man hates his city and his master and flees, and another takes (in marriage) his wife: when he returns he will have no claim to his wife.

§ 31 If a man deflowers the slave-woman of a man: he shall weigh and deliver 20 shekels of silver and the slave-woman belongs to her master.

§ 59 If a man who begat sons divorces his wife and takes (in marriage) another (woman): he shall be expelled from the house and from any possessions there may be, and he shall depart after ... [19]

Laws of Hammurabi (c. 1750 BC)

King Hammurabi (1792–50 BC) of the First Dynasty of Babylon lends his name to the most complete and comprehensive collection of legal rules from the ancient Near East. More than 50 cuneiform tablets and fragments of stelae are extant, dating from immediately after Hammurabi's reign through the mid-first millennium BC. Commentaries, extracts, catalogue entries and a bilingual extract all attest to the prevalence of the composition throughout the region. A prologue and epilogue frame approximately 300 law provisions, almost all formulated as casuistic clauses ("If such is the situation, then: this is the remedy or consequence").

The provisions selected here all involve women of the free, elite population. Those provisions dealing with priestesses, slaves or others whose circumstances are constrained by various economic, legal or social conditions are included here only when they contrast with and thus illuminate features of the provisions involving free women.

§ 108 If a tapster[20] will not accept grain for the price of beer (but) does accept silver (measured) by the "large weight" thereby reducing the value of beer relative to the value of grain: they shall charge-and-prove that woman innkeeper and they shall cast her into the water.[21]

§ 109 If there is a tapster in whose house criminals congregate, and she does not seize those criminals and lead them off to the palace: that woman innkeeper shall be killed.

§ 110 If a nadītum-priestess (or) an ugbabtum-priestess, one who does not reside within the cloister, should open a tavern or enter a tavern for beer: they shall burn that woman (var.: that nadītum-priestess).

§ 111 If a tapster gives one beer-vat as a loan: she shall take 50 silas of grain at harvest.

§ 127 If a man causes a finger to be pointed in accusation against an ugbabtum-priestess or against a wife-of-a-man but does not bring proof: before the judges they will flog that man and they will shave off half of his hair.

§ 128 If a man takes a wife but does not conclude her formal contract: that woman is not a wife.

§ 129 If a wife-of-a-man should be seized lying with another male: they will bind them and cast them into the water; if the owner-of-the-wife allows his wife to live, then the king will allow his slave to live.

§ 130 If a man pins down a wife-of-a-man who has not known a male and who resides in her father's house, and they seize him lying in her lap: that man will be killed; that woman will be released.

§ 131 If her husband accuses the wife-of-a-man and/but she has not been seized lying with another male: she shall swear an oath by the god and return to her house.

§ 132 If a finger is pointed against a wife-of-a-man because of another male and/but she has not been seized lying with another male: she will submit to the divine River Ordeal for her husband.[22]

§ 133a If a man should be captured and there are sufficient provisions in his house: his wife ...

§ 133b If that woman does not guard her person and enters another's house: they will charge-and-prove against that woman and cast her into the water.

§ 134 If a man should be captured and there are not sufficient provisions in his house, his wife enter another's house: that woman will not be subject to any penalty.

§ 135 If a man should be captured and there are not sufficient provisions in his house, before his (return) his wife enters another's house and bears sons, afterwards her husband returns and attains his city: that woman will return to her first-husband; the sons will go after their father.[23]

§ 136 If a man deserts his city and flees, and after his (departure) his wife enters another's house—if that man returns and seizes his wife: because he hated his city and fled, the wife of the fleer will not return to her husband.

§ 137 If a man should decide to divorce a šugītum-priestess who bore him sons, or a nadītum-priestess who provided him with sons: they will return to that woman her dowry and moreover they will give to her one half of the field, orchard, and property, and she will raise her sons. After she has raised her sons, they will give her a share comparable in value to that of one heir from whatever properties are given to her sons, and a husband of her choice may marry her.

§ 138 If a man should divorce his first-wife who did not bear him sons: he will give her silver as much as was her bridewealth and restore to her the dowry that she brought from her father's house, and he will divorce her.

§ 139 If there is no bridewealth: he will give her 60 shekels of silver as a divorce settlement.

§ 140 If he is a commoner: he will give her 20 shekels of silver.

§ 141 If the wife-of-a-man who is residing in a man's house should decide to leave, and she appropriates goods, squanders her house, disparages her husband: they will charge-and-prove against her; and if her husband should declare (his intention) to divorce her: he will divorce her; her travel expenses, her divorce settlement, or anything else will not be given to her.

If her husband should declare (his intention) not to divorce her: her husband may take another woman; that woman will reside in her husband's house as a slave-woman.

§ 142 If a woman hates her husband and declares, "You will not take me (in marriage)," her circumstances will be investigated by the authorities of her city quarter; and if she is circumspect and without fault, but her husband is wayward and disparages her greatly: that woman will not have any penalty; she will take her dowry and will depart to her father's house.

§ 143 If she is not circumspect but is wayward, squanders her household possessions, disparages her husband: they will cast that woman into the water.[24]

§ 144 If a man takes (in marriage) a nadītum-priestess, and that nadītum-priestess gives a slave-woman to her husband and thereby provides sons, and that man intends to marry a šugītum-priestess: they will not permit that man to do so, he will not marry a šugītum-priestess.

§ 145 If a man takes (in marriage) a nadītum-priestess, and she does not provide him with sons, and he decides to marry a šugī tum-priestess: that man may marry a šugītum-priestess and bring her into his house; that šugītum-priestess should not set herself as equal with the nadītum-priestess.

§ 146 If a man marries a nadītum-priestess, and she gives a slave-woman to her husband, and she bears sons, after which that slave-woman sets herself as equal with her mistress: because she bore sons, her mistress shall not sell her; she will place upon her the slave-hairlock and reckon her among the slave-women.

§ 147 If she does not bear sons: her mistress shall sell her.

§ 148 If a man takes a wife and la'bu-disease seizes her, and he decides to take (in marriage) another: he may take. He may not divorce his wife whom la'bu-disease seized, but she will reside in quarters he constructs and he will continue to support her as long as she lives.[25]

§ 149 If that woman should not agree to reside in her husband's house: he will restore to her dowry that she brought from her father's house and she will depart.

§ 150 If a man awards to his wife a field, orchard, house, or movable property and he makes out a sealed document for her:

after (the death of) her husband her sons will not bring a claim against her; the mother will give her estate to whichever son of hers whom she loves, she will not give it to an outsider.

§ 151 If a woman who is residing in a man's house should bind her husband by contract that no creditor of her husband may seize her, and if that man has had a debt incurred before having married that woman: his creditors will not seize his wife.

And if that woman has had a debt incurred before having entered the man's house: her creditors will not seize her husband.[26]

§ 152 If after that woman enters the man's house a debt should be incurred against them: both of them will satisfy the merchant.

§ 153 If a wife-of-a-man has her husband killed on account of another male: they will impale that woman.[27]

§ 154 If a man should know his daughter: they will banish that man from the city.

§ 155 If a man selects a bride for his son and his son knows her, and he himself afterwards lies in her lap and they seize him: they will bind that man and cast him into the water.

§ 156 If a man selects a bride for his son and his son has not known her, and he himself lies in her lap: he will weigh and deliver to her 30 shekels of silver and he will restore to her whatever she brought from her father's house, and a husband of her choice may marry her.

§ 157 If a man, after his father('s death), should lie in the lap of his mother: they will burn them both.

§ 158 If a man, after his father('s death), should be seized in the lap of his (the father's) principal wife who had borne sons: that man will be disinherited from the father's house.

§ 159 If a man who has the ceremonial-marriage-prestation brought to the house of his father-in-law and who gives the bridewealth should have his attention diverted to another woman and declare to his father-in-law, "I will not take your daughter (in marriage)": the father of the daughter will take possession of whatever had been brought to him.

§ 160 If a man has the ceremonial-marriage-prestation brought to the house of his father-in-law and gives the bridewealth, and the father of the daughter then declares, "I will not give my daughter to you": he will return twofold everything that had been brought to him.

§ 161 If a man has the ceremonial-marriage-prestation brought to the house of his father-in-law and gives the bridewealth, and his comrade then slanders him and his father-in-law declares to the owner-of-the-wife, "You will not take my daughter": he will return twofold everything that had been brought to him, and his comrade will not marry his wife.

§ 162 If a man takes a wife, she bears him sons, and that woman then goes to (her) fate: her father will have no claim to her dowry; her dowry belongs only to her sons.

§ 163 If a man takes a wife but she does not provide him with sons, and that woman then goes to her fate—if his father-in-law then returns to him the bridewealth that that man brought to his father-in-law's house: her husband will have no claim to that woman's dowry, her dowry belongs only to her father's house.

§ 164 If his father-in-law does not return to him the bridewealth: he will deduct the value of her bridewealth from her dowry and return her dowry to her father's house.

§ 165 If a man awards field, orchard, or house to his heir whom he favors and writes a contract for him, after the father goes to (his) fate, when the brothers divide (the estate): he (the preferred heir) will take the gift which the father gave to him and aside from that they will divide equally the property of the father's house.

§ 166 If a man takes wives for his sons who are grown but does not take a wife for his young son, after the father goes to (his) fate, when the brothers divide (the estate): they will establish from the property of the father's house the silver of the bridewealth for their young brother who has not taken a wife in addition to his inheritance share, and (thereby) they will enable him to take a wife.

§ 167 If a man takes a wife and she bears him sons, and later that woman goes to (her) fate, and after her (death) he takes another woman and she bears sons—after the father then goes to (his) fate: the sons will not divide (the estate) according to the mothers; they will take the dowries of their (respective) mothers and divide equally the property of the father's house.

§ 170 If a man whose first-wife bears him sons and whose slave-woman bears him sons (of whom) the father during his lifetime then declared to (or: concerning) the sons whom the slave-woman bore to him, "My sons," and he reckoned them with the sons of the first-wife—after the father then goes to (his) fate: the sons of the first-wife and the sons of the slave-woman will divide equally the property of the father's house; the (primary) heir is a son of the first-wife, he will select and take a share (first).

§ 171 And if the father during his lifetime should not declare to (or: concerning) the sons whom the slave-woman bore to him,

"My sons"—after the father then goes to (his) fate: the sons of the slave-woman will not divide the property of the father's house with the sons of the first-wife.

The freedom of the slave-woman and of her sons will be secured; the sons of the first-wife will not make claims of slavery against the sons of the slave-woman.

The first-wife will take her dowry and the marriage-settlement which her husband awarded to her and wrote for her in a tablet, and she will reside in her husband's dwelling; as long as she is alive she will enjoy (its) use, she may not sell (it); her estate will belong (as inheritance) only to her own sons.

§ 172 If her husband does not make her a marriage-settlement: they will restore to her in full her dowry, and she will take a single share of the property of her husband's house comparable in value to that of an heir.

If her sons pressure her in order to coerce her to depart from the house: the judges will investigate her circumstances and will impose a penalty on the sons; that woman will not depart from her husband's house.

If that woman decides to depart: she will leave for her sons the marriage-settlement which her husband gave to her; she will take the dowry from her father's house and a husband of her choice will take her (in marriage).

§ 173 If that woman, where she entered, bears sons to her latter husband—after that woman dies: her former and latter sons will equally divide her dowry.

§ 174 If she does not bear sons to her latter husband: only the sons of her first-husband will take her dowry.

§ 175 If a slave of the palace or a slave of a commoner takes (in marriage) a daughter-of-a-man and she then bears sons: the owner of the slave will have no claims of slavery against the sons of the daughter-of-a-man.

§ 176a And if either a slave of the palace or a slave of a commoner takes (in marriage) a daughter-of-a-man, and when he takes her she enters the house of the slave of the palace or of the slave of the commoner together with the dowry of her father's house, and subsequent to the time that they move in together they establish a house and accumulate possessions, after which either the slave of the palace or the slave of the commoner then goes to (his) fate: the daughter-of-a-man will take her dowry; furthermore, they will divide into two parts everything that her husband and she accumulated subsequent to the time that they moved in together, the slave's owner will take half and the daughter-of-a-man will take half for her sons.

MARTHA T. ROTH

§ 176b If the daughter-of-a-man does not have a dowry: they will divide into two parts everything that her husband and she accumulated subsequent to the time that they moved in together, and the slave's owner will take half and the daughter-of-a-man will take half for her sons.

§ 177 If a widow whose sons are still young should decide to enter another's house: she will not enter without the approval of the judges.[28]

When she enters another's house, the judges will investigate the estate of her former husband and they will entrust the estate of her former husband to her later husband and to that woman, and they will have them record a tablet (inventorying the estate). They will safeguard the house and they will raise the youngsters; they will not sell the household goods. Any buyer who buys the household goods of the sons of a widow will forfeit his silver; the property will revert to its owner.

§ 209 If a man strikes a daughter-of-a-man and thus causes her to miscarry her fetus: he shall weigh and deliver 10 shekels of silver for her fetus.

§ 210 If that woman then should die: they shall kill his daughter.

§ 211 If he should thus cause a daughter-of-a-commoner to miscarry her fetus by the beating: he shall weigh and deliver 5 shekels of silver.

§ 212 If that woman then should die: he shall weigh and deliver 30 shekels of silver.

§ 213 If he strikes slave-woman-of-a-man and thus causes her to miscarry her fetus: he shall weigh and deliver 2 shekels of silver.

§ 214 If that slave-woman then should die: he shall weigh and deliver 20 shekels of silver.

Middle Assyrian laws (c. 1050 BC)

MAL A (Middle Assyrian Laws tablet A) is a single large tablet from Assur and written in Middle Assyrian script probably in the eleventh century BC, recording some 60 provisions. A small fragment from Nineveh dating to the Neo-Assyrian period, some 300 years later, is a partial duplicate to the first provisions of MAL A and thus indicates that the provisions were recopied in the scribal schools.

Almost all the provisions in MAL A involve women as actors or victims. In general, the women in these Assyrian provisions are significantly less autonomous and enjoy considerably fewer rights than do women in the earlier (LH, LE) or later (LNB) Babylonian laws, though it is not easy to conclude whether this is a

158

function of the general position of women in the Middle Assyrian period or simply a function of the nature and purpose of this particular composition: as may be clear from the first and final provisions, the authority of a husband or father over his wife or daughter is constrained only by the higher authority of the temple or palace.

A § 1 If a woman, either a wife-of-a-man or a daughter-of-a-man, should enter into a temple and steal something from the sanctuary, and it is discovered in her possession or they prove the charges against her or convict her: […] a divination(?), they shall inquire of the deity; they shall treat her as the deity instructs them.

A § 2 If a woman, either a wife-of-a-man or a daughter-of-a-man, should speak something disgraceful or utter a blasphemy: that woman bears responsibility for her offense; they shall have no claim against her husband, her sons, or her daughters.

A § 3 If a man is ill or dead, and his wife should steal something from his house and give it either to a man or to a woman or to anyone else: they shall kill the wife of the man as well as the receivers (of the goods).

And if a wife-of-a-man, whose husband is healthy should steal from her husband's house and give it either to a man or to a woman or to anyone else: the man shall prove the charges against his wife and shall impose a punishment; furthermore, the receiver who received (the goods) from the wife of the man shall give (back) the stolen goods, and they shall impose a punishment on the receiver identical to that which the man imposed on his wife.

A § 4 If either a slave or a slave-woman should receive something from a wife-of-a-man: they shall cut off the slave's or slave-woman's nose and ears; they shall restore the stolen goods; the man shall cut off his wife's ears. But if he releases his wife and does not cut off her ears, they shall not cut off (the nose and ears) of the slave or slave-woman and they shall not restore the stolen goods.

A § 5 If a wife-of-a-man should steal something with a value greater than 300 shekels of lead from the house of another man: the owner of the stolen goods shall take an oath, saying, "If I incited her, saying, 'Commit a theft in my house' (may I be struck down)."

If her husband agrees, he shall hand over the stolen goods and he shall ransom her; he shall cut off her ears. If her husband does not agree to her ransom, the owner of the stolen goods shall take her and he shall cut off her nose.

A § 6 If a wife-of-a-man should place goods for safekeeping outside (of the house): the receiver of the goods shall bear liability for stolen property.

A § 7 If a woman should lay a hand upon a man and they prove the charges against her: she shall pay 1,800 shekels of lead; they shall strike her 20 blows with rods.

A § 8 If a woman should crush a man's testicle during a quarrel: they shall cut off one of her fingers.

And if a physician should bandage it but the second testicle then is affected along with it and becomes … , or if she should crush the second testicle during the quarrel: they shall gouge out both her […]-s.[29]

A § 9 If a man lays a hand upon a wife-of-a-man, behaves toward her like a bull, and they prove the charges against him and find him guilty: they shall cut off one of his fingers.

If he should kiss her: they shall draw his lower lip across the blade(?) of an ax and cut it off.[30]

A § 10 [If either] a man or a woman enters [a man's] house and kills [either a man] or a woman: [they shall hand over] the killers [to the head of the household]. If he so chooses, he shall kill them; or if he chooses to come to an accommodation, he shall take [their property]. And if there is [nothing of value to give from the house] of the killers, [he shall take] either a son [or a daughter …]

A § 12 If a wife-of-a-man should walk along the main thoroughfare, and a man should seize her and say to her, "I want to copulate with you!": she shall not consent but she shall protect herself.

Should he seize her by force and copulate with her—whether they discover him upon the wife of the man or witnesses later prove the charges against him that he copulated with the woman: they shall kill the man; there is no punishment for the woman.

A § 13 If a wife-of-a-man should go out of her house and go to a man where he resides, and should he copulate with her knowing that she is the wife-of-a-man: they shall kill the man and the wife.

A § 14 If a man should copulate with a wife-of-a-man either in an inn or in the main thoroughfare, knowing that she is the wife-of-a-man: they shall treat the copulator as the man declares his wife is to be treated.

If he should copulate with her without knowing that she is the wife-of-a-man: the copulator is clear; the man shall prove the charges against his wife and he shall treat her as he wishes.

A § 15 If a man should seize a man upon his wife and they prove the charges against him and find him guilty: they shall kill both of them; there is no liability for him.

If he seize and bring him before either the king or the judges, and they prove the charges against him and find him guilty: if the woman's husband kills his wife, then he shall also kill the man; if he cuts off his wife's nose, he shall turn the man into a eunuch and they shall lacerate his entire face. But if [he releases] his wife, he shall [release] the man.

A § 16 If a man [should copulate] with the wife-of-a-man [… by] her invitation: there is no punishment for the man; the man (i.e., husband) shall impose whatever punishment he chooses upon his wife.

If he should copulate with her by force and they prove the charges against him and find him guilty: his punishment shall be identical to that of the wife of the man.

A § 17 If a man should say to a man, "Everyone always copulates with your wife!" but there are no witnesses: they shall draw up a binding agreement, they shall undergo the divine River Ordeal.

A § 18 If a man says to his comrade, either in private or in a public quarrel, "Everyone always copulates with your wife," and further, "I can prove the charges," but he is unable to prove the charges and does not prove the charges: they shall strike that man 40 blows with rods, he shall perform the king's service for one full month, they shall shave him, and he shall pay 3,600 shekels of lead.

A § 19 If a man in private spreads rumors about his comrade, saying, "Everyone always copulates with him," or in a quarrel before people says to him, "Everyone always copulates with you," and further, "I can prove the charges against you," but he is unable to prove the charges and does not prove the charges: they shall strike that man 50 blows with rods, he shall perform the king's service for one full month, they shall shave him, and he shall pay 3,600 shekels of lead.

A § 20 If a man copulates with his comrade and they prove the charges against him and find him guilty: they shall copulate with him and they shall turn him into a eunuch.

A § 21 If a man strikes a daughter-of-a-man and thereby causes her to abort her fetus, and they prove the charges against him and find him guilty: he shall pay 9,000 shekels of lead, they shall strike him 50 blows with rods, he shall perform the king's service for one full month.

A § 22 If another man—neither her father, nor her brother, nor her son—should arrange to have a wife-of-a-man travel with him:

then he shall swear an oath to the effect that he did not know that she is the wife-of-a-man and he shall pay 7,200 shekels of lead to the woman's husband.

If [he knows that she is the wife-of-a-man]: he shall pay damages and he shall swear, saying, "If I copulated with her (may I be struck down)."

But if the wife-of-a-man should declare, "He did copulate with me," since the man has paid damages to the man, he shall undergo the divine River Ordeal; there is no binding agreement.

If he should refuse to undergo the divine River Ordeal, they shall treat him as the woman's husband treats his wife.

A § 23 If a wife-of-a-man should take a wife-of-a-man into her house and give her to a man for purposes of copulation, and the man knows that she is a wife-of-a-man: they shall treat him as one who has copulated with a wife-of-a-man, and they shall treat the procuress just as the woman's husband treats his wife the copulator.

And if the woman's husband intends to do nothing to his wife the copulator: they shall do nothing to the copulator or to the procuress; they shall release them.

But if the wife-of-a-man does not know (what was intended) but the woman who takes her into her house brings the man in to her by deceit(?), and he then copulates with her—if, as soon as she leaves the house, she should declare that she has been the victim of copulation: they shall release the woman, she is clear; they shall kill the copulator and the procuress.

But if the woman should not so declare: the man shall impose whatever punishment on his wife he wishes; they shall kill the copulator and the procuress.

A § 24 If a wife-of-a-man should withdraw herself from her husband and enter into the house of an Assyrian man, either in that city or in any of the nearby towns, to a house which he assigns to her, residing with the mistress of the household, staying overnight three or four nights, and the householder is not aware that a wife-of-a-man is residing in his house, and later that woman is seized: the householder whose wife withdrew herself from him shall [mutilate] his wife and [not] take her back; they shall cut off the ears of the wife of the man with whom his wife resided.

If he pleases: her husband shall give 12,600 shekels of lead as her value, and, if he pleases, he shall take back his wife.

And if the householder knows that it is a wife-of-a-man who is residing in his house with his wife: he shall give "triple." But if he should deny (that he knew of her status): he shall declare, "I did not know"; they shall undergo the divine River Ordeal. And if the man in whose house the wife-of-a-man resided should refuse the divine River Ordeal: he shall give "triple."

If it is the man whose wife withdrew herself from him who should refuse the divine River Ordeal: he is clear, he shall bear the expenses of the divine River Ordeal.

And if the man whose wife withdrew herself from him does not mutilate his wife: he shall take back his wife; no sanctions are imposed.

A § 25 If there is a woman residing in her own father's house and her husband is dead, her husband's brothers have not yet divided their inheritance, and she has no son, (as for) whatever valuables her husband bestowed upon her that are not missing: her husband's brothers who have not yet divided their inheritance shares shall take.

As for the rest (of the property): they shall resort to a verdict by the gods, they shall provide proof, and they shall take; they shall not be seized for the divine River Ordeal or the oath.

A § 26 If there is a woman residing in her own father's house and her husband is dead, (as for) whatever valuables her husband bestowed upon her: if there are sons of her husband, they shall take; if there are no sons of her husband, she herself shall take.

A § 27 If a woman is residing in her own father's house and her husband visits her regularly: he himself shall take any marriage settlement which he, her husband, gave to her; he shall have no claim to anything belonging to her father's house.

A § 28 If a widow should enter the house of a man and she is carrying her (dead husband's) posthumous son with her, he grows up in the house of the man who took her (in marriage), but no tablet of his sonship is written: he will not take an inheritance share from the estate of the one who raised him and he will not be responsible for (its) debts; he shall take an inheritance share from the estate of his begetter in accordance with his portion.

A § 29 If a woman should enter the house of her husband: her dowry and whatever she brings with her from her father's house, and also whatever her father-in-law gave her upon her entering, are clear for her sons; the sons of her father-in-law shall have no valid claim.

But if her husband takes control(?) of her (or: it (?)): he shall give it to whichever of his sons he wishes.

A § 30 If a father should bring the ceremonial marriage prestation and present < the bridal gift > to the house of the father-in-law of his son, and the woman is not (yet) given to his son, and another son of his, whose wife was residing in her father's house, is dead: he shall give the wife of his deceased son in *ahuzzatu*[31] to his second (younger) son to whose father-in-law's house he has presented (the bridal gift).

(Even) if the master of the daughter who is (also?) in receipt of the bridal gift does not agree to give his daughter (to the younger son): if the father who presented the bridal gift so pleases, he shall take his daughter-in-law and give her to his (younger) son. Or if he so pleases, as much as he presented, whether lead, silver, gold, or anything not edible, he shall take (back) in the quantities originally given; but he shall have no claim to anything edible.

A § 31 If a man should present the bridal gift to the house of his father-in-law, and his wife is dead, but there are (other living) daughters of his father-in-law: if he so pleases, he shall take (in marriage) a daughter of his father-in-law in lieu of his deceased wife. Or if he so pleases, he shall take (back) the silver that he gave; they shall not give (back) to him grain, sheep, or anything edible; he shall receive only the silver.

A § 32 If a woman is residing in the house of her own father and her [...] is given, whether she is taken or not taken into the house of her father-in-law: she shall be responsible for her husband's debts, transgression, or punishment.

A § 33 If a woman is residing in the house of her own father, her husband is dead, and she has sons: [... (large gap)]; or [if he so pleases], he shall give her in *ahuzzatu*[32] to her father-in-law.

If her husband and her father-in-law are both dead, and she has no son: she is a widow; she shall go wherever she pleases.

A § 34 If a man should take (in marriage) a widow, her binding agreement is not concluded, (but) she resides in his house for two years: she is a wife; she shall not leave.

A § 35 If a widow should enter into the house of a man: whatever she brings with her all belongs to her (second) husband.

And if a man should enter (the house of) a woman: whatever he brings with him all belongs to the woman.

A § 36 If a woman either is residing in her father's house or her husband settles her in a house elsewhere, and her husband then travels abroad but does not leave her any oil, wool, clothing, or provisions, or anything else, and sends her no provisions from abroad: that woman shall remain for her husband for five years; she shall not reside with a (second) husband.

If she has sons: they shall be hired out and provide for their own sustenance; the woman shall wait for her husband, she shall not reside with a (second) husband.

If she has no sons: she shall wait for her husband for five years; at the onset of(?) six years, she shall reside with the husband of her choice; her (first) husband, upon returning, shall have no valid claim to her; she is clear for her latter husband.

If he is delayed beyond the five years but is not detained of his own intention, whether because a ... seized him and he fled or because he was falsely arrested and was detained: upon returning he shall so prove, he shall give a woman comparable to his wife and he shall take his wife.

And if the king should send him to another country and he is delayed beyond the five years: his wife shall wait for him; she shall not go to reside with a (second) husband.

And if she should reside with a (second) husband before five years and should she give birth: because she did not wait in accordance with the agreement but was taken (in marriage), her (first) husband, upon returning, shall take her and also her offspring.

A § 37 If a man intends to divorce his wife: if it is his wish, he shall give her something; if it is not his wish, he shall not give her anything, and she shall leave empty-handed.

A § 38 If a woman is residing in her own father's house and her husband divorces her: he shall take the valuables which he himself bestowed upon her; he shall have no claim to the bridewealth which he brought, it is clear for the woman.

A § 39 If a man should give to a husband someone who is not his own daughter, (and) if previously her father had been in debt and she had been made to reside as a pledge: should a prior creditor come forward, he shall receive in full the value of the woman from the giver of the woman (in marriage); if he has nothing to give, he shall take the giver.

But if she had been saved from a catastrophe:[33] she is clear for the one who saved her.

And if the one who takes (in marriage) the woman either causes a tablet to be ... for him or they have a claim in place against him: he shall [...] the value of the woman, and the giver [...].

A § 40 A wife-of-a-man, or [widows], or [Assyrian] women who go out into the main thoroughfare [shall not have] their heads [bare].

Daughters of a man [... with] either a ... -cloth or garments or [...] shall be veiled, [...] their heads [... (gap) ...] When they go about [...] in the main thoroughfare during the daytime, they shall veil themselves.

A concubine who goes about in the main thoroughfare with her mistress is to be veiled.

A *qadiltu*-priestess whom a husband has taken (in marriage) is to be veiled in the main thoroughfare, but one whom a husband has not taken (in marriage) is to have her head bare in the main thoroughfare, she shall not veil herself.

A prostitute shall not veil herself, her head shall be bare.

Whoever sees a veiled prostitute shall seize her, secure witnesses, and bring her to the palace entrance. They shall not take her jewelry; he who has seized her shall take her clothing; they shall strike her 50 blows with rods; they shall pour hot pitch over her head.

And if a man should see a veiled prostitute and release her and not bring her to the palace entrance: they shall strike that man 50 blows with rods; the one who informs against him shall take his clothing; they shall pierce his ears, thread (them) on a cord, tie (it) at his back; he shall perform the king's service for one full month.

Slave-women shall not veil themselves, and he who should see a veiled slave-woman shall seize her and bring her to the palace entrance: they shall cut off her ears; he who seizes her shall take her clothing.

If a man should see a veiled slave-woman but release her, not seize her, not bring her to the palace entrance, and they then prove the charges against him and find him guilty: they shall strike him 50 blows with rods; they shall pierce his ears, thread (them) on a cord, tie (it) at his back. The one who informs against him shall take his garments. He shall perform the king's service for one full month.

A § 41 If a man would veil his concubine, he shall assemble five or six of his comrades, he shall veil her in their presence, he shall declare, "She is my wife": she is his wife.

A concubine who is not veiled in the presence of the people, whose husband did not declare, "She is my wife": she is not a wife, she is indeed a concubine.

If a man is dead and there are no sons of his veiled wife: the sons of concubines are indeed sons; they shall take the inheritance share.

A § 42 If a man pours oil on the head of a daughter-of-a-man on the occasion of a holiday, or brings dishes on the occasion of a banquet: they shall not make restoration (of gifts given).

A § 43 If a man either pours oil on the head or brings (provisions) for the banquet, (and) the son to whom he assigned the wife either dies or flees: he shall give her (in marriage) to whichever of his remaining sons he wishes, from the oldest to the youngest of at least ten years of age.

If the father is dead and the son to whom he assigned the wife is also dead, and there is a son of the deceased son who is at least ten years old: he shall take her (in marriage).

If the sons of the (dead) son are less than ten years old: if the father of the daughter wishes, he shall give his daughter (in marriage to one of them); or if he wishes he shall make a restitution (of gifts given).

If there is no son: he shall return as much as he received, precious stones or anything not edible, in its full amount; but he shall not return anything edible.

A § 44 If a male Assyrian or if a female Assyrian who is residing in the house of a man as a pledge for a debt for as much as his value has been taken for the full value: he may whip (the pledge), pluck out (the pledge's) hair, (or) mutilate or pierce (the pledge's) ears.

A § 45 If a woman is given (in marriage) and the enemy takes her husband prisoner, and she has neither father-in-law nor son: she shall remain for her husband for two years.

During these two years if she has no provisions, she shall come forward and so declare; if she is a citizen dependent upon the palace: her [...] shall provide for her and she shall do work for him.

I[f she is a wife] of a *hupšu*-soldier: [...] shall provide for her [and she shall do work for him].

And [if she is a wife-of-a-man whose] field and [house ...], she shall come forward [and declare before the judges], "[I have nothing] to eat." The judges shall question the mayor and the noblemen of the city; they shall give to her, in accordance with the going rate of a field in that city, a field and house for her provisioning for two years; she shall be resident (in that house) and they shall write a tablet for her. She shall allow two full years to pass, and then she may reside with the husband of her own choice. They shall write a tablet for her as for a widow.

If later on her lost husband should return to the country: he shall take back his wife who is taken (in marriage) outside the family; he shall have no claim to the sons she bore to her later husband; her later husband indeed shall take them. The field and house that she gave for full price outside the family for her provisioning, if it is not entered into the royal holdings(?): he shall give as much as was given, and he shall take it back.

And if he should not return but dies in another country: the king shall give his field and house wherever he chooses to give.

A § 46 If a woman whose husband is dead does not leave her house upon the death of her husband, if her husband did not deed her anything in writing: she shall reside in the house of (one of) her sons, wherever she chooses; her husband's sons shall provide for her, they shall draw up an agreement to supply her with provisions and drink as for a daughter-in-law whom they love.

If she is a second (wife) and has no sons of her own: she shall reside with one (of her husband's sons) and they shall provide for her in common.

If she (is a second wife and) does have sons, and the sons of the first (wife) do not agree to provide for her: she shall reside in the house of her own sons, wherever she chooses; her own sons shall provide for her, and she shall do service for them.

And if there is among her husband's sons one who intends to take her (in marriage): [...] shall not provide for her.

A § 47 If either a man or a woman should perform witchcraft and they (the paraphernalia) are found in their possession, and they prove the charges against them and find them guilty: they shall kill the performer of witchcraft.

A man who heard from an eyewitness to the witchcraft that he witnessed the performance of the witchcraft—(an eyewitness meaning one) who said to him: "I myself saw it"—the hearsay-witness shall go and inform the king.

If the eyewitness should recant what he reports to the king: he (the hearsay witness) shall declare before the divine Bull-the-Son-of-the-Sun-God, "If he did not say it to me (may I be struck down)"; he is clear. The king shall interrogate as he sees fit the eyewitness who spoke and then recanted and he shall investigate his matter. An exorcist shall have the man make a declaration on a day when he is purified and then he himself shall declare as follows, "No one shall release you (pl.) from the oath you swore by the king and by his son; you are bound by oath to the stipulations of the agreement to which you swore by the king and by his son."

A § 48 If a man < wants to give in marriage > his debtor's daughter who is residing in his house as a pledge: he shall ask her father[34] and he shall give her to a husband.

If her father does not agree: he shall not give her.

If her father is dead: he shall ask one of her brothers and the latter shall report to her (other) brothers.

If a brother declares, "I will redeem my sister within one full month" but if he should not redeem her within one full month: the creditor, if he so pleases, shall clear her of encumbrances and give her to a husband; [...] according to [...] he shall give her [...]

A § 49 [...] like a brother [...]. And if the prostitute is dead: because(?) her brothers declare, ... they shall divide shares [with (?)] the brothers of their mother(?).

A § 50 [If a man] strikes [a wife-of-a-man and causes her to abort her fetus, ...]: a wife-of-a-man who [...] and they shall treat him as [he treats] her; he shall make full payment of a life for her fetus.

And if that woman dies: they shall kill the man, he shall make full payment of a life for her fetus.

And if there is no son of the husband of that woman, and his wife whom he struck aborted her fetus: they shall kill the striker for the sake of her fetus.

If her fetus was a female: he shall make full payment of a life only.

A § 51 If a man strikes a wife-of-a-man who does not raise (her children) and causes her to abort her fetus: it is a punishable offense; he shall give 7,200 shekels of lead.

A § 52 If a man strikes a prostitute and causes her to abort her fetus: they shall assess him blow for blow; he shall make full payment of a life.

A § 53 If a woman aborts her fetus by her own action and they then prove the charges against her and find her guilty: they shall impale her; they shall not bury her.

If she dies as a result of aborting her fetus: they shall impale her; they shall not bury her.

If they should [conceal] that woman because she aborted her fetus [...]

A § 54 [If ...] or slave-women [...]

A § 55 If a man forcibly seizes and rapes a maiden who is residing in her father's house, [...] who is not spoken for(?), whose [womb(?)] is not opened, who is not taken (in marriage), and against whose father's house there is no outstanding claim—whether (the rape occurs) within the city, or in the countryside, or at night, whether in the main thoroughfare, or in a granary, or during the city festival: the father of the maiden shall take the wife of the copulator of the maiden and give her over to be raped; he shall not return her to her husband, he shall take her (for himself). The father shall give his daughter, she who is the victim of the copulation, to her copulator in *ahuzzatu*.[35]

If he (the copulator) has no wife: the copulator shall give "triple" the silver as the value of the maiden to her father; her copulator shall take her (in marriage); he shall not reject(?) her.

If the father does not desire it so: he shall accept "triple" silver for the maiden, and he shall give his daughter (in marriage) to whomever he chooses.

A § 56 If a maiden should willingly give herself to a man: the man shall so swear; they shall have no claim to his wife; the copulator shall give "triple" the silver as the value of the maiden; the father shall treat his daughter as he chooses.

A § 57 Whether it is a beating or [... for] a wife-of-a-man [... that is] written on the tablet [...]

A § 58 For all punishments[...] cutting off [...] and ... [...]

A § 59 In addition to the punishments for [a wife-of-a-man] that are [written] on the tablet, a man may [whip] his wife, pluck out her hair, mutilate her ears, or strike her; it bears no offense.

Neo-Babylonian laws (c. 700 BC)

A damaged tablet with script and language attributable to the Neo-Babylonian period preserves 15 law provisions, formulated as relative clauses (*amēlu ša ...*). Several provisions deal with circumstances involving marriage; others, not marriage-related, may involve women as principles.

§ 6 A man who sells a slave-woman, a claim arises against (the sale/ slave), and she is taken away: the seller shall give to the buyer the silver in its capital amount according to the sale document.

Should she bear sons: he shall give half a shekel of silver for each.

§ 8 A man who gives his daughter (in marriage) to a son-of-a-man, and the father (of the groom) commits certain properties in his tablet and awards them to his son, and the father-in-law commits the dowry of his daughter, and they write the tablets in mutual agreement: they will not alter the commitments of their respective tablets; the father will not make any reduction to the properties as written in the tablet to his son's benefit which he showed to his in-law.

Should the father, whose wife fate carries away, then take (in marriage) a second wife and should she then bear him sons: the sons of the second woman shall take one third[36] of the balance of his estate.

§ 9 A man who declares the dowry for his daughter or writes it on a tablet for her, and whose estate later decreases: he shall give to his daughter a dowry in accordance with the remaining assets of his estate; the father-in-law (i.e., the bride's father) and the groom will not by mutual agreement alter the commitments.

§ 10 A man who gives a dowry to his daughter, and she has no son or daughter, and fate carries her away: her dowry shall revert to her paternal estate.

§ 12 A wife whose husband takes her dowry, and who has no son or daughter, and whose husband fate carries away: a dowry equivalent to the dowry (which her husband had received) shall be given to her from her husband's estate.

If her husband should award to her a marriage-gift: she shall take her husband's marriage-gift together with her dowry, and thus her claim is satisfied.

If she has no dowry: a judge shall assess the value of her husband's estate and shall give to her some property in accordance with the value of her husband's estate.

§ 13 A man takes (in marriage) a wife, and she bears him sons, and later fate carries away that man, and that woman then decides to enter another man's house: she shall take (from her first husband's estate) the dowry that she brought from her father's house and anything that her husband awarded to her, and the husband she chooses shall take her (in marriage); as long as she lives, they shall have the joint use of the properties.

If she should bear sons to her (second) husband, after her death the sons of the second and first (husbands) shall have equal shares in her dowry. [...]

§ 15 A man who takes (in marriage) a wife who bears him sons and whose wife fate carries away, and who takes (in marriage) a second wife who bears him sons, and later on the father goes to his fate: the sons of the first (woman) shall take two-thirds of the paternal estate, and the sons of the second shall take one-third. Their sisters, who are still residing in the paternal home [...]

Notes

1 Bibliographical literature for all the law collections may be found in Roth, 1997, to which the major addition is the publication of a new exemplar of the Laws of Ur-Namma by Civil, 2011, 221–86. Additional literature may be found throughout the contributions in Westbrook, 2003. LE = Laws of Eshnunna; LH = Laws of Hammurabi; LL = Laws of Lipit-Ishtar; LNB = Neo-Babylonian Laws; LU = Laws of Ur-Namma; MAL = Middle Assyrian Laws.

2 This is particularly clear with the "lexical texts," those ancient word lists and "dictionaries," which compiled lists of Sumerian words and clauses and paired them with their Akkadian equivalents, and in particular with the series *ana ittišu* (published by Landsberger, 1937) and ur₅-ra I and II (published by Landsberger, 1957). On the scribal curriculum, see Veldhuis, 1997.

3 Benveniste, 1973.

4 Akkadian terms here are given in Standard Babylonian, the form of the headword in the volumes of the CAD, to which the reader is referred for further citations: *The Assyrian Dictionary of the Oriental Institute of the University of Chicago*, 1956–2011.

5 Sumerian does not distinguish grammatical gender.

6 § 6 (and also § 8) " … deflowers the not-deflowered spouse … ": Civil, 2011, 246 and note 33: " … seduces … a betrothed woman not yet married … , " with note: "Lit. 'not included (yet) in a household'," does not recognize that there is a clear relationship between the verb (a/e₂ bi₂-in-gi₄, lit. 'turns to the house') and its object (a nu-gi₄-a, lit., 'not-turned-to-the-house'). The nominal form, without the negation, a-gi₄-a, equated with Akkadian *kallatum* and translated "daughter-in-law," etc., evokes the common practice of a bride or bride-to-be entering into her husband's or father-in-law's household.

7 See note 6.

8 Sumerian tak₄ and Akkadian *ezēbum* "to leave."

9 § 11 is a subset of § 10: that is, § 10 deals with severing the relationship with a widow with whom he has been cohabiting with a formal agreement, § 11 deals with severing the relationship with a widow with whom he has been cohabiting without such a formal agreement.

10 In cases without evidence or witnesses, such as accusations of offenses done in secret (adultery, sorcery, for example), there may be recourse to divine intervention by oath or ordeal. The River Ordeal may involve one or both parties undergoing a test (swimming, floating, or some other activity) and one or both surviving. More often, one party "turns from" the ordeal, that is, refuses to undergo the process, and is declared the losing or guilty party. For oaths in judicial process, see the essays collected in Lafont, 1996. The judicial ordeal at all periods is surveyed comprehensively in Frymer-Kensky, 1977. See also Frymer-Kensky, 1981, 115–31; Durand, 1988, 509–39.

11 "Household of her man" probably refers to her natal home, but why it is expressed thus (rather than "house of her father," for example) is unclear.

12 Difficult: e₂(-)ad-da-ka(-)ti-la, but the sense is clear.

13 Or (less likely): loses her attractiveness (lit.: eye).

14 Var.: a second spouse.

15 Var.: he shall support the second spouse and the first-ranking-spouse.

16 See the comments at Introduction.

17 See note to LU § 6.

18 There is no mention of the fate of the child, who probably remains with his biological father.

19 The interpretation is difficult; see the note in Roth, 1997 to this provision.

20 The provisions LH § 108–11 fall among provisions dealing with traders and merchants, and thus should be understood to be regulating commerce (rather than regulating women's activities). For these provisions, see Roth, 1999, 445–64.

21 Variant: "they shall bind that woman innkeeper and cast her into the water." Here the casting into the water, which follows on the accusation and conviction, is clearly a punishment rather than a judicial procedure.

22 LH § 131 deals with a private accusation for which there is no evidence, and the woman takes a private oath to clear herself; § 132 deals with a public accusation, and the woman must undergo a public ordeal.

23 Compare LE § 29.

24 In this instance, casting into the water may be both a punishment and a judicial procedure (ordeal).

25 The term refers to a skin disease. Mesopotamian medical understanding attributes such afflictions to acts of divine being; see Stol, 1993, 143 with literature.

26 "Seize" in this case refers to seizing for debt-servitude.

27 See Roth, 1998.
28 The judges are authorities whose precise qualifications, selection, etc., remain unknown. Although in certain circumstances the king may act as a judge, in LH § 177 it is most likely a local authority who safeguards the deceased man's estate for inheritance by his children.
29 Possibly "eyes" or "breasts."
30 See Marti, 2004, 33.
31 An abstract noun derived from the verb translated here (passim) "to take (in marriage)." That the term refers to "marriage to a woman who was no longer a virgin" (so Lafont, in Westbrook 2003, p. 536 n. 9) is not supported.
32 See note 31.
33 That is, if she had been given in times of famine or crisis with the intention of saving her life.
34 Text, erroneously: "her father shall ask."
35 See note to *ahhuzatu* at A § 33, above.
36 "One third" refers to a normal share rather than the preferential or double share.

Bibliography

Assante, J. (1998) The kar.kid/harimtu, prostitute or Single Woman? A Critical review of the Evidence, *Ugarit Forschungen* 30, 5–96.

——(2007) Review of *Prostitutes and Courtesans. What Makes a 'Prostitute' a Prostitute? Modern Definitions and Ancient Meanings*, *Historiae* 4, 117–32.

Benveniste, E. (1973) *Indo-European Language and Society*, transl. E. Palmer (London: Faber and Faber).

Civil, M. (2011) The Law Collection of Ur-Namma, in *Cuneiform Royal Inscriptions and Related Texts in the Schøyen Collection*, A.R. George, ed. (Bethesda: CDL Press), 221–86.

Culbertson, L., ed. (2011) *Slaves and Households in the Near East* (Chicago: Oriental Institute).

Dandamaev, M. (1984) *Slavery in Babylonia from Nabopolassar to Alexander the Great*, transl. M. Powell (DeKalb: Northern Illinois University Press).

von Dassow, E. (forthcoming) *Awīlum* and *muškēnum* in the Age of Hammurabi, in *Compte Rendu de la 55è Rencontre Assyriologique Internationale (Paris, July 2009)*, Lionel Marti, ed.

Durand, J. (1988) L'ordalie, in *Archives épistolaires de Mari 1/1*, Archives royales de Mari 26/1, J. Durand, ed. (Paris: ERC), 509–39.

Frymer-Kensky, T. (1977) *The Judicial Ordeal in the Ancient Near East* (Yale University PhD diss.).

——(1981) Suprarational Legal Procedures in Elam and Nuzi, in *Studies on the Civilization and Culture of Nuzi and the Hurrians in Honor of Ernest R. Lacheman*, M. Morrison and D. Owen, eds (Winona Lake: Eisenbrauns), 115–31.

Harris, R. (1975) *Ancient Sippar* (Leiden: Nederlands Historisch-Archaeologisch Istituut te Istanbul).

Jacobsen, Th. (1993) Notes on the Word lu₂, in *Kinattūtu ša dārâti: Raphael Kutscher Memorial Volume*, A. F. Rainey, ed. (Tel Aviv: Institute of Archaeology), 69–80.

Lafont, S., ed. (1996) *Jurer et maudire: pratiques politiques et usages juridiques du serment dans le Proche-Orient ancien* (Paris: l'Harmattan).

——(2003) 'Middle Assyrian Period', in *A History of Ancient Near Eastern Law*, Vol. 1, R. Westbrook ed. (Leiden: Brill), 521–63.

Landsberger, B. (1937) *Die Serie ana ittišu*, Materials for the Sumerian Lexicon 1 (Rome: Sumptibus Pontificii Instituti Biblici).

——(1957) *The Series HAR-ra = hubullu*, Materials for the Sumerian Lexicon 5 (Rome: Sumptibus Pontificii Instituti Biblici).

Marti, L. (2004) Proposition pour le § 9 des Lois Assyriennes, *Nouvelles Assyriologiques Brèves et Utilitaires*, 33.

Mendelsohn, I. (1949) *Slavery in the Ancient Near East* (New York: Oxford).

The Oriental Institute. (1956-2011) *The Assyrian Dictionary of the Oriental Institute of the University of Chicago (1956–2011)* (Chicago: The Oriental Institute).

Renger, J. (1967) Untersuchungen zum Priestertum in der altbabylonischen Zeit, *Zeitschrift für Assyriologie* 58, 110–88.

Roth, M. T. (1987) Age at Marriage and the Household: A Study of Neo-Assyrian and Neo-Babylonian Forms, *Comparative Studies in Society and History* 29(4), 715–47.

——(1997) *Law Collections from Mesopotamia and Asia Minor*, 2nd edn. (Atlanta: Scholars Press).

——(1998) Law and Gender: A Case Study from Ancient Mesopotamia, in *Gender and Law in the Hebrew Bible and the Ancient Near East*, Bernard M. Levinson, Victor H. Matthews, and Tikva Frymer-Kensky, eds (Sheffield Academic Press), 173–84.

——(1999) The Priestess, the Prostitute, and the Tavern, *Munuscula Mesopotamica*, B. Bock, E. Cancik-Kirschbaum and T. Richter, eds (Kevelaer: Butzon und Bercker), 445–64.

——(2006) Marriage, Divorce, and the Prostitute in Ancient Mesopotamia, in *Prostitutes and Courtesans in the Ancient World*, C. Faraone and L. McClure, eds (Madison: University of Wisconsin Press), 21–39.

——(in press a) A Note on *mār awīlim* in the Old Babylonian Law Collections.

——(in press b) On Persons in the Old Babylonian Law Collections: The Case of *mār awī-lim* in Bodily Injury Provisions, in *Stolper AV*, M. Kozuh and C. Woods, eds.

——(in press c) Errant Oxen, Or: The Goring Ox Redux, in *Machinist AV*, A. Winitzer et al., eds.

Stol, M. (1993) *Epilepsy in Mesopotamia* (Groningen: Styx).

Veldhuis, N. (1997) *Elementary Education at Nippur* (PhD diss., Groningen).

Westbrook, R. (1988) *Studies in Biblical and Cuneiform Law*, Paris: Gabalda.

——(1995) Slave and Master in Ancient Near Eastern Law, *Chicago-Kent Law Review* 70, 1631–76.

Westbrook, R. ed.(2003) *A History of Ancient Near Eastern Law*, 2 vols (Leiden: Brill).

7

THE *EPIC OF GILGAMESH*

Karen Nemet-Nejat

Introduction

Modern scholars have developed a method of classifying literature into categories such as, myths, narratives, legends, epic poetry, hymns, wisdom literature, folk tales, and so on.[1] However, with few exceptions, Sumerian and Akkadian do not have words to express these genres.[2]

In an attempt to describe cuneiform literature within its own terms, Benjamin Foster created five "broad categories" of Akkadian literature namely, celebratory, didactic, narrative, effective, and expressive. Foster noted that among these classifications the boundaries are not hard and fast, and some texts may belong to more than one category. He was careful to note that this typology does not necessarily correspond to ancient classifications about which little is known.[3]

Perhaps, a better way to read and understand cuneiform literature is within its own terms. The extant literary works should be grouped as the ancients did in organizing texts[4] or descriptions within the text, as in an Old Babylonian fragment from the Hittite court in Anatolia referring to Gilgamesh as a "song," that is, a performance piece.[5] Unfortunately, Gilgamesh is not listed in any extant song catalog to date.

Versions: evolution of the epic through time

Sumerian

The extant Sumerian narratives consist of individual episodes about Gilgamesh and are dated to the late second millennium; they are *Gilgamesh and Akka, Gilgamesh and Huwawa A, Gilgamesh and Huwawa B, Gilgamesh and the Bull of Heaven,*[6] *Gilgamesh, Enkidu, and the Netherworld, The Death of Gilgamesh,* and possibly The *Gudam Epic.*[7]

However, there is no original Sumerian *Gilgamesh Epic.* Rather, the Sumerian poems provided broad outlines, which were adapted into the Akkadian version of the *Gilgamesh of Epic.*[8]

175

Akkadian

Versions of Gilgamesh, written in the Akkadian language, can be dated from ca.1700 BC (called the Old Babylonian period) to the last extant tablet ca.127 BC.[9] Foster noted that texts that could be expanded or abbreviated, without losing their contours, have the best chance of surviving from an earlier time.[10]

The Old Babylonian versions are called "Surpassing All Kings," a series consisting of an epic poem of eleven tablets and an addendum of a twelfth tablet, which is a partial translation of a Sumerian poem, which probably dated to the first millennium BC.[11]

By the first millennium many literary works had acquired a standard or what is referred to as a "canonical" form due the efforts of Kassite scribes (1595–1158 BC), who were the last of Babylonia's great creative writers.[12] The longest extant version of *The Gilgamesh Epic*, referred to as the Standard Babylonian Version, is from the seventh century BC, and is referred to as "He who saw everything," after the first few words of *The Gilgamesh Epic*; however, in catalogs and colophons[13] of the first millennium, *The Gilgamesh Epic* is simply referred to as "the series of Gilgamesh."

Oral versions

The question remains as to whether or not *The Gilgamesh Epic* originated from an oral tradition. George indicated that both the Sumerian and Old Babylonian versions were originally lays sung by minstrels. He suggested that despite a unified plot, the differences in wording signify that the narrative poem was transmitted orally.[14] Nonetheless, George was careful to point out that, even though the oral tradition may have evolved, we know only of a written tradition.[15]

Both Foster and Tigay stated that, at the present time, the oral development and transmission of narrative texts cannot be proven.[16] Foster added that, even though some scholars believe in the importance of an oral tradition in the formation of Akkadian literature, no "teller of tales" is mentioned in written Akkadian tradition; in fact, "little in Akkadian literature compels reconstructing an oral phase or tradition behind it."[17]

Addition of Tablet XII

The Epic of Gilgamesh consists of twelve tablets in the Standard Babylonian version. However, Tablet XII appears to be unrelated to Tablets I–XI. In fact, Tablet XII is, in part, a literal translation of the Sumerian composition, *Gilgamesh, Enkidu, and the Netherworld*.[18]

In the Sumerian version, the widows' children were hurt during Gilgamesh's game. Their outcry caused the ball and stick, items from a game in Tablet I, to fall to the Netherworld. The Sumerian episode was used by the Akkadian author to explain Enkidu's death. In Tablet XII, Enkidu tried to retrieve the ball and stick from the Netherworld for Gilgamesh. Gilgamesh advised Enkidu how to behave in the Netherworld but Enkidu did not listen to him, and so Enkidu was forced to remain in the Netherworld. However, the god Enki, who was the benefactor to mankind, intervened and allowed Enkidu to return from the Netherworld to answer Gilgamesh's questions and explain that those who enjoyed the most comfortable afterlife were the ones with many loving descendants who made regular offerings to their dead ancestors.

Sites where the epic was found

The Gilgamesh Epic has been found in numerous sites throughout Mesopotamia. Different versions have been found in Emar on the Euphrates, Ugarit on the Mediterranean coast, Megiddo in Israel, and in Egypt. From Hattusa in Anatolia, paraphrases of the epic were copied many times in antiquity, both in Hittite and Hurrian.[19] Because of the discovery of new editions and translations, the epic must regularly be brought up to date.

Summary of *The Gilgamesh Epic* with the female cast of characters[20]

The female characters in Gilgamesh do not have major roles. Rather, they are important in that they move the story forward. Harris stated that *The Gilgamesh Epic* was written by a male audience for a male audience.[21] Therefore, the activities and adventures of Gilgamesh and Enkidu would preclude a primary role for women.[22]

The Epic of Gilgamesh began with praise of Gilgamesh, King of Uruk, who built the Temple of Anu (the sky-god and originally chief god of the pantheon) and Ishtar (the goddess of love and war), and the city wall. According to the narrator, Gilgamesh himself wrote the epic on a lapis lazuli tablet,[23] which was deposited in the foundation of the city wall and was available for all to read.

Gilgamesh was described as a demigod, who was two-thirds divine and one-third human. His mother was the goddess Ninsun "lady of the wild cows"[24] and his father, Lugalbanda, was one of the early kings of Uruk. Gilgamesh was described as being of unusual strength and beauty.

Gilgamesh oppressed the young men of Uruk by playing a form of polo in which one man sat on the shoulders of another, as a polo player would sit astride a horse. Gilgamesh played polo until the young men of Uruk were exhausted.[25] Then he had sex with the female virgins before their husbands. The citizens cried out to the birth goddess, Aruru, who responded by creating Enkidu, a primal man, as Gilgamesh's match.

Shamhat:[26] prostitute who civilized Enkidu

Enkidu was born and raised among the wild beasts; he freed the animals caught by trappers. A trapper approached the king, who suggested the problem would be solved by the trapper bringing a harlot, Shamhat, to have sexual intercourse with Enkidu, thereby civilizing him so that he could no longer live among the animals.[27] Upon seeing Enkidu:

> Shamhat loosened her garments.[28]
> She uncovered her vagina, and he took her sexuality.
> She was not afraid; she took his virility.[29]
> She spread her garment, and he lay on her.
> She treated him, a (primitive) man to the sensuous work
> of a woman.
> In his lust, he had sex with her.
> Six days and seven nights, Enkidu, erect, pouring (semen)
> into Shamhat.[30]
>
> (Tablet I: 188–94)

Enkidu's sexual encounter with Shamhat was one step in civilizing him. Enkidu, rejected by the animals, was comforted by Shamhat:

> Enkidu, you are handsome. You have become like a god.
> Why do you roam the steppes with the wild animals?
> Come, I will lead you to Uruk-the-Sheepfold.[31]
> To the holy temple, the dwelling of Anu and Ishtar.[32]
>
> (Tablet I: 207–10 ≈ Tablet II: 6–10)

The text shifted to the dreams of Gilgamesh (below). After dreams, which interrupted the flow of the story, Shamhat brought Enkidu to the shepherds where he learned how to eat bread, drink beer, and anoint himself with oil.

(Rīmat)-Ninsun: mother of Gilgamesh

Interpreted dreams

Prior to Enkidu's arrival, Gilgamesh saw two similar dreams, which his mother, Rīmat-Ninsun interpreted as foretelling of the arrival of someone with whom Gilgamesh would share a close friendship.[33] Both dreams were similar. In the second dream, Gilgamesh told his mother:

> In a street of Uruk's main square,[34]
> An axe was lying,[35] and they gathered around it

The land of Uruk was standing around it. The land was
   gathered around it.
The men congregated around it.
I carried it and placed it at your feet.
I loved it like a wife; I made love to it.
You made it my companion.

(Tablet I: 277–85)

Ninsun interpreted his dream:

My son, the axe which you saw is my companion.
You will love it like a woman and make love to it.
And I will make it like your companion.
A strong companion will come to you, one who
   rescues his friend.
He is the mightiest in the land; he has strength.
Like a meteor of Anu, his might is strengthened.

(Tablet I: 288–93)

Enkidu eventually accompanied Shamhat to Uruk. When Enkidu saw Gilgamesh's hedonistic behavior, he challenged Gilgamesh. They wrestled, and Gilgamesh won. Enkidu acknowledged Gilgamesh as a king, divinely appointed. The two became devoted friends.

Gilgamesh suggested that he and Enkidu undertake a dangerous adventure to kill Humbaba, the monster who was appointed by Enlil[36] to guard the Cedar Forest, and to cut down a cedar, thereby achieving eternal fame. The citizens raised strong objections, but Gilgamesh was determined to go ahead with his plan. The people of Uruk cautioned Gilgamesh to allow Enkidu to lead the way.

Prayer to Shamash

Ninsun pleaded with her son not to go, but to no avail. She anointed and outfitted herself. Making an offering, Ninsun then prayed to Shamash, the sun god:[37]

She hurried up the ladder, she climbed onto the roof;
She went up to the roof, and she set up incense before Shamash.
She scattered incense before Shamash; she raised her hands
   (in prayer).
Why have you afflicted my son, Gilgamesh, with a
   restless heart?[38]
Now you have touched him so that he travels.
A distant path to where Humbaba is.
He will face a battle that he does not know.
He will travel a road he does not know.

179

Until he goes and returns,
Until he reaches the Cedar Forest,
Until he kills Humbaba the Terrible,
Until he eradicates from the land something evil that you hate,
On the day that you cross the sky,[39]
May Ayya,[40] the Bride, without fear remind you,
"Entrust him to the Watchman of the Night."

(Tablet III: 43–57)

Enkidu promised Ninsun that he would bring Gilgamesh back safely from this journey. The elders advised Gilgamesh to prepare for this adventure and gave their blessings.

Gilgamesh set off with Enkidu leading the way, taking special weapons and relying on the promised protection of the sun god.[41] During the six-day journey, they camped, and Enkidu made a magic circle of flour around Gilgamesh each night.[42]

Gilgamesh had terrifying and ominous dreams,[43] but the friends continued their journey. When they reached the Cedar Forest, Enkidu wanted to turn back; he realized the gravity of their plan. The Sun God urged them to continue, and they confronted Humbaba. Enkidu persuaded Gilgamesh to kill Humbaba, so that Gilgamesh would become famous for slaying this monster. Enkidu then cut down the tallest cedar to make a door for Enlil's Temple. They made a raft and sailed away with the Humbaba's head as proof of their conquest.

When the two friends returned to Uruk, Gilgamesh washed, dressed, and put on his crown. Ishtar, the goddess of love and war, saw Gilgamesh and wanted to marry him, offering him power and wealth.

Ishtar: goddess of love and war

Encounter with Gilgamesh

The Princess Ishtar looked with desire at Gilgamesh's beauty:

Come, Gilgamesh, and you will be my husband,
Give me your sensuality.
You will be my husband, and I will be your wife.
I will harness for you a chariot of lapis lazuli and gold
With wheels of gold and "horns" of electrum.
It will be harnessed with great storming mules.
Enter our house with the fragrance of cedar.
When you enter our house, the excellent[44] doorpost will
kiss your feet.
Kings, lords and princes will bow beneath you.

They will bring you bring produce of the mountains and
  countryside as tribute.
Your she-goats will bear triplets,[45] your ewes twins.[46]
Your pack-laden donkey foal will overtake a mule.
At the chariot your horses will gallop magnificently.
At the yoke your ox will have no match.

(Tablet VI: 7–21)

Gilgamesh rejected Ishtar and described the cruel punishments she inflicted on
her other lovers (as depicted in various myths). He also insulted Ishtar with a
series of possible proverbial sayings by comparing her unfavorably, for example:

Tar that stains the one who carries it.
A waterskin that soaks the one who carries it.
Limestone that destroys the city wall of the enemy's country.
A shoe that bites the foot of its owner.

(Tablet VI: 37–40)

Ishtar's meeting with her father to release the Bull of Heaven

Ishtar was furious at Gilgamesh's rejection and insults. She went to her father,
Anu, and mother, Antum weeping. She requested Anu to release the Bull of
Heaven:

Father, please give me the Bull of Heaven
That he will kill Gilgamesh in his dwelling.
If you do not give me the Bull of Heaven,
I will smash ... to its foundation.[47]
I will ...
And I will cause the dead to rise and eat the living,
I will make the dead outnumber the living.

(Tablet VI: 94–100)

Ishtar persuaded her father, and he gave her the Bull of Heaven. The Bull
wreaked havoc on Uruk. Both Enkidu and Gilgamesh killed the Bull. Ishtar cursed
Gilgamesh.
    Then Enkidu took the hindquarter of the Bull and flung it at Ishtar. Ishtar
gathered women of various rank to mourn this action. Gilgamesh summoned the
artisans' Bull to make a statue of his god for Lugalbanda. Then Gilgamesh celebrated in his palace. The young men slept. Enkidu had a dream in which he
would die for his actions in killing Humbaba and the Bull of Heaven. Enkidu
cursed Shamhat, but Shamash reproached Enkidu, reminding him that he
became friends with Gilgamesh because of Shamhat. Enkidu reversed his curse.

Enkidu told Gilgamesh his dream, which portended his death. He gave explicit details of the Netherworld where he would reside. Enkidu lay ill and died in twelve days.

Gilgamesh mourned his friend's death. He commissioned his artisans to make a memorial statue for Enkidu. Then Gilgamesh took off his royal garments as a sign of mourning.

Terrified by death, Gilgamesh set out on an obsessive search to find the secret of eternal life from the only person who achieved immortality, Utanapishtim "he who sought life." Along the treacherous journey he met with a scorpion creature and his mate, who guarded the passage to the sun. They warned him of the impossibility of his quest, but Gilgamesh proceeded through darkness until he reached a jeweled forest.

Siduri: the tavern keeper

The role of the tavern keeper

Ale-wives, like the philosopher of the *Epic of Gilgamesh*, were clearly an institution of city life; extant sources do not indicate whether this position was held by respectable married women.[48] The tavern was known as the place for erotic pleasure. Prostitution was an accepted trade there.[49] The walls of the taproom were decorated with clay plaques[50] showing naked women and other lascivious scenes. A clay tablet hung on the wall of the tavern, which extolled Ishtar. It referred to the tavern as her house where she could enter with her lovers.[51] In fact, in a Sumerian hymn Inanna (Akkadian, Ishtar) was described as a prostitute, who habituated the tavern. In this hymn she was described as "leaning out the window," "dressed like one of no repute," whose "seven suitors are bedding you."[52]

In taverns, fermentation of beer took place in large vessels, and beverages were usually drunk from beakers. There were many types of beer described in the lexical texts. Until Hammurabi's time (1795–1750 BC), women brewed beer, a craft protected by goddesses. In taverns these beverages had to be strained and so were drunk through drinking tubes, their ends perforated by small holes to act as a filter, from a common vat.[53]

Words of wisdom

Eventually Gilgamesh came to the tavern keeper, Siduri, who lived at the edge of the sea. He told her of his quest. Siduri tried to dissuade him:[54]

Gilgamesh, where are you roaming?
You will not find the life you are seeking.
When the gods created mankind,
They appointed death for mankind.
They held life in their own hands.

As for you Gilgamesh, let your stomach be full.[55]
Rejoice daily.
Dance and play day and night.
Let your clothes be clean,
Let your head be washed; may you be bathed in water.
Pay attention to the young child who holds your hand.[56]
Let a wife delight in your sexual desires,
For this task of mankind.[57]

(Tablet X iii 1–14)

Siduri's Information about reaching Utanapishtim

Gilgamesh insisted that Siduri tell him how to reach Utanapishtim. The tavern-keeper acceded:

There has not been any crossing at any time.
No one has ever crossed the sea.
Only the warrior Shamash has crossed the sea,
Except for Shamash, who can cross the sea.
The crossing is difficult; its ways are dangerous.
And in between are the Waters of Death, whose bar is
    impassable.
Should you, Gilgamesh, be able to cross the sea,
When you reach the Waters of Death, what will you do?
Gilgamesh, there is Urshanabi, the boatman of Utanapishtim
With him are "stone things" as he is trimming cedar in
    the forest.
Go, let him see your face.
If possible, cross with him,

(Tablet X: 70–90)

Gilgamesh did not succeed in his quest for eternal life; rather, he achieved relative immortality earned by physical creation—by building the wall of Uruk and the Temple of Ishtar that would endure. The end of the *Epic of Gilgamesh* referred to the beginning, that is, praise of Gilgamesh's wisdom and understanding of life.[58]

Purposes of *The Gilgamesh Epic*

Audience

The question remains as for what audience this literature was intended.[59] Foster indicated that Akkadian literature could be viewed as formal, written, literary work composed and possibly performed for educated people, in particular scholars and members of the royal court.[60]

Tigay suggested that "some narratives were either read or recited aloud, and also private reading was often done aloud." He also indicated that a composition may have been performed before an audience for centuries after writing.[61]

Dalley explained that this literary work has been classified as an epic because the adventures of the hero relate to a possibly heroic figure. However, she suggested that the oral form of the epic and its stories was for entertainment, "whether in royal courts, in private houses, around the campfires of desert caravans, or on the long sea voyages between the Indus and the head of the Arabian Gulf."[62]

Entertainment commissioned by the king

The Sumerian poems about Gilgamesh were probably composed at the end of the third millennium BC as court entertainment for King Shulgi.[63] Also, the courtly literature and songs of King Shulgi and his successors were adopted into the curriculum of Old Babylonian scribal schools. Large numbers of eighteenth-century tablets, discovered in scholars' houses at Nippur and Ur, have provided a set of more-or-less standardized texts, that is to say, a canon of classical Sumerian literature.

Known only in scribal circles

The extent to which literature was meant to entertain a broad reading public is not clear. The formation of Akkadian literature might have been in response to the tastes and requirements of a restricted group of literate people. Since only scribes and their students could read and write literature,[64] some compositions may have been written by them for their own education or amusement, thereby being known only within the schools.[65]

Scribes and authors

The authors of most Akkadian literary texts were usually anonymous; however, in a few instances the author was identified either in the narrative or in an acrostic. Sometimes divine inspiration or approval was acknowledged.

In the *Epic of Gilgamesh*, the scribe's name was occasionally given.[66] These scribes included Sîn-iddinam ca. 1750 BC from Nippur in central Babylonia, who wrote in Sumerian, though his native language was Akkadian. His father was a priest of Ekur, the temple of the god Enlil.[67] Sîn-lĕqi-unninni, ca. 1200 BC, was the editor of the Standard Version of the *Epic of Gilgamesh*. He was one of the few scribes known from a catalog preserved at Nineveh, which listed the authors of some of the best-known compositions. Besides being a scribe, he was also an exorcist, known for both medicine and magical rituals. He was supported by the great temple of Uruk after finishing his scribal studies.[68]

Also, known was Ashur-ra'im-napishti, an Assyrian apprentice or junior scribe, ca. 725 BC. King Ashurbanipal (668–631 BC) may have copied Tablets

III, VI–IX, XI, XII, as he was known to have been literate. At this time the Assyrian empire was the major superpower in Mesopotamia. The oldest source of Tablet XII was copied by the famous Assyrian scholar Nabû-zuqup-kěnu in 705 BC.

The most recent copy to date of Tablet X was recorded by Itti-Marduk-balātu, who became an astronomer at the temple of Marduk in Babylon in 127 BC. Eventually, 4,000 years of cuneiform studies ended in the Helleno-Parthian east.[69]

George analyzed extant tablets with their surviving colophons so that he was able to present information about who owned and who copied Gilgamesh in the first millennium BC.[70] Unlike the Assyrian sources, Babylonian tablets have been more difficult to attribute. To date, no complete set of tablets of the *Epic of Gilgamesh* has been found written by any scribe from any one place.

Educational tool

The Babylonians were unaware of the origins of their own literature, as implied by Berossus, a priest of Marduk during the third century BC. He wrote in Greek, referring to the burying of all literature in Sippar "before the Flood" and afterwards the return to Sippar to dig up the tablets and return them to mankind.[71]

The earliest extant literary texts came from the archives of Fara, Abu Salabikh, and Ebla (sometime before 2400 BC). Literature organized by Old Babylonian scribes have shown that only a fraction of Sumerian literature has survived, except in later copies.[72]

Some form of regulated education may have begun as early as 3000 BC. At the end of the third millennium, scribal education came under control of the state in order to satisfy the needs of a growing bureaucracy. The scribes also learned traditional texts, as well as creating new royal compositions. Literature about how the school operated was described in Sumerian essays, which Kramer called "School Days." These essays described in detail the organization of the staff, the student body, and the curriculum. The Sumerian compositions about school life were so detailed that I believe either disregarding them or treating them as fictional accounts of the creative mind is a matter that should be treated with the utmost care. Excavations have yet to prove these compositions as a false depiction of school life. Later, some Sumerian literature was translated into Akkadian. The grand imperial school probably can be found in levels of the Ur III and early Isin periods.[73]

To date the archaeological record of the Old Babylonian period has shown that students at Nippur and Ur were educated in private houses, none large enough to accommodate the kind of complex and large-scale academic institution described in the literature of "Schooldays."[74] Education at Nippur and Ur was similar to other cities such as Isin, Tell Harmal, and Tell ed-Der, in which scribal training was a small-scale occupation run by private individuals, in their homes, and not by the state. Classes may have been held in the courtyard[75] or in a small room.[76] At least two or three boys were taught at one time, sons, other young relatives, and, perhaps, sons of colleagues.[77]

Sumerian as a spoken language died out by the Old Babylonian period (ca. 2000–1500 BC), if not earlier, but Sumerian retained a particular prestige in education, even though more compositions were written in Akkadian, which had become the lingua franca. During the last century of the third millennium, King Shulgi probably became the patron of schools at Nippur and Ur, respectively, the religious and political centers of his empire. Or, he adopted these schools as libraries to house hymns "singing" his praises and other literature of his day for posterity. However, only a few fragments of this Neo-Sumerian literature have survived, including some fragments of narrative poems about Gilgamesh.

Toward the end of the eighteenth century, the center of power moved to the north, and the southern scribal curriculum that had kept the traditions of Sumerian literature alive for three centuries came to an end, and more Akkadian literature appeared, as *The Epic of Gilgamesh*.

Throughout the history of Mesopotamia, scribes continued to study and copy Sumerian language and literature, perhaps, to meet the needs of literate professionals, such as diviners, exorcists, astrologists, priests, and even apprentice scribes. Also, the curriculum included texts were deemed worthwhile because of their content, their broad appeal, their literary merit, and their entertainment value.[78]

Creative impulse

Akkadian has a rich and sizeable literature, which shows a creative impulse of individual writers in their use of form, content, and style, while working in a favorable cultural environment.[79] Foster explained, "Some Akkadian literary works are imitations, reworking, or translations of Sumerian prototypes," although "the two traditions are so closely connected that one can speak of a hybrid Sumero-Akkadian literary culture, even in the first millennium."[80]

In the case of *The Epic Gilgamesh*, the Old Babylonian author used the Sumerian narratives in addition to various other myths unrelated to Gilgamesh. By comparing these original source texts with the integrated Epic, the creative mind at work was revealed.[81] These texts were changed in terms of adding, deleting, and expanding the content. Both Moran and Jacobsen noted that the Old Babylonian version of Gilgamesh was a work of great originality, not only a translation from Sumerian, but rather "a poetry of remarkable freshness and simplicity."[82]

Libraries

Sumerian and Babylonian literature come mainly from two sources, the royal libraries of Ashur and Nineveh (twelfth to seventh centuries) and the scribal schools of the Old Babylonian period.

Ashurbanipal's library consisted of two types of archival documents, in both Sumerian and Akkadian, namely: (1) a rather small number of royal inscriptions, letters, and administrative texts; and (2) "library documents," namely, literary texts (myths and legends) and a considerable number of "scientific texts" (divination, omina and exorcism). King Ashurbanipal sent learned agents to search for tablets throughout Mesopotamia.[83] Ashurbanipal (668–631) wanted to collect all of traditional learning, some in multiple copies. The library of Nineveh presented a particularly valuable collection at a time when Aramaic (written in the West Semitic) had become the lingua franca and was written on ostraca, parchment, and papyrus; in fact, small numbers of court literature was written in Aramaic.[84]

Private libraries

Other first-millennium libraries, Babylonian as well as Assyrian, held random selections of the traditional texts. Usually, these collections have been found in private houses of families of the literate professional classes, who have had a scribal education for two or more generations, and also in the private homes of scribes.[85]

Historical background of the epic

Gilgamesh, King of Ur

Parents and birth name

The mother of Gilgamesh was the goddess, Ninsun, from whom he inherited two-thirds of his divinity. His father, Lugalbanda, was described as a king of Uruk, a shepherd, a man with demonic qualities, and a priest of Kullab, a district of Uruk in the Sumerian King List. Perhaps, Gilgamesh conquered Uruk and then "adopted" Lugalbanda as his father, a famous ruler and usurper of the dynasty of Uruk, a practice followed later by usurpers in Mesopotamia.[86]

The name Gilgamesh was comprised of elements that were contemporaneous in personal names, but fell out of use later. His name possibly may be translated as "Old-Man-Who-Became-a-Young-Man."[87]

The Sumerian King List

The Sumerian King List[88] listed Gilgamesh, who would have ruled ca. 2600 BC. *The Sumerian King List* should not be considered a study of the events of the past directly, but rather a composition that incorporated a variety of documents, for example, king lists, epics, anecdotes, and legends.[89]

Non-literary texts

Jacobsen has suggested that there was an actual historical figure because information about Gilgamesh traditions appear to be well-informed about the period in which he lived.[90]

Contemporaneous inscriptions of rulers of Kish and Ur were discovered. Kings of Ur may have referred to Gilgamesh in order to claim prestige for their family. Non-literary texts around the twenty-sixth or twenty-fifth century stated that Gilgamesh was a god to whom offerings were made in various towns, until the twenty-first century. By the latter time, he was considered the king and judge of the Netherworld, a position for which he was known in the first millennium in both magic and sorcery.[91]

Later inscriptions referred to his building the wall of Uruk and a shrine to Enlil in Nippur. Omens from the Old Babylonian Period (ca. 2000–1600 BC) referred to him as "the strong king who had no rival," and to other episodes, both known and unknown, from the epic. However, the Gilgamesh omens most likely do not possess any historical value.[92]

Historical evidence

The historical and biographical information about Gilgamesh in literary and non-literary texts support his date, his existence, and his association with certain historical figures; however, there are no contemporaneous inscriptions of his own. Despite information from non-literary texts, our definitive proof is lacking, so that this epic may be regarded as a legend about a king named Gilgamesh. The only historical information to date are later inscriptions stating that Gilgamesh built the wall of Uruk (its date supported by archaeological findings) and rebuilt a shrine.

Notes

1 See Morford and Lenardon, 2003, 1–15 for definitions and explanations of these terms.
2 George, 2007c, 44–79.
3 Foster, 1996, vol. 1, 39–46. See George, 2007c, who suggested defining narrative poetry as a group of long poems that are similar to Gilgamesh in form, style, and literary traditions. Some may be myths, which describe either the exploits of gods or the adventures of man. Nonetheless, like Foster, George stated there were no Sumerian or Akkadian words for either myth or heroic narrative, and certainly none for narrative poetry as a genre.
4 DelNero, 2010, 35–55.
5 Groneberg, 2003, 55–74; George, 2004, 37–66.
6 DelNero, 2010, 46 are grouped by theme, see §4.
7 Frayne, "The Sumerian Gilgamesh Poems," in Foster, 2001, 99–154.
8 Tigay, 2003, 23–30 discussed this problem at length noting the important contribution of S. Kramer in "teasing out" this issue.
9 George, 2009, 7–30.
10 Foster, 1995, vol. 1, 49.
11 Tigay, 2003, 138.

12 Rochberg-Halton, 1984, 127–33, discussed canonization as a process of "relative standardization."

13 Nemet-Nejat, 2000, 64–65, described a colophon as space reserved in the last column of literary texts for information, similar to the imprint pages in a modern book. The colophon could include any of the following data: the title of the work (that is, the shortened first line of work), the number of tablets in the series, the catch line or beginning of the next tablet, the name of owner, the name of scribe, the date of the work, comments on the original which the scribe had copied, and an invocation or curses against any unauthorized person removing the tablet.

14 George, 2003, xix–xx; Jacobsen, 1976, 195, noted that the Standard Babylonian Version incorporated unrelated sections to the epic and lacked "the freshness and vigor" of the Old Babylonian fragments.

15 George, 2003, xix–xx.

16 Foster, 1996, vol. 1, xiv, 47; Tigay, 2003, 15–16.

17 Foster, 1996, vol. 1, 47.

18 Jacobsen, 1976, 194–219; Tigay, 2003, 26–28.

19 George, 2007c, 237–54; idem., 1999, 51–58.

20 This synopsis follows the Standard Babylonian Version; on rare occasions, the Old Babylonian and even the Hittite version will be used either to illuminate sections, which are sometimes fragmentary, or to add to our understanding of the narrative.

21 Harris, 2000, 120–21.

22 Harris, 2000, 130.

23 George, 2007d, 538–39, ll. 26–28 described the lapis tablet as telling the story of the misfortunes of Gilgamesh; the tablet was placed in a cedar box with clasps of bronze.

24 Ninsun was part of the herding circle around Dumuzi; she was the mother of Dumuzi, and the mother-in-law of Inanna/Ishtar. Dumuzi and Inanna's love has been described in other myths and hymns. See Leick, 1991, 31–32, 134–35; George, 2007d, vol. 1, 147–48 described the various forms of Ninsun's name; he noted that in the Standard Babylonian version I: 36 Ninsun was described as "the exalted cow," but was also called Rimat-Ninsun, "the wild cow," throughout the myth.

25 Note the parallel with the Sumerian story of *Gilgamesh, Enkidu, and the Netherworld*, the Sumerian story translated by D. Frayne, in Foster, 2001, 134, lines 138–57. In this narrative Gilgamesh used the wood from a poplar tree planted by Inanna in Uruk to make a ball and stick for a game that Gilgamesh played while riding "piggyback on a team of orphans" until nightfall and then continued the game the next day at dawn. Klein, 2002, 193 added the game may have been connected either with fertility rites or with training for war.

26 The word shamhat(u) actually means prostitute, see CAD, Š, vol. 1, 311–12. The name is from an adjective denoting exquisite beauty par excellence and is used to refer to both men and women.

27 Westenholz and Koch-Westenholz, 2000, 438, described Enkidu as "Man without culture." The concept of the "noble savage" was a concept unknown in Babylonian literature outside the *Gilgamesh Epic*.

28 George, 2007d, vol. 2, 796–97, ll. 181//189. George translated in vol. 2, p. 549, l. 188 is "she let loose her skirts." He noted 184//191 that the prostitute took off her garment, which she spread on the ground and lay on it, enticing Enkidu to join her. Parpola, 1997, translated, this line as "Shamhat freed her breasts."

29 George, 2007d, vol. 2, 796, l. 172//190 literally translated as "to take in his breath" or "to take his scent" as a trapper would. However, ll. 189 and 190 are parallel, hence my translation.

30 George, 2007d, 797–98 l. 194 noted that the numbers 6 and 7 were often parallel in ancient Near Eastern Literature.

31 Uruk (Erech in the Bible, Warka today), was situated on the banks of the Euphrates in southernmost Mesopotamia. Uruk was a typical early urban site dating to the late fourth millennium BC. It covered approximately 30 acres and had a population of 10,000. The monumental buildings of the Early Uruk period (3500–3200 BC) suggested that a powerful elite controlled an organized, skilled labor force. Foster, 2001, xi, noted that Gilgamesh was described as the builder of Uruk's city walls, which were about approximately 10 kilometers long, with 900 towers. Traces of these walls are dated to 2700 BC. If Gilgamesh were a real king, he would have ruled Uruk at that time. See Westenholz and Koch-Westenholz, 2000, 437–51, and Jacobsen, 1976, 196; George, 2007d, 780 n. 11, noted that the reading Uruk-Sheepfold referred to the Old Babylonian version, whereas the Uruk-the-Sheepfold occurred almost throughout the Standard Babylonian version, which was about the king protecting his flock as the city wall encompassed its people.

32 George, 2007d, vol. 1, 148 noted that Uruk was the cult center of Ishtar, the goddess of sexual love; in fact, Uruk was famous for the number and beauty of its prostitutes, of which many were cultic prostitutes; see the I: 230–31.

33 Nissinen, 2010, 78, concluded, "So are there homosexuals in Mesopotamian literature? This is ultimately something that can only be decided by the community using the category of homosexuality. If love between people of the same sex, sexual coercion, random, as I believe they are not, then the answer is inevitably homoerotic encounters, and a gender-neutral sexual role are not considered expressions of homosexuality, as I believe they are not, then the answer is inevitably 'no'."

34 Tigay, 2003, 86; GE I, v, 9–15 translated the Standard Babylonian text of the second dream, which was followed by Ninsun's interpretation on pp. 86–87 G vi, 9–13; the transliteration of the dream and its interpretation are found on pp. 274–76. Tigay restored, "In the gate of my marital chamber" and continued the translation as "an axe lay down."

35 Tigay, 2003, 89 vi 13 in the Old Babylonian version Enkidu was referred to as "the axe at my side"; in fact on p. 83 n. 36, the Akkadian words for "side" and "brother" are homonyms.

36 Enlil, "lord wind," played an active role in human affairs, initially as the national god of Sumer.

37 Shamash "sun" was the god who meted justice to both gods and men.

38 This line is very long and does not fit the rest of the passage poetically.

39 For restoration of line 55, see Foster, 2001, 24.

40 Ayya was the goddess of dawn and the wife of Shamash. She was known to intercede with husband; see Leick, 1991, 16–17.

41 George, 2007b, 59–80.

42 A magic circle of flour was often used in rituals involving a patient to prevent certain demons from entering it. In other rituals it was used for apotropaic purposes; see Black and Green, 1992, 128.

43 Foster, 2001, 30–35, Tablet IV for a summary of three dreams. On p. 35, he noted that the tablet may have contained as many as five dreams.

44 Literally, Aratta, a city fabled for its wealth, in particular lapis lazuli; it is located to the far east of Sumer in what is today Iran.

45 Goats of both sexes can be fertile as early as 7 weeks. However, the best time to breed for a (dairying) goat is at 80 lb. In a single kidding gods usually 5 birth to kid, though as many as 3 kids is possible and 4–5 is unusual. Online. Available HTTP: <*http://fiascofarm.cepom/goats/kidding.htm*≥ (accessed 22 December 2010).

46 Sheep breed as early as 19 months old, with a gestation period of approximately 5 months, depending on the species. Generally, a ewe gives birth to one lamb, but twins sometimes occur. Shortly before giving birth the ewes chase off their

previous year's offspring because they have only two working teats. See B. Grizmek (ed.) *Grizmek's Animal Life Encyclopedia*, Vol. 3 of *Mammals*, pp. 501–4. This line was clearly a poetic device explaining the wealth Gilgamesh would enjoy from animals Ishtar would give to him.

47 This line and the one that followed it, Parpola, 1997, restored as "I will strike the doors and break the locks. I will smash the doorposts and turn the doors upside down." That is, George, 2007d, 840 l. 97 noted that Parpola's translation is related to *The Descent of Ishtar to the Netherworld*, that these actions would release the dead from being locked away in the Netherworld.

48 Postgate, 1992, 92.

49 Stol, 1995, 497, explained that prostitution was also an accepted trade at the harbor, or under the city wall. As in the classical world, the prostitute was pictured as leaning out of a window.

50 Pinnock, 1995, 2526, explained that erotic art was found in seals, plaques, and clay figurines. The seals were probably for administrative purposes. The plaques were for decoration and often found in showing naked women temples, possibly demonstrating a religious or official purpose. Clay figurines may have been popular art. In general, erotic art was a genre somewhere between official and popular art.

51 See Stol, 1995, 493,

52 Ibid., 493.

53 Stol, 1995, 497.

54 Kovacs 1989: 85 n. 1 included this section from the Old Babylonian version, in which the tavern keeper explained her view of life; in the Standard Babylonian version B. Foster, 2001, 75 includes this "old version" in his translation. Tigay, 2002, 166–67, noted that Siduri's speech resembled wisdom literature, that is, *carpe diem*. Harris, 2003, 124 referred to Siduri's advice as pragmatic, rather than hedonistic. Abusch, 1993, 5 made a convincing argument that Siduri's reply was not hedonistic, but rather "a prescription for healing," to draw the mourner away from the desert of grief back to city life."

55 Abusch, 1993, 16.

56 Abusch, 1993, 16 suggested that the child presented the theme of the mortal and immortal plan of Gilgamesh's life.

57 Siduri's advice has many parallels around the world, see Tigay, 2003, 169 and Abusch, 1993, 13–15; Foster, 2001, 75; Kovacs, 1989, 75 n. 1 and Jacobsen, 1976, 205 all use the Old Babylonian version here. Abusch, 1993, 17, offered a different view than *carpe diem*; he suggested that Gilgamesh's grief was so great that he was not satisfied with the rites of mourning and was unable to separate himself from the death of his friend and return to a normal life.

58 Kovacs, 1989, xxi.

59 Oates, 1986, 169–70.

60 Foster, 2001, p. xiv.

61 Tigay, 2003, 102–3, n. 72.

62 Dalley, 1991, 39–40.

63 George, 1999; 2007a.

64 See Charpin, 2004, 481–508.

65 Oates, 1986, 170.

66 George, 2007a.

67 Enlil, "lord wind," took an active role in human affairs. Enlil originally held the Tablets of Destiny, on which the fates of men and gods were decreed.

68 Walker, 1987, 48; George, 2007a.

69 George, 2003, 736–41; Charpin, 2004, 481–508, has detailed a different view of who could read and write, but in the case of the Gilgamesh epic, he concluded that this oral literature was written by apprentice scribes to preserve for the future.

70 George, 2003, 736–41.
71 Verbrugghe and Wickersham, 1996, 49–50.
72 Oates, 1986, 166.
73 Oates, 1986, 128.
74 George, 2005, 132.
75 George, 2005, 132.
76 Stone, 1987, 56–59.
77 George, 2005, 132.
78 Foster, 1996, 49–50.
79 Foster, 1996, 48–49.
80 Foster, 1996, 46.
81 Kovacs, 1989, xx; Foster, 1996, 46–47.
82 Moran, 1995, 2328; Jacobsen, 1976, 195.
83 Roux, 1964, 355.
84 George, 2007a.
85 George, 2005, 127–37.
86 Dalley, 1991, 40–41.
87 Foster, 2001, xii.
88 Jacobsen, 1976, 208.
89 Schmidt, 1995, 2340–41 suggests that *The Sumerian King List* was a propaganda tool to legitimize particular dynasties as various extant copies lists the names of different kings, the lengths of their reigns, their sequence, and number.
90 Jacobsen, 1976, 205.
91 Jacobsen, 1976, 205, 209–13; Tigay, 2002, 13–15; Foster, 2001, xii.
92 Tigay, 2003, 15.

List of abbreviations

AuOR	*Aula Orientalis*
CAD	*Chicago Assyrian Dictionary*
CANE	Sasson, J.M., (ed.), 1995. *Civilizations of the Ancient Near East*, 4 vols, New York: Charles Scribner and Sons; Hendrickson Publishers edition, Peabody, MA, 2000, 2 vols.
JAOS	*Journal of the American Oriental Society*
JCS	*Journal of Cuneiform Studies*
RA	*Revue d'assyriologie*
WO	*Dies Welt des Orients*
ZA	*Zietscrift für Assyriologie und Archaeologie*

Bibliography

Abusch, T., 1993. "Gilgamesh's Request and Siduri's Denial. Part II. An Analysis and Interpretation of an Old Babylonian Fragment about Mourning and Celebration," *Journal of the Ancient Near Eastern Society*, 22, 1–17.

Black, J. and Green, A., 1991. *Gods, Demons and Symbols of Ancient Mesopotamia*, JAOS: Austin University of Texas Press. CAD, Š, 1989. vol. 1, 311–12, s.v. Šamhatu.

Charpin, D., 2004. "Lire ou écrire," Comptes-rendus des séances de l'année … – *Académie des inscriptions et belles-lettres*, 148e année, N. 1, 481–508.

Dalley, S., 2001. *Myths from Mesopotamia: Creation, the Flood, Gilgamesh, and Others*, England: Oxford University Press. Revised edition.

DelNero, P., 2010. "Sumerian Literary Catalogues and the Scribal," *Zeitschrift für Assyriologie und Archaeologie*, 100, 35–55.

Falkenstein, A., 1948. "Der Sohn des Tafelhauses," *Die Welt des Orients*, 1, 185.

Foster, B.R., trans., 1996. *Before the Muses: An Anthology of Akkadian Literature*, 2nd edn, Bethesda: CDL Press, vol. 1.

——, 2001. trans. and ed., *The Epic of Gilgamesh*, New York: W.W. Norton & Company.

George, A.R., 1999. "What's New in the Gilgamesh Epic," *The Bulletin of the Canadian Society for Mesopotamian Studies*, 34, 51–58.

——, 2003. *The Babylonian Gilgamesh Epic: Introduction, Critical Edition and Cuneiform Texts*, New York: Oxford University Press, 2 vols.

——, 2004. "Thoughts on Genre and Meaning," in Azize, J. and Weeks, N., eds, *Proceedings of the Conference Held at the Mandelbaum House, Sydney, Australia*, Leuven: Peeters, 37–66.

——, 2005. "In Search of the é.dub.ba.a: The Ancient Mesopotamian School in Literature and Reality," in Sefati, Y., ed., *An Experienced Scribe who Neglects Nothing: Ancient Near Eastern Studies in Honor of Jacob Klein*, Bethesda: CDL Press, 127–37.

——, 2007a. "The Civilizing of Enkidu: An Unusual Tablet of the Babylonian Gilgamesh Epic," *Revue d'assyriologie*, 101, 59–80.

——. 2007b. "The Gilgamesh Epic at Ugarit," *Aula Orientalis*, 25, 237–54.

——, 2007c. "Gilgamesh and the Literary Traditions of Ancient Mesopotamia," in Leick, G., ed., *The Babylonian World*, London: Routledge, 447–59.

——, 2007d. *SB Gilgamesh I–XII, Score Transliteration*, London: Society for Oriental and Afircan Studies.

——, 2009. "Shattered Tablets and Tangled Threads: Editing Gilgamesh, Then and Now," *Aramazd, Armenian Journal of Near Eastern Studies*, 3, 7–30.

Green, A. and Black, J., 1992. *Gods, Demons and Symbols of Ancient Mesopotamia*, Austin University of Texas.

Groneberg, B., 2003. "Searching for Akkadian Lyrics: from Old Babylonian to the 'Liederkatalog' KAR 158," *Journal of Cuneiform Studies*, 55–74.

Harris, R., 2003. *Gender and Aging: The Gilgamesh Epic and Other Ancient Literature*, Norman: University of Oklahoma Press.

Jacobsen, T., 1976. *The Treasures of Darkness: A History of Mesopotamian Religion*, New Haven: Yale University Press.

——, 2004. "Pictures and Pictorial Landscape (The Burney Relief)," in Midlin, M. et al., eds, *Figurative Language in the Ancient Near East, revised edition*, London: School of Oriental and African Studies.

Klein, J., 2002. "A New Look at the 'Oppression of Uruk Episode,'" in Abusch, T., ed., *Ancient Studies in Memory of Thorkild Jacobsen: Riches Hidden in Secret Places*, Winona Lake: Eisenbrauns, 187–201.

Kovacs, M.G., 1989. trans. and intro., *The Epic of Gilgamesh*, Stanford: Stanford University Press.

Leick, G., 1991. *A Dictionary of Ancient Near Eastern Mythology*, London: Routledge.

Moran, W., 1995. " The Gilgamesh Epic: A Masterpiece from Ancient Mesopotamia," in Sasson, J., ed., *Civilizations of the Ancient Near East*, vol. 4, New York: Charles Scribner and Sons, 2327–36.

Morford, M.P.O. and Lenardon, R.J., 2003. *Classical Mythology*, 7th edn, New York: Oxford University Press, pp. 3–15.

Nemet-Nejat, K.R., 2000. *Daily Life in Ancient Mesopotamia*, Peabody: Hendrickson Publishers.

Nissinen, M., 2010. "Are There Homosexuals in Mesopotamian Literature?" *Journal of the American Oriental Society*, 130(1), 73–79.

Oates, J., 1986. *Babylon*, London: Thames and Hudson, Ltd.

Parpola, S., 1997. *The Standard Babylonian Epic of Gilgamesh*. Helsinki: SA.

Pinnock, F.,1995. "Erotic Art in the Ancient Near East," in Sasson, J., ed., *Civilizations of the Ancient Near East*, Vol. 4. New York: Charles Scribner and Sons, 1995, 2521–31.

Postgate, J., 1992. *Early Mesopotamia: Society and Economy at the Dawn of History*, London: Routledge.

Rochberg-Halton,1984. "Canonicity in Cuneiform Texts," *Journal of Cuneiform Studies* 36, 127–44.

Roux, G., 1964. *Ancient Iraq*, London: Penguin Books.

Schmidt, B., 1995. "Flood Narratives of Ancient Western Asia," in Sasson, J., ed., *Civilizations of the Ancient Near East*, vol. 4, New York: Charles Scribner and Sons, 2337–51.

Stol, M., 1995. "Private Life in Ancient Mesopotamia," in Sasson, J., ed., *Civilizations of the Ancient Near East*, Vol. 4, New York: Charles Scribner and Sons, 485–501.

Stone, E., 1987. *Nippur Neighborhoods*, Chicago: The Oriental Institute of The University of Chicago.

Tigay, J.H., 2003. *The Evolution of the Gilgamesh Epic*, 2nd edn, Wauconda: Bochazy-Carducci Publishers, Inc.

Verbrugghe, G.P. and Wickersham, J.M., 1996. intro. and trans., *Berossus and Manetho: Native Tradition in Ancient Mesopotamia and Egypt*, revised edition, Ann Arbor: The University of Michigan Press.

Walker, C.B.F., 1987. *Cuneiform*. London: British Museum Publications.

Westenholz, A. and Koch-Westenholz, U., 2000. "Enkidu–The Noble Savage?" in George, A. and Finkel, I., eds, *Wisdom, Gods and Literature: Studies in Assyriology in Honour of W.G. Lambert*, Winona: Eisenbrauns, 437–51.

8

THE DESCENT OF ISHTAR TO THE NETHERWORLD COMPARED TO *NERGAL AND ERESHKIGAL*

Karen Nemet-Nejat

Introduction

Ishtar was an important deity in ancient Mesopotamia throughout its history. She had three aspects: (1) the goddess of sex and prostitutes,[1] (2) a warlike goddess desiring power, and (3) the planet Venus, that is, the morning and evening star. Her symbols were the star or star disc and later the rosette. She was the daughter of An, the sky god, though many traditions abound as to her parentage.[2]

Ishtar's Akkadian name is related to 'Athar (a South Arabian male deity) and the Syrian goddess Astarte (Biblical Ashtoreth). Her Sumerian name, Inanna, means "Lady of Heaven." Her main shrine was Eanna "House of Heaven," in Uruk; however, the temple complex has not been located to date, although many artifacts associated with Inanna have been discovered at Uruk. In fact, numerous temples were dedicated to Inanna, indicating her importance in Mesopotamian religion. In some cities her temples have not been found but artifacts attest to their existence, such as foundation stones, votive bowls, statues, vulvae, more than fifty stone bowls, lexical lists, a record of offerings, the poems of Enheduanna,[3] tablets, seals, and sealings.[4]

The Akkadian version of *The Descent of Ishtar to the Netherworld*

The earliest Akkadian versions of *The Descent of Ishtar to the Netherworld* were found in both Babylonia and Assyria ca. fifteenth or fourteenth centuries BC and later at the palace library of Ashurbanipal at Nineveh (ca. seventh century BC). The myth consisted of approximately 140 lines. The Assyrian version included ritual instructions. Religious observance occurred in the month of Dumuzi (i.e., Tammuz = June/July) at which time Dumuzi's statue[5] was bathed, anointed, and lay in state in various cities, such as Nineveh, Arbela, Ashur, and Nimrud.[6]

195

The Sumerian version of *The Descent of Inanna* to the Netherworld

The Sumerian version, *The Descent of Inanna to the Netherworld*, was written earlier than the Akkadian version and was approximately 410 lines. This myth was a more detailed account and included the motif of the dying and rising gods in order to explain seasonal fertility.[7] In fact, the gods had intercourse to represent fertility.[8] This act, known as "the sacred marriage," was re-enacted by the king (who was deified), and possibly a priestess who represented Inanna, at the New Year's festival.[9] The sacred marriage was considered essential to the reproduction of plants and animals and usually occurred annually.[10]

Lambert added that the Sumerian and Akkadian versions of *The Descent of Inanna/Ishtar* and the Greco-Roman myth of the rape of Persephone/Prosepina explained the change of seasons; that is, the alternation between fruitfulness and decay. The goddesses represented fertility when above ground (spring and summer) and deprivation of these benefits upon their descent to the Netherworld. In fact, Lambert indicated that so many similar myths from the Aegean to the Indus Valley suggested a common way of viewing the world as early as prehistoric times.[11]

The Akkadian version lacked any ritual procedures, but, like the Sumerian myth, the goddess's cult statue made a ritual journey from Uruk to Kutha, where the gods of the Netherworld resided.[12]

The Descent of Ishtar to the Netherworld

Ishtar decided to visit the Netherworld, where inhabitants' food was dust, and their bread, clay. Those who entered lived in darkness. Their clothing was like birds with feathers, the clothing often worn by Netherworld gods.[13]

Ishtar's speech to the gatekeeper

When Ishtar arrived at the gate, she addressed the gatekeeper:

> Here, gatekeeper, open your gate,
> Open your gate and let me enter.
> If you do not open your gate for me to come in,
> I shall smash the door; I shall break the bolt.
> I shall smash the door frame; I shall overturn the doors.
> I shall raise up the dead to eat the living;[14]
> The dead will outnumber the living.
> > (*The Descent of Ishtar to the Netherworld*, lines 14–20)

Ereshkigal's reply

The gatekeeper told Ishtar to stop her violent entry, and that he would announce her arrival. Her sister Ereshkigal, Queen of the Netherworld, was disturbed by this news:

What brings her to me? What has changed her
mood toward me?
Look. I drink water with the Anunnaki (Netherworld gods).
I eat clay for bread; I drink muddy water for beer?[15]
Shall I weep for the young men who have left their wives?
Shall I weep for the young women wrenched from their lovers' laps?
Shall I weep for the baby, the infant, who was taken before
   his time?
Go, gatekeeper, open your gate for her.
Treat her according to the ancient rites.[16]
        (*The Descent of Ishtar to the Netherworld*, lines 31–38)

The undressing of Ishtar

The gatekeeper returned and opened each of seven gates for Ishtar. At each gate
he removed various items according to the "rites of the Lady of the Netherworld,"
namely the following: (1) crown, (2) earrings, (3) egg-shaped beaded necklace,
(4) toggle pins, (5) belt of birth stones, (6) bracelets on her wrists and ankles, and
(7) clothing of her upper body, as she is depicted in statues.[17]

Ereshkigal causing illness to Ishtar

Once Ishtar entered the Netherworld, she challenged Ereshkigal's position.
Ereshkigal was quick to act. She spoke to her vizier, Namtar:

Go, Namtar, take her from my presence.
Release sixty illnesses that shall overwhelm Ishtar:[18]
Disease of the eyes against her eyes,
Disease of the arms against her arms,
Disease of the feet against her feet,
Disease of the heart against her heart,
Disease of the head against her head,
Against her, all of them ...
        (*The Descent of Ishtar to the Netherworld*, lines 68–75)

Ishtar's death

After Ishtar descended to the Netherworld, all sexual activity ceased. The advisor
to the gods informed Ea, the god of wisdom, about Ishtar's death and the loss of
fertility in the country. Ea created Asushu-namir ("his appearance is bright"), an
ambivalent sexual being, who was possibly born either with genital malformation,
hermaphroditism, absence of external genitals,[19] or was castrated, self-emasculated,
a transvestite, or perhaps, a male prostitute who was the passive partner in a
homosexual relationship.[20] Ishtar herself could be either female or male.[21]

Ea instructed Asushu-namir to proceed to the gate of the Netherworld, and its seven gates would be opened for him. Ereshkigal would see him and be happy. Ea told Asushu-namir that when Ereshkigal relaxed, Asushu-namir was to have swear an oath by the great gods.

Asushu-namir's request and Ereshkigal's curse

Asushu-namir asked Ereshkigal if he could drink from the waterskin.[22] When Ereshkigal heard this request, she became furious and cursed Asushu-namir:

> You have surely requested from me that which should not
>   have been requested.
> Come, Asushu-namir, I shall curse you with a great curse![23]
> May the bread of the city's ploughs be your food.
> May the sewers of the city be your drinking place.
> May the shade of the city wall be your standing place.[24]
> May the thresholds be your sitting place.
> May the drunk and the thirsty slap your cheek.
> *(The Descent of Ishtar to the Netherworld*, lines 102–8)

Ereshkigal's decision to revive Ishtar and send her away

Ereshkigal told Namtar, her vizier:

> Go, Namtar, knock on the door of the True Temple,
> Decorate the thresholds with cowry shells,[25]
> Bring out the Anunnaki and seat (them) on gold thrones,
> Sprinkle Ishtar with the waters of life and bring her before me.
> *(The Descent of Ishtar to the Netherworld*, lines 111–14)

Namtar followed Ereshkigal's instructions. He sprinkled Ishtar with the waters of life and had her put on her clothes in the reverse order to which she undressed to enter the Netherworld. He placed the crown on Ishtar's head last, at the seventh door, and sent her away.[26]

Dumuzi as Ishtar's substitute

After Ereshkigal's instructions were followed, she said (to Namtar):

> If she does not give you a substitute for herself, bring her back![27]
> For Dumuzi, the lover of her youth,[28]
> Bathe him in pure water; anoint him with good oil,
> Dress him in a bright red garment;[29] let him play his lapis lazuli flute.
> Let the prostitutes lament him.[30]
> *(The Descent of Ishtar to the Netherworld*, lines 126–30)

Lament of Ishtar (Belili) for Dumuzi

Upon hearing the Ereshkigal's decree for Dumuzi, Belili was distraught. She lifted the eye stones,[31] and her lap was filled with them. She heard the wailing for her brother; she struck the jewelry, and the eye stones filled the face of the cow.[32] Ishtar addressed Namtar:

> Do not rob me of my only brother.[33]
> When Dumuzi rises to me, the lapis lazuli flute; and the carnelian ring will rise with him to me.[34]
> When male and female mourners come up with him,
> Let the dead rise and smell the incense.
> (*The Descent of Ishtar to the Netherworld*, lines 135–38)

Nergal and Ereshkigal compared to *The Descent of Ishtar to the Netherworld*

There are basically two versions of *Nergal and Ereshkigal*: a condensed version found at El Amarna in Egypt (ca. fifteenth or fourteenth centuries BC), which consisted of about 90 lines; and a large tablet from Sultantepe (ca. seventh century BC) and Uruk (the late Babylonian Period), which consisted of about 750 lines. The outline of *Nergal and Ereshkigal* can be reconstructed, although large parts are missing. The motifs of *Nergal and Ereshkigal* are based on their meeting, sexual passion, and eventual rule of the Netherworld.[35] The later versions of *Nergal and Ereshkigal* expanded the theme of sexuality and the role of the messengers.[36]

In both versions of *Nergal and Ereshkigal* the gods held a celestial banquet. Ereshkigal, as Queen of the Netherworld, could not attend, so she sent her vizier, Namtar, to retrieve her portion. Nergal was very rude to her vizier, so Ereshkigal sent Namtar up again to find Nergal and bring him to the Netherworld. At this point the two versions diverge.

In the version from El-Amarna, Ereshkigal wanted to kill Nergal. Ea, in his role as the god of wisdom, gave Nergal seven demons to accompany him on his journey to the Netherworld. Nergal yanked Ereshkigal by her hair from her throne and threw her to the ground in order to decapitate her. This savage courtship made sense for the gods of the Netherworld.[37] The El-Amarna myth transferred power from a solitary female to Nergal, who was given "the tablet of wisdom."[38]

In the later versions of *Nergal and Ereshkigal*, the isolation and sexual frustration of Ereshkigal were described in detail. Nergal descended to the Netherworld twice, each time through seven gates, the same number of gates as in *The Descent of Ishtar to the Netherworld*. Here Ea advised Nergal to make a chair of various types of wood, painted to look like valuable materials. The chair was perhaps a ghost's chair,[39] possibly to escape from death and from the Netherworld. Ea also warned Nergal about other ways to avoid death by refusing any food, drink and sex in the Netherworld.

Despite Ea's advice, Nergal became aroused by Ereshkigal when she stripped for a bath. They had sex for six days. Nergal woke early and tricked the gatekeeper in order to return to heaven. Later, when Ereshkigal awoke, Namtar told her that her lover had left. Ereshkigal sobbed because, as Queen of the Netherworld, she had never enjoyed the pleasures of youth and felt defiled by her sexual relationship with Nergal.[40] She stated that she could no longer continue to judge the dead. She threatened that if Nergal was not returned to the Netherworld, "I shall raise up the dead to eat the living; the dead will outnumber the living."[41]

Nergal was brought down to the Netherworld again. Possibly, he removed a piece from each of outfits at the seven gates (the tablet is broken), so he would not be completely naked when he arrived at Ereshkigal's court—unlike Ishtar, who was stripped of all her clothes in her journey to the Netherworld in *The Descent of Ishtar to the Netherworld*. As in the earlier version from El-Amarna, Nergal yanked Ereshkigal by her hair from her throne. However, in the later versions, the two made passionate love for seven days and nights as equals. Though the end of the later version is broken, Nergal seemed to remain in the Netherworld.

The Descent of Ishtar to the Netherworld began with a stock motif in Mesopotamian literature describing the Netherworld. In *Nergal and Ereshkigal*, Ea's advice to Nergal included this information:

> To the Netherworld, the Land of No Return,
> Ishtar, the daughter of Sin was determined (to go)
> Indeed, Ishtar, decided to go daughter of Sin
> To the dark house, the dwelling of Irkalla,[42]
> To the house which whoever enters cannot leave,
> To the road where those who go there is no going back,
> To the house where those who enter are deprived of light,
> Where dust is their food, clay, their bread,
> They do not see light; the live in darkness,
> They are dressed like birds (in) garments of feathers.[43]
> (*The Descent of Ishtar to the Netherworld*, ll. 1–10 = *Nergal and Ereshkigal* ii end–iii 4')[44]

Despite this account of the Netherworld, the journey was not always one way, and some gods who resided in the Netherworld did leave and return, namely: Dumuzi and his mourners in *The Descent of Ishtar to the Netherworld*, (ll. 136–37; see above); Namtar in *Nergal and Ereshkigal* in the later versions (I 51'–5',v 13', 42' and passim); and Nergal in *Nergal and Ereshkigal* (iii 36'ff. iv 45' ff, v 18') in the later versions. Also, Ishtar completely removed all of her clothing in order to enter the Netherworld; that is, she died. Nergal only removed a piece of his clothing, but the broken tablet does not offer a clear meaning.

The Descent of Ishtar to the Netherworld was concerned with the motif of fertility, which the Sumerian version explained more clearly. *Nergal and Ereshkigal* dealt with sexual passion and rulership. The items denoting authority in *The Descent of Ishtar* were a lapis lazuli flute and a carnelian ring (the rod and the ring); however, in the el-Amarna *Nergal and Ereshkigal*, Nergal, received "the tablet of wisdom" as the symbol of kingship.

The various versions of *Nergal and Ereshkigal* raise questions as to their source. The later versions might be an expansion of the earlier version from El-Amarna, or the El-Amarna version, an abbreviation of an earlier version, now lost; or, the individual versions are the same story, but told differently in different sources.[45] Though the outline of the story is known, the tablets are damaged and missing large pieces; therefore, tracing the development of the myth is speculative at this point in time.

Notes

1 In the Standard Babylonian Version of *The Epic of Gilgamesh* Tablet VI, Gilgamesh rejected Ishtar and listed the cruel punishments she inflicted on her other lovers in various myths, including Dumuzi, in the *Descent of Ishtar to the Netherworld*.
2 Borger, 1963, 87; Black and Green, 1992, 108–9; P. Lapinkivi, 2010, 35; see also n. 23. For example, in *The Descent of Ishtar*. Ishtar is the daughter of Sin, the moon god.
3 These are the first poems of a known author, a priestess and daughter of Sargon. These works have been studied by Hallo and van Dijk, 1968.
4 Collins, 1994.
5 Many statues of the deities were made from wood with an overleaf of gold and dressed with decorated garments. The statues were washed, dressed, given food and drink, and provided with a lavishly adorned bedroom. That is, the gods were conceived in human terms.
6 Dalley, 1985, 381.
7 Yamauchi, 1961, 80–88, discussed at length the various scholarly opinions as to the theme of dying/rising god throughout the ancient Near East and concluded that this theory was untenable.
8 Black and Green, 1992, 157; Leick, 1991, 145.
9 Collins, 2004, noted those hymns from ca. 2100–1800 also depicted the sacred marriage. Here Dumuzi, called Amaushumgalanna, was considered to be the consort of Inanna, and the sacred marriage ritual was centered at Uruk.
10 Nissinen, 2001, 93–136.
11 Lambert, 1995, 1825.
12 Dalley, 1997, 381.
13 Green, 1995, 1834–35. The clothing of the inhabitants of the Netherworld and its various connotations have been summarized by Lapinkivi, 2004, 37–42. The description of the Netherworld in *The Descent of Ishtar to the Netherworld* lines 1–10 (Foster, 1996, 403; Dalley, 1997, 381) was repeated in *Nergal and Ereshkigal*.
14 Lines 19–20 were identical to the curse uttered by after Nergal absconded after having made love to her in *Nergal and*; see Foster, 1996, 425 v 2.7'–8', Dalley, 1997, 386.
15 Bread and beer were staples in ancient Mesopotamia.
16 Katz, 1995, 221–28, indicated that these rites referred only to the undressing Inanna/Ishtar to render indicated that these rites were created of undressing were only

in reference to Inanna/Ishtar to render her powerless and subjugate her to Ereshkigal. Parpola, 2000, 197–99 discussed the possible significance of Ishtar's clothing.

17 Lapinkivi, 2004, 55–64, summarized the opinions of various scholars in great detail.

18 Reiner,1985, 49, n. 7, noted that even though sixty diseases are mentioned, in fact, only five are noted; Reiner suggested only those diseases of body parts which were protected by divine items were mentioned.

19 Leick, 1994, 138; Lapinkivi, 2010, 159.

20 Harris, 2000, 165, 170–71 discussed the androgyny of Ishtar's cultic personnel.

21 Lapinkivi, 2010, 156–59.

22 Lapinkivi, 2004, p. 83 ll. 98–99; p. 88 ll. 109–18; pp. 90–91 ll. 131–34.4, discussed the problem as to whether the waterskin represented the dead body of Ishtar; he noted that water was neither poured nor sprinkled from the waterskin. Neither of the previous concepts was explicitly stated. The waterskin may, in fact, be a waterskin (á la Gertrude Stein), and Ereshkigal was upset because it did contain the waters of life (see line. 114 below).

23 Other texts have variant readings: "I will decree a fate for you that will not be forgotten" and "I will decree a fate that will not be forgotten forever."

24 Kilmer, 1971, 301, n. 17, suggested that this curse referred to the male prostitute. Stol, 1995, 493, noted that prostitution was a trade found at the city walls, the harbor, and the tavern.

25 Cowrie shells resemble a woman's sexual organ. See Lapinkivi, 2004, 64, l. 54.

26 There are three texts with different translations for line 118: "Go, Namtar and take Ishtar away"; "If she does not give you her substitute, bring her back," and "Namtar took her to the gates."

27 Hallo, 1995, 1874, discussed the banishment of the god of fertility, here Dumuzi, as part of the seasonal cycle, Lambert, 1995, 1825. In the Sumerian version, Inanna considered various alternatives before settling on Dumuzi, who would spend one-half year in the Netherworld, Lapinivki, 2004, 90, 92.

28 Dumuzi was not Ishtar's brother, but her lover, as described in the Dumuzi–Inanna love songs. The term brother may have been used here in an emotional relationship, see CAD, A$_1$, p. 195 mng. 2. V.

29 Dalley, 1997a, 383a, n. 24, stated that corpses were wrapped in red cloth for burial as traces of red cloth have occasionally been found at some burials. Tammuz was purified and clothed for burial.

30 Ibid., the prostitutes belonged to Ishtar's temple.

31 The eyestones were probably agate and cut so that they resembled an eye, that is, with the white or lighter color around the dark pupil. These beads were used in making jewelry.

32 Parpola, 2000, 192–94 referred to Ishtar as the cow.

33 This line is confusing, since in l. 127 Dumuzi/Tammuz, is referred to as Ishtar's lover, as he is in a series of songs and Gilgamesh. In the Sumerian story Geshtinanna, Dumuzi's sister pleads for his release. See Safati, 1998, *Love Songs in Sumerian Literature*.

34 Dalley, 1997, 384, n. 27, noted that in the Sumerian version, Inanna took the "rod and ring," emblems of either kingship or divinity, down to the Netherworld. The lapis lazuli flute and the carnelian ring in *The Descent of Ishtar* may have represented the "rod and the ring."Lapinkivi, 2004, 93, compared the significance of this line to a mural from the royal palace at Mari in which the investiture of a king was depicted with his holding a red ring and a blue rod.

35 Jacobsen, 1976, 229.

36 Foster, 1996, 413.

37 Jacobsen, 1976, 230; Harris, 2000, 134.

38 In *Enuma Elish* ii 40–45, "the Babylonian Creation Myth," kingship of the gods was symbolized by the "Tablets of Destiny."
39 Nemet-Nejat, 2000, 142 explained that a dying person was given a funerary bed and a seat at the left. An incantation was recited to free the soul from its corporeal body, and the chair became the seat for the soul. In fact, the soul received its first funeral offerings on the chair. Scurlock, 2005, added that a bed frame and a chair were given in this context, see pp. 26 and 52; see notes 374 and 675. Harris, 2000, 130, viewed this passage differently and suggested that the chair or throne was a compensatory gift.
40 Harris, 2000, 145–46, discussed how a woman's erotic feelings provided a strong basis for marriage; however, monogamy and sexuality were true for human beings, Mesopotamian gods could have different mates depending on the period and the "story."
41 Foster, 1996, 425; Dalley, 1997, 386.
42 Lapinkivi, 2004, 36–37 discussed various scholars possible translation of the term, which seems to mean Netherworld; Horowitz, 1998, 288–89.
43 See Scurlock, 1995, 1892.
44 See Foster, 1996, 420; Dalley, 1997, 386.
45 Foster, 1996, 410, 413; Dalley, 1997, 384, has suggested that these versions represent the harmonizing of two different traditions.

Bibliography

Black, J. and Green, A., 1992. *Gods, Demons and Symbols of Ancient Mesopotamia: An Illustrated Dictionary*, Austin University of Texas Press.

Borger, R., 1963. *Babylonisch-Assyrisch Lesestücke*, 3 vols., Rome: Pontificum Institutum Biblicum. CAD, A1, p. 195 mng. 2. V.

Collins, P., 1994. "The Sumerian Goddess Inanna (3400–2200 BC)," *Papers from the Institute of Archaeology* 5, 1994, Online. Available HTTP <http://ancientworldonline.blogspot.com/2009/11/soas-research-online.html>.

Dalley, S., 1997a. "The Descent of Ishtar to the Underworld," in W.W. Hallo (ed.) COS, 381–84.

——, 1997b. "Nergal and Ereshkigal," in W.W. Hallo (ed.), Leiden & New York: Brill, 384–90.

Foster, B.R., 1996. trans., *Before the Muses: An Anthology of Akkadian Literature*, vol. 1, 2nd edn, Bethesda: CDL Press.

Green, A. 1995. "Ancient Mesopotamian Religious Iconography," in J.M. Sasson (ed.), *Civilizations of the Ancient Near East*, vol. 3: New York: Charles Scribner's Sons, 1837–55.

Green, A. and Black, J., 1992. *Gods, Demons and Symbols of Ancient Mesopotamia: An Illustrated Dictionary* (illustrations by Tessa Richards), Austin, Texas: University of Texas Press.

Hallo, W.W. (ed.), 1997. The *Context of Scripture: Canonical Compositions from the Biblical World*, vol. 1, Leiden & New York: Brill.

——, 1995. "Lamentations and Prayer in Sumer and Akkad," in J.M. Sasson (ed.), *Civilizations of the Ancient Near East*, vol. 3, New York: Charles Scribner's Sons, 1871–81.

Hallo, W.W. and van Dijk, J.J.A., 1968. *The Exaltation of Inanna*, New Haven: Yale University Press.

Harris, R. 2000. *Gender and Aging in Mesopotamia: The Gilgamesh Epic and Other Ancient Literature*, Norman: University of Oklahoma Press.

Horowitz, A., 1998. *Mesopotamian Cosmic Geography*, Winona Lake: Eisenbrauns.

Jacobsen, T., 1976. *The Treasures of Darkness: A History of Mesopotamian Religion*, New Haven: Yale University Press.

Katz, D., 1995. "Inanna's Descent and Undressing the Dead as Divine Law," *Zeitschrift für Assyriologie* 85, 221–28.

Kilmer, A., 1971. "How was Queen Ereshkigal Tricked?" A New Interpretation of the Descent Ishtar, *Ugarit-Forschungen* 3, 221–33.

Lambert, 1995. "Myth and Mythmaking in Sumer and Akkad," in J.M. Sasson (ed.), *Civilizations of the Ancient Near East*, vol. 3, New York: Charles Scribner and Sons, 1825–35.

Lapinkivi, P., 2004. *The Sumerian Sacred Marriage in the Light of Comparative Evidence*, Helsinki: Helsinki University Press.

——, 2010. *The Neo-Assyrian Myth of Ishtar's Descent and Resurrection*, Helsinki: Helsinki University Press.

Leick, G., 1994. *Sex and Eroticism in Mesopotamian Literature*, London and New York: Routledge.

——, 1998. *A Dictionary of Ancient Near Eastern Mythology*, London: Routledge.

Nemet-Nejat, K.R., 2000. *Daily Life in Ancient Mesopotamia*, Peabody: Hendrickson Publishers.

Nissinen, M. 2001. "Akkadian Rituals and Poetry of Divine Love," *Melammu Symposia II*, in R.M. Whiting (ed.), Helsinki: University of Helsinki Press, 93–136.

Parpola, S., 2000. "Monotheism in Ancient Assyria," in B.N. Porter (ed.), *One God or Many: Concepts of Divinity in the Ancient World*, Casco Bay, Maine, 165–209.

Reiner, E., 1985. *Your Thwarts in Pieces, Your Mooring Rope Cut: Poetry from Babylonia and Assyria*, Ann Arbor: University of Michigan.

Scurlock, J., 1995. "Death and Afterlife in Ancient Mesopotamian Thought," in J. Sasson (ed.), *Civilizations of the Ancient Near East*, vol. 3, New York: Charles Scribner and Sons, 1883–93.

Sefati, Y., 1998. *Love Songs in Sumerian Literature*, Israel: Bar-Ilan University Press.

——, 2005. *Magico-Medical Means of Treating Ghost-induced Illnesses*, Leiden: Brill.

Stol, M., 1995. "Private Life in Ancient Mesopotamia," in J.M. Sasson (ed.), *Civilizations of the Ancient Near East*, vol. 1, New York: Charles Scribner's Sons, 485–501.

Yamauchi, E., 1961. "Cultic Clues in Canticles?" *Bulletin of the Evangelical Theological Society* 4, 80–88.

9a

AKKADIAN TEXTS—WOMEN IN LETTERS

Old Assyrian Kaniš

Cécile Michel

The important number of letters, dated mainly to the first half of the nineteenth century BC and discovered in the merchant harbour of Kaniš, was generated by the long distance—more that a thousand kilometres—between Aššur and Kaniš, main stations of the Old Assyrian international trade route, as well as by the geographical break-up of families. Letters were the only medium to send news; they have been kept by the merchants because of the many data they contained about current trading operations, mixing sometimes commercial and private affairs. Some letters belonging to the correspondence between Assyrians and their wives and families tackle many aspects of daily life.[1]

Most of the female authors of letters discovered in Kaniš did not follow their husbands in Anatolia and stayed in Aššur, at the head of their household. There, they represented their husbands in commercial transactions, participated in international trade and accomplished many daily tasks. They weaved textiles to dress their children and servants, but the most important part of their production was exported to Asia Minor. Their know-how was appreciated and their production considered by their husbands, who knew what was valuable on the Anatolian market. With the gold and silver earned from the sale of their textiles, they bought barley to feed children and servants, and regularly repaired their house. When they lacked money, they used to send complaints to their husbands.

These women educated their younger children, giving them also a moral and religious background. They reminded men of their religious duties and asked them to engage in correct behaviour. Assyrian ladies were helped in their daily tasks by a domestic staff whose importance depended on their social level. They were concerned about offering their neighbours the image of a prosperous and harmonious family.

Some Assyrian women undertook the long trip to Anatolia in order to visit family members or to get established there by marrying an Assyrian or a local man. Assyrian ladies in Anatolia were supposed to follow their husbands during all their professional trips inside Anatolia, being thus assured to have food and a place to live.

Some women seem to have been able to write their own letters. There were official scribes working for big firms or the administration of the trading post. But the important amount of letters found in Kaniš implies that a significant proportion of the Assyrian population was able to read and write, sometimes making mistakes in the use of signs or grammar. Thus, it is not unlikely that a few women received a basic education in writing.

The women living alone, widows, priestesses and those separated from their husband, are the best-documented. Through their correspondence, we imagine women with strong personalities, being treated as equals with men and enjoying a great influence inside their family.

Producing textiles[2]

Lamassī writes to her husband that she has some difficulties in finding transporters for her textiles. She denies producing low-quality textiles.

Say to Pūšu-kěn: thus (speaks) Lamassī.

Kulumāya is bringing you 9 textiles, Iddin-Sîn: 3 textiles; Ela refused to take textiles (for transport); Iddin-Sîn refused to take 5 (another) textiles (for transport). Why do you always write to me: "The textiles you used to send me are not good!" Who is the fellow living in your house who is decrying the textiles when they arrive before him? As to me, on my side, I try my best to make and send you textiles in order that from each caravan trip (at least) 10 shekels of silver may accrue to your house.

Lament for money[3]

Tarām-Kūbi writes to her husband stressing her financially critical situation. She accuses him of having left nothing in the house and complains that she has no more money to buy barley.

Say to Innaya: thus (speaks) Tarām-Kūbi.
You wrote me as follows: "Keep the bracelets and rings which are available (there). Let them serve for your sustenance." Certainly, you had Ilī-bāni bring me ½ mina of gold, but which are the bracelets that you left me? When you left, you did not leave me silver, not even a single shekel! You emptied the house and took (everything) out! After you had gone, there was a severe famine in the City (of Aššur and) you did not leave me barley, not even a single litre! I constantly have to buy barley for our sustenance. And,

as to the goods for the temple collect, I gave an emblem in/ among […] and I spent my own possessions. So I just paid the City Hall for [what] the house of Adada owed. What are the complaints you keep writing me about? There is nothing for our sustenance and (for sure) we keep making complaints! I have collected what I had at my disposal and sent it to you. Today, I am living in an empty house. Now is the season, take good care to send me, in exchange for my textiles, silver from what you have at hand, so that I can buy barley, about 10 ṣimdu measures (ca. 300 ltr).

Concerning the tablet bearing (the list) of witnesses that Aššur-imittī, son of Kura, took, he caused many troubles (at) home, took maids as pledge, then your representatives settled the matter. But I finally had to pay 2/3 minas of silver. Before you arrive, he must not sue. At your arrival, you will discuss (together). Why do you keep on listening to slander and sending me heated (letters)?

Repairing the house and managing a daughter-in-law[4]

A widow writes to her son about repairs that have to be made to their house. She also complains about the wrong behaviour of her son's young wife who refuses to live with her while her husband is abroad.

Say to Enlil-bāni: thus (speaks) Tarīš-mātum.

Concerning the house in which we live, I was afraid that the house has become weakened so, during spring, I had bricks made and I stacked (them) in piles. Concerning the beams about which you wrote me, send me the necessary amount of silver so that here they [will buy] beams [for you] (lacuna).

He wastes […] and you […] You (are) my brother, in [whom else should I trust?] And you in whom else should y[ou trust? On] your arrival, you will learn that the share of silver of our father's house is so that you and I may be at ease. Don't pay heed to slander and gossip!

Before your departure, you gave me some instructions concerning our daughter-in-law as follows: "Do not let her go to the house of her father; it is with you that she has to live in the house and keep a watch on the house after you." When you left, there had never been any instance of misconduct or misdeed on her part. (But) now, for 8 months she [re]fuses to sta[y] with me, she fights with me, at night, she always go her father's house and I keep on hearing bad things about her; at last she refuses to hear my words!

CÉCILE MICHEL

Rebuking a son[5]

Ištar-bāšti reprimands her son, asking him to pay attention to his parent's affairs. She intends to travel to Kaniš.

Thus (speaks) Ištar-bāšti: say to Puzur-Ištar.
Why should I write you many words? If not you, who else do we have over there? If not you, your father has nobody else over there! Be a gentleman, pay heed to the instructions of your father, keep the tablets of your father safe and ask (all the concerned persons) to pay all his outstanding claims. And sell the merchandise of your father then get ready and come here so that you may see the eye of (divine) Aššur and of your father and thus please your father!
Do you not know that today I will not scold you? Come quickly so that I can depart with you and watch over your father's house and yours in Kaniš and thus no one will create troubles to the house of your father.

Preaching at men[6]

Two sisters accuse their brother of loving money at such a level that he neglects everything else, even his god.

Say to Imdī-ilum: thus (speaks) Tarām-Kūbi and Šīmat-Aššur.
Here (in Aššur) we consulted the women who interpret dreams, the women diviner, and the spirits of the dead, and (divine) Aššur keeps on warning you: You love (too much) money; you hate your life! Can't you satisfy (divine) Aššur (here) in the City (of Aššur)? Please, when you have heard the letter (then) come here, see (divine) Aššur's eye and save your life! Why don't you send to me the proceeds from my textiles?

Social success[7]

Lamassī reminds her husband of his parental responsibilities and religious obligations; she envies her neighbour who keeps on extending his house.

Say to Pūšu-kěn: thus (speaks) Lamassī.
You hear that mankind has become bad, one tries to swallow up the other! Be a man of honour, come and break your obligations! Put our young (daughter) under the protection of the god Aššur. (Here), in the City (of Aššur), wool is expensive. When you put silver at my disposal, (about) 1 mina, put it within the wool.

The *mūṣû*-official[8] asked me for your export duty of every mina of silver which you sent me, and I was afraid for you but I did not give (anything); I told (him): "The eponym may come in and take away (everything from my) house (but I will not give anything)!" Your sister sold a slave girl but I myself released her for 14 shekels (of silver).

Since you left, Šalim-ahum built two times a house; when will we be able to do (the same)? As for the textile(s) which Aššur-malik brought you previously, could not you send the silver?

Wise advice to a sister separated from her husband[9]

The priestess Ummī-Išhara writes from Aššur to her sister Šalimma, who is living in Kaniš with her mother, a widow. Ummī-Išhara, as a wise elder sister, gives advice to Šalimma in order to preserve the couple. Šalimma's husband feels lonely in Aššur while his wife prolongs her stay in Kaniš, and Ummī-Išhara is afraid that he might decide to divorce her sister.

Say to Lamassatum and Šalimma: thus (speaks) Ummī-Išhara. Concerning the letter you sent me, in which (you wrote) as follows: "Why does he not send me someone?" His messenger did arrive but it was me who sent (him). I talked to him several times, but each time he flares up, saying: "Several times a letter of mine went to her, but she refused to come here! What should I send to her more that the many messages that already reached her?"

The gentleman has become very annoyed by the matter saying: "Since she refuses to come, you must not speak to me again!" If you are my sister, do not keep writing me lies (and) do not write to him for any silver. I wrote to him concerning the silver, and he (said): "Should I really oblige her mother or her brothers for all the half mina of silver for her expenses? Or is there not silver available from my outstanding claims, (at least) 10 shekels? And if there are not, let her ask for 10 shekels of silver for her expenses for her mother or her brothers, and myself, here I will give it back (only if) she comes here."

Do not keep on sending to me all kinds of words or letters. You have brought me into conflict with the gentleman (and) he (tells) me: "Since, not being my *amtu*-wife,[10] she refuses to come here, you must not mention her name again to me, lest you will not be my sister anymore!" Why are others ruling your children and your household while you are staying over there? Please, do not make your children waste away and do not take me away from the gentleman's house! If there is a possibility for you to come here, get ready and leave for here before the gentleman changes his mind! The day Pilah-Ištar arrived here, since you did not came with him, he (the gentleman) felt very unhappy and for five days he did not went out (of his home). Write me if you are searching for another husband, so that I know it. If not, then get ready and leave for here.

If you do not come here, you will bring me into conflict with the gentleman, and you will make your children waste away, and I, I will never mention your name again! You will no longer be my sister, and you must not write me anymore.

Assyrian wife in Anatolia trying to follow her husband[11]

Ištar-nādā is supposed to follow her husband during all his travels through Anatolia. But she is always one town late and complains that he left her behind.

Say to Ina-Sîn: thus (speaks) Ištar-nādā.

You left me in Burušhattum and really I got out of my husband's mind (litt. of my husband's hands) and you do not take care of me! I came here and in Kaniš, you denigrated me and during one (full) year you did not let me come to your bed. You wrote to me from Timilkiya as follows: "If you do not come here, you are not anymore my *amtu*-wife! I will make it even worse than in Burušhattum." From Timilkiya, you went to Kaniš saying: "I will leave again within 15 days." (But) instead of 15 days, you did stay there one year! From Kaniš you wrote to me as follows: "Come up to Hahhum!" Today, I am living in Hahhum since one year and in your consignments, you even do not mention my name! Your representatives who live there at your side have seen my (long lonely) days; they said: "We, we spoke to him as follows: 'At (...)

Abbreviations

AAA	Annals of Archaeology and Anthropology (Liverpool).
BIN	Babylonian Inscriptions in the Collection of J. B. Nies.
CCT	Cuneiform Texts from Cappadocian Tablets in the British Museum.
KTS	Keilschrifttexte in den Antiken-Museen zu Istanbul.
Kt	Kültepe.
k	kārum.
MAH	Museum siglum of the Musée d'Art et d'Histoire, Geneva.
TC	Textes cunéiformes, Musées du Louvre.

Notes

1 Michel, 2008b, 117–40.
2 BIN 6, 11 edited by Veenhof, 1972, 113–44, and translated by Michel, 2001, no. 302.
3 CCT 3, 24 edited by Michel, 1991, vol. II, no. 3, and Michel, 2001, no. 348. Lines 1–38 have been quoted by Dercksen, 2004, 23–24.
4 AAA 1/3, 1 collated by Kawasaki, 1998, 85, and translated by Michel, 2001, no. 320.
5 KTS 1, 1b translated by Michel, 2001, no. 352. For the women of this family, see Kryszat, 2007, 210–18.
6 TC 1, 5 translated by Larsen, 1982, 214; Michel, 2001, no. 348; and K. Hecker, 2007, 77–100.
7 MAH 16209 published by Garelli, 1965, 156–60, no. 25, and translated by Michel, 2001, no. 306.
8 The *mūṣû*-official is involved in the levy of the export tax in Aššur.
9 KT 91/k 385 published by Veenhof, 2007, 285–304. A piece of the envelope, Kt 91/k 386, bears the following text: [Seal of Ummī-Išhara. To Lamassatum] and Šalimma, the wife of Irma-Aššur.
10 There are two words for the "wife": the *aššatu*-wife corresponds to the main wife and the *amtu*-wife to the second wife. They have the same status considering their relations with their husband but it seems that the children of the *amtu*-wife have less rights than the children of the *aššatu*-wife.
11 Kt h/k 73 published by H. Sever, "Yeni Belgelerin Işığında Koloni Çağında Yerli Halk İle Asurlu Tüccarlar Arasındaki İlişkiler", *Belleten* 59, 1995, 14, and translated by Michel, 2006a, n. 56 and 2008, 29–30, n. 29. The tablet has been collated in May 2005 and is complete; thus, the end of the text must have been written on a second page or a tablet supplement.

Bibliography

Dercksen, J. G., 2004. *Old Assyrian Institutions*, Leiden: Brill.

Garelli, P., 1965. 'Tablettes Cappadociennes de Collections Diverses', *Revue d'Assyriologie* 59, 149–76.

Hecker, K., 2007. 'Altassyrische Briefe', *Texte aus der Umwelt des Alten Testaments Neue Folge 3* 2007, 77–100.

Kawasaki, Y. 1998. 'An Unpublished Old Assyrian Tablet in the "Prof. Garstang Collection", Housed in Liverpool Museum', *Oriento* 33, 79–87.

Kryszat, G., 2007. 'Eine Dame mit Namen Zizizi', *Altorientalische Forschungen* 34, 210–18.

Larsen, M. T., 1982. 'Your Money or your Life! A Portrait of an Assyrian Businessman', in N. Postgate. (ed.), *Societies and Languages of the Ancient Near East, Studies in Honor of I. M. Diakonoff*, Warminster: Aris and Phillips, 214–44.

——, 2001. 'Affect and Emotion', in W. van Soldt *et al.* (ed.), *K. R. Veenhof Anniversary Volume*, Leiden: Nederlands Instituut voor het Nabije Oosten, 275–86.

Michel, C., 1991. *Innāya dans les tablettes paléo-assyriennes*, Paris: Editions recherches sur les civilisations.

——, 2001. *Correspondance des Marchands de Kaniš au Début du IIe Millénaire Avant J.-C.*, Paris: Cerf.

——, 2006a. 'Bigamie Chez les Assyriens du Début du IIe Millénaire', *Revue Historique de Droit Français et Etranger* 84, 155–76.

——, 2006b. 'Femmes et Production Textile à Aššur au Début du IIe Millénaire Avant J.-C.', *Techniques & culture* 46, 281–97.

——, 2008a. 'Femmes au Foyer et Femmes en Voyage: le Cas des Épouses des Marchands Assyriens au Début du IIe Millénaire Av. J.-C.', *Clio, Histoire femmes et sociétés* 28, 17–38.

——, 2008b. 'La Correspondance des Marchands Assyriens du XIXe s. av. J.-C.: de l'Archivage des Lettres Commerciales et Privées', in L. Pantalacci (ed.), *La Lettre d'Archive. Communication Administrative et Personnelle dans l'Antiquité Proche-orientale et Égyptienne*, Le Caire: Institut français d'archéologie orientale, 117–40.

——, 2009a. 'Femmes et Ancêtres: le Cas des Femmes des Marchands d'Aššur', *Topoi*, Suppl. 10, 27–39.

——, 2009b. 'Les Filles de Marchands Consacrées', *Topoi*, Suppl. 10, 145–63.

——, 2009c. 'Les Femmes et l'Écrit dans les Archives Paléo-Assyriennes (XIXe s. av. J.-C.)', *Topoi*, Suppl. 10, 253–72.

—— (forthcoming) 'Women in the Aššur and Kaniš according to the private archives of the Assyrian merchants at the beginning of the IInd millennium BC,' *Writing from the Ancient World*, SBL: Baltimore.

Veenhof, K. R., 1972. *Aspects of the Old Assyrian Trade and its Terminology*, Leiden: Brill.

——, 2007a. 'Sisterly Advice on an Endangered Marriage in an Old Assyrian Letter', in M. T. Roth (ed.), *Studies Presented to Robert D. Biggs, June 4, 2004*. Chicago: Oriental Institute, 285–304.

——, 2008. 'The Death and Burial of Ishtar-Lamassi in *karum* Kanish', in R. J. van der Spek (ed.), *Studies in Ancient Near Eastern World View and Society Presented to Marten Stol on the Occasion of his 65th Birthday, 10 November 2005, and his retirement from the Vrije Universiteit*, Bethesda: CDL Press, 97–119.

9b

AKKADIAN TEXTS—WOMEN IN LETTERS

The Neo-Assyrian period

Sarah C. Melville

Of the thousands of Neo-Assyrian letters that have come down to us, only a few involve women and many of these are too fragmentary to provide much useful information. Since the majority of letters from this period come from the royal archives and therefore deal with matters of state, rather than from private residences where we would expect to find personal correspondence, it is not surprising that women are under-represented in the letter corpus. Nonetheless, letters to, from, or about women help to reveal the place of women in Assyrian society.

A number of conventions governed Assyrian epistolary practices: letters were not dated, usually identified the king or other royals by title only, and naturally assumed that the reader remembered and understood the context, thus leaving us to determine the original circumstances, sense, and ramifications of the correspondence.

The following are examples of the most characteristic and best-preserved letters in which women figure prominently. In the translations, square brackets indicate breaks in the text, while words in parenthesis do not appear in the text but have been added to aid in reading or to explain.

Letters concerning domestic matters

The king to the queen mother (presumably, Esarhaddon to Naqi'a)[1]

There is nothing personal about this letter and it does not reveal much about the relationship between the king and his mother. However, it is clear that the two communicated regularly when they could not meet face to face and that the king took his mother's advice, at least in some instances. The formal address—the fact that the king does not refer to himself or his

213

mother by name—simply reflects conventional scribal practice and should not
be understood to signify that the two had a strained relationship.

> Word of the king to the mother of the king: I am well. May it be
> well with the king's mother. Regarding the servant of Amūšu
> (Amos) about whom you wrote: As the king's mother ordered,
> I have ordered. What you said to me is very good. Why should
> Ḫamunāya go?

The consort's palace[2]

The king maintained palaces in every major city in Assyria, while other members
of the royal family enjoyed a range of options: some lived in the palace; some
retained private estates, and some did both. It appears that the king usually paid
for separate residences for the consort in various locations, though she might
have administered them herself.[3] Legal documents show that royal women
(consort, queen mother) oversaw their own estates, but it is likely that these
reverted to the crown when the women died.[4]

> To the king, my lord: your servant, Bel-iqiša. May it be well with
> the king, my lord. May Nabu and Marduk bless the king, my lord,
> very very much!
>   With regard to the (construction of the) consort's palace in
> Kilizi which the king, my lord, delegated to me: I have cleared the
> (old) palace; the foundation is open; the bricks are in stock for
> laying the foundations. If the king, my lord, commands, let the
> order be made for the chief of the builders to come and lay the
> foundations.

Šērūa-ēṭirat to Libbāli-šarrat[5]

The only surviving Neo-Assyrian letter certainly authored by a woman is a
short missive from the daughter of Esarhaddon, Šērūa-ēṭirat, to her sister-in-law,
Libbāli-šarrat, who was the wife of Ashurbanipal. Since the letter refers to
Ashurbanipal as crown prince, it must have been written sometime between 672
(the year he was designated heir) and 668 (his accession year). This short note is
usually interpreted as an admonishment meant to put Libbāli-šarrat in her
place.[6] However, an alternative reading in which Šērūa-ēṭirat encourages (albeit
brusquely) the younger woman to fulfill her new duties is just as plausible and
would better explain why the letter became part of the official archive. Even if
she had been groomed for her position, Libbāli-šarrat had a big adjustment to
make as the wife of the crown prince, and the woman closest to her in rank
(a princess) might well have written to prod her into fulfilling her role as "Lady of

the House."[7] The letter, which clearly states that the future queen should be able to read and write, raises intriguing questions about the extent of literacy among elite women (and, by association, men) at court.[8] At the very least it indicates that during Esarhaddon's reign, some royal women received basic scribal training.

> Word of the daughter of the king to Libbāli-šarrat:[9] Why do you not write your tablet and do your schoolwork? If (you do) not, they will say, "Is this the sister of Šērūa-ēṭirat, the eldest daughter of Succession Palace of Aššūr-etel-ilāni-mukīnni,[10] great king, mighty king, king of the world, king of Assyria?" For you are a daughter-in-law, the "lady of the house" of Ashurbanipal, the crown prince of the Succession Palace of Esarhaddon, king of Assyria.

Greetings and blessings

From Ašarēdu to the queen mother[11]

Ašarēdu wrote this letter of assurance to the queen mother (presumably Naqi'a/ Zakūtu) from the Babylonian city of Cutha, as is evident from the invocation of the gods Nergal and Laṣ in the greeting formula. The letter is not dated and there is some doubt as to the identity of the author. During the reign of Ashurbanipal, Ašarēdu served as the governor of Cutha, while another man of that name is known to have been a scholar in Babylonia during Esarhaddon's reign. Since the letter to the queen mother contains phrases typical of both a governor ("It is well with the city and the temples of the king") and a scholar ("I am keeping the watch of the king"), it is not possible to identify the author with certainty. Although the letter is no more than a standard report, the fact that it was written to the queen mother indicates that some official found it politic to keep her informed, presumably when the king himself was absent, otherwise occupied, or ill.

> To the mother of the king, my lord: your servant, Ašarēdu. May Nabû and Marduk bless the mother of the king, my lord. Every day I pray to Nergal and Laṣ for the lives of the king and the mother of the king, my lords. It is well with the city and the temples of the king, and now I am keeping the watch of the king, my lord.

Ištār-šumu-ēreš, chief scribe, to the queen mother[12]

This fragmentary letter of greeting is remarkable for the rather extravagant compliment that Ištār-šumu-ēreš pays the queen mother, in effect, elevating her to the level of the king, at least metaphorically.[13] What remains of this letter and other letters written to Naqi'a contain no indication that she wielded executive power or held any type of official position other than the one she held by virtue of being queen mother. However, they do reveal that she was both a formidable presence at court and someone whose favor was well worth cultivating.

> To the mother of the king, my lord: your servant, Ištār-šumu-ēreš. May it be well with the mother of the king, my lord. May Nabû and Marduk bless the mother of the king, my lord [...] [the verdict of the mother of the king, my lord] is as final as that of the gods. What you bless is blessed; what you curse is cursed. Regarding what the mother of the king, my lord wrote to me [...]
> May Mullissu grant [...] and give longevity, happiness, joy [...] to the king, [...] and the name [...]

Nabû-nādin-šumi to the daughter of the king[14]

Hoping to curry favor at the Assyrian court, an official (perhaps a priest?) wrote to the king's daughter from Babylon (judging from the gods invoked in greeting formula). Presumably, Nabû-nādin-šumi had met the king's daughter or had received a temple donation from her.[15] Although the context of the letter is unfortunately lost, it shows that royal women, other than the consort or the queen mother, traveled or were otherwise involved in foreign affairs.

> To the king's daughter, my lady: your servant, Nabu-nadin-šumi. Every day I pray to Bēl, Zarpānītum, Nabû, Nanāya and Tašmētum for the lives of the king of the world, my lord, and the king's daughter, my lady.
> Zarpānītum, exalted lady, has made your heart happy. As I have prayed to Bēl and Nabû for the well-being of the king of the world, my lord, and the king's daughter, my lady, may Bēl and Nabû set the happy faces of the king of the world, my lord, and the king's daughter, my lady, toward me.

The ghost of the dead consort blesses the crown prince[16]

This broken letter from Adad-šumu-uṣur, Esarhaddon's chief exorcist, was written shortly after Ashurbanipal became crown prince.[17] The letter quotes Ashurbanipal as crediting his mother's purity and blameless behavior for his elevation to crown prince. Here Ashurbanipal is making use of a long-standing royal trope by which the crown prince or king establishes his legitimacy through his relationship to his mother, often claiming to have been singled out while still a child or even in his mother's womb.[18] According to Adad-šumu-uṣur, Ashur-banipal has done an admirable job fulfilling his duty to his mother's shade, presumably by making funeral offerings on a regular basis.[19]

[beginning broken]

"Aššur and Šamaš decreed for me to be the crown prince of Assyria on account of her virtue." Her ghost blesses him as he has venerated the ghost. "May his name (and) his descendents rule over Assyria!" Fear of the gods engenders goodness; fear of the gods of the underworld establishes order.

[remainder broken]

Letters of political significance

The governor's wife 'mourns' the death of the king[20]

This intriguing text apparently describes events in Aššur after the news of Sennacherib's murder reached the city.[21] When the governor learned of the king's death he immediately went to the palace to get his wife, who had previously been living there, but in what capacity (e.g. as king's wife/concubine or harem administrator) is not stated. There are various ways to interpret this letter,[22] but it seems to me that the governor reacted to the crisis in a logical and effective manner. He acted swiftly to secure the city, maintain order, and return everything to 'normal' by trying to carry out the appropriate mourning rituals. Since women played an important role in mourning rites and Sennacherib's mausoleum had already been built in Assur, it seems natural that the governor would go straight to his wife, the woman he knew best at the palace, to get the rituals started. That this was a time of crisis in Assyria is clear from the ad hoc way the rituals were conducted and the dramatic events reported in the second-half of the letter. It is also likely that the governor was attempting to come through the crisis politically unscathed, if not with an improved power base.

> The king received the governor's woman and caused her to enter the palace. On the day we heard the king was dead and the Inner City people were crying, the governor released his wife from the palace. She roasted a young she-goat; he installed his eunuch as mayor. His eunuchs stood in front of the mayor wearing robes and decked in gold jewelry. Qīsāya, the singer, and his daughters sang before them. As for what we said …

[about ten fragmentary lines …]

> We went to Dannāya. He unwound the rope of the gate and let Dannāya to go out. We left to weep for the body (of the king). We saw the governor with his troops clad in armor and armed with swords. We were awed and spoke thus to the vizier and to Ḫambi, "Why are we crying? The governor and his troops are armed with swords and standing guard (lit. standing ahead of us)."

217

He went to the palace, to the succession palace immediately, saying "Open the door for me!" For the sake of the governor, we will take over. [...] is killing the sons of Zazakki.

Na'id-Marduk to the queen mother[23]

This text represents the only Neo-Assyrian letter with clear political content that was addressed to a woman, in this case, the queen mother Naqi'a. In the letter, Na'id-Marduk, the Governor of the Sealand (in Babylonia), reports an Elamite raid and pleads for the king to send reinforcements. He also claims to have rebuffed Elamite diplomatic advances and affirms his continued loyalty to Assyria. Although the letter is not dated, the events described most likely occurred around 675 BC.[24] Na'id-Marduk's comment that he has previously written to the queen mother invites speculation about the basis of their relationship. Was Na'id-Marduk writing to the queen mother as his official superior (that is, was she in charge of part of Babylonia)? Was Naqi'a ruling while the king was incapacitated or away? Or was Na'id-Marduk simply trying to get the king's attention by writing to someone he knew well and knew to be influential? Since there is no evidence to corroborate the supposition that Naqi'a acted in an official capacity (as a governor, for example) anywhere in the empire, it seems best to take this letter as Na'id-Marduk's personal entreaty to the queen mother, whose opinion he knew to be important to the king.[25]

To the mother of the king, my lord: your servant, Na'id-Marduk. May it be well with the mother of the king, my lord. May Aššur, Šamaš and Marduk invigorate the king, my lord. May they decree happiness for the mother of the king, my lord.

From Elam they came against us and seized the bridge. When they came, I wrote to the mother of the king, my lord. Now they have dismantled the bridge but they have kept the pontoons from the bridge. They have not let them go. We do not know whether or not they will go. If they do go, I will write to the mother of the king, my lord. May the troops reach us, my lord!

The son of Nikkal-iddina has written to the king of Elam and to Ḫuban-nikaš [. ...] the king of Assyria and his camp [...]

[Break in text]

The mother of the king, my lord, knows that the words are trustworthy and someone among the Chaldeans has written accordingly. By the gods of the king, my lord, (I swear) that a messenger of the king of Elam did bring messages, but did not come before me. I did not see him and no one opened his letter before he left. On the second day of Ab, his messenger came to me across the border. I made him withdraw and I sent my messenger to the palace. My lord should know that my heart is entirely with the house of my lord!

Letters concerning cultic matters

A number of letters in the corpus indicate that high-ranking royal women took part in day-to-day rituals, funeral services, and some other cult-related events. In addition, female servants sometimes participated as stand-ins in particular rituals. Nevertheless, the details and context of women's ritual activity are not given in the letters and so full understanding of their religious roles continues to elude us. We do know that royal women contributed regularly to temples and that the highest ranking women (queen mother and consort) took part in some rituals. Note, however, that even when performing a ritual on behalf of one of the royal women, officials usually required the king's permission.

Nergal-šarrāni, priest of the Nabû temple at Kalhu, to the queen mother[26]

To the mother of the king, my lord: your servant, Nergal-šarrāni. May it be well with the mother of the king, my lord. May Tašmētum, whom you worship, take your hands. May you behold a thousand years of the kingship of Esarhaddon.

Concerning what the mother of the king, my lord, wrote to me: "what goes into the ritual?" Sweet oil, wax, and sweet-scented aromatics, myrrh, cannabis, and sadidu-plants. I will certainly do whatever the mother of the king has ordered. On the [xth] day they will do the whole-offerings: one bull, two white sheep, and a duck. Damqāya, the queen mother's maid, cannot take part in the ritual. Whoever the mother of the king, my lord, orders should open the basket and do the ritual.

[Nergal-šarrāni] to the queen mother[27]

[beginning broken] May Nabû and Marduk bless the mother of the king, my lord. Concerning the offerings about which they wrote to me: "Before whom are they made?" They are all done before Tašmētum: a bull, two rams, and a duck. This is all.

Nabû-šum-līšir to the queen mother[28]

The Assyrians considered eclipses to be particularly portentous events that could signal a grave threat to the king. Hence, in the event of a negative eclipse interpretation priests took every precaution to safeguard the king and his family. Several letters to Esarhaddon concern eclipse rituals, which sometimes included the enthronement of a substitute king.[29] Evidently the queen mother felt the need to get involved as well, although it's likely that any ritual performed on her behalf was less elaborate than those done for the king or the crown prince.[30]

> To the mother of the king, my lord: your servant, Nabû-šum-līšir. May Šhamašh and Marduk look after the health of the mother of the king, my lord.
> The slave girl who is in the house of Šama' (and) who was consigned to my care, since the eclipse ritual is ready, it will be performed on her. The queen mother said, "Let them give rams." If it is welcome to the mother of the king, let them delegate that the rams be given to the chief of accounts of the palace.

Marduk-šākin-šumi, chief exorcist, to the king about a royal funeral

This letter almost certainly refers to the state funeral of the king's wife, Ešarra-hammat, who died in 673. Women of the court and other suitable women traveled to take part in the funeral rites, which were elaborate and lengthy.[31] This letter contrasts markedly to the ad hoc arrangements described above in "The governor's wife 'mourns' the death of the king" (C1).

> To the king, my lord: your servant, Marduk-šākin-šumi. May it be very well with the king, my lord. May Nabû and Marduk bless the king, my lord. May Ištar of Arbela give joy and well being to the king, my lord. May she satisfy the king with old age, extreme old age. May she bestow long-lasting days on the king, my lord.
> Now I am constantly performing the ritual and I have collected the articles for the king's burning rite in a warehouse in the Inner City. Concerning those women about whom the king, my lord, spoke to me, the house where they are staying is not healthy for eating, drinking, and anointing the head because they are so numerous and staying there together. If it is acceptable to the king, let them be made to dwell someplace else.
> Alternatively, if we do the ritual by the 14th day, they can go to the river. May the king, my lord, write to his servant how it is proper for us to do the ritual, and for them to go where (they should) go, and we will act accordingly. And what are the king, my lord's, orders regarding that female servant who is with them? Should the ritual be performed for her together with them?
> [remainder broken]

Adad-aḫu-iddina, a temple official in Nineveh, writes to the king about a prophetess[32]

Prophecy played an important role in royal planning during the Sargonid period of Assyrian history. Most prophets were women, who were associated with the cult of Ištar, although the deity invoked by the prophetess in this letter is not named.[33] This letter reveals a dispute over who had custodial authority over an important piece of cultic furniture. Evidently the writer was more worried about getting the king's permission than about fulfilling the seer's vision.

> To the king, my lord: your servant, Adad-aḫu-iddina. May it be well with the king, my lord. May Aššur, Mullissu, Nabu and Marduk bless the king, my lord.
>
> Mullissu-abu-uṣur, the prophetess who brought the king's garments to Babylon, has prophesied in the temple … "the throne from the temple [.] May you let the throne go. I will destroy my king's enemies with it." (I answered) thus: "without (the order of) the king, my lord, I will not hand over the throne." What the king, my lord, orders, we will do accordingly.

Urad-Nabû to the king[34]

A priest in Kalhu (Nimrud), Urad-Nabû here informs the king that he has found a couple of suitable girls whom he has chosen to take part in some ritual or perhaps to be trained as priestesses. Of note is his rather obsequious and long greeting, as well as his attention to the girls' living conditions and patrimony.

> To the king, my lord: your servant, Urad-Nabû. May it be well with the king, my lord. May Aššur, Sin, Šamaš, Bēl, Zarpanītum, Nabu, Tašmētum, Ištar of Nineveh, and Ištar of Arbela, these great gods who love your kingship, let the king, my lord, live 100 years. May they let the king, my lord, be sated with old age, extreme old age.
>
> On the 7th, in the temple I beheld beautiful little girls. One was the granddaughter of Qannasusi. I sent and had the house looked at. The other one's name is Urkittu-reminni. She is the daughter of [NN], the bodyguard. I saw her on the royal road. I sent and had (her) house inspected.

(remainder of letter broken)

Letters concerning women's health

A large number of Neo-Assyrian letters deal with health matters. Although most of these relate directly to Esarhaddon's health, which we know to have been poor, various other letters reveal that every effort was made to treat the illnesses of other people associated with the palace, including women and children.[35]

The queen mother's illness

A series of four letters written to the king by his physicians over the course of a few days or a couple of weeks tracks their treatment of the queen mother's illness.[36] The letters probably date to the period immediately following the coup-d'état attempt in 670.[37] The incantations used to cure the queen mother (Naqi'a) indicate that her physicians believed her illness had been caused by witchcraft and it is possible that after the political crisis abated, and in reaction to it, the queen mother suffered a brief period of what we would now recognize as severe post-traumatic stress.[38] However, as no symptoms are mentioned in the letters, it is best to be cautious about a diagnosis.

Adad-šumu-uṣur, chief exorcist, to the king[39]

To the king, my lord: your servant, Adad-šumu-uṣur. May it be well with the king, my lord. May Nabû and Marduk bless the king, my lord. May the great gods establish great good health for the mother of the king, my lord.

    When Bēl removed the king's illness ...

    (break in text)

    ... rituals [...] are being carried out. We are performing many quality anti-witchcraft rituals.

Adad-šumu-uṣur to the king[40]

To the king, my lord: your servant, Adad-šumu-uṣur. May it be well with the king my lord. May Nabu and Marduk and the great gods of heaven and earth bless the king my lord very, very much!

    The mother of the king is doing exceedingly well; the king, my lord can be very happy.

    (break in text)

    The incantation "Ea, Šamaš, Asalluḫi" of "Breaking the Curse;" the incantation "You, River, Creator of All" – she has performed 10 tablets with their rituals and she is very well. The king, my lord should be very happy.

Nabû-nādin-šumi to the king[41]

Nabu-nadin-šumi, one of Esarhaddon's exorcists, wrote this letter to the king regarding an unidentified ritual that the king had ordered performed on behalf of his sister, Šaddītu. The treaty mentioned probably refers to Esarhaddon's

Succession Treaty, which allows us (tentatively) to date the letter to the first or second month of 672.[42] The letter is also a good example of the competition for royal patronage among exorcists. Nabû-nādin-šumi is incensed that another exorcist would dare to come in from Kalhu (Nimrud) to Nineveh and interfere with his ritual in his jurisdiction. Šaddītu, like her brother, Šamaš-mētu-uballiṭ (see next letter), did not have the authority to consult the king's exorcist on her own behalf.

> To the king, my lord: your servant, Nabû-nādin-šumi. May it be well with the king, my lord. May Nabû and Marduk greatly bless the king, my lord.
>   The king, my lord directed me: "Go and carry out the ritual for Šaddītu." I did, (but) I did not produce the rest of the ritual; I had to go to the treaty. Why did Šumaya rush from Kalhu and say to Šaddītu, "I will set up and perform this ritual for you"?
>   (several fragmentary lines)
>   The king sent me. Why did he act quickly to do (the ritual)? He is incompetent! I shall do it. Alternatively, should I learn from his hands?

Šamaš-metu-uballiṭ, the king's son, to the king[43]

In this brief letter, one of the king's sons writes to ask that medical attention be provided to one of the women of the court. The patient, Bābu-gāmilat, is referred to as a gemé šá lugal (lit: slave girl of the king), but since it seems unlikely that a prince would write to the king about the king's own slave, it has been suggested that this phrase denotes someone of much higher rank.[44] In any case, the letter indicates that even the king's son did not have direct access to the royal physicians, but had to seek the king's intervention directly.

> To the king, my lord: your servant, Šamaš-mētu-uballiṭ. May it be well with the king, my lord. May Nabû and Marduk bless the king my lord, very very much.
>   Now, Bābu-gāmilat, the king's maid, is very sick. She cannot (even) eat flatbread. Now, may the king, my lord, give orders for a doctor to come and look at her.

Miscellaneous letters

Concerning the procurement of women for deported Aramaeans[45]

During the Neo-Assyrian period, the wholesale deportation of conquered peoples from their homelands to far regions of the empire became one of the most common means of pacification. Aššur-matka-tera was an official in charge of deportees during the reign of Sargon II (721–705 BC).[46] Evidently, he had been trying to arrange marriages between the deportees and an unidentified group of women, who refused to go through with the marriage until the Aramaeans came up with silver for the bride price/dowry. The extent to which the government was involved (would they have supplied the silver?) remains uncertain, but it is clear that the Assyrians realized that encouraging deportees to start families and settle down was a good way to establish social order and stability.

> To the king, my lord: your servant, Aššur-mātka-tēra. May it be well with the king, my lord. Concerning the Aramaeans of whom the king spoke thus: "let them get women for them"—the women say, "We have observed that the Aramaean men do not agree to make payment. They say, "(not) until they give us silver." May they themselves give silver that they themselves may marry."

Sending a woman to the king[47]

This intriguing but fragmentary letter concerns a woman who was attached to the household of the governor of Nippur (an important pro-Assyrian Babylonian city), probably during the reign of Ashurbanipal (669–c. 627 BC).[48] Whatever the circumstances—whether political or personal—the situation was important enough for the king to intervene and have the woman brought to him. That the letter refers to Re'indu by name rather than station (as servant or wife, for example), suggests that she enjoyed a relatively high status. Unfortunately, this name does not appear in any other Neo-Assyrian texts and at present there is no way to resolve the mystery surrounding her (possible) flight from Nippur and eventual removal to Assyria.

> (beginning destroyed)
> I pray. … Concerning Re'indu of the house of the Governor (of Nippur) about whom the king, my lord, wrote. I sought her in Babylon, but I did not see her. Because I asked and because I investigated, (I discovered) she dwelt in Dilbat. I led her out from Dilbat and I am sending her to the king, my lord, in the hands of the eunuch, Na'id-ilu, who brought the sealed letter of the king to me.
> (reverse broken).

Abbreviations

PNA	K. Radner (ed.), *The Prosopography of the Neo-Assyrian Empire* (Helsinki 1998ff.).
SAA	State Archives of Assyria.
SAAS	State Archives of Assyria Studies.

Notes

1   SAA XVI, 2.
2   SAA XVI, 111; PNA I/III, 316 dates this to the reign of Ashurbanipal.
3   In addition to the present letter, see Sennacherib's dedication to Tašmetum-šarrat elsewhere in this volume.
4   See, for example, SAA VI, 90, 265, 325 and SAA XIII, 90, 101, 108. After his mother's death, Sennacherib appears to have given her estate at Šabbu to Naqi'a. See SAA XII, 21–23.
5   SAA XVI, 28.
6   See, for example, SAA XVI, p. xxviii.
7   On the possibility that this title represents an official position of some kind, see Svärd and Luukko, 2009, 278–93.
8   Livingstone, 2007, 98–118 and Parpola, 1997a.
9   The opening of the letter leaves no doubt that the king's daughter outranked the king's daughter-in-law. See, Svärd and Luukko, 2009, 285, n. 37 for a discussion of the significance of the greeting formula.
10 Another name for Esarhaddon.
11 SAA XVIII, 10. See also SAA X, 154, a similarly mundane greeting from another official to the queen mother.
12 SAA X, 16–17, translated here as an amalgamation.
13 Parpola, SAA X, 17, restores "the verdict of the mother of the king" as part of the standard royal blessing that follows. Its appearance here is unusual because it is a complement that is typically reserved for kings. For further discussion, see Parpola, 1983, 27, 231.
14 SAA XVIII, 55. Reign of Esarhaddon or Ashurbanipal.
15 Royal women did travel occasionally and were also known to make donations to temples. See Melville, 2004 and Macgregor, 2012.
16 SAA X, 188.
17 Adad-šumu-uṣur can be identified as the author on orthographic grounds. See Parpola, 1983, 132, who also establishes the probable date.
18 For further discussion, see Melville, 2004, 55–56.
19 For more on funerary practices, see Postgate, 2008, 179–80. See also the Neo-Assyrian consort's funerary inscriptions in this volume.
20 SAA XVI, 95.
21 For the date, see Frahm, 1997, 184.
22 See, for example, Frahm, 1997, 184.
23 SAA XVIII, 85.
24 For discussion of the letter's date, see Melville, 1999, 64–67 and Waters, 2000, 38–40.
25 SAA XIII, 76
26 SAA XIII, 77. The letter can almost certainly be attributed to Nergal-šarrani.
27 SAA X, 313.
28 For further discussion, see Parpola, 1983, xxii–xxxii.
29 For tentative dating of this letter and further discussion, see Melville, 1999, 56–58.
30 SAA X, 233.
31 SAA XV, 37. See also Nissinen, 1997, 78–81.
32 For more on prophecy during this period, see Nissinen, 1997 and Parpola, 1997b.
33 SAA XV, 65.
34 See also SAA X, 293 (a letter concerning a royal childbirth), 301, 302, and 305 (all concerning royal babies).
35 Two of these, SAA X, 197 and 244 are not included here because they simply mention that the Queen Mother has recovered.
36 See Parpola, 1983, 138 for dating.

37 For further discussion of the Queen Mother's illness, see Melville, 1999, 84–85.
38 SAA X, 200.
39 SAA X, 201.
40 SAA X, 273. The author of this letter is not the same man who wrote to the king's daughter in the letter B3 translated above.
41 For argumentation, see Parpola, 1983, 211.
42 SAA XVI, 26.
43 Teppo, 2007, 407.
44 Saggs, 2001, 92.
45 Radner, 1998, 194.
46 SAA XVIII, 20.
47 Parpola, 2002, 1037.
48 The letter refers to the šandabakku, the title used to designate the governor of Nippur.

Bibliography

Cole, S. and P. Machinist. 1998. *Letters from Priests to the Kings Esarhaddon and Assurbanipal* = SAA XIII. Helsinki: Helsinki University Press.

Frahm, E. 1997. *Einleitung in die Sanherib-Inschriften.* Wien: Institut für Orientalistik der Universität.

Kataja, L. and R. Whiting. 1995. *Grants, Decrees and Gifts of the Neo-Assyrian Period* = SAA XII. Helsinki: Helsinki University Press.

Kwasman, T. and S. Parpola. 1991. *Legal Transactions of the Royal Court of Nineveh, Part I* = SAA VI. Helsinki: Helsinki University Press.

Livingstone, A. 2007. "Ashurbanipal: Literate of Not?" *Zeitschrift für Assyriologie* 97, 98–118.

Luukko, M. and G. Van Buylaere. 2002. *The Political Correspondence of Esarhaddon* = SAA XVI. Helsinki: Helsinki University Press.

Macgregor, S. L. 2012. *Beyond Hearth and Home: Women in the Public Sphere in Neo-Assyrian Society.* SAAS 21. Helsinki: The Neo-Assyrian Text Corpus Project.

Melville, S. 1999. *The Role of Naqia/Zakutu in Sargonid Politics* = SAAS IX. Helsinki: Helsinki University Press.

——. 2004. "Neo-Assyrian Royal Women and Male Identity: Status as a Social Tool," *Journal of the American Oriental Society* 124, 37–57.

Nissinen, M. 1997. *References to Prophecy in Neo-Assyrian Sources* = SAAS VII. Helsinki: Helsinki University Press.

Parpola, S. 1983. *Letters from Assyrian and Babylonian Scholars to the Kings Esarhaddon and Ashurbanipal.* Kevelaer: Butzon & Bercker.

——, 1993. *Letters from Assyrian and Babylonian Scholars* = SAA X. Helsinki: Helsinki University Press.

——, 1997a. "The man without a scribe and the question of literacy in the Assyrian empire," in B. Pongratz-Leisten, H. Kühne and P. Xella (eds), *Ana šadî Labnāni lū allik: Festschrift für Wolfgang Röllig,* Kevelaer: Butzon & Bercker, 315–24.

——, 1997b. *Assyrian Prophecies.* = SAA IX. Helsinki: Helsinki University Press.

——, 2002. *The Prosopography of the Neo-Assyrian Empire: III/1. P–S.* Helsinki: the Neo-Assyrian Text Corpus Project.

Postgate, N. 2008. "The Tombs in the Light of Mesopotamian Funeral Traditions," in L. al-Gailani Werr, D. Collon, J.E. Curtis and H. McCall, eds, *New Light on Nimrud:*

Proceedings of the Nimrud Conference, 11th–13th March 2002. London: BISI and the British Museum, 177–80.

Radner, K., ed., 1998. *Prosopography of the Neo-Assyrian Empire 1/I: A.* Helsinki: the Neo-Assyrian Text Corpus Project.

——, ed., 1999. *Prosopography of the Neo-Assyrian Empire 1/III: B-G.* Helsinki: the Neo-Assyrian Text Corpus Project.

Reynolds, F. 2003. *The Babylonian Correspondence of Esarhaddon* = SAA XVIII. Helinski: Helsinki University Press.

Saggs, H. W. F. 2001. The Nimrud Letters, 1952. *Cuneiform Texts from Nimrud V.* Trowbridge: the British School of Archaeology in Iraq.

Svärd, S. and M. Luukko. 2009. "Who Were the 'Ladies of the House' in the Assyrian Empire?" in M. Luukko, S. Svärd and R. Mattila, eds. *Of God(s), Trees, Kings, and Scholars: Neo-Assyrian and Related Studies in Honour of Simo Parpola.* Helsinki: The Finnish Oriental Society, 279–94.

Teppo, S. 2007. "Agency and the Neo-Assyrian Women of the Palace," *Studia Orientalia* 101, 381–420.

Waters, M. 2000. *A Survey of Neo-Elamite History* = SAAS XII. Helsinki: Helsinki University Press.

10a

WOMEN IN NEO-ASSYRIAN TEXTS

Sarah C. Melville

As authors and subjects males dominate the written sources that have survived from the Neo-Assyrian period (c. 1000–1605 BCE); yet females, too, appear in every kind of text, including monumental inscriptions, temple dedications, funerary tablets, and labels on personal items. The picture that emerges is one in which (elite) women worked together with men and played important roles in pursuing personal and family interests, and even, on some occasions or in certain capacities, running the country. The texts included here are representative of women's various activities, although administrative and economic documents are excluded because they merely name participants.[1]

Boundary stele (Pazarcik stele) of Adad-nīrārī III and Sammu-ramāt[2]

This royal inscription offers the only Assyrian example of a woman taking part in a military campaign. As Queen Mother, Sammu-ramāt (Semiramis of legend), accompanied her (probably young) son, Adad-nīrārī, (810–782 BCE) when he campaigned against the king of Kummuḫ. In accordance with Assyrian ideology, the part of the text that describes the actual fighting reverts from the first person plural (we) to the first person singular (I) so that the king can take sole credit for the victory. Nevertheless, Sammu-ramāt did share recognition for extending Assyrian territory and setting up a boundary stone – both activities that were the traditional preserve of kings. There is little doubt that this woman wielded real power and possibly even acted as regent during the early years of her son's reign.[3]

> Boundary stone of Adad-nīrārī, king of Assyria, son of Šamšī-Adad, king of Assyria (and of) Sammu-ramāt, consort of Šamšī-Adad, king of Assyria, mother of Adad-nīrārī, mighty king, king of Assyria, daughter-in-law of Šalmanu-ašarēdu, king of the four quarters.
>
> When Ušpilulume, king of Kummuḫ, caused Adad-nīrārī, king of Assyria (and) Sammu-ramāt, consort, to cross the Euphrates River; I smashed Attar-šumkī, son of Abī-rāmi, of the city

Arpad, together with eight kings, who were with him at the city Paqarḫubunu, their boundary and land. I deprived them of their camp. In order to save their lives, they went up (the mountains).

In that year they put up this boundary stone between Ušpilulume, king of Kummuḫ and Qalparuda, son of Palalam, king of Gurgum.

Whoever takes it away from the possession of Uspilulume, his sons, his grandsons, may the gods Aššur, Marduk, Adad, Sin, (and) Šamaš not support his lawsuit. Prohibition of Aššur, my god, (and) Sin, who dwells in Harran.

The building inscription of Naqi'a/Zakūtu

Naqi'a (also known as Zakūtu)[4] enjoyed a long and illustrious life at the Assyrian court as a secondary wife (and perhaps eventually consort) of the king Sennacherib (704–681 BCE), the mother of King Esarhaddon (680–669 BCE) and the grandmother of King Ashurbanipal (668–627 BCE).[5] Her origins and early career are obscure, but she became prominent after Sennacherib unexpectedly chose Esarhaddon, his youngest son and his only son by Naqi'a, to be crown prince in about 683 BCE. There is no evidence to support the oft stated speculation that Naqi'a was responsible for Esarhaddon's promotion, although once her son was king, as queen mother Naqi'a became *ipso facto* the most important woman in the Assyrian Empire.

A variety of sources, almost all of them dating to Esarhaddon's reign, bear witness to Naqi'a's diverse activities, some of which are truly remarkable for a woman of the time. However powerful Naqi'a might appear in retrospect, it is important to remember that her social and political status derived from her relationship to a male king – be it husband, son, or grandson. This is not to deny that as the most prominent female of the realm she enjoyed a measure of personal authority and frequently acted autonomously. One of Naqi'a's more noteworthy accomplishments was the construction of a palace at Nineveh for Esarhaddon sometime between c. 677 and 673 BCE.[6]

In the ancient Near East monumental building projects were an important indicator of royal competence and the fiscal health of the state. One of the king's chief duties was to sponsor construction of palaces, temples, aqueducts, quays, and military installations as proof of his power and ability to provide for his people. Public works projects were implemented throughout the empire at sights chosen both for their propaganda value and in response to need.[7] For anyone other than the king – especially a woman – to build on the king's behalf was unprecedented in Assyria and might easily have been misconstrued as a sign of royal weakness. What kind of king would let his mother/a woman build a palace for him? Could he not build one for himself? However, the fact that Esarhaddon undertook numerous building projects at Nineveh, elsewhere in Assyria, and in other parts of the empire undoubtedly mitigated any negative impact his mother's project might have had. On the contrary, Esarhaddon most likely endorsed Naqi'a's involvement in a large scale building project in order to proclaim publically that she was an important figure at court.

Normally the Assyrians celebrated public building projects with com-memorative inscriptions, which could be buried in foundation deposits so that later kings (and the gods) would know who had undertaken construction, or displayed on walls, floors, or stelae in order to reach a wider audience.[8] Late Assyrian kings of the eighth and seventh centuries were especially attentive to this practice and many elaborate examples survive. Texts describing royal con-struction projects follow a fairly standard pattern: introductory passage including titles and genealogy; description of labor and materials; location of the building; furnishings; sacrifices made to the gods; celebratory banquet, and finally, a description of the building's lavish splendor and purpose. Naqi'a's building inscription follows this basic formula with modifications that reveal the scribe's careful attention to the protocols and etiquette of rank. That is, Naqi'a's inscription is intentionally shorter and more modest than the typical royal type; she does not overstep her position. For example, while a typical example of royal building inscription mentions inviting "all of the gods of Assyria" to the grand opening party,[9] Naqi'a limits her invitation to the gods of the city. Her inscrip-tion also explicitly states that Esarhaddon rather than Naqi'a supplied both the labor and the expensive wood for the palace doors. These refinements demonstrate a respect for convention and ideal mother-son regard, while they also reassure potential critics that the whole project was actually underwritten by the king himself.

Three fragmentary copies of the inscription survive and they are translated here in composite form including some restorations.[10] Unrestored breaks in the text are indicated by square brackets. Additional explanatory words appear in parenthesis.

Naqi'a/Zakûtu, consort of Sennacherib, king of the world, king of Assyria, daughter-in-law of Sargon, king of the world, king of Assyria, mother of Esarhaddon, king of the world, king of Assyria. (The gods) Aššur, Sin, Šamaš, Nabû, Marduk, Ištar of Nineveh, (and) Ištar of Arbela were pleased and they gladly put Esarhaddon, my offspring, on the throne of his father. From the top of the upper sea to the lower sea they constantly patrolled [. ...] no rival.

They destroyed his (Esarhaddon's) enemies and they put the nose rope on the kings of the four quarters. People of all the lands, enemy captives that were his part of the plunder, he gave as my lordly portion and I had them carry the hoe and the dirt basket and they made bricks. A piece of undeveloped land in the midst of Nineveh behind the Sin and Šamaš temple [...] for a royal residence of Esarhaddon, my beloved son [...]

[. ...] I stretched across it. Door leaves of cypress, a gift of my son, I hung side by side in its gates. That house I constructed, completed, and filled with splendor. Aššur, Ninurta, Sin, Šamaš,

Adad and Ištar, Nabû and Marduk, the gods who dwell in
Nineveh, I invited inside and I made before them pure, extravagant
offerings.

[. ...] the king [. ...] on [...] whatever [. ...] the one who
dwells [...] may (the protective deities) the Šedu and the
Lamassu [...] care for its interior and constantly keep watch.
I had set [. ...] Esarhaddon, king of Assyria, my beloved son,
I invited inside and held a banquet [...]

Everything valuable, furnishings of a palace, symbols of
kinship, for Esarhaddon, my beloved son [...]

The Zakûtu Treaty

Loyalty oaths were a common way for late Assyrian kings to bind their subjects to
them, attempt to forestall conspiracies, or secure the public's allegiance to a newly
designated crown prince.[11] The best known examples of this type of treaty
involve the Assyrian king Esarhaddon (680–669 BC) and his heirs. Just before
Esarhaddon ascended the Assyrian throne in the wake of his father's murder and
the ensuing rebellion, he had all of Assyria take an oath of allegiance.[12] In 672 BC,
perhaps motivated by failing health, Esarhaddon designated his heirs and required
the population to swear to uphold his choice.[13] Just two years later, after
Esarhaddon violently suppressed a coup attempt, he imposed yet another loyalty
oath.[14] Given the royal penchant for oath-taking, it should come as no surprise
that when Esarhaddon died en route to Egypt the Assyrians were made to swear
allegiance to their new king, Ashurbanipal. What is particularly remarkable about
the resulting *adê* agreement, known as the Zakûtu Treaty, is that Ashurbanipal's
grandmother, Naqi'a, implemented the new oath rather than Ashurbanipal himself.

The Zakûtu Treaty is unique; it is the only example of a loyalty pledge initiated by someone other than the Assyrian king, and it also marks the only time
(with the possible exception of Sammu-ramāt) that a woman had the political
clout to stand in for a king. Yet however eminent Naqi'a's status among the
Assyrian elite, there is no evidence that Ashurbanipal needed her help to take
the throne or that once he was on it, his grandmother ever acted publically
again. The treaty's brevity and omissions (e.g. leaving out Ashurbanipal's name
in the opening) indicate that it was implemented hastily and automatically when
news of Esarhaddon's death abroad arrived at court.[15] Ashurbanipal's assumption
of the throne proceeded afterwards without incident.

The nearly complete treaty is part of the British Museum's collection of
tablets from the royal archives at Nineveh. Unrestored breaks in the text are
indicated by square brackets. The translation given here includes some restorations.
Words in parenthesis do not appear in the text.

Treaty of Zakûtu, consort of Sennacherib, king of Assyria, mother
of Esarhaddon, king of Assyria, (grandmother of Ashurbanipal,

king of Assyria) with Šamaš-šum-ukīn, his equal brother, with Šamaš-mētu-uballiṭ and the rest of his brothers, with the king's relatives, with the officials and the governors, the bearded and the eunuchs, the courtiers, the exempted people, and everyone who enters the palace, with the people of Assyria, small and great:

Anyone who (concludes) this treaty which Zakûtu, the queen dowager, has imposed on all the people of Assyria on behalf of Ashurbanipal, her favorite grandson, anyone who should [...] lie and carry out a deceitful or evil plan or revolt against Ashurbanipal, king of Assyria, your lord; in your hearts plot evil intrigue (or) speak slander against Ashurbanipal, king of Assyria, your lord; in your hearts contrive (or) plan an evil mission (or) wicked proposal for rebellion (and) uprising against Ashurbanipal, king of Assyria, your lord; [...] or conspire with another for the murder of Ashurbanipal, king of Assyria, your lord:

May [...] Jupiter, Venus, Saturn, Mercury, [...]

(two lines missing)

(And if) from this day on you (hear) an evil (plan) of conspiracy (and) rebellion against Ashurbanipal, king of Assyria, your lord, you shall come and report to Zakûtu, his (grand)mother and Ashurbanipal, king of Assyria, your lord; and if you hear of a (plot) to kill or destroy Ashurbanipal, king of Assyria, your lord, you shall come and report to Zakûtu, his (grand)mother and Ashurbanipal, king of Assyria, your lord; and if you hear of evil intrigue being contrived against Ashurbanipal, king of Assyria, your lord, you shall speak (of it) in the presence of Zakûtu, his (grand) mother and Ashurbanipal, king of Assyria, your lord; and if you hear and know that there are men who agitate or conspire among you – whether bearded men or eunuchs, whether his brothers or royal relatives or your brothers or your friends or anyone in the whole country – should you hear or know, you shall seize and kill them and bring them to Zakûtu, his (grand) mother and Ashurbanipal, king of Assyria, your lord.

Neo-Assyrian dedicatory inscriptions

Public dedicatory monuments naming or depicting women are very rare and contain little information other than the woman's name and conjugal line, making it clear that her status largely depended on her patrilineage, husband, or son. In the privacy of the women's quarters of the palace, in the temple, or in the grave, we are afforded a glimpse into the more intimate lives of women, but even here, their relationships with men dominate. Even so, it would be wrong to view these women as passive or to assume that they did not actively participate in court life, sometimes in very important roles. The following are examples of the three types of text that could be dedicated by or to women: monumental inscriptions; temple dedications, and funerary texts.

Inscriptions on monuments

Stelae from Aššur

Three of the so-called *stelenreihen* of Aššur were dedicated to Neo-Assyrian consorts, although only two female names are still legible. The name on the third stele, which was dedicated to one of Sennacherib's wives, is broken. While the function of these stelae remains ambiguous, it is clear that only important men and exceptional women had the right to erect one.[16]

STELE OF SAMMU-RAMĀT[17]

> Stele of Sammu-ramāt, consort of Šamši-Adad, king of the world, king of Assyria, mother of Adad-nērāri, king of the world, king of Assyria, daughter-in-law of Šalmaneser, king of the four quarters.

STELE OF LIBBĀLI-ŠARRAT[18]

In addition to its identifying inscription, Libbāli-šarrat's stele boasts a portrait depicting the consort in formal pose, wearing the characteristic mural crown, and making a ritual gesture with an aromatic plant.[19]

> Image of Libbāli-šarrat, consort of Ashurbanipal, king of the world, king of Assyria.

STELE OF THE CONSORT OF SENNACHERIB[20]

This stele probably belonged to the mother of one of Sennacherib's older sons rather than to Naqi'a, the mother of Esarhaddon, although Dalley, having recently re-examined the stele, asserts that the broken name could be restored Zakûtu, the Akkadian version of Naqi'a.[21]

> Stele of [...], consort of Sennacherib, king of the world, king of Assyria

In praise of Tašmētum-šarrat[22]

This unique text, which was inscribed on a bull colossus guarding the doorway to the women's quarters of Sennacherib's palace at Nineveh, is remarkable for its personal and romantic nature. Unfortunately, since Tašmētum-šarrat is known otherwise only from labels on two vases found at Aššur, her exact status remains uncertain. It is likely that she was the mother of one or both of Sennacherib's elder sons, Aššur-nādin-šumi and Urdu-Mullissu.[23] Note that the text refers to two locations: the domestic wing of the palace where the inscription was set up and another domicile that Sennacherib had built elsewhere for Tašmētum-šarrat. In Assyria it was common for the king and other members of the royal family to own estates in various places, so mention of two palaces is not particularly unusual, though it certainly indicates Tašmētum-šarrat's high standing. The overtly affectionate language of the inscription is truly remarkable, however.

> And for Tašmētum-šarrat, the consort, my beloved wife, whose appearance the goddess Bēlet-ili has made perfect above all women, I had a palace of loveliness, celebration, and joy built and I set sphinxes of white limestone in its doorways. At the command of Aššur, father of the gods, of Ištar, the queen, may she be endowed with days of good health and a happy heart inside both these palaces, and may she have her fill of pleasure, and may the benevolent Alad and the benevolent Lamma deities[24] linger beside these palaces forever and never leave them.

Temple dedications

Along with the other members of the Assyrian ruling class, royal women regularly donated to temples and made lavish dedications to the gods in hopes of securing divine support.[25] While it now seems certain that by the reign of Sennacherib (704 – 681 BCE) the consort played an expanded role in state religious practice, the scope and requirements of that role remain elusive.[26]

Sammu-ramāt's dedication of an "eye-stone" to Ištar.[27]

> To Ištar, her lady, Sammu-ramāt, consort of Šamši-Adad, king of Assyria, dedicated (this) for her well-being.

Naqi'a's dedications noted on a cuneiform tablet[28]

> To the Queen Mullissu, who dwells in Ešarra, great queen, her lady, Zakûtu, consort of Sennacherib, king of the world, king of Assyria, daughter-in-law of Sargon, king of the world, king of Assyria, mother of Esarhaddon, king of Assyria dedicates a piece of gold jewelry, covered with obsidian, carnelian, and banded agate, weighing 7½ mana, 5 shekels, for the life of Esarhaddon and for herself, her own life, the length of her days, the stability of her dynasty (and) her well-being.
>
> To Ištar of Nineveh, who dwells in Emašmaš, great queen, her lady, Naqi'a, consort of Sennacherib, king of Assyria, daughter in law of Sargon, king of the world, king of Assyria, dedicates a pectoral of red gold set with precious stones weighing 3¾ mana

for the lives of Esarhaddon, her son and herself, for her life (and) the stability of her dynasty (and) her well-being.

Naqi'a's dedication of an agate bead[29]

To the deity [. ...] Zakûtu, consort of Sennacherib, king of Assyria, has donated (this agate) for the life of Esarhaddon, king of Assyria, her son, and for herself and her own life.

Dedication inscription of Libbāli-šarrat, consort of Ashurbanipal[30]

[For the goddess, DN g]eat [Lady], her Lady. [Libbāli-šarrat, Consort of Assurb]anipal, king of the world, king of Assyria, [she has made it ... of] red gold [for the life and health of] Assurbanipal, her beloved, (for) his length of days, the longevity of his throne and for herself, for her life, her length of days, and the well-being of her dynasty. May (the goddess) make her words pleasing to the king, her husband and may she (the goddess) make them grow old together. (Thus) she has made (it) stand and donated (it).

Funerary inscriptions

In 1989 a team of Iraqi archaeologists excavating Aššurnaṣirpal's palace at Nimrud discovered two tombs which contained the burial goods of four Neo-Assyrian royal women. Tomb II contained inscriptions of Yabâ, consort of Tiglath-pileser III (745–727), Bānītu, (dowager?) consort under Šalmaneser V (726–722), and Atalia, wife of Sargon II (721–705). Tomb III contained the sarcophagus and inscription of Mulissu-mukanniš at-Nīnua, consort of Aššurnasirpal II and (dowager?) consort under Šalmaneser III.[31] Among the extraordinarily rich finds were two funerary inscriptions, several objects with cuneiform labels, inscribed bricks, a couple of inscribed amulets, and a large quantity of very finely crafted gold jewelry and vessels.[32] The fact that both inscriptions attempt to prevent the theft of funerary goods or the later re-use of the tomb indicates that such disturbances were all too common, and indeed, both tombs were broken into a fairly short time after the original interment.

Funerary text of Yabâ[33]

Neo-Assyrian burial customs are not fully understood, but evidence indicates that the dead were often buried under the floors of houses and that after burial offerings of food and drink were poured into the tomb through a libation pipe embedded in the floor.[34] That Yabâ was buried under the floor of the palace is entirely in keeping with what we know of Assyrian funerary practice. In her inscription, Yabâ invokes the underworld deities to protect her last resting place from theft or the intrusion of additional burials. However, her curses did not frighten sufficiently, nor her wishes inspire compliance, for archaeologists found that a second skeleton, probably belonging to Atalia, had been interred with her at a later date.

> By the name of Šamaš, Ereškigal and the Annunaki, the great gods of the land, mortal destiny overwhelmed the life of Yabâ, the consort and she went on the path of her fathers. Whoever after – whether consort, who sits on the throne, or a concubine, who is the king's darling – removes me from my tomb or puts someone else in with me, or puts a hand on my jewelry with an evil heart, or breaks the seal of that tomb, above under the sun's rays, may his ghost wander outside in thirst, below in the underworld, when libations of water are poured, he must not receive beer, wine or flour as a funerary offering with the Annunaki. May Ningišzida and the great door-keeper, Bitû, (and) the great gods of the underworld impose restlessness on his corpse and ghost forever.

Sarcophagus inscription of Mullissu-mukannišat-Ninua[35]

Although it makes no reference to personal belongings, this inscription is similar to that of Yabâ in its attempt to prevent anyone from disturbing the sarcophagus by adding another body to it. What is unique about this text is that Mullissu-mukannišat-Nīnua names her father, who is a high official at court. Both father, who was the king's chief cupbearer, and daughter have good Assyrian names and most likely belonged to the old aristocracy. No other Assyrian consort, royal wife, or concubine has left an inscription that names a male other than a king (husband or father-in-law) or crown prince (son).

> Belonging to Mulissu-mukannišat-Nīnua, consort of Aššurna-ṣirpal, king of Assyria, of Šalmaneser, king of Assyria. Let no one after – whether servant or consort – put (another) inside, or remove this sarcophagus from its place. Whoever removes this sarcophagus from its place, his ghost will not receive funerary offerings with (other) ghosts: it is a prohibition of Šamaš and Ereškigal – daughter of Aššur-nīrka-da"inni, great cupbearer of Aššurnaṣirpal, king of Assyria.

Notes

1 For the most recent studies of Assyrian women, see Macgregor, 2012 and Svärd, 2012.
2 Grayson, 1996, 204–5. For further discussion, see Dalley, 2005; Asher-Greve, 2006, 324–29; and Siddall, 2011.
3 Sammu-ramāt's position continues to be debated. For different views, see Shramm, 1972; Dalley, 2005; Siddall, 2010, 159–73 and Svärd, 2012, 102–4.
4 Naqi'a is a West Semitic name meaning "pure". In some texts the name is paired with its Akkadian translation, Zakûtu.
5 For more information about Naqi'a, see Melville, 1999; Ornan, 2002, Streck, 2001 and Svärd, 2012.

6 Melville, 1999, 37–38.

7 See especially Porter, 1993 and 2003.

8 Few people were literate. See, Russell,1991, 223–40 and Porter,1993, 105–6 for a discussion of "audience."

9 See for example, Luckenbill, *ARAB II*, 47 (Sargon's palace) and 178 (Sennacherib's palace).

10 Borger,1956, 115–16 and 1988, 5–11.

11 For extant examples of Neo-Assyrian treaties and loyalty oaths, see Parpola, 1987, and Parpola and Watanabe, 1988. For discussion of loyalty oaths in the Near East, see Weinfeld, 1976; Tadmor, 1982; Brinkman, 1990; and Holloway, 2001.

12 Parpola and Watanabe, 1988, 22–23.

13 First published by Wiseman, 1958 and subsequently updated by Parpola and Watanabe, 1988, 28–58.

14 Parpola and Watanabe, 1988, 59.

15 For a full discussion, see Melville, 1999, 86–90 and Svärd, 2012, 74–75 and 113–14.

16 Miglus, 1984, 133–40 suggests that they were removed from a nearby temple when it got too crowded with dedicatory monuments.

17 Andrae, 1913, 5.

18 Andrae, 1913, 6–8.

19 For the mural crown, see Ornan, 2002, 473–74.

20 Andrae, 1913, 4.

21 Dalley, 2005, 17 n. 36. For a different view, see Frahm, 1997, 185.

22 Galter, Levine, and Reade, 1986, 32.

23 For further discussion of Tašmētum-šarrat's possible status, see Reade, 1986, 141.

24 These and the sphinxes mentioned earlier refer to the human headed winged bull and lion statues (Akkadian *šēdu, lamassu* and *apsasāti*), which guarded the entryways to Assyrian palaces.

25 For more on the temple contributions of royal women, see Melville, 2004. For temple contributions in general, see Menzel, 1981.

26 For more on the consort's religious role, see Menzel, 1981: T 66 and 68; Reade, 1986, 141–42; and Macgregor, 2012.

27 Seymour, 2008, 104. For queens and eyestones, see Clayden, 2009, 47.

28 *ARU* 14. See also Melville, 1999, 43.

29 Van De Mieroop, 1993, 259–61.

30 ADD 644. Deller, 1983, 22–24.

31 It is possible that Yabâ and Bānītu were the same person, since the latter could be an Akkadian translation of the former which is West Semitic. For the tombs and inscriptions, see Fadhil, 1990a, 1990b; Damerji, 1998 and Al-Rawi, 2008. For different views on the status of these women, see Melville, 2004, 44–47, Dalley, 2008, and Svärd, 2012, 91–92. For a discussion of the origins of some of these women, see Dalley, 1998 and Younger, 2002.

32 For all the inscribed objects from the tombs, see Al-Rawi, 2008; for the jewelry and other objects, see Collon, ed. 2008, 105–18.

33 Fadhil, 1990b; Kamil,1998, and Al-Rawi, 2008, 119–20.

34 Postgate, 2008, 180.

35 Fadhil, 1990a and Al-Rawi, 2008, 124–25.

Bibliography

Al-Rawi, F., 2008. "Inscriptions from the Tombs of the Queens of Assyria," in *New Light on Nimrud: Proceedings of the Nimrud Conference 11–13th March 2002*. J.E. Curtis, H. McCall et al., eds. London: the British Museum, 119–38.

Andrae, W., 1913. *Die Stelenreihen in Assur*. Leipzig: J.C. Hinrichs.

Asher-Greve, J. M., (2006). "From 'Semiramis of Babylon' to 'Semiramis of Hammersmith'", in, *Orientalism, Assyriology and the Bible* (Hebrew Bible Monographs 10), edited by S.W. Holloway. Sheffield: Sheffield Phoenix Press, 322–73.

Borger, R., 1956. *Die Inschriften Asarhaddon König von Assyrien*. Graz: E. Weidner.

———, 1988. "König Sanheribs Eheglück", *Annual Review of the Royal Inscriptions of Mesopotamia Project* 6, 5–11.

Brinkman, J.A., 1990. "Political Covenants, Treaties, and Loyalty Oaths in Babylonia and Between Assyria and Babylonia," in *I trattati nel mondo antico. Forma, ideologia, funzione*. L. Canfora, M. Liverani and C. Zaccagnini, eds. Rome: "L'Erma" di Bretschneider, 81–111.

Clayden, T., 2009. "Eye-Stones." *Zeitschrift für Orient-Archäologie*, 2: 36–86.

Collon, D. (ed.), 2008. "Nimrud Treasures: Panel Discussion," in *New Light on Nimrud: proceedings of the Nimrud Conference 11–13th March 2002*. J.E. Curtis, H. McCall et al., eds. London: the British Museum, 105–18.

Dalley, S., 1998. "Yaba, Atalya, and the Foreign Policy of Late Assyrian Kings." *SAAB* 12: 83–98.

———, 2005. "Semiramis in History and Legend," in *Cultural Borrowings and Ethnic Appropriations in Antiquity*. Erich S. Gruen, ed. Stuttgart: Franz Steiner Verlag, 11–22.

———, 2008. "The Identity of the Princesses in Tomb II and A New Analysis of Events of 701 BC," in *New Light on Nimrud: Proceedings of the Nimrud Conference 11–13th March 2002*. J. Curtis, H. McCall et al. eds. London: the British Museum, 171–75.

Damerji, M. S. B., 1998. "Gräber Assyrischer Königinnen aus Nimrud," *Jahrbuch des Römisch-Germanischen Zentralmuseums Mainz*, 45: 1–83.

Deller, K., 1983. "Zum ana balāṭ-Formular einiger assyrischer Votivinschriften," *Oriens Antiquus* 22: 13–24.

Fadhil, A., 1990a., "Die Grabinschrift der Mullissu-mukanniša̮t-Ninua aus Nimrud/Kalhu und andere in ihrem Grab gefundene Schrifttrager," *Baghdader Mitteilungen* 21, 472–82.

———, 1990b. "Die in Nimrud/Kalhu aufgefundene Grabinschrift der Jaba," *Baghdader Mitteilungen* 21, 461–70.

Frahm, E. 1997. *Einleitung in die Sanherib-Inschriften*. Archiv für Orientforschung Beiheft 26. Vienna: Institut für Orientalistik.

Galter, H., Levine, L. and J. Reade, 1986. "The Colossi of Sennacherib's Palace and their Inscriptions," *Annual Review of the Royal Inscriptions of Mesopotamia Project* 4, 27–32.

Grayson, A. K., 1996. *Assyrian Rulers of the Early First Millennium BC, II (858–745 BC). Royal Inscriptions of Mesopotamia, Assyrian Periods 3*. Toronto: University of Toronto Press.

Holloway, S., 2001. "The GISkakki Aššur and Neo-Assyrian Loyalty Oaths," in *Historiography in the Cuneiform World, Part 1: Proceedings of the XLVe Rencontre Assyriologique Internationale*. P. Steinkeller, P. Machinist, J. Huehnergard, P.-A Beaulieu, I. T. Abusch and C. Noyes, eds. Bethesda: CDL Press, 239–65.

Kamil, A., 1998. "Inscriptions on Objects from Yaba's Tomb in Nimrud," *Jahrbuch des Römisch-Germanischen Zentralmuseums Mainz* 45, 13–18.

Kohler, J. and A. Ungnad, 1913. *Assyrische Rechturkunden*. Leipzig: Eduard Pfeiffer.

Luckenbill, D.D., 1927. *Ancient Records of Assyria and Babylonia Volume II: Historical Record of Assyria from Sargon to the End*. Chicago: The University of Chicago Press.

Macgregor, S. L., 2012. *Beyond Hearth and Home: Women in the Public Sphere in Neo-Assyrian Society*. SAAS 21. Helsinki: The Neo-Assyrian Text Corpus Project.

Melville, S., 1999. *The Role of Naqia/Zakutu in Sargonid Politics*. SAAS 9. Helsinki: Helsinki University Press.

———, 2004. "Neo-Assyrian Royal Women and Male Identity: Status as a Social Tool," *Journal of the American Oriental Society* 124, 37–57.

Menzel, B., 1981. *Assyrische Tempel*. Rome: Biblical Institute Press.

Miglus, P., 1984. "Another Look at the 'Stelenreihen' in Assur," *Zeitschrift für Assyriologie* 74, 133–40.

Ornan, T., 2002. "The Queen in Public: Royal Women in Neo-Assyrian Art," in *Sex and Gender in the Ancient Near East: Proceedings of the 47th Rencontre Assyriologique Internationale, Helsinki, July 2–6, 2001*. S. Parpola and R.M. Whiting, eds. Helsinki: The Neo-Assyrian Text Corpus Project, 474–77.

Parpola, S., 1987. "Neo-Assyrian Treaties from the Royal Archives of Nineveh," *Journal of Cuneiform Studies* 39, 161–89.

Parpola, S. and K. Watanabe., 1988. *Neo-Assyrian Treaties and Loyalty Oaths*. Helsinki: Helsinki University Press.

Porter, B.N., 1993. *Images, Power and Politics: Figurative Aspects of Esarhaddon's Babylonian Policy*. Philadelphia: American Philosophical Society.

———, 2003. *Trees, Kings, and Politics: Studies in Assyrian Iconography*. Fribourg: Academic Press, and Göttingen: Vandenhoeck and Ruprecht.

Postgate, N.J., 2008. "The Tombs in the Light of Mesopotamian Funeral Traditions," in *New Light on Nimrud: Proceedings of the Nimrud Conference, 11th–13th March 2002*. J.E. Curtis et al., eds. London: BISI and the British Museum, 177–80.

Reade, J.E., 1986. "Was Sennacherib a Feminist?" *Comptes rendus des séances de l'Académie des Inscriptions et Belles-Lettres* 33, 139–45.

Russell, J.M., 1991. *Sennacherib's Palace without Rival at Nineveh*. Chicago: University of Chicago Press.

Schramm, W., 1972. "War Semiramis eine assyrische Regentin?" *Historia* 21: 513–521.

Seymour, M., 2008. "Babylon's Wonders of the World: Classical Accounts," in *Babylon: Myth and Reality*. I. Finkel and M. Seymour (eds.). London, The British Museum Press: 104–109.

Siddall, Luis R., 2011. *A Historical and Ideological Analysis of the Reign of Adad-nīrārī III, King of Assyria*. Unpublished Ph.D. dissertation. School of Oriental and African Studies, University of London.

Streck, M., 2001. "Naqi'a," in *The Prosopography of the Neo-Assyrian Empire, volume 2 part II: L-N*. Heather D. Baker, ed. Helsinki: The Neo-Assyrian Text Corpus Project, 929–30.

Svärd, S., 2012. "Power and Women in the Neo-Assyrian Palaces." Ph.D. Dissertation, University of Helsinki.

Tadmor, H., 1982. "Treaty and Oath in the Ancient Near East: a Historians Approach," in *Humanizing America's Iconic Book: Society of Biblical Literature Centennial Addresses*, G.M. Tucher and D.A. Knight, eds. Chico: Scholars Press, 127–52.

Van De Mieroop, M., 1993. "An Inscribed Bead of Queen Zakutu," in *The Tablet and the Scroll: Near Eastern Studies in Honor of William W. Hallo*. M. Cohen, D.C. Snell and D.B. Weisberg, eds. Bethesda: CDL Press, 259–61.

Weifenld, M., 1976. "The Loyalty Oath in the Ancient Near East," *Ugarit Forschungen* 8, 379–414.

Wiseman, D.J., 1958. "The Vassal Treaties of Esarhaddon," *Iraq* 20, 1–100.

Younger, Jr., K.L., 2002. "Yawheh at Ashkelon and Calah? Yahwistic Names in Neo-Assyrian." *VT* 52: 207–18.

10b

WOMEN IN NEO-ASSYRIAN INSCRIPTIONS

Neo-Assyrian oracles

Karen Nemet-Nejat

Introduction

Oracles refer to a message from a god channeled through a human intermediary, who was either a male, a female or gender-neutral prophet.[1] Most of the extant prophecies focused on the king and guaranteed his success over his enemies and legitimate succession.[2]

The oracles may have been spoken as the phrase "from the mouth of" suggests. Then the message was probably disposed soon afterward, as only twenty-nine individual oracles are extant, of which seven are found on their original tablets.[3] These twenty-nine oracles deal with prophecies of only two Neo-Assyrian kings, Esarhaddon and Ashurbanipal.[4] The individual oracles have no formal structure.

Neo-Assyrian prophetic oracles are of two main types: (1) records of one oracle on one tablet and (2) collections of oracles on larger tablets, which list oracles, letters, treaties, and other documents, which were placed in archives. In addition, there are diverse tablets, which refer to prophets, their activities, and their actual prophecies.[5] There is no single word in Akkadian, Egyptian, Hebrew, and other West Semitic languages that are used to mean prophet.[6]

Though kings were usually the recipients of prophecies,[7] Both Esarhaddon (681–669 BC) and Ashurbanipal (668–627 BC) received oracles when they were crown princes. Also, in a few oracles the god spoke to Naqi'a, the (a) wife of Sennacherib, the mother of Esarhaddon, and the grandmother of Ashurbanipal. Naqi'a's name is West Semitic and means "purity"; however, she adopted the name Zakutu, which is an Akkadian translation of "purity."[8]

The king and the royal family were especially interested in prophets and the worship of their patron goddess, Ishtar of Arbela,[9] who was called "the lady of Arbela" or the "lady who resides in Arbela."[10] Ishtar protected the king and fought for him. The temple of Arbela was one of the major temples in Assyria.

The oracles discussed here are all messages spoken by female prophets. Numbers 68, 74, 75, and probably 90 refer to Esarhaddon's war against his brothers and his rise to power as King of Assyria in 681 BC. Most of the prophecies can easily be dated to historical events.[11] Prophecies were of particular importance in acceptance by the people when endorsed by the gods.[12]

Oracle spoken to Esarhaddon

Nissinen #68 = Parpola, SAA 9 1.1 (lines 4'–29') Ishtar-la-tashiyat, meaning "Do not neglect Ishtar,"[13] spoke to Esarhaddon and promised to destroy his enemies.

> "Esarhaddon, king of all the lands, do not be afraid.! What wind[14] has risen against you whose wings I have not broken?[15] Like ripe apples,[16] your enemies will continually roll at your feet."
>
> "I am the Great Lady, I am Ishtar of Arbela' who throws your enemies at your feet. Which of my words that I have spoken to you (that) you could not rely?"
>
> "I am Ishtar of Arbela. I will flay your enemies. I will deliver them. I am Ishtar of Arbela. I will go before you and behind you."[17]
>
> "Do not be afraid. You are paralyzed, but, during (your) suffering, I will rise up and sit down."[18]
>
> (From the mouth of Ishtar-la-tashiyat, a woman from Arbela.)[19]

Oracle to Naqi'a, the Queen Mother (part of tablet lost)

Nissinen #74 = Parpola, SAA 9 1.7 (column v lines 1–11).

Ishtar-beli-da'in, meaning "Ishtar, strengthen my lord," spoke to Naqi'a, the Queen Mother[20] stating that Esarhaddon's enemies at home would be conquered because Esarhaddon was the legitimate king.

The beginning of the text is lost.

> "[...] He decided. He will not receive [...] colluding weasels,[21] and polecats.[22] I will dismember them at his feet. You are who you are (i.e. you know who you are). The king is my king."
>
> (From the mouth of Ishtar-beli-da'in, a votaress)

Oracle to Naqi'a, the Queen Mother

Nissinen #75 = Parpola, SAA 9 1.8 (column v lines 12–20).[23]

Ahat-abisha "Sister of her father" spoke to Naqi'a, the Queen Mother, reassuring her that, although Esarhaddon was sent away because he faced more and more opposition, Sennacherib would not change the order of succession despite the growing popularity of Esarhaddon's brothers.

> I am the Lady of Arbela (Ishtar).
> To the king's mother:[24]
> Since you implored me, saying, "The one (is) on the right[25] and the other on the left you have placed in your lap. My own son you have driven out to roam the steppe?"[26]
> "Now, king, do not be afraid! Kingship is yours. Power is also yours."[27]

Oracle to Naqi'a, the Queen Mother

Nissinen #90 = SAA 9 5 (pp. 34–35).

Word of Ishtar of Arbela to the Queen Mother by an unknown female prophet indicated that the succession of Esarhaddon had divine approval. Ishtar of Arbela was waiting in a chapel in anticipation of the king's return for the New Year's festival, a festival that required his presence.

> Word of Ishtar of Arbela [to the king's mother]:[28]
> "My knees are bent for Esarhaddon, my king. Mulissu[29] has heard the cry [of her calf]. Get ready![30] [...] As to Esarhaddon, the king of Assyria, Ninurta[31] goes at the right and left of my king. He [tramples the enemies beneath his feet.]"
> I will go to the Palace of the Steppe[32] [...] I will protect[33] Esarhaddon, king of Assyria. His enemies in [...] The enemy of [...] The enemy of [...] we will cast at his feet.[34] We will go [...] Praise Mullissu! [...] of Shamash, they are until my father.

Abbreviations

CAD	Chicago Assyrian Dictionary
JSOTSup	Journal of Old Testament Studies.
OIS	Oriental Institute Seminars.
RAI	Rencontre assyriologique internationale.
SAA	State Archives of Assyria.
SAAS	State Archives of Assyria Studies.
SBLSym	Sym Society of Biblical Literature Symposium.

Notes

1 M. Nissinen, 2003, 98; and 2010, 344.
2 Nissinen, 2003, 100–101.
3 Ibid., 2003, 97–98.

4 Bonnet and Merlo, 2002, 81–82.
5 Huffmon, 2000, 57–59. Nissinen, pp. 97, 133.
6 Huffmon, 2000, 57–59; Nissinen, 2003, 98; 2010, 341–42.
7 Nissinen, 2003, 99.
8 Melville, 1999, 13–16.
9 Nissinen, 2003, 99–100; 2010, 344.
10 Nissinen, 2001, 176–80.
11 Jean, 2010, 270–71.
12 Jean, 2010, 270–71; Nissinen, 2010, 343–46; See F.M. Fales and G.B. LaFranchi, 1997, 104–5, for equivalent phrases which mark divine speech.
13 Nissinen, 2003, 100, noted that the names of the prophets were significant, and that Arbela was an important base, where the Temple of Ishtar was located.
14 Parpola, 1997, 4 note i: 6 that "wind" referred to the enemy.
15 Parpola, 1997, lxvii.
16 Simānu refers to the time when apples are ripe; see Parpola, 1997, 4–5, 1. n. I 9.
17 See M. Streck, 1916, 48, ll. 100–101, "I (Ishtar of Arbela) will go before Ashurbanipal, the king whom my hands created."
18 Nissinen, 2003, 103 n. c, suggested the "getting up" and "sitting down" probably referred to Ishtar's rescuing and fighting for the king and finally returning to her place.
19 Nissinen, 2010, 346, pointed out that the phrase "from the mouth of" indicates the oral nature of the prophecy. Nissinen, 2003 103 n. f, noted that the sign in text actually indicated a male before the prophet's name. However, the scribe erased this symbol and replaced it with the female notation.
20 Melville, 1999, 24–29.
21 *Kakkišu* and *pušhu* are names or rodents, mustelids and insectivores; here these names refer to Esarhaddon's domestic enemies. For translation, see Parpola, 2007, 9, n. 3ff.
22 Parpola, 1993, No. 352, ll. 22–25, r. 1–6.
23 This oracle refers to the Esarhaddon's two older brothers, who were in a position of power, see Nissinen, 1998, 23; Parpola, 1997, n. 9 15f; Parpola, 2007, vol. 2, part 11, 22; Parpola, 1980, 175, 180–81.
24 Parpola, 1997, n. v 15f; 2007, vol. 2, part 11, p .22; 1980, 175, 180–1; 1997, 9 v 15.
25 Esarhaddon, the favorite son of Sennacherib, outsmarted his brothers ("the one on the right and the one on the left"). With the help of his mother Naqi'a, Esarhaddon became the crown prince, referred to as "as the one in your lap." See Parpola, 1993, nos. 185 ll. 5–12, but, in this text, the same wording of the oracle refers to Ashurbanipal.
26 Sennacherib sent Esarhaddon away to the capital of the western provinces as Esarhaddon faced more and more opposition. Sennacherib did not change the order of succession despite the growing popularity of Esarhaddon's brothers, see A. Kuhrt, 1995, 521, discussed that Arad-Mullissu killed his father in order to gain kingship; Parpola, 1980, 171–82.
27 Nissinen, 1998, 22 indicated that the prophetess was referring to Esarhaddon, stating that the succession arranged by Sennacherib and Naqi'a had divine approval.
28 Nissinen, 1998, 23 discussed how this prophecy referred to the battle and indicated the acute situation for which Naqi'a implored Ishtar on her son's behalf as he was now at war; Parpola, 1997, lxv explained the phrase "word of Ishtar"; it occurred mostly at the beginning of the oracle in combination with the person addressed, similar to royal letters, i.e., "The word of the king to So-and-so." This phrase is identical to דברה׳ "the word of God."
29 Parpola, 2000, 194–95, discussed the role of Mullissu as the divine mother of the king and an element of Ishtar, the goddess of love. In Assyria Ishtar was the queen of heaven and consort of the god Ashur. She was described as the "wild cow" and

through her horns with the moon, a heavenly aspect of Ishtar, the "Daughter of the Moon." Green and Black, 1992, 53.

30 CAD, R, 97b.

31 Assyrian kings worshipped Ninurta as a warlike god who would aid them in fighting their enemy, see Black and Green, 1992, 142–43.

32 The Palace of the Steppe is a shrine of Ishtar in Milqi, which is near Arbela. Ishtar resided there during the king's absence while waiting for him to return from victory; see Nissinen, 2001, 183–86.

33 The concept of "safety" refers both to physical safety and reconciliation with the gods, see Nissinen, 2001, 181.

34 We refers to Esarhaddon and Naqi'a, Parpola, 1997, 34, "5 n. R 5.

Bibliography

Bonnet, C., and Merlo, P. 2002. "Royal Prophecy in the Old Testament and in the Ancient Near East: Methodological Problems and Examples," *Publicaciones del Instituto de. Epigrafici Studi sul Vicino Oriente e linguistici Antico*, 19 77–86.

Fales, F.M. and Lanfranchi, G.B., 1997. 'The Impact of Oracular Material on the Political Utterances and Political Action in the Royal Inscriptions of the Sargonid Dynasty', in Heinz, J-G., ed., *Oracles et prophéties dans l'antiquité, Actes du Colloques de Strasbourg 15–17 Juin 1995*, Université des Sciences Humaines de Strasbourg, Travaux du Center de recherche sur le Proche-Orient et la Grèce antiques 15, Paris: de Boccard, 99–114.

Green, A. and Black, J., 1992. *Gods, Demons and Symbols of Ancient Mesopotamia: An Illustrated Dictionary* (illustrations by Tessa Richards), Austin: University of Texas Press.

Huffmon, H., 2000. "A Company of Prophets: Mari, Assyria, Israel," in Nissinen, M., ed., *Prophecy in Its Ancient Near Eastern Context: Mesopotamian, Biblical, and Arabian Perspectives*, SBLSym 13. Atlanta: Society of Biblical Literature, 47–70.

Jean, C., 2010. "Divination and Oracles at the Neo-Assyrian Oracles: The Importance of Signs of Royal Ideology," in Annus, A. ed., *Divination and Interpretation of Signs in the Ancient World*, Oriental Institute Seminars 6, Chicago: Oriental Institute, 267–76.

Kuhrt, A., 1995. *The Ancient Near East c. 3000–330 BC*, vol. 2, London: Routledge.

Melville, S., 1999. *The Role of Naqia/Zakutu in Sargonid Politics*, State Archives of Assyria Studies vol. 9, The Neo-Assyrian Text Corpus Project, Helsinki: University of Helsinki.

Nissinen, M., 1998. *References to Prophecy in Neo-Assyrian Sources*, State Archives of Assyria, vol. 7, Helsinki: Neo-Assyrian Corpus Text Project, Helsinki: University of Helsinki.

——, 2001. "City as Lofty as Heaven: Arbela and Other Cities in Neo-Assyrian Prophecy," in *Every City Shall be Forsaken: Urbanism and Prophecy in Ancient Israel and the Ancient Near East*, Haak, R.D. and Grabbe L.L., eds., Journal for the Study of the Old Testament Supplement Series 330, Sheffield: Sheffield Academic Press, 172–209.

——, 2003. *Prophets and Prophecy in the Ancient Near East*, Society of Biblical Literature Symposium 12, Atlanta: Society of Biblical Literature.

——, 2010 "Prophecy and Omen Divination: Two Sides of the Same Coin, in Divination and Oracles at the Neo-Assyrian Oracles: The Importance of Signs of Royal Ideology," in Annus, A., ed., *Divination and Interpretation of Signs in the Ancient World*, Oriental Institute Seminars 6, Chicago: Oriental Institute Seminars, 341–46.

Parpola, S., 1980. "The Murderer of Sennacherib," in Alster, B., ed., *Death in Mesopotamia: 26th Rencontre assyriologique internationale*," Mesopotamia 8, Copenhagen: Akademisk Vorlag, 171–82.

———, 1993. *Letters from Assyrian and Babylonian Scholars*, State Archives of Assyria, vol.10, The Neo-Assyrian Text Corpus Project, Helsinki: University of Helsinki.

———, 1997. *Assyrian Prophecies*, State Archives of Assyria, vol. 9, The Neo-Assyrian Text Corpus Project, Helsinki: University of Helsinki.

———, 2000. "Monotheism in Ancient Assyria," in *One God or Many: Concepts of Divinity in the Ancient World*, Porter, B.N., ed., Transaction of the Casco Bay Assyriological Institute 1, Chebeague Island: Casco Bay Assyriological Institute, 165–209.

Parpola, S., ed., 2001. *The Prosopography of the Neo-Assyrian Empire*, vol. 2, part 11, The Neo-Assyrian Text Corpus Project, Helsinki: University of Helsinki.

———, 2007. *Assyrian English-Assyrian Dictionary*, The Neo-Assyrian Text Corpus Project, Helsinki: University of Helsinki.

Streck, M., 1916. *Ashurbanipal und die Lutzen assyrischen Könige bis zum Untergange Niniveh's*, vol. 2, Leipzig: J.C. Hinrichs.

Villard, P., 2001. "Les Prophètes á l'époque néo-assyrien," in Lemaire, A., ed., *Prophètes et rois et Proche-Orient*, Paris: Cerf, 55–84.

11

WOMEN IN HITTITE RITUAL

Billie Jean Collins

The limitations of the written evidence have left us woefully ignorant of the standing and role of women in Hittite society. From priestesses of high status to singers and musicians, they took part in festival activities.[1] In the area of domestic religion we are fortunate to have relatively rich documentation, nevertheless, no systematic study has yet been done on gender and Hittite ritual. Clearly certain clusters of rituals, birth rituals, for example, were customized for female clients (see Bachvarova, this volume). But women take part in rituals in multiple capacities. They could commission rituals, serve as ritual "objects" key to the rite's implementation and success, or construct and conduct the rituals. Women might also be the source of the misfortune the ritual is meant to address.

The women who were primarily (though not exclusively[2]) responsible for overseeing ritual performance fell into a category of professionals who bore the label (written with Sumerian logograms) ᴹᵁᴺᵁˢŠU.GI, which is commonly translated "Old Woman" (in German "Alte"). In fact we know very little about the demographic to which such practitioners belonged, and the label "Old Woman" evokes infelicitous images of the witches of modern folklore. German *Beschwörerin* "conjurer" is less problematic, though it also carries negative connotations that simply do not apply in a Hittite context. The Hittite reading for the Sumerian term is *hasauwa-*, which originally meant "(she) of birth," indicating her connection with rituals of childbirth (Beckman 1993: 37; but cf. Puhvel, *HED* 3, 229 who questions the etymological connection to *has(s)-* "give birth"). The term evolved to encompass any woman with special knowledge of the rites that could aid with a broad spectrum of problems. Thus, here I use the translation Wise Woman, which better reflects the respect with which such women were evidently regarded in Hittite society. Numerous examples of Wise Women operating in concert with male practitioners (e.g., no. 1), such as augurs, physicians, and diviners, indicate that they operated as part of mainstream belief and practice. Beckman notes (1993: 37 n. 73) that thirty-six of the rituals listed in the CTH include the title ŠU.GI, and (p. 36) that thirty-eight of the seventy-one individuals attested by name as authors of rituals in the CTH are women.[3] In at least some cases they were slaves. Some were attached to the royal household and were well rewarded for their service. We know nothing about how such women learned their craft; we may speculate that their skills were passed between family members, though not necessarily from mother to daughter. The Wise Woman Anniwiyani, for example, is identified as the mother of Armati the Augur, servant of Hurlu.[4]

In the texts translated here, we encounter these ritual specialists alongside women with a special religious status, including a seeress, an AMA.DINGIR ("mother of the deity") priestess, a hierodule (MUNUS-ŠUHUR.LAL), and a consecrated girl, as well as women of no special status, including a "young girl" and a woman who was perhaps a deportee.

Tunnawiya's *Ritual of Impurity* or *Ritual of the River* (CTH 409)[5]

The Wise Woman responsible for this ritual must have been a practitioner of some renown given that no fewer than five rituals were attributed to her. Originally from Tunna, a town in the easternmost part of what would later be Tarhuntassa (the Ereğli Valley; see Miller 2004: 453), she was a resident of Hattusa. The rituals belong to the beginning of the Empire period (fifteenth century BC). In one of the rituals attributed to her she bears the title midwife, suggesting the close connection between the two mentioned above (Beckman 1993). That the ritual treated here was not performed exclusively by Tunnawiya is indicated by the statement that it was also known by another name (see §2). Whether Tunnawiya was indeed the source for the rituals attributed to her has been called into question (see Miller 2004: 519–22), and indeed we may well question whether she was a true historical personage at all.

This ritual targets a range of maladies relating in particular to reproduction, both male and female (§§1–2). The instructions differ depending on whether the client is male or female; for example, matching the items of clothing and the gender of the animal to the gender of the client (§§3–4).[6] The Wise Woman begins by enlisting the aid of the mother goddess Hannahanna of the Riverbank. Following the list of ritual ingredients in §§3–5, Tunnawiya heads to the riverbank "to instruct" the goddess. There, the night before the ritual begins, she gathers clay from the riverbed amidst offerings meant to ensure the goddess's blessings on the proceedings (§§6–8). Most of the ritual takes place in an uncultivated place where a hut has been set up (§§9–32). The purification is accomplished primarily through lifting a series of objects over the client (§§11–15), a ritual cleansing of the client, which involves scraping and combing the impurity from the body of the client onto a clay figurine (§§23–26), and passing through gates (§§28–32). At the conclusion of the purificatory rites, the Wise Woman returns to the riverbank to make more offerings to the goddess, attributing her with the purification. Offerings are then made to the Sun God, both at the riverbank and near a fruit tree. Tunnawiya appeals to him for blessings on behalf of the client (§§33–36). A final offering is made to Hannahanna back at the hut, concluding the ritual (§§37–38).

I have used the feminine pronoun in the translation when referring to the ritual patron. Note that Tunnawiya is assisted by a MUNUS-ŠUHUR.LAL, a kind of priestess, usually translated "hierodule." Pikku, the scribe responsible for this copy, was active in the reigns of Hattusili III and Tudhaliya IV, providing a date for the copy in the latter part of the thirteenth century.[7]

§1 According to Tunnawi, the Wise Woman, if a person, either a man or a woman, is placed in any impurity; or anyone else has named him/her for impurity; or a woman's children keep dying or her fetuses keep miscarrying; or if a man's or woman's body parts are disabled[8] by words of impurity,

§2 and that person is faced with[9] the impurity, then that person, whether man or woman, performs the Ritual of Impurity in the following way. Some call it the Ritual of the River. This ritual is one and the same.[10]

§3 If (the ritual patron is) a man they take a black ram,[11] if (it is) a woman they take a black ewe; one black piglet, one black puppy—a male piglet if a man, (a female) if a woman. For a woman: one pair of black shirts; one black belt; one black hood; one pair (of) black leggings, unadorned; one pair of black shoes; one tunic; one black felt tunic; and the woman plugs her ears with black wool.

§4 But if (it is) a man, one pair of black shirts; one pair of black leggings; and he plugs his ears with black wool. Nine small combs of boxwood; one small *sarra* of boxwood; two black *TIYADU*s; nine soldier breads; [...]; six small black asphalt utensils; two black *pahhunali*-containers; four small black pots; [four] large black [pots]; eight black lids; three black pitchers; two black pitchers; two black water jugs.

§5 One sheep, one lamb, three hot breads of a double handful; one cheese; one curd; one *huppar* of beer; oil cake; meal; one *hanissa*-container of wine for libations. As soon as she arranges all this, at nightfall the Wise Woman takes [two] flat breads, one pitcher of wine, one oil bread, (and) meal, and goes to the riverbank to instruct the Mother Goddess of the Riverbank.

§6 As soon as she arrives at the riverbank, she breaks one flat bread for the Mother Goddess of the Riverbank and places it on the riverbank. She scatters the oil cake and meal over. She pours a libation of wine and says:

§7 "Mother Goddess of the Riverbank, I have now returned to you. From whichever riverbank this clay was taken, may you, O Mother Goddess of the Riverbank take it in your hand and rub this ritual patron with it and cleanse the twelve parts of his body." Thereupon she takes the clay of the riverbank and then goes to the spring. She breaks one flat bread. She takes it, namely, the mud of the spring. She scatters the oil bread and meal, libates the wine, and says:

§8 "Just as you, O spring, keep welling up mud back up from the dark earth, in the same way remove evil uncleanness from the body parts (of) this person, the ritual patron." Thereupon she takes clay of the spring. But while the Wise Woman collects these things, before the river reed huts have already been set up. Where they set (it) up—where(ever) no cultivation is near and the plough has not come, there the hut is set up.[12]

§9 The Wise Woman carries the clay of the riverbank and the clay of the spring there. [Two cl]ay [figurines]; twelve clay tongues *halupant*-back; two clay cows; two clay *wawarkima*;[13] a little [blue wool]; a little red wool; rushes and red wool are braided together;[14] an eagle's wing; a little bone; a little allin; seed of [.]. ... ; a little bit of fig; [a little] *zinakki*; a little [heart]; a little liver; a piglet of dough; a morsel of *wagessar* bread; a morsel [of] *harnanda*-[bread]; a morsel of cucumber bread; one figure of wax; one figure of sheep fat, and they are wrapped in fat. All this she arranges on a reed tray.

§10 One *usantari*-cow[15]—but if a man then she provides a bull. When morning arrives the ritual patron comes to the hut. When she arrives she dresses in black. Then the Wi[se] Woman takes [blue wool] and red wool and unravels it.

§11 She throws it over the body (of the ritual patron). Then she takes one black sheep and lifts it over her and the Wise Woman recites the incantation of lifting over: "Storm God of the mountains, run above heaven; heaven, run above earth."[16]

§12 Afterward she lifts the piglet over her and recites the incantation of the piglet. Then she lifts the puppy over her and recites the incantation of the puppy.

§13 Afterward she lifts the clay tongue over her and recites the incantation of the tongue. Next she lifts the two (clay) figurines over her. Next she lifts the *wawarkima*[17] over her. Next she lifts the clay oxen over her; next the dough; next the string. Next she takes the feather and waves it over and away from[18] (her), and she continues to recite the (appropriate) incantations. They have already been treated on a tablet.[19]

§14 Next she lifts the two *TIYADU* over her and says as follows: "Whatever persons were *t*.-ing and *e*.-ing her form, bones, and flesh with this impurity, now I am *t*.-ing and *e*.-ing in return the form, bones, and flesh of the sorcerer of the impurity." She puts the *TIYADU* on the tray.

§15 Next she lifts the figurines of wax and sheep fat over her and says: "Who were making this person impure, I am now holding these two magical[20] figurines and I am now *t.*-ing and *e.*-ing this." Then she melts them down and says: "Let the evil persons who were making her impure likewise be melted down."

§16 When she is finished she stands up and washes her hands with wine. They hold heated pebbles from the *pahhunali*-vessel next to her and she incants—they (the incantations) have been recorded already.

§17 Thereupon she washes with water. They hold pine cones from the *pahhunali*-vessel next to her and she recites—they (the incantations) have been recorded already. Then she takes the blue wool and red wool from her body and recites[21] as follows:

§18 "(Those) who were making her black, making her green, making her impure; whoever either made her impure before the gods or whoever made her impure before the dead, or whoever made her impure before humanity, I am hereby performing the Ritual of Impurity.

§19 "I am taking it away from her. I am taking the evil impurity, sorcery, *astayaratar*, anger of the gods from the twelve parts of her body. I am taking terror of the dead from her. I am taking the slander of the masses from her." Then she sets the blue and red wool down on the tray.

§20 Thereupon the black shirt that she (the ritual patron) has been wearing, the Wise Woman rips it from her top to bottom. And she pulls the black leggings off her feet (and) takes the black plugs out of her ears. She says as follows:

§21 "I am now taking from her the blackness (and) greenness (caused by) the words of impurity. On account of which words of impurity she became black and she became green, I am taking the *astayaratar* (away)." Then the black (clothes)[22] that she (the ritual patron) has been wearing, she (the Wise Woman) takes them off her and puts them down in one place.

§22 Thereupon she waves an empty pot over and away from her, breaks it, and incants. Then she sets pots at her feet and says: "I am now performing the Ritual of Impurity. I hold the black implement of impurity. Remove it! The evil impurity, sorcery, *astayaratar*, anger of the gods, terror of the dead, the cruelty of humanity—remove it!

§23 The ritual patron goes to wash. The Wise Woman sends in the nine combs of boxwood and she sends in one figurine of clay and she sets the figurine of clay at her feet for washing and she washes above. But a hierodule < takes > the combs and combs it (the figurine) once with each comb.

§24 Meanwhile the Wise Woman recites as follows: "I am now cleansing every body part. Let evil impurity, sorcery, *astayaratar*, anger of the gods, and terror of the dead be combed out of her![23]

§25 "I am now holding a *sarra*. Whoever disabled (her) twelve [body parts] with evil impurity—now I am separating off from each of your twelve body parts the evil impurity, sorcery, *astayaratar*, anger of the gods, and terror of the dead. Let them be completely separated off from her!"

§26 The combs, the *sarra*, the wing, the [black] shirt, the black [leggin]gs, whatever was on her, she dedicates it to the river. They bring [dow]n the remnants fr[om the hu]t and the figurine, and [thr]ow it into the river.

§27 [But the pupp]y (and) piglet they bring to another location and burn [them] on [a flame]. Meanwhile she keeps [...]. But the Wise Woman [constructs a gate] of hawthorn [in front] of the hut on the [up]per side. She [binds] it around with white wool.

§28 [In fro]nt three thick breads, meal [...] she [sca]tters [on this side] and [she scatters] on that side. [But on the lower side] she makes a gate of *alanza*-wood and she binds [it around] with black wool. [...] she places in the same way. [As soon as] they arrange [all this], [...] they come to the place [... re]ports.

§29 [...] pure hut [... the ritual patron, whether male o]r female, [passes through] the hawthorn gate and says [as follows:]

§30[24] "[You hawthorn in spring clothe yourself in] white, [but in autumn] you clothe [yourself in blood-red]. The sheep passes through you and you pull out its fleece. The ox passes through [you] and you pull out its hair.

§31 "In the same way let it pull out evil, impurity, sorcery, *astayaratar*, divine anger, perjury, the slander of the masses, and a short life." Then she (the ritual patron) throws a flat bread behind and the Wise Woman says: "Let the grain send away from behind her the evil impurity."[25]

§32 Further, she passes through the gate of *alanza*-wood and she says "Just as this *alanza*-wood purifies a thousand (or even) ten thousand shepherds and cowherds, let it in the same way purify the twelve body parts of this ritual patron of the evil impurity, sorcery, *astayaratar*, perjury, bad dreams, the anger of the gods, terror of the dead. Then she throws a flat bread behind and the Wise Woman speaks in exactly the same way.

§33 She goes to the riverbank and breaks one flat bread at the riverbank. She sets it on the riverbank, scatters oil cake and meal, libates wine once, and says: "Mother Goddess of the Riverbank, now the twelve body parts are scrubbed from impurity by your hand (and) purified." Thereupon she goes to the spring, breaks one flat bread, scatters oil cake and meal, libates wine once, and says: "O Sun God[26] my lord, now the twelve body parts are scrubbed (from impurity and) purified by means of clay from the spring."

§34[27] She next takes the *usantari* cow by the horns and says: "Sun God, My Lord, behold. Just as this cow is *usantari* and (is) in a *usantari* pen and she keeps filling the pen with bull-calves and cow-calves; may likewise the ritual patron be *usantari* too, and may she fill her house with sons and daughters and progeny and brood!" Then they drive the [cow] back to the pen.

§35 [Then] where there stands a tree covered with fruit, she goes [th]ere. She goes and tak[es] it [and she says: "O S]un God my Lord, just as this tree is cov[ered and just] as it has driven up shoots [... , in the same way let] life, health, str[ength, and long years ... for the ritual patron]. Let the [ritual patro]n [be] cov[ered] and in the same way. [Let her fill her house] with grandchildren [and great grandchildren]!"

§36 Then [she steps] oppo[site] the Sun God and consecrates [one sheep and one lamb] to the Sun God and s[ays: O Sun God my Lord come] and eat! Now [the twelve body parts are] scrubbed [and purified from whatever impurity] by [your] words O Sun God. You, O Sun God [have] released [them].

§37 Then [she sets (out)] the three hot breads, one cheese, and [one curd]. The coo[ked] liver and heart [she sets on them. She libates either beer] or wi[ne three times]. She goes to the hut [...] The Mother Goddess of the Riverbank [...] she says as follows: "[...] you eat! [...] let her eat! From what [...] This ritual patron [...].

§38 [Now] they have purified the twelve body parts. [...] *ilatar*. And the liv[er and heart ...]. Then she l[ibates] wine three times [...] and she toasts the river three times. Thereafter she toasts the [Mother Goddess of the Riverban]k three times. Then she d[rive]s up to the city.

Colophon: One tablet of the Ritual of Impurity and of the River. This ritual of Tunnawiya, Wise Woman, is finished. Pikku copied (it).

A ritual for the Protective Deity of the *kursa* and his Heptad (CTH 433.2)[28]

Sometimes the Wise Women operated in concert with male practitioners. In this ritual, from western Anatolia and dating to the early Empire period, a Wise Woman presides over a ritual designed for the royal family, as well as for the augurs who are attached to the king's retinue. In addition to being the beneficiaries of the ritual, the augurs also aid the Wise Woman in its implementation, as does a priest. The tablet is the second of the composition, containing the activities of three days of the multi-day ritual. The first and fourth columns of the ritual are not fully preserved, and thus neither are the name of the ritual expert or the official purpose of the ritual. It has the goal of placating the Tutelary Deity of the *kursa*, whose anger has been aroused by an unfavorable bird omen, as well as the demonic Heptad. The Tutelary Deity of the *kursa* was protector of wildlife, including birds, and thus augury fell within his sphere. The deity's anger may have been the result of a failure on the part of the augurs to interpret the omens correctly.[29] This would explain the rite to purify them in col. ii §§8–10. In any event, his anger is also directed at the royal family, on whose behalf the omen was solicited. Only the better-preserved columns ii and iii are translated here.

Col. ii

§1' [...] and him [...] nine charcoal (pieces?),[30] nine [...] the Wise Woman, the augurs, and the priest [go] out to the gate. The Wise Woman pours out [...] the same way. As they did on the fir[st day] now they do the same.

§2' [...] the Wise Woman goes away?. Next in the same way [...].and when [they] come before the deity in the temple the [Wi]se Woman [agai]n speaks those same words in front of the deity.

§3' Afterwards the Wise Woman takes [...] and a small quantity of lentils and sprinkles them on the hearth and says the following: "Now for you, O Protective Deity of the *kursa*, new [...] cast off the evil again from the soul (of the ritual patron?) [...] ... take!

§4' "Be favorably disposed toward the [king, que]en, and [pri]nces and be favorably disposed [to] the augurs.

§5' "Even as by day humankind surrounds you, O Hearth, by night the gods surround you. And if the gods ask you as follows, 'what did they do that they invoked the Protective Deity of the *kursa* and the Heptad?'

§6' "Then you, O Hearth, convey (only) good things to the Protective Deity of the *kursa*, the Heptad, and all the gods. (O gods) be favorably disposed to the king, the queen, and the princes and give them life and strength!

§7' "And you, O Hearth, the king, queen, princes, and their grandchildren and great-grandchildren will surround forever. And you (o gods) always show them the path, always show the path to the augurs."

§8' The Wise Woman takes one small sweet cake and crumbles it in her hand and kneads it with sheep fat to make an oil cake.

The Wise Woman takes a little of the oil cake from her hand and puts it back for the Protective Deity of the *kursa*. And for the augurs she puts fat cake in their mouths saying as follows: "Protective Deity of the *kursa* and Heptad,

§9' remove the evil, anger, and sullenness and oil cake will be placed in your mouths as well (or: once again). And for them the fat should flow out from the mouth. If some augur has spoken an evil word before the deity or if some (augur) has enraged you,

§10' then let also the augurs, that is, their mouth(s), be wiped off with fat cake." And the oil cake that is sitting before the Protective Deity of the *kursa*, the Wise Woman takes it up and throws it in the hearth. Day two (is finished. The ritual) is not finished.

Col. iii

§1 As soon as it is light on the third day, the Wise Woman goes before the Protective Deity of the *kursa*. She takes a little *kars*-grain (and) barley and roasts it on a flame and scatters it, that is, the flour.[31] Then she waves (it) over and away from the Protective Deity of the *kursa* and she waves (it) also over and away from all of the augurs.

§2 As she does this she speaks as follows: "The words that are evil and terrible, may they go away! But let good, pleasant, and wise (words) come in!" Then the Wise Woman produces the *kars*-grain and the barley and where there are rocks she scatters it there.[32]

§3 When darkness falls, [...] by foot. Three small, sweet thick breads, among them one sweet cake is stacked; the one is bound to the other above. They take a pitcher of wine and a billy goat. Afterwards the Wise Woman and all the augurs go. They bring them before the deity and hold them out to the deity while she speaks as follows: "Protective Deity of the *kursa* I am going now. I give the goat to the male (gods). Be once again tranquil toward me! Let the Heptad also take the offering for themselves."

§4 The Wise Woman detaches from the deity the white wool that was tied to (the statue of) the Protective Deity of the kursa and the *parhuena* that was bound to the deity. And the white wool that was tied to the necks of the augurs and the white wool that was tied to the logs, the Wise Woman detaches them and puts them in a *hulta*-garment.

§5 Then she brings three small sweet cakes, one pitcher of wine, and one billy goat out from the gate and all the augurs go behind. To the right of the path she lays down foliage and sets the three small sweet cakes on it. She consecrates the billy goat to the Heptad and breaks two small sweet cakes for

254

Hannahanna. She then consecrates the billy goat to the male gods. They slaughter the billy goat upward on the foliage. She speaks as follows:

§6 "O Heptad, we have just given you this offering. Eat and drink! May the terrible Heptad step off the road again. May you bestow kindliness on the Protective Deity of the *kursa*. May you be favorably disposed to the king, queen, and princes! Show them the path! And be favorably disposed to the augurs and show them the path! May he ... ! May he ... !"[33]

§7 The raw sections of the goat are cooked on a flame. She sets down [...] for the Heptad. Afterward the liver and heart are cooked on a flame. On the foliage [...] wine is libated.

§8 [...] the augurs co[nsu]me it [...] but the [bru]sh is brought in and it [...] is sprinkled on the goat hide. [...] The Wise Woman to the Protective Deity of the *kursa* to [...] the Wise Woman [...] them [...] The Wise Woman speaks [...]

§9 [...] the g[oat] hide [...]

Ritual for the Sun God of Blood and the Storm God, against the sorcery of the king's sister[34]

Sorcery, or rather the perception of sorcery (see Miller 2010b), was a relatively common occurrence in the Hittite royal court; numerous instances are known to us. Two rituals are preserved that relate to one particular instance that allegedly occurred in the reign of King Tudhaliya II (ca. 1400 BC). The king's sister Ziplantawiya, presumably desirous of advancing the political interests of her own children at a politically turbulent moment with regard to the succession, allegedly performed, or solicited, sorcery against the king and his family. One of the texts, which is not well preserved, may contain a ritual performed by Ziplantawiya on behalf of her son Attai (Kassian 2000, 107). In this text she bears the title queen.[35] The second, better-preserved ritual, which is translated here, was certainly performed to counter Ziplantawiya's curses and restore the gods' goodwill toward the royal house.

The ritualist is not identified and we cannot be certain (contra Kassian 2000: 9–10 with n. 2) that it was performed by a Wise Woman as opposed to a male ritualist. Following the incipit, which lists the ritual ingredients (§§1, 2), the statement of the problem and the desired outcome of the ritual (§§3, 4), the activities are divided into two closely related parts. The focus of the first part (§§3–19') is on nullifying the sorcery by placing the tongues representing the curses into a container of honey and burying them beneath a rock, followed by breaking thick breads representing, in turn, anger, well-being, peace, and withholding (of evil). The goal is to turn the curses back on Ziplantawiya. The focus of the second part (§20'–34') is, first, on the cutting of colored threads (in the fragmentary §§21'–25'), and then on the sacrifice of rodents for the chthonic deities whose anger the ritualist seeks to pacify. Both sections rely heavily of course on incantations. Finally, a colophon identifies the scribe.

Col. I[36]

§1 [Whe]n they propitiate[37] the Sun God of Blood and the Storm God they take [these thing]s: two *kurtali*-containers of dough; into one are thrown seven tongues of dough and into the other are thrown seven tongues of dough. A *waksur*-measure of sheep fat, a *waksur*-measure of honey, two lambs, twenty *turuppa*, one *sutu*-measure of *emmer*. She places it on thick loaves. One puppy, seven fingers of dough, seven tears of dough. They are thrown into a basket. One linen thread.

§2 Silver, gold, lapis lazuli, Babylon-stone, *parasha*-stone, rock crystal(?), *lulluri*-stone, tin, copper—he/she takes a little of each. He/She takes one set of scales of wood. Forty wooden figurines, four small carts, six wooden (carts) for sitting in, one wooden (cart) for sitting and standing in, five cups, two small *KUKUB*-vessels, one *hanessa*-vessel of wine. He/She arranges them.

§3 [And] they carry (these items) into the lord's house.[38] He/She takes one (of the) *kurtali*-containers of dough with < the tongues > and says as follows: "These evil, ... tongues—Ziplantawi[ya] made (them). [N]ow the evil tongues—Ziplantawiya [made] them from the mouth into which (*kurtali*-container?). Now Ziplantawiya's soul[39] is wide, her [li]mbs are good (and) beautiful, her mouth is [goo]d, her tongue is good. What evil she has spoken (is) against Tuthaliya, Nikalmati, and their sons. She [ma]de the tongues against them. She has conveyed evil (about) them to the Sun God of Blood and the Storm God. And she has been bewitching them.

§4 "[... b]ehold, we are propitiating the Sun God of Blood and the Storm God. [These] e[v]il tongues (are) demonic(?).[40] Let them (the tongues) seize Ziplantawiya [together wit]h [h]er son[s] instead! At the top let them seize her head. Let them seize her heart, her womb, her [kn]ees, her hands, her feet! [Wh]atever she has inflicted upon her brother, we are [p]ropitiating it for the lord together with his wife (and) his sons. Let these evil tongues se[i]ze Ziplantawiya together with her sons instead!"

§5 [...] (he/she takes) the (other) *kurtali*-container and pou[rs] fat and honey from above (into it) and s[a]ys as follows: "Behold, we have [p]laced the evil sorcerou[s] tongues, [wh]ich Ziplanta-wiya had made, into the honey. O Sun God of Blood and Storm God, b[e] appeased! Let these evil sorcerous tongue[s tu]rn (from) the lord together with his wife, his sons, his household! Let

256

them [seiz]e Ziplantawiya together wit[h her sons]! Let them give to the lord (together with) his wife and his sons life, cou[rage] (and) youthful vigor! Let the gods give him a straight-pointing w[eap]on! Let him raise his grandsons and great-grandsons and let him satiate the land!"

§6 He/she sticks the figurines [under a rock?][41] and says as follows: [" …]. Behold, [the evil sorcer]ous tongues, which Ziplantawiya has made against the lord and against his wife (together with) [h]is sons, [. t]o the son adults [… per]fect […]. (approximately 3 paragraphs broken)

§7' […] whe[n … t]hrown […] And [she says] as foll[ows: " …] Ziplantawiya […] the lord [… B]ehold, Ziplantawiya [… her [sou]l is wide [… the evi]l sorcerous [tongue … let it seiz]e. Her heart, [her] womb [… And] let it seize [Ziplantawiya together with] her [son]s [instead! …] And them? […] into […]
Col. II

§8' We [b]rought the figurines to [the]ir [place.] And they stuck them under another rock. (He/she takes) the *kurtali*-container of dough where the fat and honey have been poured, and sets it on the rock. She breaks three small thick [lo]aves, libates wine and says as follows: "Just as t[his] rock (is) eternal, may the lord and his wife (and) [h]is so[ns] in the same way be eternal! And let his weapon b[e] pointed straight ahead!" And he/she libates the *turuppa* with wine.

§9' He/she says as f[ol]lows: "Mouth, tongue, tooth! Behold, I have consecrated to you a pu[r]e, perfect, white shee[p] not be[a]ten with a stick. Again cast off the evil, and speak well of the lord together with his wife and his sons!"

§10' They poured out the evil tongues [fro]m the *kurtali*-container [and] said as [f]ollows: "Just as these (tongues), which Ziplantawiya has made against the lord with his wife (and) his son[s], perish, [so] let Ziplantawiya's sorcery and her evil word [per]ish in the same way! And let it not come back again!"[42]

§11' He/she places the foliage on the ground and breaks three thick breads to the Sun God of Blood and to the Sun God's male gods. He/she offers *turuppa*-bread (and) wine and says: "O Sun God (and) the Sun God's male gods, behold I have given you the thick bread of anger. What Ziplantawiya has inflicted upon the lord, let it be inflicted back on her!"

§12' And he/she consecrates three thick breads and a *turuppa* to the Storm God and (his) male gods in the same way and speaks in the same way. He/she roasts the *turuppa* on a flame,[43] cuts them off, and sets them out for the Storm God and his male gods, (and) for the Sun God and his male gods, and says as follows: "O Sun God and the Sun God's male gods, O Storm God and the Storm God's male gods, we have cut these. Let it be cut off—Ziplantiya's evil word (and) sorcery! Let it be turned back on Ziplantawiya!" He/she takes up the foliage with the thick breads and the *turuppa* and places them in front of the figurines.

§13' T[hen] they took (some) other [fo]liage and again con-secrated the thick breads (and) *turuppa* in the same way. And they said as foll[ow]s: "O Sun God of Blood, Storm God (and) the male gods! Behold, I broke for you thick breads of well-being, (so) destroy the e[vi]l! Let there once again be well-being for the lord (along with) his wife (and) his sons. O Sun God and Storm God restore well-being, life, youthful vigor, and a straight-pointed weapon!

§14' They took up the foliage and placed it in front of the figurines. Again they placed other foliage, offered the thick breads and *turuppa* of peace to the Sun God, the Storm God and the male gods in the same way and said as follows: "O Sun God of Blood, Storm God, and the male gods, [beho]ld, I have broken the thick bread of peace for you, so be reconci[le]d with the lord together with his wife and his sons!"

§15' He/she throws silver, gold, stones, ... -stones on the balance. They weighed (them) six times before the Sun God and said as follows: [O Sun Go]d [of Blood] and Storm God, behold, the lord with his wife and his sons (are before) you. [O Sun G]od [of Blood] and Storm God, be appeased! Guard! [...] anything." They placed [the thick bread] of peace on the ground(?). And the silver, gold, stones, [. ... An]d they left them in their place.

§16' [... he/she sai]d: "O Sun God and Storm God, [...]"
(*About 3 lines broken.*)

[...] one lamb [...] And [...] she said:

§17' ["O Sun God of Blood, Storm God, and male gods! Beho]ld, [I have broken the thick bread] of withholding for you. [... they p]lough. And it [...] we take away oil and emmer;[...]. And away the lord's [...] we took [grand]sons and great grandsons?. [... And] again to him back away [...]. [Be atten]tive [to Ziplantawiya (with evil intention)], but do not be attentive to the lord (with evil intention)."[44]

§18' [...] they roast on a flame [... the th]igh and the sh[oul]der-blade [...] these lambs together with ... they placed the foliage on the hearth [and b]urnt [it up.]

§19' [...] And they cut up the puppy. [...] It is finished.

§20' [When] they propitiate [the Sun God of Blood and the Storm God], they take these things: ... [one] blue [threa]d, one red thread [one white thread, one bla]ck [thread], one green thread, […] piglet, a *waksur*-measure of mutton fat, [a *waksur*-measure of honey, …], five cups, two small *KUKUB* vessels, [… And them] everywhere […] they stand. […] they roast.

§21' [… w]hich she t[akes].

(*About 3–4 lines broken to lower edge.*)

Col. III

§22' [… what Ziplantawiya] on the l[ord] with his wife and his sons [has inflicted …]

§23' [… He/she says as follows:] "For him [a rope] is [pull]ed up. [Just as] I have cut [off] this (rope), in the same way l[e]t [the evil word and sorcery of Ziplantawiya] be cut [off]!"[45]

§24' […] And [he/she says] as follows: ["What Ziplantawiya] has inflicted on the lord's wife, [we are p]ropitiating [it for the lord (together with) his wife and his sons. …] And it […] let be! [… I have c]ut. And Ziplantawiya's […] let it be cut! [… And] let him seize [Ziplantawiya together with] her sons [instead]!" And he/she places it in the basket.

§25' […]. And she says as follows: [… What she] has inflicted on […], so [it …] And it [… Z]i […]

§26' [… A]smuheba[46] [… And] she p[laces it] in the basket.

§27' He/she [s]ticks [the figurines …] and [says] as follo[ws: " … Behold, the evil sorce]rous tongues that Ziplantawiya [has made] against the lord and his wife [and his sons, … to the l]ord, to his wife and his sons […] perfect […]. Let them release Tuthaliya! […] Let them seize [Ziplantawiya toge]ther with her sons [instead]!

§28' "[And] let them give [to the lord and his wife and his sons lif]e, long years, [courage, and youthful vigor!] And to him let [the gods] give [the straight-pointed weapon]! Let them raise his grandsons and great-grandsons [and] let them satiate the land! [… let him sa]tiate!"

§29' He/she takes [u]p [the …]. And the houses [… Af]terwards the puppy […] they sweep in. And the ashes […] … they carry away. And […]. They put it down.

§30' […] they dug. […] I cleaned the figurines. […] they put [them] down, but they did not bury them; they set them [beneath a rock]. He/she sets the *kurtali*-container where the fat and honey [are poured] on the rock. Down in front he/she [sets] foliage, [and] breaks a thick bread. He/she offers one *gaparta*-rodent [and] he/she says [as foll]ows: "Mouth, tongue, tooth, may you eat!

§31' "Just as [this r]ock is eternal, so may the lord and his wife and his sons [be ete]rnal! And cast off evil, [and] speak well once again [of the lor]d together with his wife and his sons!" They poured out the [evi]l tongues from the *kurtali*-container and said as follows: "Just as these (tongues) perish,

§32' "that Ziplantawiya has made for the lord together with his wife and his sons, so let Ziplantawiya's sorcery and her evil words perish in the same way! May they (the tongues) not return." And the *gaparta*-rodent that he/she has sacrificed to the evil tongue, he/she roasts (its) liver and shoulder blade and leaves it on the rock. He/she puts the gaparta-rodent on the hearth and burns it up.

§33' Afterward, he/she puts foliage in three places. He/she broke three thick breads to the Storm God of Oath and his male gods. He/she sacrificed a *gaparta*-rodent and let the blood (flow) over the thick breads. Afterward he/she broke three offering breads to the Sun God and his male gods. He/she sacrificed a *gaparta*-rodent and let the blood (flow) over the offering breads. Afterward he broke three offering breads to the Storm God of Heaven and his male gods. He sacrificed a *gaparta*-rodent and let the blood (flow) over the thick breads. Then they roasted the meat, liver, (and) shoulder blade over a flame.

Col. IV

§34' […] to the Sun G[od] (and) the Storm God of Heaven [… he/she sa]crificed, and sa[ys] as follows: [… "O Sun God (and)] Storm God of [Hea]ven, behold, [the thick bread] of ang[er] to you […]. To the lord (and) to his wife (together with) his sons [… And] do not release her […] looks. […] look favorably [at the lord] (with) his [wi]fe (and) his sons! And them […] Give (him) [grandso]ns and great-grandsons!"

(*A few illegible signs of the first line are all that is preserved of the next paragraph. There is a gap of several (five?) paragraphs before the colophon.*)

Colophon: When […] The hand (of) SUKUR-anza.

(*Erased to the lower edge.*)

Ritual at the river (CTH 433.6)[47]

Only a small portion of the middle of the ritual is preserved, so we cannot be sure of its overall purpose or who is conducting the rite. In this portion of the ritual, the client, who may be either male or female, is made to stand over a pit into which a piglet has been slaughtered.[48] The incantations that accompany this rite are directed at the Sun God, who is asked to free the client from his or her state of impurity. What is interesting and highly unusual here is the presence of priest, augur, wise woman, and seeress at the rite.[49] References to seeresses are rare in Hittite texts and we know nothing about them, other than that they are connected with divination. Also of interest is the use of a young girl, although the context is too broken to enlighten us as to her function within the ritual. As with Tunnawiya's ritual above, the purification requires a river and appeals to the Sun God, whose role is clarified here as the dispenser of justice. The presence of Anuwanza as scribal supervisor dates the copy to the beginning of the reign of Tuthaliya IV (r. ca. 1237–1209).[50]

obv. i

[As soon as] it is [l]ight [on the Nth day], they [...]. [...] the hut, rem[nants ...][51] and he/she goes to the river. But the [hu]t and the cloth ... the earth is dug. They truss a pig and they [kill] it down in the pit. They then bridge over (the pit) for the sake of his/her (i.e., the ritual patron's) purity.

The ritual patron steps over the pig.

"Sun God my lord, king of heaven, the ritual patron has now completed (the ritual). Further, the Priest, the Augur, the Wise Woman, and the Seeress (are present). (The ritual patron) went to the mountain; she/he went to the meadow, and no one sustained him/her.

"And now she/he has come again to you, O Sun God, king of heaven, in humility. You O Sun are king in heaven, and you are the shepherd of humanity. You judge the case of humanity, O king of heaven. And who from which [...], you O Sun God, king of heaven, sustain him/her!

"The ritual patron (is) now in (a state of) evil impurity, in ... , bewitchment, infliction, ... cruelty. The oath deities [...] in terror. While indeed for the ritual pa[tron ...] in. And she/he t.-ed him down. And it ... [...] he/she cannot conquer. But if the charioteer and ... [...], he t.-ed the terror of the deer of the field, the human of the field. Then [he bega]n to carry it off [...]

"Together with a yoked pair he ... -s. They harness the ... and [...] and they unharness it. And [...] the neck he ... -s and they release it. Then they have ... carried off.

"O Sun God, [release?] the [rit]ual [patron] from evil impurity, bewitchment, infliction, [...], terror.

"[...] ... the terror of the deer [of the] fie[ld], [of the human] of the [field] [...]
(Of col. ii only the initial signs of lines 1–9 are preserved. Col. iii is lost altogether. Col. iv is restored based on B ii?).
rev. iv

(first three preserved lines are untranslatable) ... he/she sets and says, "What for him/her [...] now the Wise Woman has left it above and now the mother of the deity and the W[ise]

Woman[52] are bringing it down for him/her. And grain, dough, and *huri*-bread are scattered before the pig(let) [and the pig]let eats. But what remains they leave behind the river.

Further, they dig (at) that place and the brazier they dedicate to the river. The frog, the image of clay, and the puppy likewise. The cloak, the headband, and the tablets [they] le[ave] behind the river.

Colophon: Second Tablet: Ritual of the River. Not finished. Hand of Zuzzu, son of AMAR.UTU before Anuwanza, chief scribe.

B continues:

When for the ritual patron the remnants down [...] and they bring in a young girl and the ritual patron [...] forth (his) hand to her [...]

And he says as follows: "O Sun God my lord [...] a young girl and now the young girl [...] ... man the dark(?) earth [...] ... of this of the young [girl ...] ...

Paskuwatti's ritual against a man's failure to procreate[53]

Paskuwatti's ritual, written down in the early Empire period (fifteenth century), is an invocation to the Luwian goddess Uliliyassi, as per the catalogue tablet KUB 30:65 i 6 ("One tablet, words of Paskuwatti: when I invoke Uliliyassi"), whom Hoffner (1987: 281; followed by Hutter 2003: 238) supposes was a patroness of plant and animal fecundity. Traditionally understood as a ritual against impotence, it has recently been reinterpreted as addressing homosexuality (Miller 2010a). In any event, the problem is that the man who is the client here lacks progeny. The ritual employs two main strategies. The first is the use of a young girl to try and entice the patient into a sexual response. The precise nature of the girl's ritual status is an open question. She appears to enjoy a special state of purity, whether that implies virginity, or that she is consecrated to the deity, or both, though it is by no means a given that virginity was especially prized by the Hittites. Was this a temporary state or a permanent one? The other strategy is a dream incubation in which it is hoped that the goddess will appear to the man in a dream and have sex with him. This eventuality will be an indication of his cure.

§1 According to Paskuwatti, woman of Arzawa, who [however] resides in Parassa. If some man lacks the ability to procreate or he is not a man with respect to a woman.

§2 I make an offering on his behalf to Uliliyassi and invoke her for three days. On the first day I do as follows: One soldier bread is piled up, and these (things) are laid down with it: three sweet thick breads (made) of moist flour weighing one *tarna*, figs, raisins, *kallaktar*, *parhuena*, meal of the deity—a little bit (of) each in turn—a tuft of wool from an *iyant*-sheep, a pitcher of wine, and the [garment]s or the cloak of the man who is the ritual patron, are (all) [pla]ced on the soldier bread.

§3 A consecrated girl[54] carries [th]em off, and the ritual pat[ron], having bathed, follows them. [...] is bathed. We take them to a different place in the countryside and take up a position. [The girl] (continues to) hold the soldier bread raised and I construct gates of reeds.

§4 I tie them together with red and white wool.[55] I place a spindle and a distaff in the ritual patron's [hand], and he comes [out] through the gates. When he emerges from under the gates, I take the spindle and distaff away from him. I give him a bow and [arrows] as I recite the following: "I have just taken womanliness away from you and given you back manliness. You have cast off/ rejected the (sexual) behavior[56] [of women]; [you have adopted] the behavior of men!"

§5 ... At the same time I [spe]ak as [follows]: " ... to you ... and to him/her the *hattar* [...] or of the consecrated girl [...]. She? went down to his? loins,[57] but this mortal (is) one of shit, one of piss.[58] He did not find you.[59]

§6 "But now he has come to you on his knees for help[60] and is seeking you—your divinity—O Goddess. Whether you are on the mountain, whether you are in the meadow, whether you are in the valley—wherever you are, come in good will to this man! Let the wind and rain not batter your eyes!

§7 "He will proceed to make you his (personal) goddess. He will provide a place for you. He will give you a house. He will give you servants and he will give you livestock. He will make you a recipient of vows.

§8 "I am just now entreating and invoking you. So come! Bring with you the moon, the star(s), and the Sun Goddess of the Earth.[61] Let servants run before you! Let the gods and [goddesses] run before you! Come beside this man! You are his wife for his progeny! So take care of him! Turn to him and speak to him! Turn your maidservant over to him, and he will become a yoke. Let him take his wife and produce for himself sons and daughters! They will be your servants. They will continually give you offerings, thick breads, meal, and libations.

§9 "This man has not known you. But now he has sought you. Since it is you (instead of another deity) that this one has sought, you, O goddess, must step toward him in favor. The matter

263

about which we are entreating you on earth, O goddess, reveal your divinity and make it good! Let him experience[62] your divinity, O goddess! It will happen that he will make you [his personal goddess]." I put [the crumbled thick breads] back on the soldier bread, and we go back into the house. In the house in which I perform (the ritual) a new table is set up. I place (the crumbled thick breads) on top of the soldier bread upon the table. Down in front (of it) I place a pitcher.

§10 I take a little of the crumbled thick breads that are lying on the soldier bread and give (it) to the man who is the ritual patron. He puts it in his mouth and toasts Uliliyassi three times. When night falls, the ritual patron lies down in front of that same table. They place a bed down in front of that table for him.

§11 The garments or the cloak that are lying on the soldier bread he will spread out by night. I perform it (the ritual) over three days. On each day I entreat three times: (once) at dawn, once at midday, and once at dusk. And while doing so, I speak those very same words.

§12 At dawn I break some thick breads, other thick breads I break at midday, (still) others I break at dusk. I also scatter another (portion) of meal. Next I present one sheep to Uliliyassi, and they slaughter it down in front of the table. They carry the sheep out and [butch]er [it]. Then [they …] it. [They take] the [raw] meat, the breast (and) shoulder [of the shee]p, and they set them […] on the table. They co[ok] the liver [and heart] on [a flame and. … They crumble] two thick breads and [they set] (them) on the table for her.

§13 (too fragmentary for translation.)

§14 (first several lines are too fragmentary for translation) "Turn [your maidservant] over [to him] and he will become a yoke for her. Let him take his wife, let him produce children! Let him produce sons and daughters! You, O goddess, reveal your divinity!

§15 "Let him experience your power! He will make you his personal deity. He will make you a recipient of vows." Once again they spread out a bed for him down in front of the table. They also spread out below for him the garments or cloak that has been lying on the soldier bread. The ritual patron sleeps (to see) if he sees the goddess incarnate in a dream (and if) she goes to him and sleeps with him. Throughout the three days in which [I] entr[eat] the goddess he reports whatever dreams he sees, whether the goddess reveals her eyes to him (or) whether the goddess sleeps with him.

§16 It will happen that he will make (her his personal) deity. Moreover, if she prefers a pithos vessel, he will install her as a pithos vessel. But if not, he will install her as a *huwasi* stone. Or he will fashion her (as) a statue. But the new table that was set up for the invocation ritual becomes the goddess's alone.

§17 But [if he does not see] (her) incarnate, (if) the goddess [does not sleep] with him in a dream, I will keep on performing (this ritual). (*Remainder of column lost.*)

Ashella's ritual against plague[63]

The ritual attributed to Ashella comes from western Anatolia, and may have been introduced into the Hittite chancellory during the reign of Mursili II (r. ca. 1321–1295 BC).[64] It is frequently cited for its close similarities to the biblical scapegoat rite described in Leviticus 16. In this case, however, in addition to a ram, a woman is used to carry the impurity to the camp of the enemy. This occurs on the first day of the four-day ritual. The ritual's purpose is to remove the plague that is infecting the land or army. The source of the malignancy is some malevolent deity, who it is hoped, will accept the rams as a substitute for the afflicted. The activities of day two focus on an offering of a special nature to a deity whose identity is not preserved; the human participants are not invited to dine with the deity. This is followed by a purificatory rite involving passing between fire and a communal meal with the Protective Deity of the Ritual Paraphernalia. The final two days of the ritual are concerned with presenting offerings, first to the deity who caused the plague, then to the Storm God, the Sun God, and all the gods. These are also followed by communal meals.

The status of the woman used to transport the miasma is not specified. As the bearer of impurity, she herself may be considered "impure" in some way, on the principle of like attracting like. Based on what we know of Hittite practice, it is unlikely that she was a woman of high or even moderate social standing, that is, "one of their own." It is more likely that she was someone who was considered expendable, such as a slave or a deportee, although in the absence of evidence, this is merely a surmise. Note that the woman is given food and drink for her journey.

§1 According to Ashella, man of Hapalla: If a plague occurs in the land or in the army camp (dupl. C: if the army suffers a ruinous year), I perform this ritual.

§2 I do the following:[65] When day turns to night, all who are army commanders, every one prepares a ram. Nothing is prescribed as to whether the rams should be white or black. I wind twists of white, red, and green wool and he weaves them into one.[66] I string one pearl(?) and one ring of iron and lead and I tie them to the necks and horns of the rams. They tether them (the rams) before the tents for the night, and as they do so, they say the following: "Whatever deity is stirring (or: wandering) below, whatever deity has caused this plague, for you I have secured these rams. Be satisfied with (these)!"

§3 Then in the morning I drive them to the countryside. With each ram they bring one pitcher of beer, one thick bread, and one cup of [...]. At the tent, before the king, he seats an ornamented woman. He sets one *huppar* of beer and three thick breads at the foot of[67] the woman.

§4 Afterwards the camp commanders place their hands on the rams and recite as follows: "The deity who has caused this plague, now the rams are standing here and their liver, heart, and thigh are very succulent. May human flesh be repulsive to him (the deity) once again, and may you (o deity) be satisfied with these rams." The army commanders bow down to the rams and the king bows to the ornamented woman. Afterwards, they take the rams, the woman, the bread, and the beer through the army and drive them to the countryside. They go and abandon them at the enemy border (so that) they do not end up at any place of ours. Thereupon they recite as follows: "Whatever evil was among the men, cattle, sheep, horses, mules, and donkeys of this army, these rams and the woman have just carried it away from the camp. Whoever finds them, may that land receive this evil plague."

§5 At daybreak on the second day they prepare six rams, six billy goats, twelve ... jugs, twelve cups, twelve thick breads, one *huppar* of beer, and three small bronze knives. They drive them (the animals) to yet another place in the countryside carrying all these things along. When they move to the countryside, they "stick" them on the ground[68] and cook them whole. They spread out foliage below and arrange the meat, offering breads, and a small knife thus. Then they fill the cups and jugs with beer. In addition, at the same time [they say] the follow[ing: " ...] promptly for the first time [...] we have released. Now [to you o deity] we have given cooked food, including meat, bread, and beer, and ra[w food].[69] O Deity, eat and drink like a god. Don't cast it aside!"[70] Then they bow down, and come away. While they are worshipping the deity, no one shall place (any) utensil on the ground. It is not permitted; nor shall one take it up for himself.[71]

§6 When they leave the ritual, they pour salt into the water. He washes their hands with it. Then they ignite a fire in two places and they pass through them. They arrange two goats, one *huppar* of wine, and five thick breads. The two goats are dedicated to the Protective Deity of the Ritual Paraphernalia. He sets the cooked breast, right shoulder, liver, and heart on (some) foliage. He toasts the Protective Deity of the Ritual Paraphernalia three times and they eat. Then they come away.

§7 At daybreak of the third day, they drive in one billy goat, one ram and one pig. Afterward they prepare three thick breads and one *huppar* of beer and then drive them into the countryside to another place. They spread out branches and set down. They return the three thick breads. The billy goat, the sheep (i.e., ram), and the pig they present to that very deity who made this plague in the army (saying): "May that deity eat. May that deity drink. And in the land of Hatti and in regard to the army of the land of Hatti may there be peace. May he (the deity) be turned in favor (to the army)." They eat and drink. Then they come away.

§8 At daybreak on the fourth day, they drive in one bull, one ewe, and one wether—but (it must be) a ewe to which a ram has not yet gone—ten thick breads, one *huppar* of beer, one *huppar* of wine. They drive them to yet another place in the countryside and they present the cow (i.e., bull) to the Storm God. But the ewe they present to the Sun God(dess?).[72] And they present three sheep to all the gods. Then they spread foliage on the ground. He sets the cooked breast, the right shoulder, the liver, the heart, and thick bread on the foliage. Then he toasts the Sun God of Heaven, the Storm God, and all the gods three times, and they eat. Then they come away.

Colophon: One ritual, the word of Ashella, when a plague occurs in the land or in the army camp. (Dupl. B: One tablet, complete, containing three rituals. When a plague occurs in the land or in the army camp. Dupl. C: The plague ritual of Ashella, man of Hapalla, finished.)

Abbreviations

CHD	1980ff. *The Hittite Dictionary of the Oriental Institute of the University of Chicago,* Chicago: Oriental Institute.
CTH	L. Laroche, 1971. *Catalogue des textes Hittites.* Paris: Klincksieck.
FHL	Durand, J.-M., and E. Laroche, 1982. 'Fragments hittites du Louvre', *in Mémorial Atatürk, Études d'Archéologie et de Philologie Anatoliennes,* Paris: Editions Recherche sur les civilisations, S. 73–107.
HED	J. Puhvel, 1984ff. *Hittite Etymological Dictionary,* Berlin: de Gruyter.
KBo	Keilschrifttexte aus Boghazköi
KUB	Keilschrifturkunden aus Boghazköi
VBoT	A. Goetze, 1930. *Verstreute Bogazköi-Texte.* Marburg: a.d. Lahn.

BILLIE JEAN COLLINS

Notes

1 See Taggar-Cohen, 2006.
2 Midwives, hierodulae, temple singers, and priestesses could also conduct rituals; Taracha, 2009, 151.
3 He aligns this with the preponderance of healing goddesses; 1993, 36, n. 68.
4 CTH 393: A. VBoT 24; B. KBo 12.104.
5 Text: KUB 7.53 + KUB 12.58. Editions: Goetze, 1938; Cornil, 1999.
6 See Hutter, 2003, 260–61 for idea that the distinction between the sexes is particularly prevalent in Luwian rituals.
7 Miller, 2004, 482 n. 813.
8 Literally "separated off." See *CHD Š*, 235, sub *sarra*-D.
9 For this translation, see Puhvel, *HED* 1:240, sub *au(s)*-.
10 Following *CHD* P, 215–16, sub-*pát*.
11 The color black throughout the ritual symbolizes the pollution that is to be removed. See §18.
12 See Miller, 2004, 482, for the understanding of this passage.
13 See Kloekhorst, 2008, 990–91 for discussion. "object in which the door-axle is fixed and turns."
14 For the translation of this sentence, see Kloekhorst, 2008, 782.
15 See Kloekhorst, 2008, 929 for discussion of the meaning of *usantari* as "bringing gains, bringing blessings."
16 A Luwian incantation, which appears in Hittite elsewhere in Tunnawiya's corpus. Translation follows Hutter, 2003, 248.
17 Miller, 2004, 520 translates *"hinge."*
18 Melchert, "Marginalia to the Myth of Telipinu," paper presented at the 221st AOS meeting, Chicago, IL, 2011 understands *ser arha wahnu* as "whirl over and away from," that is, picking up the evils with the inward arc and removing them with the outward arc.
19 Translation follows Miller, 2004, 520. On the implications of incantations kept on a separate tablet, see pp. 520–21.
20 In the sense of sorcerous, i.e., dolls used for black magic.
21 Goetze (1938) translates "in each case she speaks" which may be the correct sense of the iterative form here.
22 That is, all the rest of the black garments listed in §3.
23 Literally "down from" her.
24 On Old Hittite motifs in this ritual, see Miller, 2004, 455–58.
25 That is, so that the impurity does not follow behind her.
26 Cf. the ritual at the river (CTH 433.6), translated below, which explains that the Sun God as judge has the power to relieve the patient's suffering.
27 For this paragraph, see Kloekhorst, 2008, 929.
28 Text: KBo 17.105 + KBo 34.47. Edition: Bawanypeck, 2005, 84–105.
29 As suggested by Bawanypeck, 2005, 233–34.
30 Translation of this word follows Bawanypeck, 2005, 98–99, with bibliography.
31 *QÉMANNAM* is a hapax. Bawanypeck, 2005, 100 takes it from Akkadian *qĕmu(m)* "Mehl."
32 Presumably so that it will not take seed.
33 Two verbs of unknown meaning.
34 Text: A. KBo 15.10 + KBo 20.42; B. KUB 57.39. Edition: Kassian, 2000, 20–104.
35 For a discussion of this obscure period in Hittite history and the possible identity of Ziplantawiya, see Forlanini, 2005, esp. 240–42.
36 This translation is based on the transliteration of Kassian, 2000, 20–75.

37 Kassian uses variously conciliate, placate, pacify, etc., to translate *lilai-*. However, "propiate" is the appropriate term when the goal is to forestall the anger of someone who has the power to injure you. See the *New Oxford American Dictionary*.

38 That is, the lord of the ritual, i.e., the one for whom the ritual is performed.

39 Accepting Kassian's, 2000, 80–81 understanding of *addi-* here.

40 Cf. KUB 20.73 iv 7–8, where *hatestanti-* is parallel with the gods. Cf. HED H, 265.

41 Restoration based on §8'. The symbolism is that the rock, eternal like the royal house, will hide/crush/bury the figurines of fingers and tears, which symbolize the evil or its effects.

42 See Rieken, 2004, 246 on the meaning of *-apa* "back" in this instance.

43 The *turuppa*-bread is symbolic of the evil; roasting them, like cutting them, will analogously destroy the evil. See Haas, 2003, 394.

44 For the reconstruction and interpretation of this line, see Kassian, 2000, 89–90, though my translation differs slightly from his.

45 For the restoration of this paragraph, see Torri, 2003, 157.

46 Another royal personage of uncertain identity. Freu, 1995, 140, proposed that she could be the wife of Hattusili II, predecessor of Tudhaliya II, according to his reconstruction.

47 Text: A. KUB 36.83; B. KBo 34.49. Edition: Bawanypeck, 2005, 265–73. Otten and Siegelová, 1970: 37 suggested that this text belongs to another ritual, preserved primarily on unpublished tablets, for the Guls deities. See also McMahon, 1995, 263.

48 On pig sacrifice among the Hittites, see Collins, 2006.

49 These are the same personnel, less the seeress, found in CTH 433.2 translated above.

50 Mascheroni, 1984, 165; for more on Zuzzu and Santa, see Marizza, 2010, 88.

51 Compare §26 of Tunnawiya's Ritual. Perhaps this has to do with the disposal of the ritual objects previously used.

52 The duplicate has "the woman of the deity," and omits the Wise Woman altogether. The "mother of the deity" is a category of priestess, for which see Taggar-Cohen, 2006, 335–68.

53 Text: KUB 9.27 + KUB 7.5 + KUB 7.8. Editions: Hoffner, 1987; Mouton, 2007, 129–41.

54 DUMU.MUNUS *suppessar*: Kloekhorst, 2008, 789, translates "priestess, 'purified woman'," presumably since *supp(a)i-* implies a sacrilized state rather than simply "unsullied." Though the two things certainly are not mutually exclusive (Mouton [2007: 136] translates "fille de pureté sacrée," "très certainement une vierge" [n. 121]), it is by no means a given that virginity was particularly valued in Hittite society.

55 Symbolic of menstrual blood and semen, respectively, as per Melchert, 2001, 406–8; 2003, 283.

56 Literally, behavior or custom. Translation follows Hoffner. See Miller, 2010a, 85 on the significance of the word *saklai-* in understanding this as a ritual against homosexuality.

57 Translation follows Miller, 2010a, 86.

58 Following Miller, 2010a, 86–87.

59 "You" meaning the goddess. That is, he fails to access the goddess's inspiration and respond to the girl.

60 Following Hoffner's understanding of *appa* here; 1987, 284.

61 That is, the nocturnal sun.

62 Literally "look up at."

63 Text: A. KUB 9.31; B. HT 1; C. KUB 9.32; D. KUB 41.18; E. KUB 41.17; F. KBo 13.212; G. FHL 95; H. KBo 44.15. Edition: Dinçol, 1985. The many minor variations between the duplicates are not taken into account in this translation.

64 See Collins, 2010.
65 Following C. Duplicates A, B, and D have "I take these things … ," but the expected list of ingredients does not follow.
66 See Miller, 2004, 485–87 on the use of (and shifting between) first and third person in the ŠU.GI rituals.
67 Lit. "below."
68 That is, they kill the animals by stabbing them with the bronze knives.
69 Duplicates B and C, both of which are only partially preserved, seem to differ here. This translation follows C, as restored by B.
70 Cf. CHD P: 53b (sub *pai-*) "but do not give(?) yourself under a human being."
71 Translation of these last two sentences follows Cohen, 2002, 55.
72 We expect the solar deity here and the Sun God of Heaven who appears five lines later, to be one and the same, however it is odd that the male Sun God would have been offered a ewe. For this reason I prefer to understand the solar deity here as the Sun Goddess.

Bibliography

Bawanypeck, Daliah, 2005. *Die Rituale der Auguren*, Heidelberg: Winter.
Beckman, Gary, 1993. "From Cradle to Grave: Women's Role in Hittite Medicine and Magic," *Journal of Ancient Civilizations* 8, 25–39.
Cohen, Yoram, 2002. *Taboos and Prohibitions in Hittite Society. A Study of the Hittite Expression natta āra ('not permitted')*, Heidelberg: Winter.
Collins, Billie Jean, 2006. "Pigs at the Gate: Hittite Pig Sacrifice in Its Eastern Mediterranean Context," *Journal of Ancient Near Eastern Religions*, 6, 155–88.
——, 2010. "Hittite Religion and the West.", in Yoram Cohen, Amir Gilan, and Jared L. Miller, eds, *Pax Hethitica: Studies on the Hittites and Their Neighbors in Honour of Itamar Singer*, Wiesbaden: Harrassowitz, 5–17.
Cornil, P., 1999. "La tradition écrite des texts magiques hittites," *Ktema* 24, 7–16.
Dinçol, Ali M., 1985. "Ashella Rituali (CTH 394) ve Hititlerde Salgın Hastalıklara Karşı Yapılan Majik İşlemlere Toplu Bir Bakış [Das Ritual von Ashella (CTH 394) und ein überblick über die magischen Handlungen gegen die Seuchen bei den Hethitern]," *Belleten* 49, 1–40.
Forlanini, M., 2005. "Hattušili II.—Geschöpf der Forscher oder vergessener König?" *Altorientalische Forschungen* 32, 230–45.
Freu, Jacques, 1995. "De l'ancien royaume au nouvel empire: les temps obscurs de la monarchie hittite," *Atti del II congresso internazionale di hittitologia, Pavia 28 giugno – 2 luglio 1993*, Pavia: Gianni Iuculano Editore.
Goetze, Albrecht, 1938. *The Hittite Ritual of Tunnawi*, New Haven: American Oriental Society.
Haas, Volkert, 2003. *Materia Magica et Medica Hethitica. Ein Beitrag zur Heilkunde im Alten Orient*, Berlin: de Gruyter.
Hoffner, Harry A. Jr., 1987. "Paskuwatti's Ritual against Sexual Impotence (CTH 406)," *Aula Orientalis* 5, 271–87.
Hutter, Manfred, 2003. "Aspects of Luwian Religion," in H. C. Melchert, ed., *The Luwians*, Leiden: Brill, 211–80.
Kassian, Alexei S., 2000. *Two Middle Hittite Rituals Mentioning ᶠZiplantawija, Sister of the Hittite King ᵐTuthalija II/I*, Moscow: Paleograph.
Kloekhorst, Alwin, 2008. *Etymological Dictionary of the Hittite Inherited Lexicon*, Leiden: Brill.

Marizza, Marco, 2010. "La Papponimia nel Mondo Ittita: Casi Accertati e Casi Presunti," *Kaskal* 7: 85–97.

Mascheroni, Lorenza M., 1984. "Scribi Hurriti a Bogazköy: Una Verifica Prosopografica," *Studi Micenei ed Egeo-Anatolici* 24: 151–73.

McMahon, Gregory, 1991. *The Hittite State Cult of the Tutelary Deities*, Chicago: The Oriental Institute of the University of Chicago.

——, 1995. "A Public Ritual for the Tutelary Deity of the Hunting Bag and the Heptad," in *Atti del II congresso internazionale di hittitologia, Pavia 28 giugno – 2 luglio 1993*, Pavia: Studia Mediterranea, 263–268.

Melchert, H. Craig, 2001. "A Hittite Fertility Rite?," *Studien zu den Bogazköy-Texten* 45, 404–9.

——, 2003. "Hittite *antaka*-'loins' and an Overlooked Myth about Fire," in G. Beckman, R. Beal and G. McMahon, eds., *Hittite Studies in Honor of Harry A. Hoffner Jr. on the Occasion of His 65th Birthday*. Winona Lake: Eisenbrauns, 281–87.

Miller, Jared, 2004. *Studies in the Origins, Development and Interpretation of the Kizzuwatna Rituals*, Wiesbaden: Harrassowitz.

——, 2010a. "Paskuwatti's Ritual: Remedy for Impotence or Antidote to Homosexuality?," *Journal of Ancient Near Eastern Religions* 10, 83–89.

——, 2010b. "Practice and Perception of Black Magic among the Hittites," *Altorientalische Forschungen* 37, 167–85.

Mouton, Alice, 2007. *Rêves hittites: Contribution à une histoire et une anthropologie du rêve en Anatolie ancienne*. Leiden: Brill.

Otten, Heinrich and Jana Siegelova, 1970. "Die hetitischen Gula-Gottheiten und die Erschaffung der Menschen." *Archiv für Orientforschung* 23, 32–38.

Puhvel, Jaan, 1991. *Hittite Etymological Dictionary Vol 3: Words beginning with H (Trends in Linguistics Documentation 5)*, Berlin: de Gruyter.

Rieken, Elisabeth, 2004. "Die hethitische 'Ortsbezugspartikel'-*apa*.", in Th. Poschenrieder, ed., *Die Indogermanistik und ihre Anrainer. Dritte Tagung der vergleichenden Sprachwissenschaftler der neuen Länder (Greifswald in Pommern, 19.-20. Mai 2000)*, Innsbruck: Institut für Sprachen und Literaturen der Universität Innsbruck, 243–58.

Taggar-Cohen, Ada, 2006. *Hittite Priesthood*, Heidelberg: Winter.

Taracha, Piotr, 2009. *Religions of Second Millennium Anatolia*, Wiesbaden: Harrassowitz.

Torri, Giulia, 2003. *La similitudine nella magia analogica Ittita*, Rome: Herder.

12

HURRO-HITTITE STORIES AND HITTITE PREGNANCY AND BIRTH RITUALS

Mary Bachvarova

Hurro-Hittite stories

The libraries of the Hittite capital provide us access to the myths of a variety of cultures in a variety of languages, including indigenous (pre-Hittite) Hattic and imported Hurrian stories. Indeed, Hattusa is currently our primary source for Hurrian mythology, both in the original Hurrian and in Hittite. Most of the translations provided here are of a set of texts that belong more or less securely to the Hurro-Hittite genre of narrative poetry; oral-derived texts drawn from a bilingual oral poetic tradition that was originally the province of Hurrian-speakers, but was adopted by Hittite-speakers.[1] Hurro-Hittite song addressed a shared set of concerns about the interactions between mankind and the divine, superior and subordinate, and men and women. At least some Hurro-Hittite songs were performed during festivals,[2] although other settings can also easily be imagined, such as entertainment at court, or to provide an admonitory example in magic rituals.

The following texts, extracts of which are translated here, include canonical examples of Hurro-Hittite narrative song: the *Song of Birth* (originally called by modern scholars the *Song of Kumarbi* or the *Song of Kingship in Heaven*),[3] the *Song of Hedammu*, and the *Song of Ullikummi*. I also include a fragment about Mt. Wasitta in labor, a fragment of an episode involving the goddess of sexuality and the Mountain Pishaisha, and the *Song of Keshshi*. Overall we get a sense of respect for women's power to conceive and to seduce and manipulate men through their sexuality, but the misogynistic attitude of the ancient Greeks and Romans is refreshingly absent. Acknowledgment of women's special ability to harness and interpret the magical power of words also comes through, complementing the portrait of Anatolian sorceresses in the magical incantations translated in other sections of this volume.

I translate only Hittite versions here, unless otherwise specified.[4]

Hurro-Hittite songs I: the Kumarbi cycle

The Kumarbi cycle is a set of songs grouped together by modern scholars because they share a common theme: the ascent of the Storm-god, in Hurrian

Teshshub, in Hittite Tarhun, to kingship in heaven and his subsequent battles to maintain control against the chthonic god Kumarbi. They include the *Song of Birth*, the *Song of Hedammu*, and the *Song of Ullikummi*. Translations of these stories are widely available, but the transliteration of the *Song of Birth* has been updated, leading to new readings, and I offer some new interpretations of the texts. There are thematic connections with the two fragments translated in the next section, as well as with the Hittite birth rituals.

The Song of Birth

This text presents the rise to power of the Storm-god, born from the unnatural union of the gods Anu and Kumarbi. It is our most graphic description of childbirth outside of the birth rituals and provides insight into the role of midwives. There are obvious comparisons with the myths of the castration of Ouranos by his son Kronos, the swallowing and subsequent vomiting forth of his children by Kronos, when fed a rock by his wife Maia, and with the birth of Aphrodite, who issues forth from the head of her father Zeus, who had swallowed her mother Metis to prevent her from giving birth to a child more powerful than him.[5] But, whereas the Greek myth has misogynistic overtones, providing the powerful virgin goddess with a lineage untainted by femininity, the Hurro-Hittite story provides for the perfect combination of heaven (Anu) and earth (Kumarbi) in a single god, who is therefore invincible. Notable is the absence in Hurro-Hittite myth of examples of female deities attempting to bring forth young on their own, as found in Greek myth with the Python and Typhon, both products of parthenogenesis, and in Mesopotamian myths with Ninmah and Tiamat.[6]

The exact phrasing of the implanting of Anu's sperm in Kumarbi can tell us about ideas concerning the woman's role in the conception of the child. It is imagined as the uniting of Anu's "manliness" with the "heart" or "inside" (ŠÀ, Hitt. *kard-*, *ištarna-*) of Kumarbi,[7] just as bronze is formed from white tin (sperm) and red copper (mentrual blood, often considered to nourish the fetus in traditional belief systems).[8] We can compare the twining of red and white wool in a Hittite fertility ritual.[9] The term "heart" or "inside" is used in the myth to refer to the space in which the "burden" of the child is placed. The comparison with the creation of bronze from the two metals tin and copper suggests, first of all, that Hurrians and Hittites thought that the process of gestation involved heating the fetus to achieve the change of state, a common theory cross-culturally,[10] and, more specifically, that the metaphor of the womb as crucible, found in Mesopotamian texts,[11] was familiar farther west.

As with the Sumerian myth *Enki and Ninhursag*, there is the question of how the child will exit Kumarbi's body, which lacks the proper orifice. In the end, he emerges from the "Good Place."[12] What this place is, is unclear, but it appears to be at or near the top of the head. Therefore, it may refer to the three sutures in the human skull, where the plates are joined. In that case the sutures represent the seamlines where the Fate-goddesses close up Kumarbi's skull after Tarhun

273

comes out. The Hittite Fate-goddesses were called *Gulšeš*, "inscribers," an action done on wood or stone. Thus, they had the expertise to mend the break in the skull.

There is a second pregnancy and birth, twins engendered by Tarhun's wagon with the Earth in the Abzu, the primordial waters, but how that fits into the larger trajectory of the story is unclear. The Abzu is given the determinative that marks it as a city, rather than a cosmic place, so it is unclear whether it is imagined to be a meeting place for the tryst between the two entities, heavenly[13] and chthonic, or the place in which the fetus is gestated. The messenger who reports the good news receives gifts.

The tablet translated here is the first tablet of a longer work, of which no more has been preserved. It is a New Hittite copy of a worn original. I translate here only the opening and the passages relevant to conception, pregnancy, and birth.[14]

(§1, 1.A i 1–4) [...] who are the [F]ormer Gods, let the great [Form]er Gods listen, let Na[ra, Napshara, Mink]i, Ammunki listen, let Amme[z]zadu, [Alulu,], father (and) mother listen.[15]

(§2, 1.A i 5–11) Let [Enlil (and) Abad]u, father (and) mother of Ishhara,[16] listen. Let Enlil [(and) Ninli]l, who are great (and) mi[g]hty gods [below] and [ab]ove, [...] and [the s]hining one[17] listen. Long ago, i[n f]ormer years, Alalu was king in heaven. Alalu was on the throne, and Great Anu, foremost of the gods, was stepping before him, and he kept bow[i]ng down at his feet and kept putting drinking cups in his hand.

(§3, 1.A i 12–17) As just nine years were counted off Alalu was king in heaven, and in the ninth year Anu [w]ent in batt[le] against Alalu. He defeated him, Alalu. He ran away before him. Down he went into the Dark Earth. He went down into the Dark Earth, and Anu seated himself on the throne. Anu was sitting on the throne, and great Kumarbi kept giving him to drink. He kept bowing down at his feet and putting drinking cups in his hand.

(§4, 1.A i 18–24) As just nine years were counted off Anu was king in heaven, and in the ninth year Anu went in battle against Kumarbi.[18] Kumarbi, the seed of Alalu, went in battle against Anu, and Anu was no longer able to withstand the eyes of Kumarbi. He broke away from Kumarbi and from his hands. Anu ran, he set off for heaven. Kumarbi assaulted him from behind. He grabbed Anu (by) the feet and dragged him down from heaven.

(§5, 1.A i 25–9) He bit his buttocks[19] and his manliness fused with Kumarbi's heart like bronze. When Kumarbi swallowed down the manliness of Anu, he rejoiced and laughed. Anu turned back to him and began to say <to> Kumarbi, "Did you rejoice before [yo]ur heart because you swallowed my manliness?

(§6, 1.A i 30–6) "Don't rejoice before your heart. I have put a burden inside your heart. First, I have impregnated you with Tarhun, the august one. Second, I have also impregnated you with the River Aranzah (the Tigris), not to be resisted. Third, I have also impregnated you with august Tashmishu. I have also placed three terrifying gods as burdens inside your heart.[20] You will proceed to finish (the pregnancy?) by smashing the cliffs of Mt. Tassa with your head."

(§7, 1.A i 37–41) When Anu finished speaking, [he] went up to heaven and he concealed himself. [K]um[arbi] spat forth from his mouth, the wise king spat forth from his mouth s[pit and manliness][21] mixed together. What Kumarbi s[pat] forth, [M]t. Ganzura ac[cepted] as a fearsome god.

(§8, 1.A i 42–46) [Kuma]rbi, upset(?), [went to] Nipp[ur ...] went. On the lordly ... him [...] sat down Kumarbi ... not [...] [c] ounts off. The seventh month arriv[ed ...] in his heart [...].

There is a gap of about 45 lines before we pick up the narrative in column ii.

(§9', 1.A ii 1–3) ["...] Kumarbi. Let him come [f]orth from his vigorous [...], or [...] come f[o]rth from his *hu[wa]lpanzana*,[22] or let come forth from his 'goo[d p]lace'."

(§10', 1.A ii 4–15) A.GILIM (an epithet of Tarhun) [began] to speak words before Kumarbi, in his heart (i.e., from inside him), "May you be living,[23] l[or]d of wisdom (and) the headwaters,[24] if/when to come out [...], Kumarbi, you bit[25] below. Which ones [...]. Earth will give me her power. Heaven will g[ive] me [hi]s h[er]oism, and Anu will give me [hi]s manliness, and Kumarbi will give me his wisdom. Nara will give me his powerfulness, and Napshara will give me [his ...], En[li]l will give me his power, [his ...], his fearsomeness, and [hi]s wisdom. [...] all. ... heart ...

The text of the rest of this paragraph, and most of the next two paragraphs, are too fragmentary to translate. There is mention of other attributes presumably given to Tarhun, including his bull Sheri and a wagon in which the Storm-god will ride. His brother Suwaliyat will give him something. Anu speaks, saying, "Let him come." There is mention of "like a woman," and where Tarhun will emerge is again discussed. I pick up the narrative at the end of §12'.

(§12', 1.A ii 28) " ... come. If it is good, [come] from the 'good [place']."

(§13', 1.A ii 29–38) He began to speak to Kumarbi in his heart, "[...] they stand ... the place. If I [come from X,] he will break [the X thing]s like a reed. I[f] I come [f]orth from the 'good place'

I will defile myself in that way also. In heaven, on earth [...]. I will defile myself inside by means of the ear. But, if I come forth from the 'good place' [...] l[ike] a woman (nom.) [...] he will moan for my sake. When me, Tarhun of Heaven in [...] ... he decreed it within. He broke him [li]ke a stone, Kumarbi, his skull. He came forth from him by means of his skull, Shining-Faced One, the hero, the king."[26]

(§14', 1.A ii 39–45) When he went, he stepped before Ea, Kumar[bi b]owed. He fell down, Kumarbi. From [...] he was [a]ltered. [Kumarb]i so[ught] out the god Abundance.[27] In front of Ea [he began to] speak, "Give me the [ch]ild. I will eat [hi]m up. Which woman to me [doe]s [X]. And which ones to me Tarhun (direct object) [...] I will eat [u]p. Like [a re]ed I will crus[h him]."

The next few lines of the paragraph are too fragmentary to be translated. It appears that a rock is prepared to be given to Kumarbi to eat. I pick up the translation in line 50.

(§14', 1.A ii 50–54) [... began] to l[ook] at him. [...] Kumarbi began to e[a]t [...]. But the [basal]t [broke off/damaged] Kumarbi's teeth in his mouth. [W]hen his teeth in his mouth were [broken/injured] he began to weep.

(§15', 1.A ii 55–65) [... Kum]arbi (nom.). [He began to] spea[k] words, "[I] was afraid of, [...]." Like old age Kumarbi (nom.) [...]. To Kumarbi he began to speak, "Let them call [it X]. Let it lie in [X place]." And, the basalt he threw in [... a hol]e. "Let them proceed to call you [...]. Let [weal]thy [men], heroes, (and) lords [sac]rifice cattle [(and) sheep] to you, and let poor men make offerings with [groats] to you."

At this point the text becomes too fragmentary for translation. The gist appears to be the establishment of sacrifices among the lands for the rock, in commemoration of Tarhun's birth.[28]

(§16', 1.A ii 71–75) [The rich men] began to sacrifice with [cattle (and) sheep]. [The poor men] began to make an offering with [gr]oats ... they began to [...]. His skull like a garment [they closed up]. They closed up Kumarbi, his skull, from [which] place the hero, Tarhun, came forth.

(§17', 1.A ii 76) [... the Fa]te-[goddess]es. His "good place" like a garment [they closed up].

The rest of the paragraph is too poorly preserved to translate, but "the Aranzah river ... came forth," "they birthed him, Kumarbi ... like a woman of the bed."[29] Then there is mention of Mt. Kanzura, and again we are told that "the hero came forth … from the 'good place'," and there is mention of Anu.

We pick up the text in column iii of the reverse. Teshshub appears to have seized power, and Kumarbi begins to think of ways of deposing him. Teshshub utters curses against his enemies, then is warned by his bulls Sheri and Tauri to be careful how he speaks, while Ea too is upset at Teshshub's dangerous words.

Only the last three paragraphs of column iv and the colophon are preserved. I pick up the translation when the impregnation of Earth is being described.

> (§27''', 2.A iv 6'–16') [When] the sixth [mon]th came, the Wagon […] the manli[ness] of the Wagon […] the Wagon [went?] back to the (city) A[bzu?]. He took [wis]dom to his mind […] Ea, lord of wis[dom] did [X]. But Earth we[nt] to the city Abzu [… kn]ows. And Ea, [lord of] wisdom, [c]ounts. The first month, the [second month, the third month went]. The fourth [mo]nth, the fifth month, the sixth month went. [The seventh month], the eighth [m]onth, the ninth month went. The ten[th] month [arrived]. In the tenth month Earth [began to] cry out.
>
> (§28''', 2.A iv 17'–27') When Earth cried out [s]he gave birth to [two] children. A messenger went […]. E[a] on [h]is throne approved […] brough[t] the fine word: "[…] Earth h[as] borne two children […]." Ea [he]ard the words. To him […] by [mo]uth the mess[enger] who went. […] the king repeatedly ga[v]e a gift. To him/her a garment [for his] b[ody]. To him a pull-over garment for his chest […], and an *ipantu*-garment of silver fo[r the mes]senger. Around their middle [a piece of clothing] s/he wind[s].

The Song of Hedammu

In this story we learn of how Tarhun vanquished the deposed Kumarbi again by defeating his sea-serpent son Hedammu, fathered off the sea-god's daughter. We learn here indirectly about marriage negotiations in the human world.

Rather than using force against Hedammu, Tarhun turns to the seductive charms of his sister *IŠTAR*. The scene of seduction by music and dance on the shore of the sea is reminiscent of the actions of the Sirens in the *Odyssey*, who were famous for luring sailors to their death. The goddess, whose name was typically written with the Akkadogram *IŠTAR* in texts from Hattusa, is in Hurrian versions of the Hurro-Hittite narrative tradition the Hurrian goddess Shawushka, who was merged with the Mesopotamian Ishtar in the Hurrian-controlled city of Nineveh by early in the second millennium. In Hittite versions she is the Hittite goddess Anzili, who also appears in birth incantations.[30] From these texts we see that Anzili shared traits with the Mesopotamian goddess and could be syncretized with her via Shawushka. However, the Hurrian and Hittite goddesses were also closely connected to magic, and more generally in Anatolia magic was the special province of goddesses such as Kamrusepa and—in the mortal realm—women (often "Old Women", or, as Collins translates, "Wise Women"), as discussed in this volume in the sections on Kamrusepa and Hittite magic rituals.

I translate only the passages relevant to women's life in the ancient Near East. The text, extending over several tablets, is in fragments, with duplicates and parallels, whose precise order is yet to be determined. Thus, I do not number the paragraphs, and fragment numbers are intended only for reference.

The following passage begins partway through the first paragraph on the tablet, which is probably the second tablet in this recension.[31]

> (2.A i 1–14) [The Sea] heard. [(His mind inside) rejoi]ced. [He put] his foot on a s[tool]. They put a rhyton in the hand of the Sea. The grea[t Sea] [began to] spe[ak] a word in reply to Kumarbi, "[To u]s the matter is good, Kumarbi, [fa(ther) of] the gods. Come [(to me)] on the seventh day, in my house, [...] my daughter [She]r-tapshuruhi is [...] in length and in [wi]dth she is one mile. Her, [Sh]ert[ap]shuruhi, [you will drink] like sweet milk." When Kumarbi heard, he rejoiced [in]side, and when night time arrived [... They] led [fo]rth the great Sea from Kumarbi's house with [...], *arkammi*-drums, and g[*algaltur*]i-cymbals of bronze and (with toasts) from rhyta of bronze. They led him away [t]o his house. In [his hous]e he sat on a beautiful chair. The Sea looked forward to Kumarbi('s visit) on the seventh day.[32]

When the child is born, in the form of a sea-snake, he devours aquatic creatures at a great rate. A meeting between Kumarbi and the Sea to ask him to provide a wet-nurse for the child is set up by a discussion with Kumarbi's "vizier" Mukishanu, during which they take precautions that they will not be overheard by IŠTAR (Anzili) of Nineveh by blocking off the windows and eliminating any crawling or slithering creature.[33] Anzili catches sight of the monster and is horrified. She listens in on the conversation between Kumarbi and the Sea by turning herself into a snake, despite their precautions, then goes to report to her brother the Storm-god.[34] We can compare her actions in *Elkunirsa and Ashertu*, in which she disguises herself as a cup and a bird in order to listen in on a conversation for her brother.[35]

I pick up the translation in the second paragraph preserved in this particular fragment. The first mentions Hedammu three times, and "my sin."

> (9.A ii 7'–11') [As ...] finished [speaki]ng, s/he [went] a[(way)] (and) Anzil(i) wen[t] into the bath-house. [...] she went [(in)] to [(bathe)]. She bathed [... she (did) X], and [(with)] sweet [(fine oil)] she anointed herself. [(She)] ornament(ed) herself, [(and beauty was)] running after [(her)] like puppies.

(9.A ii 12'–16') [Anzili] began to speak [to Ninatta (and) K]ulitta,³⁶ [" ...] take the [galgaltu]ri-cymbals. On the sho[re] of the sea [(with the arkammi-drum strike) on the right side] and on the [le]ft strike the galgalturi-cymbals [(for kingship) ...] perhaps the message [he] wi[ll] hear [...]. We will see him when [...].³⁷

There are at least two parts to the scene in which Anzili meets and seduces Hedammu. In the first part she exposes her naked limbs to the snake; he is aroused and asks who she is. In the second, she feeds him a potion, apparently putting him to sleep. The snake ejaculates copiously, swamping many towns on the shore with his ejaculate, which I envision as resembling frog spawn. It is the latter part I translate here:

(4.A iv 3'–10') [...] In heaven the clouds [...] from the [powe]rful waters [...] when [Anzil]i went, the queen of Nineveh, [(she approved. She sprinkled beaut)]y, šaḫi, and [parnull]i³⁸ in the powerful waters. The beauty, š[aḫi], (and) parnulli dissolved in [(the waters and when Hedammu) tasted the sce]nt, the beer, [a sweet] dream seized victorious Hedammu, [(hi)s (mental powers)]. He was dreaming like an ox or an a[(s)]s. [...] and he recognized [no]thing and was eating frogs and lizards.
(4.A iv 11'–18') [Anzili] began to speak [(to Hedammu)], "C[ome] up again, from the po[(werful) water]s come straight up, cutting through the middle. 90,000 [...] pulls the place from the earth, and Anzili holds forth [before Hedammu] her naked limb[s]. Hedammu [...] his manliness springs forth. His manline[ss ...]. He impregnates repeatedly [pl. object ...] 130 towns [he] did [X]. And with his belly/embryo(s)³⁹ [...] 70 towns [...] in [... pl. obj.] he finished off. [...] heaps of heads he heap[ed up].⁴⁰

The Song of Ullikummi

Once again Kumarbi tries to defeat his rival Teshshub, this time creating a deaf and blind stone monster that is impervious to Anzili's charms, just as Odysseus has his crew members fill their ears with wax to keep out the sound of the Sirens' songs. The story has Caucasian parallels, both in the birthplace of Ullikummi (his name means 'destroy Kummi!', the home of Teshshub), which seems to have originally been near Lake Van, and in the notion that a child can be conceived by ejaculation onto a rock, a way to circumvent the need for a feminine receptacle for the fetus.⁴¹ Hittite does not mark male or female gender, but it is best to assume that the rock (perunaš) is male, since the deity Perwa, god of cliffs and horses, was male.⁴² So, Ullikummi, like Teshshub, is the product of a male-male union.

IŠTAR, Queen of Nineveh, is called tarš[i]kantaš MUNUŠ-aš 'woman of things said over and over again', that is, 'woman of incantations'.⁴³ This seems to acknowledge her involvement in Hurro-Hittite magic, in which *IŠTAR*, that is, Shawushka/Anzili, is a frequent character.[44] In addition, Kumarbi explicitly acknowledges that Anzili/Shawushka is a great sorceress by worrying that she will be able to injure his child with her incantations.

I translate here only the opening and the subsequent sections in which the birth and fostering out of the child is described and in which *IŠTAR* fails to seduce the monster:[45]

(§1, 1.A i 1–4) [...] I sing Kum[arb]i, [father of] al[l the gods] w[ho] repeatedly [t]akes in his mind w[isdom].

(§2, 1.A i 5–8) Kumarbi [repeatedly] ta[kes] wi<s>dom before his mind. [(He repeatedly)] rai[(ses up)] an evil day, an evil being. He se[eks] evil against Tarhun. [(He repeatedly)] raise[(s up)] a rival against Tarhun.

(§3, 1.A i 9–10) Kumarbi repeatedly takes wis[(dom)] before his mind. He [(repeatedly lines)] it [(up)] l[(ike)] stone bead(s).

(§4, 1.A i 11–16) When Kumarbi [(took)] w[(isdom in his mind)], [(he immediately got)] up from his throne. He took his staff with his hand [and (he put)] o[n his feet] the swift wind[s] as shoes. (He set off from)] Urkesh, [(the city)], and [he arrived at] the cool l[(ake.)]

(§5, 1.B i 13–20) [...] in the cool la[ke] a great cliff lies. In length it is three leagues, [and] in width [it is ... leagues] and half a league. What it holds below, [to sleep with it] his desire sprang forth. He slept [wi]th the r[ock]. To it his manliness insid[e ...]. He took it five times, [...] he took it ten times.

(§6, 1.B i 21) [...] he [too]k [th]at staff [...] ...

Kumarbi consults with the Sea about the child. We then pick up the narrative in the middle of a paragraph part way down column iii of exemplar A.

(§10", 1.A iii 7'–9') [She/They] help[ed] to birth him. [...] the rock (nom./gen.) from [...] the child ... Kumarbi [...].

(§11", 1.A iii 10'–14') The [...] women helped to birth him. The Fate-goddesses, the G[reat] Goddess[es lifted up the child].[46] They bounce[d him] on [K]um[arbi's] [k]nees. [Kumar]bi beg[an] to amuse tha[t s]on. [He] be[gan] to sit him upright. He began to [g]ive [him] a fine name.

(§12", 1.A iii 15'–25') Kumarbi began to [sp]eak before [his] mi[nd], "What name [shall I give] to him? Which child the Fate-goddesses, the Great Goddesses gave to me, he sprang from my body like a spear. Com[e], let (his) name be Ullikummi. Let him go up to [kingsh]ip in heaven, let him crush down Kummi, [the beau]tiful city, and let him strike Tarhun. Let him grind [him] completely like [c]haff, and let him pulverize him with his foot [like] ant(s), and let him shred apart Tashmishu like a britt[le re]ed, and let him scatter all the gods down from [heaven] like birds, let him sha[t]ter them [like] empty vessels."

(§13", 1.A iii 26'–36') When Kumarbi fi[nish]ed spe[akin]g words, he [began] to speak before his mind, "To [who]m shall I give him, this child? Who [will take] him for themselves, will treat him as a gift? […], will [take] him into the [dark] earth? L[et] the Sun-god of [Heaven and the Moon-]god [n]ot see him, and le[t] the Storm-god [of] the city Kumm[i], the [h]eroic king, not [see him]. Let him not kill him. Let Anzili, queen of Nineveh, woman of inc[ant]ations, no[t] see him. Let her not shred him apart l[i]ke a brittle reed.

(§14", 1.A iii 37'–45') Kumarbi began to speak to Impal[ur]i, "Impaluri, which words I speak [to you], hold your ear c[o]cked to my words. Take your staff, and pu[t] the swift winds o[n yo]ur [feet] (as) shoes. Go down to the Irsirra-goddesses and say before the Irsirra-goddesses these weight[y] words, 'Come, Kumarbi, father of the gods, calls you to the house of the gods. For which ma[tt]er he calls you, […], come immediately.'"

(§15", 1.A iii 46'–8') "[The Irsirra-goddess]es will take the child. Those ones [will take] him [down into the dark] earth, and the Irsirri-goddesses […] the heroes, and not the great ones […]."

(§16", 1.C iii 4'–8') [When] Impaluri [hear]d [the word, he took] his staff with his hand, he put [his shoe]s [on his feet]. He [wen]t [forth], did Impaluri. He arrived at [the Irsirr]a-[goddesses.]

(§17", 1.C iii 9'–19') [Impaluri] began to [speak in turn] to the Irsirri-goddesses, "Come, Kumar <b> i, father of the gods, [calls yo]u, and for which matter [he calls] you, you [(do not) know]. Hurry! Come!" [(When) the Irs]irra-goddesses hea[(rd), they hur-ried,] they [h]astened. They [got up] from their chairs, and they went all the way to Kumarbi's house without stopping. [(Kumarbi)] began [(to)] s[(peak)] to the [I]rsirra-goddesses.

(§18", 1.B iii 10'–19') "[T]ake [(this)] child] and [(tre)a]t him as a gift. Tak[e] him to the Dark Earth. [(H)]urry, hasten. Place him as a spear on Ubelluri's right shoulder. In one day let him grow a cubit, and in one month [le]t him grow an IKU (3,600m²), but whatever rock strikes his head, let his eyes be covered (against it)."

(§19", 1.A iv 6'–12') When the Irsirr[a-]goddesses heard the [wo]rds, they took [the child] from Kumarb[i's] knees, and the Irsir[ra-]goddesses lifted the child. They pressed [him] in t[heir] bosom like a garment. They lifted him [lik]e the wind[s]. They bounced him on Enlil's knees. [En]lil raised his eyes and gaze[d] at the child. He was standing in front of the divinity, and his body was made of stone, of b[a]salt.

Enlil wonders at the child and worries that the conflict between Kumarbi and Tarhun is entering a new phase. The child is placed on Ubelluri's shoulder and grows rapidly until the Sun-god notices him and goes to Tarhun's house to report this new problem. At this point we switch to the second tablet, of which there are seven exemplars. Tarhun now goes with his brother Tashmishu to discuss the issue with Anzili, who warns him about his new rival, and seems to complain about the fact that she is not male, and thus is allowed only certain courses of action.

(§33", 2.A i 14'–28') [And, a]fter [the Sun-god] of Heaven (left), Tarhun t[ook wi]sdom before his mind. Tarhun a[nd] Tashmishu took each other [b]y the h[and]. [Fro]m the *kuntarra*-building, from the temple they w[(ent)] forth […], and Anzili cam[(e)] away from heaven with heroicness. [(An)]zili spoke in turn to her mind. "Wher[(e)] are they running inside, the two brothers?" She sw[ift]ly(?)[47] stood, Anzili. Before her two [brothers] she stood up. They to[o]k each other by the hand. They went up to Mt. Hazzi, and the king of Kummi was setting his eyes, he was setting his eyes on the dreadful basalt. At the dreadful basalt he looked, and he was altered […] because of anger.

(§34", 2.A i 29'–42') Tarhun sat on the ground, and his tears were flowing [for]th like canals. Tarhun, [w]eeping, speaks the word, "Who [th]en will behold the strife caused by this one? Who will [do b]attle? Who then will behold the fearsome qualities of [this] one?" Anzili speaks [in ret]urn to the Storm-god, "My brother, he does not [kn]ow even a little mental force, although heroism[48] has been given to him tenfold. […] which child they help to birth […] you do not know [his] mental force. […] we were in the house of Ea […] I was a man, [b]ut you … him […]. I will go […].

After about 26 lost or broken lines, we pick up the narrative in column ii of version A, as Anzili attempts to seduce the rock monster.

(§36"', 2.A ii 5'–12') She got dressed. [She] or[namented herself.] She [went away] from Nineveh. [She took] her lyre (and) *galgalturi*-cymbals [with her] ha[nd.] Anz[ili] set out [to the sea]. She burne <d> cedar as incense, and she struck her [ly]re (and) *galgaltur-i*-cymbals. She made her golden (ornaments) flutter. She took up a song, and heave[n] and [e]arth [we]re singing responsively with her.

(§37''', 2.A ii 13'–25') Anzili sings, and she puts on a stone of the sea and a pebble. There is a great wav[e] from the sea. The great wave says to Anzili, "Before whom are you singing, and before whom are you filling your mouth with wi[nd]? The man is deaf, and he doe[s not] hear. He is blind in his [ey]es, and he does not see. He h[as] no mercy. Go away, Anzili, and [f]ind your brother, while he is not yet heroic, while the skull of his head has not yet become terrifying."

(§38''', 2.A ii 26'–30') When Anzili heard this, she extinguished the c[edar], and she threw away her lyre (and) [ga]/galt[uri]-cymbals, and her gold (ornament)s [...]. Crying out, she [...] she set out [...].

The gods proceed to a cataclysmic battle, but the gods are unable to vanquish Ullikummi until Ea advises them to take the primeval copper cutting tool from the "grandfatherly" storehouse and cut him off from the shoulder of Ubelluri, as if his umbilical cord is finally cut.

Hurro-Hittite song II: fragments

Mt. Wasitta in labor

This New Hittite fragment may belong to an alternate texualization of the myth of Ullikummi.[49] Normally, mountains were conceived of as male. Thus, we have another example of imagining a world in which the feminine power to gestate and give birth could be co-opted by male entities. As with the birth of the rock monster, the story appears to explain volcanic activity.[50] The story depends on the double meaning of the verb *tuḫḫai* "smoke; moan, cry out," that allows the cries of labor to be equated with the smoke and steam that pours forth with a pyroclastic flow.[51]

(§1', i/iv 3'–11') [...] body [...]. He [k]nows/[ex]periences, Kumarbi, [...]. He [keeps] co[unting] the days. [...] He keeps marking off the [mo]nths. [...] with [t]his table [...]. The days [...]. The first [mo]nth went by, the second month arrived, [the third month, the fourth month], the fifth [month], the sixth month, the seventh month, the eighth month arrive[d, the ninth month, the tenth month arrived. He was] ready to [e]mit smoke/ to [c]ry out (in labor).

(§2', i/iv 12'–22') [M]t. Wasitta moaned. Kumarbi heard the [mo]aning [...] in [his house (or: city)]. Mt. Wasitta [m]oaned. All the mountains [w]ent to him t[o] see. To Mt. Wasitta all the mountains began to say, "Mt. Wasitta, [w]hy are you [cr]ying out? You have not known the cries of labor since childhood. The Fates

283

have [n]ot inscribed it for you, nor would your mother have given birth [to y]ou for it." Mt. Wasitta began to answer all the mountains, "I have not known the cries of labor since childhood. The fates have not inscribed it for me, nor did my mother give birth to me for it.

(§3', i/iv 23'–9') "[…] when among the mountains a stranger [came], he made me sleep with him. From that moment on […] I began to cry out […] … wise ones. The next [month. …] The ninth [month we]nt by. The tenth month arrived. [I was r]ead[y] to cry out. […] smok[e]/moani[ng …

Ishtar and Mt. Pishaisha

In this New Hittite fragment, the Syrian Mount Pishaisha takes advantage of *IŠTAR*/Shawushka/Anzili (with whom he was often partnered in cult), raping her as she sleeps. The story thus has parallels with the Sumerian *Inanna and Shukaletuda*, in which a gardener rapes the sleeping Inanna.[52] Haas (2006: 212) further compares it to the Greek myth of the Anatolian goddess Agdistis, raped on a mountainside. To appease the enraged goddess and save his life, the mountain tells her a story that fills in some gaps in the cycle of extant stories about how the Storm-god seized and maintained his kingship. It is the earliest attestation of the narrative conceit that provides the frame of *A Thousand and One Arabian Nights*, but there it is the sultan who has been sexually betrayed by an unfaithful wife, and, embittered, decides to marry then immediately execute a series of virgins, only to be seduced by the story-telling powers of Scheherazad.[53]

(§1', ii? 2'–20') The mount[ain] he [saw?] Anzili, her [naked][54] limbs. His desire to sleep [with her sprang] f[orth]. Mt. Pishaisha slept with [Anzili …] Anzili […] leapt up. [Her] limb[s …] "Who at this time […] did dishonor to me? To Tarhun not […] furthermore another enemy. […] an enemy to him. Anzili in her anger sa[id] this. Mt. Pishaisha heard ang[ry] Anzili, her words, and he was afraid, and he gro[veled] down a[t Anzili's] knees like a (bent) apple tree. [He said,] "Don't kill me. I will speak to you […] life. With what […] Tarhun of Heaven contests the Sea, [and with] w[hat] the a[ngry] mountains contest in battle Tarhun of Heaven. Long ago Na[mni] and Hazzi, the mountains, …

Hurro-Hittite song III: the Song of Keshshi

The New Hittite *Song of Keshshi* tells the story of a hunter who loved his wife so much he neglected his mother and the gods and could no longer be successful in the hunt. In the Hurrian *Song of Keshshi*, the hunter and his wife Shinda(li)meni face each other in the assembly of elders, just as in the story of the *Sun-god, the*

Cow, and the Fisherman pits the fisherman's two sons, "Good" (*ḫandanza*) and "Bad" (*ḫuwappaš*), against each other in a public argument before the assembly. As Shinda(li)meni's brother is explicitly described as a "bad man" in the Hittite version, it appears that Shinda(li)meni is meant to represent the side of wrong, or at least is influenced by her evil brother.[55] Her characterization thus presents a negative example that allows for an exploration of the conflicts and choices a woman needs to make when she marries and must shift her loyalties to her husband's family, to help maintain his family line rather than her original family. Shinda(li)meni appears in a Hurrian childbirth incantation as a midwife.[56] Clearly, we are unable to fully appreciate the back story attached to this character.

As for the scene in assembly, it is not impossible that it refracts a reality in which women could appear in public to argue their case. Certainly we have evidence of women throughout Hittite history for which such an occasion would arise; for example, the disloyal sister of the Old Hittite king Hattusili I, whom he banishes along with her son, whom he had chosen as his successor; or the stepmother of the New Hittite king Mursili II, whom he suspected of causing his wife's death; or the daughter of King Benteshina of Amurru, whose divorce from King Ammistamru II of Ugarit was an international affair.[57]

Finally, Keshshi's mother interprets a set of seven dreams, a sequence of events also found twice in the Akkadian *Epic of Gilgamesh*. There his mother Ninsun interprets the first set, and his companion Enkidu interprets the second set. That older women were considered to be particularly adept at dream interpretation is suggested by the fact that this is one of the tasks that "Old Women" carry out at the Hittite court.[58]

This narrative is unusual in that its Hurrian version is relatively well-preserved, enough to distinguish at least five separate tablets. At least one recension of the Hurrian version (which differs markedly from the Hittite one) was very long, on the face of it more than fourteen tablets, although it is safer to say more than six tablets.[59] There is also a piece of an Akkadian version from Amarna in Egypt.[60]

What remains of the Hurrian version is quite different from the Hittite one. Here the concern seems to be a demand from a steward that Keshshi provide a part of his harvest of emmer wheat, which causes Keshshi to weep and pray to the gods. He has dreams in this version, but they appear to be about the crisis involving the wheat, rather than hunting and illness. There is mention of a man Urumzi and a woman Tadi[zuli], who bears the same name as the betrothed of Gurparanzah, whose story is translated below. Dijkstra suggests they are Keshshi's parents. His ancestor god does play an important role, as in the Hittite version, and the old men, who are the people who make up the assembly before whom he and his wife argue their case, also appear in the Hittite version. It may be that Keshshi is a man who finds himself going from one disaster to another.[61]

I present here what remains of the Hittite version.[62]

(§1', 1.A ii 2'–3') [...] Keshshi (nom. sing.) the gods [...] he became a hunter [...] every[one].

(§2', 1.A ii 4'–8') [...] a bad [m]an, Udubsharri, his sister Keshshi [took] as [h]is w[if]e. The name of the woman was Shindalimeni. She was perfect, endowed w[ith] everything. Keshshi only list[ened] to his wife, and Keshshi was no longer paying [att]ention to the gods, the offering(s) with thick bread. He wasn't going into the mountains to hunt any longer. He only listened to [his] wife.

(§3', 1.A ii 9'–14') His mother began to speak to Keshshi, "You love your wife alone, and you no longer go into the mountains to hunt. You don't bring back anything for me." Keshshi took up his spear, and he called his little dogs (to follow) behind him. He went into Mt. Natara to hunt. The gods were angry with Keshshi over the offering(s), and they hid away all the game from him.

(§4', 1.A ii 15'–19') [K]eshshi wandered three months in the mountains, but he did not want to return empty-handed to his city in hunger (and) thirst, and [e]vil illness holds Keshshi in the third month. Keshshi [...] on a tree [...] the gods, the sons [o]f the mountains. Keshshi (acc.) to eat [...], but the father-god [of] Keshshi down from the mountain [...].

(§5', 1.A ii 20') "[Wh]y do you eat him, K[eshshi], in the mountains?"

The rest of the paragraph is too fragmentary to translate. In column iii we learn of some of Keshshi's seven dreams. In the third one someone brings something from Mt. Natara to a city, and female servants are mentioned. For the fourth and following dreams we switch to column ii of another tablet, which overlaps with what we have of the end of 1.A, although this version is not identical.

(§9", 2.A ii 4'–6') He also < saw > a fourth dream. A weighty [b(asal)]t rock fell from heaven. It crushed maid-servants [and (a man)] of god.

(§10", 2.A ii 7'–8') He also saw a fifth dream. The father-gods of Keshshi began to light a fire.

(§11", 2.A ii 9'–10') He also saw a sixth dream. Keshshi, a stock lies [(on his) n(eck)], and below on him li[e] the fetters of a woman.

(§12", 2.A ii 11'–13') He saw a seventh[!] dream. Keshshi [(went)] after some lion[(s)]. He ran forth at the gate, but in front of the gate he found water-snakes in the household space.[63]

(§13", 2.A ii 14'–16') [When it] became light, the [S]un-god came with his rays. Keshshi rose from [s(wee)]t sleep. He began to tell in tu[(rn to)] his mother the dreams of the night.

(§14", 2.A ii 17'–25') [K(eshshi)] began to speak to his mother, "How [will we] a[ct]? Will we go [i(n the mountain)]? We will die in the mountain. Let the mountains [d]e[v]our me." His mother began to speak to Keshshi, "The meaning [of] the dr[eam] is this: The grass grows high. Dreams (acc.) [...] city. The river fl[ows] away down from it/him. [...] But the forest ... on the day [...] the rushing [o]f [the river]. We also [...] we will die, her[e ...] blue [wo]ol [...]

The last line of the fragment only preserves three signs, but a recent join allows us to continue into the next paragraph, of which the beginnings of lines are preserved. It opens with mention of Keshshi's mother weeping. Keshshi is engaging in dialogue with her. A spear is mentioned, something "broke off," spears are mentioned again, someone "went back," "young men" appear, and eating is mentioned. Column iii only preserves parts of two paragraphs, and we can read "in the third month."[64] In another fragment, we learn that "she bor[e] a son," there is mention of the city Perumna and "old men," someone "began to cry," something happened "[i]n the seventh month," someone "[took] the girl in wife-ship," and the "king" is involved.[65]

Other mythical narratives

I present here only one more of the possible candidates for inclusion in this volume, the *Legend of Gurparanzah*, which has not been included in any English-language collections of translations of Hittite myths. Other pertinent stories that touch upon the powers of women, on the themes of pregnancy and birth, have been translated by Harry A. Hoffner, Jr., in his *Hittite Myths* (2nd edn, 1998): *Elkunirsha and Ashertu, Legend of Appu, The Sun-god, the Cow, and the Fisherman.*

The heroic deeds of Gurparanzah

The New Hittite story of Gurparanzah (Hurrian 'quiver of the Tigris'), king of the otherwise unknown town of Ailanuwa, is only preserved in frustratingly scanty fragments. What we have tells something about his marriage to Tadizuli (Hurr. 'she whose face inspires love'), the daughter of the king of Akkade, who bears the unetymologizable name Impakru.

It provides information (although perhaps fantastically presented) about marriage customs and the involvement of the bride, who here seems to have some say in the matter. The groom strikes the attention of the king through his exploits on a hunting expedition, in which "sixty kings, seventy champions" participate. The contest with the bow, which occurs, if not as the rite by which the bridegroom is chosen, at least during the wedding, has parallels with Odysseus' archery contest with the suitors of Penelope.[66] The wedding is supposed to be consummated in the palace of the king of Akkade, but complications ensue, separating the bride and groom, which require the attentions of the river Aranzah (the Tigris), who can move about in the form of an eagle. All these elements have interesting parallels with Turkic epic; for example, the wide-spread *Alpamish*.[67]

The story does not seem to be a song, but does show Hurrian influence, and the colophon is broken at the crucial point at which the genre of the text is mentioned. Its function and even its point can only be conjectured, but Pecchioli Daddi (2003: 492) is right to point out that "[s]ince the young man's god and protector turns to the Mother Goddess [Hannahanna] and Fate Goddesses that preside over birth, it is reasonable to suppose that the consummation of the stymied union between the king of Ailanuwa and the daughter of the Akkad king is the theme of the story together with the prelude of the birth of a child who is presented as heir of the Hurrian and Akkadian traditions." In addition, if Pecchioli Daddi (2003: 479) is right to conjecture the verb "ins[cribe]" in §3",

thus producing the sentence, "To us [they have] ins[cribed] the woman in man-ness," we speculatively can flesh out the themes of the story further, based on further parallels with Turkic epic, in which the theme of the lone daughter (often required to assume male traits) as inheritor of her father's kingdom is common. The daughter then has a say in her choice of suitor, as it seems Tadizuli does here.

I translate parts of columns ii and iii of one tablet, and column i of another tablet.[68]

In ii 1'–7', the king of Akkade discusses "in the role of son-in-law" in regard to "the king of Ailanuwa." We pick up part way through the next paragraph.

> (§3", 3.A ii 10'–15') [Impa]kru came forth. [...] stepped (forward). Impakru spoke as follows to the sixty kings, (to) the seventy champions: "And look! The king of Ailanuwa took *ḫakḫari* from us. To us [they have] ins[cribed] the woman in man-ness."
>
> (§4", 3.A ii 16'–24') [Six]ty kings, seve[nty champion]s, Eniadali [...], to Eshiadali ... for[th ...]they [sa]id, "Eshiad[ali ... to Impakr]u my lord sa[id] this [...], listen! [...] the woman (nom.) Gurparanzah. ... [They called] to eat (and) to drink seventy [champions]. Like that one [...] s/he did not s[ay].

In the first paragraph preserved in col. iii, we have a hunting scene involving Gurparanzah, in which "Impakru won."

> (§6"', 3.A iii 9'–14') In [the stepp]e the wildlife [... a leopa]rd, a bear (acc.) Gurparanzah [... immed]iately killed. The steppe (acc.) forth [... The]n they went into Aggade [...] in Aggade, the city, Impakru [did X. Si]xty kings, seventy champions we[nt] in.
>
> (§7"', 3.A iii 15'–23') He sat Gurparanzah, that one's son-in-law [...], down in front and separately [...]. They ate (and) drank with them. It for them [...]. They requested bows, they [X]-ed a

quiver (and) pillar. When they brought (them), they set them down in front of Gurparanzah. Gurparanzah shoots. From his bow his arrow crosses like a bird. He won the shooting (contest) against the sixty kings, the seventy champions.[69]

(§8"', 3.A iii 24'–32') Impakru went to bed. He went to sleep. And, Gurparanzah went to bed, as they sprinkled fine oil before him. […] they covered the ways wit[h …]. It/them [in the inner] chamber […]. He go[t] onto the bed by means of the step-ladder. His wife Tadizuli … another da[y …] s/he established. To Gurparanzah [she] s[aid, " …] you [as]saulted/violated. Do not, until […] you […]. For us the […] of the inner chamber […]."

The last paragraph preserved in this column (§9"', 3.A iii 33'–8') is too fragmentary for continuous translation, but Tadizuli does something, and there is reference to a storehouse and to one set of iron objects.

We pick up the narrative again in column i of 4.A, all that is preserved of this tablet. In §10"" (i 1–6) we are in the middle of a conversation which involves a "girl," and the words, "if to/for me m[y] lord […]/ you will unite/are uniting." Pecchioli Daddi suggests that one of the interlocutors is Gurparanza's bride, Tadizuli, who has taken matters into her own hands and is consulting with the Aranzah river.[70]

(§11"", 4.A i 7–13) "From [Ag]gade with/from the house […]. For you the name […]. [A]nd I will inscribe the name […] my lord sp[eaks] wisdom. In Aggade I will go. […] What Gurparanzah gives/will give […] there/from there also let (it) be."

(§12"", 4.A i 14–22) The river Aranzah left in the guise of an eagle. He went into Aggade. He reached the city Nuadu. He sat on the step-ladder. Gurparanzah was grieving aloud,[71] the champions were (grieving) antiph[on]ally with him. The river Aranzah said to Gurparanzah, "Why do you cry aloud? (Why) did tears run from your pure eyes?

(§13"", 4.A i 23–25) ["King of the land of] Ailanuwa, [w]hy [do you] cry aloud?" [Gu]rparanzah [said] to the river [Aranzah], "[…]. In this pla[ce] you still […]."

(§14"", 4.A i 26–33) Thus (spoke) the river Aranzah: "I […] of the personal Storm-god,[72] the head-water […] of the father, of the mother the watch[er …]. Thus (spoke) Gurparanzah, "The girl [… .] Which dowry she will give me, […] and from Aggade happi[ly … .] And I will adorn myself […] you will go with/down/back [… .]

(§15"", 4.A i 34–39) The river Aranzah heard. He left from [the land of Ailanuwa] in the guise of an eagle. He went with Hannahanna i[n …]. The Fate-goddesses […] they saw the river Aranzah […] they gave to drink. H[e] ate […] one time, two times, three times, four times, five times, six times, seven times […].

In the last paragraph of the column there are mentions of Aranzah and the Fate-goddesses. The colophon states that it is the second tablet of the [story?] of Gurpara[nzah …].

Hittite pregnancy and birth rituals

An abundance of pregnancy and birth rituals from Hattusa has been preserved.[73] Unlike the Mesopotamian materials, which are the product of learned male practitioners, the texts present themselves as dictated to male scribes by illiterate performers, some male, some female. The rituals presented here draw on many of the different cultural threads out of which Hittite culture as attested at Hattusa was woven, including the indigenous pre-Hittite Hattic culture, based in central and north-east Anatolia, and the culture of Plain Cilicia (Kizzuwatna), in which Hurrian and Luwian elements were mixed.

Purificatory precautions, "When a woman becomes pregnant"

In this text, prescriptions regarding purity during pregnancy and after birth are collected in two different versions: one on the obverse of the tablet, the other on the reverse. They reflect the practices of Hurro-Luwian Kizzuwatna.[74] I translate the requirements as presented on the obverse of version A, of Middle or early New Hittite date. Cross-cultural parallels for the restrictions regarding intercourse, diet, dining, attendance at events, and physical and mental purity are easy to find, and in the prohibitions we catch a glimpse of normal daily life for women. Also noteworthy is the difference in timing for a purificatory ritual performed for the baby, at three months for a boy, at four for a girl.[75]

(§1, A obv. 1–4) [Thus says X: W]hen a woman becomes pregnant, in her house she […]. She does not sit on the [birth-s]tool … opened up […]. She goes. [She] cleanses herself with *kunzigannaḫit*-stone. […]

(§2, A obv. 5–6) [When the seventh month arrive]s, her husband no longer approa[ches] his wife. [i]n the seventh month she offers the *māla*-offering of pregnancy.

(§3, A obv. 7–9) Th[en, which … -r]aya rites are before [her], [she] offer[s] them completely […]. She offers the *māla*-offering that was just mentioned. Then, [she] offer[s] for the flesh and bloo[d] rites.[76] […] she gives.

(§4, obv. 10–13) [When] it becom[es] light (i.e., the next morning) […] purifies [her mouth …] in the following way. The exorcist (ᴸᵁAZU) […] in a cera[mic] pitcher, and [insi]de he throws some ḫarnai-resin,[77] and he puts [in]side cedar-wood, oliv[e]-wood, [tamarisk-wood]. She purifies her mouth.[78] But, [how] he speaks [meanwh]ile in Hurrian, it is (on) a separate tablet.

(§5, obv. 14–16) It is [no] longer right for her to […] back. And, if someone invites her, [let] her [not g]o to the house [of] the fea[st]. And, as is the injunction [of] the cl[ea]ns[ing] and the purification of the birth-stool, so [tho]se also are in this very way.

(§6, obv. 17–19) It is not right for her to eat (or) drink *aštauwar*, [and she does no]t eat *tapi*. Crus[h]ed "cress" she does not e[a]t. [She] eat[s] "[c]ress" [of] the garden.[79] The *aštauwar* < of > a woman a man eats, [but] a woman does not eat the [ašt]auwar o[f] a man.

(§7, obv. 20–3) And, [i]f her husband is with her, that one also is washed[80] in a pure manner. Wheneve[r] there is [(eat)]ing, he is with her, but a table is [pres]cribed both for her husband and it is prescribed [fo(r)] his wife, and a (separate) bowl is prescribed for (each of) the[m], and although he is with her, nevertheless the woman does not eat [w(ith him)].

(§8, obv. 24–26) [Both (wooden) utens(ils and ceramic utensils, the st)]ool and the bed, [they (take)] all new (and) [(empty,)] but which bronze tools there are, they sterilize inside by burning. […] they take. There is no word (about it).

(§9, obv. 27–30) [(And,) the woman (gives birth. Wh)]ile the seventh day is passing, [(the *māla*-offering of)] the one born [is offered]. […] meanwhile on that seventh [day] they offer. Then, [(if a boy is born] on [(wh)]ich month. … If […] the third [da]y […] remains.

(§10, obv. 31–33) […] from [that] month let them [(cou)]nt [(off)]. When [the third month arrives], they cleanse [the boy (with *ku*)]*nzi* [(*ganaḫit*)]. [(But,) the doctors (kn)o]w the *kunziga*[(*naḫit*)] they offer.

(§11, obv. 34–36) [(But,) if (a girl is)] bo[(rn)], from [(th)]at month [(they)] count, [(and when) the fourth] mon[th arrive]s, th[ey (c)leanse] the girl with *kunzigannaḫit*.

(§12, obv. 37–39) [But, (w)]hen it is the festival [(of) bi(rth)], when she gives birth, how they do the festival [is writt]en [on a writing board]. It is in Kizzuwatna. The festival [they did not teach] me orally [by heart]. I will bring [it] from there.[81]

(§13, obv. 40–3) And, [wh(ile)] it is being completed, they do [(not)] harm (or) fight [(a)ny(one)], nor do they commit a sin against anyone. If (someone) angers (someone), he [(does) not[82]] < go > back, but when he steps forward, they see him [and] they [inquire].

(§14, obv. 44–6) [But,] when [a woman] becomes pregnant, [bring] back the Great Goddesses of the Body,[83] […] how they do the festival then for them, it is (on) a separate tablet. How/ When […] of the days have arrived, that too is (on) a separate tablet.

(§15, obv. 47–50) [when] the woman is pregnant, [they do] the festival of the month for the Great Goddesses of the Body. [...] they give repeatedly. They keep possession of them (i.e., the statuettes of the goddesses) on the return trip. But, when the[y] do [X], they seat them inside the house < of > the birth-stool. [...] the exorcists give repeatedly in the same way.

(§16, obv. 51–5) [When a woman gives birth], on which day she gives birth, on [th]at day [they do] the festival of birth for the Great Goddesses [of the Body and Hebat].[84] [...] for them from that also they complete the festival. [...] they send away. They [offe]r to the Great Goddesses and Hebat as much as is good for the client of the ritual.

Purification by the patili-priests

The *patili*-priest was a magico-religious officiant originating from Kizzuwatna. An expert in purification, he served in both death and birth rituals.[85] In this Middle Hittite ritual one priest among a group of at least two engages in a variety of suggestive activities that connect both to purification and to sexual activity, a successful pregnancy, and birth, such as pegging and binding (used in purificatory rituals to render evil inactive), sealing closed the birth chamber and opening it again, and leading the woman in and out of the room. The binding, sealing, and closing are all ways to magically ensure that the womb remains closed until the proper term of the pregnancy has been reached. As discussed earlier, the red wool used in the ritual is symbolic of menstrual blood, thought to nourish the baby. Whereas in a ritual meant to promote the fertility of the king and queen, red and white wool is intertwined and used as a belt for one of the rite's participants,[86] here a bundle of sticks of cedar, tamarisk, and olive-wood tied together with red wool is tucked into the woman's girdle. The girdle is significant in birth rituals, because it must be untied when the woman gives birth.[87] It may be that the "blood ritual" used to purify the birth-stool also alludes to the woman's contribution to the baby, as well as to the blood that will be discharged during delivery, again besmearing the chair. As in the previous ritual, the woman's mouth is purified, both to maintain the proper state of mind for the woman and prevent ill omen, and as a proxy for the vagina.[88] Finally, we have a hint of a connection between birth and cosmogony, with the manipulation of a special bread decorated with the moon, sun, and stars.

We basically have only the second and third column of exemplar A, which is filled in by five duplicate or parallel texts.[89]

(§7', C 2') And, the pegs above [...]
(§8', C 3'–4') [He] tak[es anot]her bowl. [...] the pegs above with [...].

(§9', C 5'–9') Wh[ich] birth stool […], of that one [he hammers a peg on this side] and on that side [he hammers] a pe[g…] on this side [and on] that side he ties together[90] [cedar-wood, tamarisk-wood] (and) olive-wood […].

(§10', C 10', A ii 1–3) He takes two pitchers of wine. On [top cedar-wood, (tamarisk-wood, (and) olive-wood)] are [ti]ed [together].[91] One on th[is] side [(and one on that side)] he [(han)]gs.

(§11', A ii 4–8) [(And, which inner chamber the woman)] is inside of, [(aro)]und the outside [(of that inner chamber)] he [(hamm)]ers two pegs, [(one peg on this side)] and one on [(that)] side (of the door). [(Then,)] he ties on the pegs [(cedar-wood, tamarisk-wood,)] and [(o)]live-wood.

(§12', A ii 9–11) The pitcher [… breads (shaped like grape-)] bunches (are) ha[(nging)] down, and [(a ball of wool)] they [cut] o [(ff)] in front.

(§13', A ii 12–14) A *patili*-priest [(wave)s] with a [(shel)]duck (over) [(the chair)] of the woman, [(the table, the b)]ed, the stan[d, (the birth-stool, and the woman.)]

(§14', A ii 15–17) [(The woman)] offer[(s inside) the inner (chamber)] for the [(bl)]ood-rite. She washes [(her hands.)] They bring her in, [(in front of the birth-stool.)]

(§15', A ii 18–21) S/he [(offer)]s one goo[(se for the path,)] and one goose for the *ḫapi*, [(for the purification ritual,)] for the *kulamuši* [(s/he)] offe[(rs)]. They bl[oo]dy the [(birth-)]stool and the pegs.[92]

(§16', A ii 22–7) The cedar-[w]ood, the tamarisk-wood, the olive-wood are tied together with red wool. A *patili*-priest takes it. He puts it on the girdle[93] of the woman, and he pours fine oil on her head,[94] and on her hand he binds red wool.

(§17', A ii 28–30) Then, a *patili*-priest takes the *ḫarnai*-resin from the bowl, with the cedar-wood, the tamarisk-wood, the olive-wood. He purifies the mouth of the woman.

(§18', A ii 31–7) A *patili*-priest puts the bowl (containing) the *ḫarnai* on top of the pegs. He covers it over. The woman proceeds to bow to the birth-stool. Then, she puts forth her hand over the birth-stool. Then, she sits (on it). Her husband, the *patili*-priests, and the *katra*-women come.[95] They bow to the woman.

(§19', A ii 38–43) A *patili*-priest sea[l]s in front of the birth-stool. And, which *ḫarnai* is poured into the *kappi*-vessel, (and) which two pegs he hammers around in front of the door-leaves of the inner chamber, he puts on top (of those pegs) the *kappi*-vessel (with that *ḫarnai*) and [t]hen covers it over.

(§20', A ii 44–49) They give to eat to the *patili*-priests and the *katra*-women, and they go away. [B]ut, when it becomes night time, (and) a sta[r] leaps up, a *patili*-priest g[o]es in. He open[s] (i.e., breaks the seal on the door) in front of the birt[h] stool.

(§21', A iii 1–5) [He] lead[s] the woman inside. She bow[s] to the birth stool. [Th]en, she puts forth her hand over (it). She goes forth [f]rom the inner chamber. [A *patil]i*-priest sea[l]s in front of the inner chamber.

(§22', A iii 6–10) The woman sits on a wooden [...]. [At her h]ead he puts one wickerwork table. [T]hen, he puts on top a *naḫiti*-bread. Made on the top of [n]aḫiti[-bread] are the Moon, the Sun, and [...] star(s).

(§23', A iii 11–15) The cedar-wood, tamarisk-[woo]d, oli[ve]-wood bound [to]gether with red wool that the *pat[i]li*-priest put in the girdle of the woman, it he takes away. He puts it down on top of the *naḫiti*-bread.

(§24', A iii 16–19) The *patili*-priest gives a pitcher of wine to the woman, and [th]at one p[r]offers two kids to her. The woman offers them with the wine. A *patili*-priest leads them away.

(§25', A iii 20–23) When he arrives [a]t the crossroads, he [of]fers one kid to the male [god]s of the *šinapši*-structure, and he [off]ers one kid to the male gods of the city.

(§26', A iii 24–28) [The *pat]ili*-priest comes back and he bows [in front] of the inner chamber. He [bo]ws to the woman, and he calls out (in Hurrian), "Well-being!" They give him to drink. [(He)] goes away.

(§27', A iii 29–32) But, [(when)] it becomes light, the woman washes herself. If the woman is pure according to the dream, a *patili*-priest leads her [(i)]nside to the birth-stool.

(§28', A iii 33–34) She bows, and she puts [forth] her hand [(over)] the birth-stool.

(§29', A iii 35–41) If she is not pure according to the dream, she bows [(in front)] of the door (of) the inner chamber. Then, she [(puts)] forth her hand all aro[(und)] the birth-stool, and when it is night, (and) a st[ar l]eaps up, he [l]eads the woman inside to the birth-stool. She bows to the birth-stool, and she puts forth her h[and] over (it). She goes fort[h].

(§30', A iii 42) A *patili*-priest [seal]s [in front of] the inner chamber. ...

It appears that the ritual at the crossroads is repeated.

Hannahanna's allotments

This incantation, probably of Middle Hittite date, explains how Hannahanna ("Granny") was given jurisdiction over the fertility of humans. The Anatolian goddess was featured in invocation rituals with parallels to the Demeter myth. The incantation mentions a series of indigenous Hattic and/or Anatolian deities, residing in towns in central and northeast Anatolia: the chthonic deity, the Sun-goddess of Arinna, who represented the sun when it was below the horizon; the symbol of kingship, the personified throne Halmasuitt; Hatepinu, daughter of the Sea, wife of the vegetation god Telipinu, who was also the main character in invocation rituals; the tutelary deity, a type of god or goddess associated with deer, hawks, hunting, and wild spaces; and the god Huzziya.[96]

(§1, obv. 1–3) [When] a woman gives birth, the midwife ge[t]s ready these things: [2 stoo]ls, 3 leather chair coverings. On each stool one leather chair covering lies.

(§2, obv. 4–8) And, she spreads out [one] leather chair covering on the ground between the stools. When the child falls down, the woman sits on the stools, and the midwife holds a cloth. She incants as follows:

(§3, obv. 9–15) "Among the gods they distribute shares. The Sun-goddess sat in Arinna, and Halmasuitt likewise in Harpisa, Hatepi <nu> likewise in Maliuha, the tutelary deity likewise in Karahna, fearsome Telipinu likewise in Tauniya, Huzziya likewise in Hakmissa, but [Hann]ahanna had no place, (so) her place remained among humans.

(§4, obv. 16–19) "[…] among … is the <p>lace. That thing [there is n]o. … There is no window. […] it is a place of [a pilla]r. […] lay …

Tunnawiya's birth ritual

Tunnawiya was a respected practitioner, to whom several rituals were attributed, including one translated in the previous chapter. She was an expert in expelling evil, and (also) spoke Luwian. This Middle Hittite ritual, of which only the beginning and end sections are retained, has three notable features: first, a live ewe is apparently waved over the laboring woman to attract any evils away from the human, a challenging maneuver to execute; second, the Hittite theme of the everlasting rock, a symbol of righteous kingship predicated on the support of the royal ancestors, is invoked;[97] finally, it shows that girls were as valued as boys were, but they were differentiated by gendered tasks.[98]

We only have parts of the first and fourth columns of the tablet.[99]

(§1, i 1'–4') [… on the one side] and on the other side […] s/he sits.The ea[rth …]. The child [falls] do[wn …].

(§2, i 5'–8') Two sma[ll] stools […]. One stool [is put] in f[ront] of the woman, and one stool [is put] beh[ind] her. The midwives se[at] themsel[ves].

(§3, i 9'–13') [W]hile the woman c[ries out, the midwife] incants the incantation [of] c[rying out]. Whenever the woman [begins to] c[ry out, the midwife] incants, an[d] from one tablet [...]. The tablets of the incantation are separ[ate].

(§4, i 14'–17') And when the woman b[egins] to cry out, they prepare already beforehand (for) the child. In that month, during those days that the [child] [is] born, the[y] have already prepared him/her beforehand.

(§5, i 18'–24') And, [w]hile the [wo]man i[s] still crying out, which ewe is prepared, [wh]ether she is pregna[nt] or empty, they lead her into the inner chamber, and when the woman [is] giving birth (and) the child is falling, that ewe they wave (over) the woman, [(i.e.,) over her head,] three times, and at the same time the midwife [sp]eaks [as follows]:

(§6, i 25'–7') "Those who [do X] to [th]at woman, [...] her away [... let them] release the woman.

(§7, i 28') [...] hea[d ...]

The column breaks off here. Columns ii and iii are not preserved.

(§8', iv 1'–2') "[...] lif[e ...]. The rocky peak[100] [...].

(§9', iv 3'–6') "To this [child ...], the <eter> nal rocky peak [...] which dow[n]. Keep alive [...]. [K]ee[p ...].

(§9', iv 7'–12') "Co[m]e. [Like] the wind [a]nd the rai[n] do not m[ove] the rocky peak in its place, likewi[se] also, w[ha]t was born to these, let an evil word [not] move [his/her life] in its place. [Let i]t be protected likewise. Let it be forever living."

(§10', iv 13'–15') Whenever a bo[y] is born, the midwife speaks a[s follows]: "Now her[e I] broug[ht] the goods of a boy, but in the following y[ea]r may I bring the goods of a girl!"

(§11', iv 16'–18') [But,] if it is a gi[rl], she speaks as follows: "No[w] here I brought the goods [of a gir]l, but in the following year may I bring the goods [of a bo]y.

(§12', iv 19'–22') [X tablet: "Whe]n a woman gives birth." Not finished. [Word of Tunn]awiya, midwife, [...] for/of all.

Pittei's ritual

This Late New Hittite pair of incantations, attributed to a certain woman named Pittei, is presented in Hittite heavily influenced by Luwian. It shares parallels with Hattic, Luwian, and Akkadian incantations. Pittei has used standard building blocks of anti-black-magic motifs, particularly resonant with the concerns of birth, to produce an original work addressing a specific event, the birth of a baby boy with some sort of medical problem, which is blamed on two factors: the evil omen of a red moon and malevolent sorcerers.

The inverse movements of good and evil described in the two incantations evoke the movement of the baby down the birth canal, and the extractive imagery in the second incantation also alludes to the process of birth. The ingredients of the ointment to be applied to the baby boy's ears, the "stone of the assembly" and the "living rock," attempt to enhance the masculine powers of the child, for the assembly is the place for adult men and the living rock, as discussed earlier, is a symbol of secure kingship and masculinity.

While Giorgieri (2004) has argued that the omen was a lunar eclipse, Bachvarova (2013) suggests that it was a more common event, since the moon can appear red when it rises over the horizon, especially if there is much moisture or particulate matter in the atmosphere, which scatters light at the blue end of the spectrum. The imagery of the Moon-god approaching in a threatening manner matches the movement of the moon rising over the horizon; in a lunar eclipse, on the other hand, the moon shades from white to red to white again.

In his edition of the text, Beckman suggested that the incantation draws on themes also found in the wide-spread Mesopotamian myth of the Moon-god Sin and the Cow-Maiden.[101] Although the Moon-god's role is inverted here, his suggestion can be supported by the fact that the recipe for the ointment matches key elements of recipes for ointments that appear on the same tablets as versions of the Akkadian incantation, as can be seen in the translation here.[102]

(§1, rev. 1–18) [Thus says] Pittei when (a woman) gives birth to a child. "Heaven was clothed in darkness. *duwiš* was clothed. And, the Moon-god was clothed in blood. He girded himself with skins of blood. He took his arrow(s) of death. He took his bow of death. In one hand he held blazing fire; in the other hand he held drawn swords. He proceeded inside quickly. Mighty one, s/he ... the gates [...] the girl. He was born before him/her, the *zammantiš* child. *IŠTAR* of the field form[erly]. She was filled with fear, she was afraid. Her mouth went sideways. Her eyes likewise. Her nine limbs likewise. She (the midwife) treated her, her head, (while) she was pressing her from above. The mother (of) the son cried aloud. The Storm-god looked down from heaven. 'What is that? How is there nothing?' He (the Storm-god) recounts it all afterwards in the same way." "Here we are taking from somebody. Let the Great Goddesses come." Before her let the midwives take the *karšikarši*-ointment, the *ḫaršānin*. Let them take the *kuwari* (dust?) of the road. Let them take the dust of ... Let them [take] the stone of the assembly, let them take the fruit of the rock, ... [...] let them take. Let them take the living rock. Let them grind it. [Let them mix] it wit[h] butter. Let them apply to the son, in his ears. And, [let them] cl[ean] the mother below. "Go away! You are *zunnumiš* (and) *mannaimiš*. But, this [...]. It was good. Let it come as a good thing. Furthermore, it [... his] h[ead ...]." She says a second spell:[103]

(§2, 22–34) "'Tongues, tongues, where are y[ou] going?' 'We are going to flatten out the rock. ... We are going to brea[k] the obsidian. Likewise to confine the lion. Likewise to fetter the wolf. Likewise to lift the *zammantiš* son.'" She turns them back. "There they come, the sorceress women!" She [t]akes the obsidian from the *ḫūwanda*. Likewise the apple. She holds the knife. "[She] confronts them, the [m]*anniš* woman, the midwife. Let her cut off her tongue with the obsidian. Let them blind her, her eyes with the knife. Let them take her teeth with the apple. Woman, turn away the evil tongues. Eat up their lord. Who contrives evil for this child, let him/her see heaven flattened. Let him/her see the earth opened. Likewise the great god Zilipuri blazing. Let him/her see Ishtar *papartama* (neut. n./a. s.). Likewise death *zappian*. Likewise the lion confined. Likewise the wolf fettered. Likewise the feet [of] the snake, who ... this child, who contrives evil for him." This she turns back.

Abbreviations

ABoT	Balkan, K., 1948. *Ankara Arkeoloji Müzesinde Bulunan Bogazköy Tabletleri*. Istanbul: Millî Eğitim Basımevi.
CTH	L. Laroche, 1971. *Catalogue des textes Hittites*. Paris: Klincksieck.
EA	El-Amarna tablets.
ETCSL	Electronic Text Corpus of Sumerian Literature <http://etcsl.orinst.ox.ac.uk>
HED	Puhvel, J. 1984ff. *Hittite Etymological Dictionary*, Berlin: Walter de Gruyter.
HEG	Tischler, J. and G. Neumann (1983–2010). *Hethitisches etymologisches Glossar*. Innsbruck: Institut für Sprachwissenschaft der Universität Innsbruck.
IBoT	Istanbul Arkeoloji Müzelerinde bulunan Bogazköy tabletleri.
KBo	Keilschrifttexte aus Boghazköi.
KhT	Konkordanz der hethitisch Texte (www.hethport.uni-wuerzburg.de/hetkonk/)
KUB	Keilschrifturkunden aus Boghazköi.
RlA	Reallexikon der Assyriologie (und Vorderasiatischen Archäologie) (Berlin 1928 ff.)
TUAT NF	Texte aus der Umwelt des Alten Testaments. Neue Folge.

Notes

1 For the concept of oral-derived texts, texts that refract an oral tradition, even if they may be composed by scribes, see Foley (1990). On the prehistory, form, function, and setting of Hurro-Hittite narrative song, see Bachvarova (forthcoming).
2 See Rutherford (2001).
3 On the correct title for the *Song of Birth*, see Corti (2007).
4 I refer to the numbers assigned to each text based on Laroche's *Catalogue des textes hittites* (1971), and additional bibliography can be found through their CTH numbers on the electronic database, Konkordanz der hethitischen Texte (http://www.heth-port.uni-wuerzburg.de/hetkonk/). I also note the publication information for the tablet fragments. Modified versions of the translations of the Kumarbi appear in *Ancient Mediterranean Myths*, ed. C. López Ruiz (Oxford University Press).
5 All are told in Hesiod's *Theogony*. The parallels have been much studied. See, for example, West (1997: 276–305), and most recently López-Ruiz (2010).
6 Told in, respectively, the *Homeric Hymn to Apollo*, Hesiod's *Theogony*, *Enki and Ninmah*, and the *Epic of Creation*.
7 Cf. the term ^{MUNUS}ŠÀ.ZU "midwife," lit. "knowing the heart."
8 See Melchert (2001b: 407, note 4), Stol (2000: 14).
9 See Melchert (2001b).
10 In Hippocrates: see Hanson (1995: 302–4).
11 The womb as crucible: Cohen (1976: 134), Stol (2000: 63, note 94).
12 Bernabé (2009: 26) suggests the "good place" is the phallus.
13 The wagon was probably the Big Dipper constellation, which was also known to the ancient Greeks as the "Wagon" (*Il.* 18.487).
14 CTH 344.A = KUB 33.120+. The tablet we have is also worn and damaged and is therefore very hard to read. I use the new transliteration of Rieken (2009), posted on the electronic Konkordanz der hethitischen Tontafeln under CTH 344, which supersedes the transliterations of García Trabazo (2002: 15–75) and Laroche (1965, 1968: 153–47). For earlier full translations see Hoffner (1998: 42–45) and Haas (2006: 133–43).
15 The Former Gods are the previous generation of gods deposed by the Storm-god, and are thus analogous to the Titans in Greek mythology.
16 Ishhara was a Syrian goddess partially assimilated to Shawushka of Nineveh, on whom see below, note 30. She is emblematic of female sexuality and fertility. See Prechel (1996: 90–103) on Ishhara in Hattusa, and Archi (2002: 27–33) on her relationship with the Former Gods.
17 Following Haas (2006: 134).
18 Perhaps the scribe has slipped here, switching the roles of the two gods.
19 *paršēnaš* means "cheeks" (see Kloekhorst 2008: 641–42).
20 On the identity of the three other gods, see Bernabé (2009).
21 Following García Trabazo (2002: 168).
22 Rieken (2009) suggests: "swelling" (see note 14).
23 A polite greeting.
24 Here Kumarbi is syncretized with Mesopotamian Enki. See Archi (2004).
25 Taking *waggatatta* as 2s. pret. pl.
26 Bernabé (2009: 25–26) argues that the Shining-Faced One (^{d}KA.ZAL) is *IŠTAR*.
27 See García Trabazo (2002: 173) for this god.
28 The worship of baetyls was common in Syria and Anatolia. See Hutter (1993) and Fick (2004). We may compare the *omphalos* ('navel') rock at Delphi, which was thought to be the rock swallowed by Kronos.
29 Following Hoffner (1998: 44).

30 On Shawushka generally see Wegner (1981), also Popko (1995: 98). On *IŠTAR* of Nineveh, see Reade (2005), Beckman (1998) and Haas (1979). On *IŠTAR-i/IŠTAR-li* representing Anzili, see Wilhelm (2010).

31 CTH 348. I use the transliteration of Siegelová (1971). Also see Rieken et al. (2009ff) on KhT, Groddek (2001–2), Stefanini (2004), and Dijkstra (2005), with a proposal for re-ordering some fragments, the earlier, fuller translation by Hoffner (1998: 50–55), following the order of fragments proposed by Siegelová, and the German translation and discussion by Haas (2006: 153–56).

32 CTH 348 I.2.A = KUB 8.67.

33 See Groddek (2001–2) on the Hittite version of the latter scene (CTH 348.I.26.A = KBo 26.94, 27.A = KBo 26.83), and Dijkstra (2005) on the Hurrian one (CTH 348.II.1 = KUB 45.62+ i). Compare the use of the Irsirra-goddesses as wet-nurses in the *Song of Ullikummi* tablet 1, §16–18, translated below.

34 Hittite: CTH 348.I.1.B = KUB 8.65, I.5.A = KBo 19.112; Hurrian: CTH 348.II.1 = KBo 12.80+ iv; see Dijkstra (2005: 321–22).

35 See trans. of Hoffner (1998: 90–92).

36 Her two attendants.

37 CTH 348.I.9.A = KUB 33.88 rev. 8'–11', filled in with CTH 348.I.11.A = IBot 2.135 obv. 6–10 (translit. Siegelová 1971: 54).

38 Fragrant plant-based substances.

39 ᵁᶻᵁ*šarḫuwantit.*

40 CTH 348.I.4.A = KUB 33.84+, with B = KBo 19.111 (translit. Siegelová 1971: 58, 60).

41 On the lovely rock upon which Kumarbi ejaculates, a landmark in Lake Van, see Singer (2002). More than one Caucasian tradition records how a stone was impregnated by ejaculation onto the earth, producing the hero Sosruquo, while the Circassian Toterash forces Sosruquo to plough the sky with his shoulder, just as the stone Ullikummi, created when Kumarbi ejaculated on a huge rock, is set on the right shoulder of Ubelluri, on whom the earth and sea rest, and grows up into the sky. See Abaza Saga 47: "How Sosruquo Was Born" (trans. Colarusso 2002: 185–87), Ubykh Saga 86: "The Birth of Soseruquo" (trans. Colarusso 2002: 388–97); Circassian Saga 23: "Two fragments of the Ballad of Sawseruquo" (trans. Colarusso 2002: 112–23). See Colarusso *ad loc.* and Haas (1982: 148).

42 See Bachvarova (unpublished).

43 CTH 345.1.A = KUB 36.7a+ iii 34', see Beckman (1998: 5). The key word *tar-š[i-i]k-kán-ta-aš* unfortunately straddles a break between two fragments. García Trabazo (2002: 196, with note 129) avoids transliterating the two signs in question, and Hoffner (1998: 58) avoids translating.

44 Haas (1979: 399), Wegner (1981: 7, 55–59, 65–66), Beckman (1998: 6).

45 CTH 348. 1.A (Late New Hittite) = KUB 33.96+, 1.B (New Hittite) = KUB 33.98 +, 1.C = KUB 33.102+; 2.A = KUB 33.87, 2.C = KUB 33.92+. I follow the transliteration of Rieken et al. (2009-) on KhT for 1.A and 2.A, although I occasionally use the conjectures used by García Trabazo (2002: 176–251), which often stem from Güterbock (1951, 1952). Also see the fuller translations of Hoffner (1998: 55–65) and Haas (2006: 157–75).

46 On the Great Goddesses as divine midwives see most recently Taracha (2010).

47 So García Trabazo (2002: 213).

48 "Heroism": UR.SAG-*tar* = *ḫaštaliyatar*, lit. 'bone-hardness', cf. *ḫašta-/i-*'bone'.

49 For the concept of textualization, writing down a version of a relatively flexible oral narrative, see Honko (2000).

50 See Gadjimuradov (2004) on the representation of volcanic activity in Hurro-Hittite myth.

51 *Fragments of the Kumarbi Myth*: CTH 346.5.A = KUB 33.118, translit. Rieken et al. (2009ff.) on KhT, trans. Haas (2006: 159). See Archi (2009: 215–16).

52 See trans. of ETCSL 1.3.3.

53 *Fragments Mentioning Ishtar (Mt. Pishaisha)*: CTH 350.3.A = KUB 33.108 ii? 2–20, translit. Rieken et al. (2009ff.) on KhT. Also see G. Wilhelm in "Meer. B. Bei den Hethitern," in RlA 8.5 and trans. of Haas (2006: 212–13).

54 Filled in from the New Hittite parallel text CTH 350.2.A = KUB 36.33 4'.

55 Haas (2005).

56 *Ritual of Shalashu*: CTH 788.7 = KBo 27.176 10' (translit. Haas and Wegner 1988: 419), see Haas (2006: 209).

57 See Bryce (2005: 93, 207–10, 311–12).

58 Mouton (2007: 52–53).

59 Dijkstra (2008: 210, 214).

60 EA 341, translit. Izre'el (1997: 17–19).

61 For a full discussion of the Hurrian fragments and the possible storyline that can be extracted by combining the Hittite and Hurrian versions, see Dijkstra (2008).

62 CTH 361, translit. of the Hittite version Friedrich (1950: 234–43, 253–55). For earlier translations, see Hoffner (1998: 87–89), and Haas (2006: 206–11). Also see Dijkstra (2008). I translate or discuss CTH 361.I.1.A = KUB 33.121+, 2.A = KUB 17.1+, 3. A = KBo 22.89.

63 For this translation see Melchert (2001a).

64 CTH 361.I.2.A = KUB 36.63.

65 CTH 361.I.3.A = KBo 22.89.

66 Morris (1996: 621).

67 On the characteristic plots of "romantic" Turkic epic and possible connections between *Alpamish* and the *Odyssey*, see Reichl (1992: 143–70, esp. 169–70, 339, 351).

68 CTH 362.3.A = KUB 36.67+, 4.A = KUB 17.9. For transliteration and English translation see Pecchioli Daddi (2003). Also see German translation and discussion of Haas (2006: 217–20). I follow Pecchioli Daddi's switching of the obverse and the reverse of KUB 36.67+, which makes the hand copy's obv. ii into rev. iv and rev. iii into obv. i. The numbering in the electronic *Korpus den hethitischen Tontafeln* follows the old order. CTH 362.1.A = KBo26.104, a fragment too small for continuous translation, and 2.A = KBo 22.98, are (indirect) joins to KUB 36.67, and therefore should be fragments 2 and 3 while KUB 36.67 + ABoT2.19 is fragment 1. See Pecchioli Daddi (2003: 493–94) and Akdoğan (2007) for discussion. I do not translate three small fragments that have been linked with this narrative, although they do not explicitly mention any important characters other than the river Aranzah (KUB 36.64). Two mention sleeping and/or a bed (KBo 22.70; KBo 22.96, with parallels to KUB 36.67 iv 28'–31').

69 Written the with the Sumerogram GURUŠ, usually translated as "young man," or Hitt. *šarku-*"powerful."

70 Pecchioli Daddi (2003: 486).

71 Lit.: "saying '*alala*'."

72 Lit.: "Storm-god of the head."

73 See Hoffner (1968), Beckman (1983), Pringle (1993), Mouton (2008).

74 See Mouton (2008).

75 CTH 489.A = KBo 17.65+, with B = KUB 44.59 (NH), translit. and trans Beckman (1983: 133–75), (Mouton 2007: 109–22), trans. J. Klinger in TUAT NF5 (2010: 184–87); partial trans. and discussion Wilhelm (2008: 23). For the most part I follow the edition of Mouton, although I occasionally use the edition of Beckman, where Mouton eschews reconstructing the text.

76 On the flesh and blood rite see Feder (2010: 102).

77 *ḫarnai* is a plant-based material burned in rituals (Haas 2003: 324). There is a pun here with *ḫarnau*-"birth stool."

78 Other translators opt for the exorcist purifying the woman's mouth. I see the woman as purifying her own mouth because of the presence of the reflexive particle *-za*.

79 Perhaps the distinction is between dried and fresh "cress."

80 So B = *KUB* 44.59 obv. 4'.

81 See Miller (2004: 517–19) on the reference to other written versions.

82 My own conjecture.

83 For such a ritual, see perhaps *Pittei's Ritual* below. The Great Goddesses (DINGIR. MAḪ.MEŠ) are often translated as Mother Goddesses, but in the singular the Great Goddess is Hannahanna "Granny." Thus, they themselves are not conceived of as fertile. Rather, they promote the fertility of other women, as a grandmother cares for her pregnant daughter or daughter-in-law and her newly born grandchildren. Also see Taracha (2010).

84 The north Syrian Hebat was the consort of the Storm-god.

85 Beckman (1983: 235–38).

86 Melchert (2001b).

87 Loosening girdle in birth in the Classical sources: Pindar, *Olympian* 6.39, Callimachus, *Hymn to Delian Apollo* 209, 222 (King 1993: 121).

88 For the connection between the mouth and vagina in Classical sources, see King (1998: 28).

89 CTH 477, translit., trans., and discussion Beckman (1983: 86–115), Mouton (2008: 83–94), with electronic edition and translation booked under CTH 477 in KhT, partial trans. and discussion Wilhelm (2008: 14–23). I follow Mouton's edition primarily, using her paragraph numbering, but also incorporate conjectures of Beckman that she eschews in her more conservative edition, as well as from Wilhelm. The exemplars used here are A = KUB 9.22, B = KBo30.lt ABoT 1.17 (used to fill in A), C = KUB 7.39.

90 See discussion of Mouton (2008: 84, note 4).

91 See Mouton (2008: 84, note 4) for a discussion about the issues filling in the lacunae in this paragraph.

92 See Feder (2010: 107) for this reading and for the ritual purification with blood.

93 "Girdle": *ipulliyaš*. This object can be made of wool, and is formed off the verbal root *app-/epp* "take, grasp." See HEG I-K: 365, but with the definition "(hand-)grip(?)." The plural form is used because the girdle is made up of multiple cords.

94 Anointing of the head is part of the betrothal ceremony, as Wilhelm (2008: 18) notes, although discounting its relevance here and preferring to see it as solely purificatory.

95 The *katra-/i*-women are important priestesses, associated with Kizzuwatnean religious practices; see Taggar-Cohen (2005: 388–89), and Miller (2002).

96 CTH 430 = KUB 30.29, translit. and trans. Beckman (1983: 22–31), trans. J. Klinger TUAT NF 5 (2010: 181–82), Wilhelm (2008: 13–14).

97 On living rock as a symbol of kingship see Hoffner (2007: 127), with reference to the Illuyanka myth and Hoffner (2010: 137), with reference to the Hattic-derived Old Hittite *Benedictions for Labarna* (CTH 820.1 = KUB 36.110, translit. Neu 1980: 227–28).

98 See further Hoffner (1966).

99 CTH 409.III = KBo 17.62+, translit. and trans. Beckman (1983: 32–41), trans. J. Klinger, TUAT NF 5 (2010: 182–83).

100 The (eternal) rocky peak, (SAG.UŠ/*uktūri*) ^{NA4}*ḫekur*, was a rocky outcropping associated with the veneration of a particular royal ancestor. The term, which refers to the physical form of the place, partially overlaps with É.NA₄ "stone house," which

describes the function of the place, to house the royal dead. On the $^{NA_4}hekur$ and the
É.NA$_4$, see van den Hout (2002), Archi (2007: 50–53), and Singer (2009: 169–72).

101 See Bachvarova (2001) for a discussion of the Cow-Maiden myth. Also see Stol (2000:
124) on the myth and ointments to be applied during childbirth.

102 CTH 767.7 = KBo 13.241+, translit. and trans. Beckman (1983: 176–99), translit.
Starke (1985: 233–36), discussion and trans. Giorgieri (2004), Haas (2006: 240–41s),
translit., trans. and discussion Bachvarova (2013), where a modified version of this
translation appears. The tablet is a *Sammeltafel*, in which two unrelated texts are
inscribed, one on the obverse, one on the reverse.

103 A section belonging to the unrelated text on the obverse interrupts here.

Bibliography

Akdoğan, R., 2007. "Gurparanzah Destanına Birleşen Bir Tablet Parçası." *Studi Micenei
Egeo-Anatolici* 49, 1–20.

Archi, A., 2002. "Formation of the West Hurrian Pantheon: The Case of Išhara," in
Recent Developments in Hittite Archaeology and History: Papers in Memory of Hans G. Güterbock,
eds. A. Yener and H. A. Hoffner, Jr. Winona Lake: Eisenbrauns, 21–32.

——, 2004. "Translation of Gods: Kumarpi, Enlil, Dagan/NISABA, Halki." *Orientalia, N. S.*
73, 319–36.

——, 2007. "The Cult of Royal Ancestors at Hattusa and the Syrian Practices," in *VITA:
Belkıs Dinçol ve Ali Dinçol'a Armağan, Festschrift in Honor of Belkıs Dinçol and Ali Dinçol*, eds.
M. Alparslan, M. Doğan-Alparslan, and H. Peker. Istanbul: Ege Yayinlari, 49–57.

——, 2009. "Orality, Direct Speech, and the Kumarbi Cycle." *Altorientalische Forschungen*
36, 209–29.

Bachvarova, M. R., 2001. "Successful Birth, Unsuccessful Marriage: Using Near Eastern
Birth Incantations to Interpret Aeschylus' *Suppliants*." *NIN* 2, 49–90.

——, 2013. "*CTH* 767.7: The Birth Ritual of Pittei: Its Occasion and the Use of
Luwianisms," in *Luwian Identities: Culture, Language and Religion between Anatolia and the Aegean*,
eds. A. Mouton, I.C. Rutherford, and I. Yakubovich. Leiden: Brill, 135–57.

——, forthcoming. *From Hittite to Homer: The Anatolian Background of Greek Religion and Literature*. Cambridge: Cambridge University Press.

——, unpublished. "Wisdom of Former Days: The Manliness of the Hittite King and the
Foolishness of Kumarbi, Father of the Gods." *Presented at "Mapping Ancient Near Eastern
Masculinities,"* University of Pennsylvania, March 25, 2011.

Beckman, G., 1983. *Hittite Birth Rituals*. 2nd edn. Wiesbaden: Harrassowitz.

——, 1998. "Ištar of Nineveh reconsidered." *Journal of Cuneiform Studies* 50, 1–10.

Bernabé, A., 2009. "El extraordinario embarazo de Kumarbi," in *Reconstruyendo el Pasado
Remoto: Estudios sobré el Proximo Oriente Antiguo en homenaje a Jorge R. Silva Castillo*, eds.
D. A. Barreyra Fracaroli and G. del Olmo Lete. Aula Orientalis—Supplementa 25.
Barcelona: Editorial AUSA, 25–32.

Bryce, T. R., 2005. *The Kingdom of the Hittites*. 2nd edn. Oxford: Oxford University Press.

Cohen, M. E., 1976. "Literary Texts from the Andrews University Archaeological
Museum." *Revue d'assyriologie et d'archéologie orientale* 70, 129–44.

Colarusso, J., 2002. *Nart Sagas from the Caucasus: Myths and Legends from the Circassians, Abazas,
Abkhaz, and Ubykhs*. Princeton: Princeton University Press.

Corti, C., 2007. "The So-called 'Theogony' or 'Kingship in Heaven': The Name of the
Song." *Studi Micenei ed Egeo-Anatolici* 49, 109–21.

Dijkstra, M., 2005. "The Myth of Apši 'the (Sea)dragon' in the Hurrian Tradition: A New Join (KBo 27, 180)." *Ugarit-Forschungen* 37, 315–29.

——, 2008. "New Joins in the Hurrian Epic of Kešši and their Ramifications." *Ugarit-Forschungen* 40, 205–24.

Feder, Y., 2010. "A Levantine Tradition: The Kizzuwatnean Blood Rite and the Biblical Sin Offering," in *Pax Hethitica: Studies on the Hittite and Their Neighbours in Honour of Itamar Singer*, eds. Y. Cohen, A. Gilan and J. L. Miller. Wiesbaden: Harrassowitz, 101–14.

Fick, S. M. E., 2004. "Zur Bedeutung der Baityloi in der Hoch- und Volksreligion," in *Offizielle Religion, lokale Kulte und individuelle Religiosität: Akten des religionsgeschichtlichen Symposiums "Kleinasien und angrenzende Gebiete vom Beginn des 2. bis zur Mitte des 1. Jahrtausends v. Chr." (Bonn, 20.-22. Februar 2003)*, eds. M. Hutter and S. Hutter-Braunsar. Münster: Ugarit-Verlag, 157–71.

Foley, J. M., 1990. *Traditional Oral Epic*. Berkeley: University of California Press.

Friedrich, J., 1950. "Churritische Märchen und Sagen in hethitischer Sprache." *Zeitschrift für Assyriologie und vorderasiatische Archäologie* 49, 213–55.

Gadjimuradov, I., 2004. "Die vulkanische Urheimat der altanatolischen Sukzessions- und Steingeburtsmythen." *Altorientalische Forschungen* 31, 340–57.

García Trabazo, J. V., 2002. *Textos Religiosos Hititas: Mitos, Plegarias y Rituales: Edición Bilingue*. Madrid: Editorial Trotta.

Giorgieri, M., 2004. "Das Beschwörungsritual der Pittei." *Orientalia N. S.* 35, 409–26.

Groddek, D., 2001–2. "'[Diese Angelenheit] höre Ištar von Nineveh nicht!': Eine neue Episdoe einer Erzählung des Kumarbi-Kreises." *Die Welt des Orients* 31, 23–30.

Güterbock, H. G., 1951. "The Song of Ullikummi: Revised Text of the Hittite Version of a Hurrian Myth." *Journal of Cuneiform Studies* 5, 135–65.

——, 1952. "The Song of Ullikummi: Revised Text of the Hittite Version of a Hurrian Myth (Continued)." *Journal of Cuneiform Studies* 6, 8–42.

Haas, V., 1979, "Remarks on the Hurrian Ištar/Šawuška of Nineveh in the Second Millennium BC." *Sumer* 35, 397–401.

——, 1982. *Hethitische Berggötter und hurritische Steindämonen. Riten, Kulte und Mythen. Eine Einführung in die altkleinasiatischen religiösen Vorstellungen*. Mainz am Rhein: P. von Zabern.

——, 2003. *Materia Magica et Medica Hethitica: Ein Beitrag zur Heilkunde im Alten Orient*. Berlin: W. De Gruyter.

——, 2005. "Die Erzählungen von den zwei Brüdern, vom Fischer und dem Findelkind sowie vom Jäger Kešše." *Altorientalische Forschungen* 32, 360–74.

——, 2006, *Die hethitische Literatur: Texte, Stilistik, Motive*. Berlin: Walter De Gruyter.

Haas, V. and I. Wegner, 1988. *Die Rituale der Beschwörerinnen* ^{SAL}*ŠU.GI*. Rome: Multigrafica Ed.

Hanson, A. E., 1995. "Paidopoiïa: Metaphors for Conception, Abortion, and Gestation in the *Hippocratic Corpus*," in *Ancient Medicine in its Socio-Cultural Context, Vol. I*, eds. P. J. van der Eijk, H. F. J. Horstmanshoff, and P. H. Schrijvers. Amsterdam: Rodopi, 291–307.

Hoffner, H. A., Jr., 1966. "Symbols for Masculinity and Femininity and their Use in Second Millennium Magic Ritual." *Journal of Biblical Literature* 85, 326–34.

——, 1968. "Birth and Name-Giving in Hittite Texts." *Journal of Near Eastern Studies* 27, 198–203.

——, 1998. *Hittite Myths*. 2nd edn. Atlanta: Society of Biblical Literature.

——, 2007. "A Brief Commentary on the Hittite Illuyanka Myth," in *Studies Presented to Robert D. Biggs*, eds. M. T. Roth, W. Farber, M. Stolper, and P. von Bechtolsheim. 27. Chicago: Oriental Institute of the University of Chicago, 119–40.

——, 2010. "The Political Antithesis and Foil of the Labarna in the Old Hittite Texts," in *Ipamati kistamati pari tumatimis: Luwian and Hittite Studies Presented to J. David Hawkins on the Occasion of his 70th Birthday*, ed. I. Singer. Tel Aviv: Emery and Claire Yass Publications in Archaeology, Institute of Archaeology, Tel Aviv University, 131–39.

Honko, L., 2000. "Text as Process and Practice: The Textualization of Oral Epics," in *Textualization of Oral Epics*, ed. L. Honko. Berlin: M. de Gruyter, 3–54.

Hutter, M., 1993. "Kultstelen und Baityloi: Die Ausstrahlung eines Syrischen Religiösen Phänomens nach Kleinasien und Israel," in *Religionsgeschichtliche Beziehungen zwischen Kleinasien, Nordsyrien und dem Alten Testament. Internationales Symposium Hamburg 17.-21. März 1990*, eds. B. Janowski, K. Koch, and G. Wilhelm. Orbis Biblicus et Orientalis 129. Freiburg: Schweiz: Universitätsverlag, 87–108.

Izre'el, S., 1997. *The Scholarly Amarna Tablets*. Groningen: Styx.

King, H., 1993. "Bound to Bleed: Artemis and Greek Women," in *Images of Women in Antiquity*, eds. A. Cameron and A. Kuhrt. Detroit: Wayne State University Press, 109–27.

——, 1998. *Hippocrates' Woman: Reading the Female Body in Ancient Greece*. London: Routledge.

Kloekhorst, A., 2008. *Etymological Dictionary of the Hittite Inherited Lexicon*. Leiden: Brill.

Laroche, E., 1965, 1968. "Textes mythologiques en transcription." *Revue Hittite et Asianique* 23, 61–178, and 26, 5–90.

——, 1971. *Catalogue des Textes Hittites*. Paris: Klincksieck.

López-Ruiz, C., 2010. *When the Gods Were Born: Greek Cosmogonies and the Near East*. Cambridge: Harvard University Press.

Melchert, H. C., 2001a. "Hittite *damnaššara*-'domestic'/ᵈ*Damnaššareš* 'household deities'." *Journal of Ancient Near Eastern Religions* 1, 150–57.

——, 2001b. "A Hittite Fertility Rite?," in *Akten des IV. Internationalen Kongresses für Hethitologie. Würzburg, 4.-8. Oktober 1999*, ed. G. Wilhelm. Wiesbaden: Harrassowitz, 404–9.

Miller, J. L., 2002. "The *katra/i*-Women in the Kizzuwatnean Rituals from Ḫattuša," in *Sex and Gender in the Ancient Near East: Proceedings of the 47th Rencontre Assyriologique International, Helsinki, July 2–6, 2001*, eds. S. Parpola and R. M. Whiting. Helsinki: The Neo-Assyrian Text Corpus Project, 423–31.

——, 2004. *Studies in the Origins, Development and Interpretation of the Kizzuwatna Rituals*. Wiesbaden: Harrassowitz.

Morris, S. P., 1996. "Homer and the Near East," in *A New Companion to Homer*, eds. I. Morris and B. Powell. Leiden: Brill, 599–623.

Mouton, A., 2007. *Rêves hittites: Contribution à une historie et une anthropologie du rêve en Anatolie ancienne*. Leiden: Brill.

——, 2008. *Les rituels de naissance kizzuwatniens: Un exemple de rite de passage en Anatolie Hittite*. Paris: De Boccard.

Neu, E., 1980. *Althethitische Ritualtexte in Umschrift*. Wiesbaden: Harrassowitz.

Pecchioli Daddi, F., 2003. "From Akkad to Ḫattuša: The history of Gurparanzaḫ and the river that gave him its name," in *Semitic and Assyriological Studies Presented to Pelio Fronzaroli by Pupils and Colleagues*. Wiesbaden: Harrassowitz, 476–94.

Popko, M., 1995. *Religions of Asia Minor*. Warsaw: Academic Publications Dialog.

Prechel, D., 1996. *Die Göttin Išḫara: Ein Beitrag zur altorientalischen Religionsgeschichte*. Münster: Ugarit-Verlag.

Pringle, J., 1993. "Hittite Birth Rituals," in *Images of Women in Antiquity*, eds. A. Cameron and A. Kuhrt. Detroit: Wayne State University Press, 128–41.

Reade, J., 2005. "The Ishtar Temple at Nineveh." *Iraq* 67, 347–90.

Reichl, K., 1992. *Turkic Oral Epic Poetry: Traditions, Forms, Poetic Structure*. New York: Garland.

Rutherford, I. C., 2001. "The Song of the Sea (ŠA A.AB.BA SÌR): Thoughts on KUB 45.63," in *Akten des IV. Internationalen Kongresses für Hethitologie. Würzburg, 4.-8. Oktober 1999*, ed. G. Wilhelm. Wiesbaden: Harrassowitz, 598–609.

Siegelová, J., 1971. *Appu-Märchen und Ḫedammu-Mythus*. Wiesbaden: Harrassowitz.

Singer, I., 2002. "The Cold Lake and its Great Rock," in *Gregor Giorgadze von Kollegen und ehemaligen Studenten zum 75. Geburtstag gewidmet*, ed. L. Gordesiani. Tblisi: Institut der Erforschung des westlichen Denkens, 128–32.

——, 2009. "'In Hattuša the Royal House Declined'. Royal Mortuary Cult in 13th century Hatti," in *Central-North Anatolia in the Hittite Period: New Perspectives in Light of Recent Research. Acts of the International Conference Held at the University of Florence (7–9 February 2007)*, eds. F. Pecchioli Daddi, G. Torri, and C. Corti. Rome: Herder, 169–92.

Starke, F., 1985. *Die Keilschrift-Luwischen Texte in Umschrift*. Wiesbaden: Harrassowitz.

Stefanini, R., 2004. "The Catch Line of Ḫedammu 10 (KUB 33.103, Rs.)," in *Šarnikzel: Hethitologische Studien zum Gedenken an Emil Orgetorix Forrer (19.02.1894–10.01.1986)*, eds. D. Groddek and S. Rößle. Dresden: Verlag der Technischen Universitä Dresden, 627–30.

Stol, M., 2000. *Birth in Babylonia and the Bible: Its Mediterranean Setting*. Cuneiform Monographs 14. Groningen: Styx.

Taggar-Cohen, A., 2005. *Hittite Priesthood*. Heidelberg: Winter.

Taracha, P., 2010. "Anatolian Ḫannahanna and Mesopotamian DINGIR.MAḪ," in *Investigationes Anatolicae*, ed. J. Klinger. Wiesbaden: Harrassowitz, 301–10.

van den Hout, T. P. J., 2002. "Tombs and Memorials: The (Divine) Stone-House and Ḫegur Reconsidered," in *Recent Developments in Hittite Archaeology and history: Papers in Memory of Hans G. Güterbock*, eds. K. A. Yener and H. A. Hoffner, Jr. Winona Lake: Eisenbrauns, 73–92.

Wegner, I., 1981. *Gestalt und Kult der Ištar-Šawuška in Kleinasien*. Kevelaer: Butzon und Bercker.

West, M. L., 1997. *The East Face of Helicon*. Oxford: Clarendon Press.

Wilhelm, G., 2008. "Rituelle Gefährdungsbewältigung bei der Geburt nach altanatolischen Quellen," in *An den Schwellen des Lebens: Zur Geschlechterdifferenz in Ritualen des Übergangs*, ed. B. Heininger. Berlin: LIT, 11–26.

——, 2010. "Die Lesung des Namens der Göttin *Ishtar-li*," in *Investigationes Anatolicae*, ed. J. Klinger. Wiesbaden: Harrassowitz, 337–44.

INDEX

Ninurta 88, 230, 242, 244 n31
Nippur 19, 30, 37, 43, 47, 52 n30, 53
    n44, 60, 62, 64, 65, 72 n63, 89, 148,
    149, 184, 185, 224; shrine to Enlil 188
Nisaba 17, 29, 33–37, 92–93, 97 n91
Noah: Babylonian 90; Sumerian 88
Nunbaršegunu 29, 30–33, 34
Nunnamir 32, 52 n32
nursemaids 62, 64, 69 n21, 71 n46
Nuska 30, 32, 33, 36

oaths of allegiance 108–9, 231–32
Obliging Slave, The 78–79
Odysseus 279, 287
Odyssey (Homer): Sirens 277, 279
oil, poured on head 166–67
Old Man and the Young Girl, The 65–67, 68
Old Women 278, 285
omens and prophecy 89, 188, 221, 243
    n19, 252–55, 297; dreams 18, 19,
    43–45, 178–79, 180, 182, 208, 285,
    286–87; oracles 240–41
omphalos 299 n28
oracles 240–41; to Esarhaddon 240, 241,
    243 n27, 244 n34; to Naqi'a 240,
    241–42, 242, 243 n21, 244 n34
oral tradition 79, 80, 91, 176
Ouranos, castration of 273

Pabilsag 19
Pace (Aristophanes) 85
palace households 17, 214
Palace of the Steppe 242, 244 n32
parallel universe paradigm 20–23, 24
Paskuwatti's ritual against a man's failure
    to procreate 262–65
patili-priests 292–94
Pazarcik stele 228–29
pea flour 69 n14
Penelope 287
"Perfect pick-up line" charm 107
"Performance anxiety" charm 108
performance pieces 91
Persephone, rape of 196
Perumna 287
Perwa, diety 279
Peštur 51 n13
PG800 14
PG1163 14
PG1237 14
philology 5
Pikku, the scribe 248

Pishaisha, Mt 284
Pittei's ritual 296–98
Plain Cilicia 290
plaques 17–18, 19, 24 n2
poetry 40, 184, 188 n3
popular sayings 87–88
post-partum complications, charms and
    spells 110–14
potter's oven 123, 139 n92
power: abuse of 89; loss of 86–87, 96 n61
prayers 16; for children 89; to Shamash
    179–80
pregnancy and childbirth 84, 273–77,
    283–84, 290–92; baby boys with
    medical problems 296–98; child-bed
    fever 112–13; conception 273–77; and
    cosmogony 292, 294; death in 118,
    134–35; difficult labor charms 128–35;
    fostering 276–80; Marduk invoked in
    131, 132, 133, 134, 135, 140 n117;
    medicine and healing magic 119–35;
    miscarriage 116–17, 121–28, 139 n71,
    248; prognosticating 119–21;
    purification by patili-priests 292–94;
    purificatory precautions 1–3, 290–94,
    302 n78, 302 n94; rituals surrounding
    123–35, 247–52, 290–98, 302 n94;
    sex-prediction 120–21, 130
pregnancy tests 119–20
priestesses 19–20, 23, 152, 153, 166, 206,
    221; in legal usage 146–47; letters from
    209–10; "mother of the deity" 269 n52;
    royal women as 18–20, 23
priests 289–91
private accusation 153, 172 n22
property 83, 154–55, 157–58
prophetesses 221, 240, 241
prophets 240
Prosepina, rape of 196
prostitutes 52 n39, 86, 89, 90, 91, 169,
    189 n26, 189 n28, 190 n32, 191 n49,
    195, 202 n30; Inana as 182; Ishtar as
    182; legal position of 150; male 88,
    197, 202 n24; veiling of 166; *see also*
    temple prostitute
Protective Deity of the Ritual
    Paraphernalia 265, 266–67
Proverbs 88
proverbs, Akkadian 79–81; admonitions
    88–91; adultery 84–85; bilingual
    collections 81, 89; compared to Biblical
    wisdom literature 84, 88; female slaves